The Challenge of Reform in Indochina

Harvard Studies in International Development

Other volumes in the series include:

*Jointly published by the International Center for Economic Growth.

The Challenge of Reform in Indochina

EDITED BY

Börje Ljunggren

Harvard Institute for International Development
Harvard University

Distributed by Harvard University Press

Published by Harvard Institute for International Development
January 1993

Distributed by Harvard University Press

Editorial management: Vukani Magubane
Editorial assistance: Nancy Soukup, Deborah McCarthy
Design and production: Editorial Services of New England, Inc.

Library of Congress Cataloging-in-Publication Data

The Challenge of reform in Indochina / edited by Börje Ljunggren.
     p. cm. — (Harvard studies in international development)
   Includes bibliographical references and index.
   ISBN 0-674-10712-8
    1. Indochina—Economic policy. 2. Indochina—Economic conditions.
  3. Indochina—Social policy. 4. Indochina—Social conditions.
  5. Indochina—Politics and government. I. Ljunggren, Börje.
  Series.
  HC441.C46   1992
338.959—dc20   92-26516
                                                 CIP

Printed in the United States of America

Contents

v

Contributors

Nayan Chanda is Deputy Director of the *Far Eastern Economic Review*. He has reported on Asian politics and economy for over two decades. He is the author of *Brother Enemy: The War After the War* and coauthor of a number of books on Southeast Asia. He was a Senior Associate at the Carnegie Endowment of International Peace. He holds an M.A. degree in history from Jadavpur University, Calcutta.

David Dapice is a development economist with appointments as an Associate Professor in the Department of Economics at Tufts University and a Faculty Associate at HIID. He has worked as a Brookings Policy Fellow at the World Bank, and served on the Social Science Research Committee. He has worked extensively on a variety of topics in Indonesia, Thailand, Vietnam, and other countries. He received his B.A. degree in political economy from Williams College and his M.A. and Ph.D. from Harvard University.

David Dollar is a Senior Economist for Vietnam at the World Bank. His published research includes works on socialist economies in transition, North-South technology transfer, and productivity growth. Before joining the World Bank he taught at UCLA and the Chinese Academy of Social Science. He holds a B.A. in Asian studies from Dartmouth College and a Ph.D. in economics from NYU.

May Ebihara is Professor of Anthropology at Lehman College and the Graduate Center of the City of New York. She received a B.A. in anthropology from Reed College and a Ph.D. in anthropology from Columbia University. She is the only American anthropologist who did field research among peasants in prerevolutionary Cambodia, and is presently restudying the village she originally investigated.

Adam Fforde is Director, ADUKI Pty Ltd (consultants), Chairman of The Vietnamese Educational Trust and is currently conducting research at the Economics Department, Research School of Pacific Studies, Australian National University. From 1987 to 1992 he was a consultant to the Swedish aid programme in Vietnam and also served as a socioeconomic advisor to the Development Cooperation Office (SIDA) of the Swedish Embassy in Hanoi. He studied at Oxford and Birkbeck College in London and received a Ph.D. from Cambridge University.

Bernard Funck is an economist at the World Bank, East Asia and Pacific Region. From 1988–91 he was the World Bank economist for Laos. In 1992 he led a group of economists who conducted the first economic study of the Cambodian economy in 20 years, *Cambodian Agenda for Rehabilitation and Reconstruction*. Before joining the Bank in 1987, he worked as a research economist with the Belgian Government (Planning Bureau), the EEC, and the National Bank of Belgium. He holds masters degrees in economics and philosophy from the University of Louvain (Belgium).

Joan Kaufman is a Senior Analyst at Abt Associates, Inc., in Cambridge, Massachusetts, and a lecturer in Population Sciences at the Harvard School of Public Health. She holds masters degrees in Asian studies and health and medical sciences from the University of California at Berkeley, and a D.P.H. in Public Health from Harvard. She has consulted and worked in the international population and health fields since 1980, including four years in China with the U.N. She conducts research and publishes on family planning, women's health, population, and AIDS policy and programs.

Börje Ljunggren is Deputy Director General of the Swedish International Development Authority (SIDA) and head of its Department for Asia and the Middle East. He is the author of *Indiens Ekonomi* (1972) and articles on a wide variety of development issues. Ljunggren has worked on Indochina since the early 1970s. He was posted there in 1978–80 as the first Swedish Chargé d'affaires to Laos. In 1990/91 he was a Visiting Scholar at the Harvard Institute for International Development where he was responsible for organizing the Institute's seminar series on Indochina. He holds a Ph.D. in political science from Southern Illinois University.

Hy V. Luong is Associate Professor of Anthropology at the University of Toronto. He received his B.A. from the University of California at Berkeley, and a Ph.D. from Harvard University. He has regularly conducted field research in Vietnam on language, social structure, and political economy, and is the author of *Discursive Practices and Linguistic Meaning,* and *Revolution in the Village: Tradition and Transformation in North Vietnam, 1925–1988.*

Dwight H. Perkins is Director of the Harvard Institute for International Development and H.H. Burbank Professor of Political Economy at Harvard University. He is the author, coauthor or editor of eleven books and many articles on economic development in Asia, particularly China and Korea, as well as on more general issues of development. He has visited and lectured in Vietnam. He received a Ph.D. in economics from Harvard University.

Gita Sen is a Visiting Professor at the Harvard Center for Population and Development Studies, and a Fellow at the Centre for Development Studies in Trivandrum, India. She received her B.A. in economics from the University of Poona, an M.A. from the Delhi School of Economics, and a Ph.D. from Stanford University. She is a development economist whose research focuses especially on gender and development. Recently she has been researching the gender dimensions of population policies.

C. Peter Timmer is Thomas D. Cabot Professor of Development Studies, At Large, Harvard University. He has been a resident advisor in Indonesia and has worked on food and agricultural policy in China, Japan, the Philippines, Sri Lanka, and Vietnam. He received his A.B., M.A., and Ph.D. degrees in economics from Harvard University and has taught at Stanford and Cornell Universities. He is Faculty Fellow of the Harvard Institute for International Development and teaches economic history, the economics of the world food system, economic development of Southeast Asia, and business and government relations. He is lead author of *Food Policy Analysis,* which has been translated into Vietnamese, and contributing editor of *Agriculture and the State: Growth, Employment, and Poverty in Developing Countries.*

William S. Turley is Professor of Political Science at Southern Illinois University-Carbondale. He was Fulbright-Kennedy Visiting Professor at Chulalongkorn University in Bangkok in 1982–84. His research interests center on Vietnamese politics, foreign policy, and reform under socialism. He received his A.B. in political science from Whitman College and M.A. and Ph.D. from the University of Washington.

Preface

This book began rather modestly in the summer of 1990 when Börje Ljunggren, of the Swedish International Development Authority, proposed that he use his forthcoming year as a visiting scholar at the Harvard Institute for International Development (HIID) to organize a seminar series on economic reform issues in Indochina. With financial assistance from the Mac-Arthur Foundation and HIID, the seminar series brought scholars and experts to Harvard to present papers and exchange ideas on progress and problems in the process of economic and political reform in Indochina. Those papers, revised several times to keep pace with a rapidly changing environment, form the core of this book.

During the academic year 1990–91, many seminar participants were surprised to learn of the extensive economic reforms already carried out in socialist Indochina. The heady political reforms that had exploded throughout Eastern Europe and the Soviet Union and the failure of political reform to move forward in China after the Tiananmen incident captured nearly all of the attention of those interested in socialist countries. Any interest in Indochina focused on the boat people fleeing a repressive regime in Vietnam and on the continuing tragedy in Cambodia, where warfare continued in the aftermath of the bloody reign by the Khmer Rouge. Laos had apparently disappeared from the face of the earth. Talk of market economies emerging in these circumstances struck many observers as premature at best, utter lunacy at worst.

In mid-1992, such talk is accepted as reality. In Cambodia, a peace process mediated by the United Nations is under way, however tenuous in the face of Khmer Rouge hostility. Multinational corporations from around the world are eagerly waiting for the United States to lift its economic and political blockade of Vietnam so that they can invest in the transformation of the next Asian "tiger" into a newly industrializing country. Laos has become the darling of the aid agencies as it privatizes and promotes markets in its still largely rural and feudal economy.

Most of the chapters in this volume support the view that the reform process in all three countries is well under way in the economic sphere. Following the pattern of East and Southeast Asia, the process of political reform lags considerably behind the economic reforms. This lag presents a challenge of its own to Western donors, who seem more comfortable with the sequencing of reforms in Eastern Europe and the former Soviet Union, where political revolution and the dismantling of communism led to popular support for market-oriented policies. But if those policies fail to deliver benefits fairly immediately, a political backlash might threaten the economic reform process as well. There is much to learn from the Asian experience with reforms—including the Chinese experience, where the Chinese Communist Party has remained in political power while overseeing, in Guangdong Province, the world's fastest economic growth. Economic performance has been the pragmatic standard for policy change as well as the continued justification of communist regimes for retaining political power.

This interplay between economic and political reforms can be seen clearly in Indochina. Most Western analysts feel that democracy and free markets are ultimately inseparable, and a reform process that starts with one must inevitably lead to the other. In its extreme form, this Western view argues that both democracy and free markets are needed to stimulate economic growth. Many Asian observers are perplexed by this idea. In their experience, authority is as important as popular sentiment in governing large countries, and government interventions are as important as free markets in stimulating rapid economic growth. Balance in both economic and political systems, rather than extremes in either, is the Asian key to long-run development.

Whatever the degree of progress in economic and political reform in Indochina—and this book argues that it is substantial—this balance has not yet been achieved. The process of political reform in Cambodia is challenged by the intransigence of the Khmer Rouge and their tacit allies in the Thai military. Further economic reform in Vietnam is slowed or even thwarted by elements in the Communist party who fail to see their future in rapid economic growth. In Laos, the state may not have the capacity—politically, financially, and bureaucratically—to maintain stability of basic macroeconomic variables, much less design and implement a strategy for rapid economic growth.

Far from being resolved, then, the challenge of reform in Indochina is just beginning. Explaining the nature of this challenge is necessarily a lengthy and convoluted process. In the end, the optimistic tone of many chapters in this book might be premature. By the time this book appears in print, it is indeed possible that the peace process in Cambodia will have collapsed and that economic reforms in Vietnam will have been blocked by those who oppose the restructuring of state enterprises or the banking system.

But rosier scenarios are possible as well. They build on the important, difficult, and positive steps already taken, steps described and analyzed by various authors. If these chapters accurately depict the beginning of economic and political reform in Indochina rather than its premature end, the volume will serve as a basis for judging how the many challenges on the road to reform are met and overcome.

A framework for understanding these challenges, as socialist societies attempt to build market-oriented economies, is presented by Dwight Perkins in Chapter 1. Drawing on the experience of China as well as Eastern Europe and the former Soviet Union, Perkins argues that four elements are needed for successful restructuring: goods and services must be available in markets for sale and purchase; the prices in these markets must reflect real scarcities in the economy; the markets must be reasonably competitive; and producers must act to minimize costs or maximize profits in the face of market prices. None of these elements can be successful alone, and substantial progress on all four fronts is needed before there can be increased economic productivity and growth. A simple strategy that fosters free markets and privatization may do little to dislodge the entrenched bureaucracy that runs a socialist economy, and economic collapse is as likely as economic growth. Perkins provides an analytical framework for understanding why the reform process in Vietnam is in danger of stalling.

Nayan Chanda's chapter also contributes to this understanding. His central theme is that the countries of Indochina were faced with new challenges to their development policies and to international relations as a result of the end of the Cold War and the collapse of communism in Eastern Europe. Cambodia, Laos, and Vietnam were suddenly deprived of their principal sources of economic support and were faced with a fundamental threat to their identities as countries committed to building socialism. The dramatic changes in Eastern Europe are likely to complicate further the process of economic and political reform—and, in Vietnam and Laos, the transition of political leadership. According to Chanda's assessment, the historically rooted conflict in Cambodia and the tension between Cambodia and Vietnam are likely to continue in the post–Cold War era, as will the traditional rivalry between Vietnam and China and other regional disputes over territory and resources. Ideological fervor in the countries of Indochina might be declining, but disputes over political power and the embers of old rivalries in the region are likely to remain sources of instability and conservatism in political change.

The two chapters in the volume by Börje Ljunggren provide the core material on the process of reform itself, its historical evolution in each of the three countries of the region, and an optimistic perspective on the extent to which both political and economic reform are now self-generating, beyond the capacity of vested interests to stop. Ljunggren's overview of the reform process in Chapter 3 begins with the pre-reform model and the limited reform measures undertaken in 1979 and emphasizes various dimensions: the role of the state; the dismantling of central planning; price reforms and marketization; decollectivization; autonomy and privatization of enterprises; and attitudes toward the international economy and the corresponding views of the international community toward Vietnam's reform effort. Ljunggren argues that, in practice, the reforms go beyond "socialist renovation." Despite the ideological rhetoric and heavy intervention by the government and party, mixed market economies are emerging.

In his concluding chapter, Ljunggren expands on four critical issues that continue to challenge the reform process in all three countries: state capacity to manage structural reforms and conversion to a market economy, with the vastly different tasks required of government; domestic resource mobilization and the role of aid in countries where Western tax systems have yet to replace the "profits" of state enterprises as the chief source of government finance; the impact of reform on the social sectors and the difficulty in maintaining popular support for economic reforms in the face of widening income disparities and the loss of public welfare services; and the political dimension of reform, which continues to plague all countries in Asia where the Communist party is in control.

In Chapter 4, Bernard Funck analyzes the reform issue in Laos that he considers especially crucial: the conflict between the country's need for macroeconomic control and the lack of state capacity to exert control over the economy. A weak state and a relative flood of foreign aid risk corrupting the entire public sector while simultaneously inhibiting the development of a productive private sector.

May Ebihara is the only American anthropologist who has conducted fieldwork in a Khmer village inside Cambodia. In Chapter 5, she addresses issues of reform from the perspective of this village, which she first visited in 1960. After her return to the village in 1989–90, she described what had happened during the intervening thirty years. The majority of the population did not survive the Pol Pot years, and memories of those years remain a source of great trauma. How this trauma can be healed nationally while the Khmer Rouge retains significant influence in current affairs in Cambodia must be answered before meaningful economic reforms can take root.

My chapter on food policy and economic reforms in Vietnam grows out of collaborative work with Professor Vo-Tong Xuan of Can Tho University. For several years, we have been arguing that the rural economy in general, and agriculture in particular, should provide the main impetus to economic growth. While not disagreeing with other economists, including several represented in this volume, that exports of labor-intensive manufactured goods must be the medium- and longer-run basis of rapid economic growth, we feel that agriculture is capable of stimulating rapid growth immediately. The transformation of Vietnam from a famine-prone rice importer in the mid-1980s to the world's third-largest rice exporter from 1989 onward is ample testimony of the capacity of the Vietnamese rural economy to respond quickly to a more favorable economic environment, without having to wait for the full set of institutional reforms that are needed for the industrial sector to take off. My chapter concludes with an extensive discussion of further market reforms and pricing policies that are needed to maintain this momentum.

In Chapter 6, David Dapice addresses Vietnam's prospects for rapid development. Although some have suggested that Indonesia, South Korea, Taiwan, or Thailand might logically be a model for Vietnam, the situation today in Vietnam is substantially different from that of other Asian countries in the early stages of the development process. South Korea, Taiwan, and Thailand began with much higher incomes per capita, relatively developed market systems, low debt, and capital stock that was in much better condition. Indonesia received generous debt relief, foreign aid, and a major boost from oil exports—none of these seem likely for Vietnam. Compared with the experience of Indonesia and Thailand, rapid growth for Vietnam would require a greater degree of foreign investment and emphasis on early development of labor-intensive exports.

In Chapter 8, David Dollar argues for a more optimistic assessment of Vietnam's development prospects. A careful review of the country's success with macroeconomic stabilization from mid-1989 to mid-1990 reveals the crucial importance of a free exchange rate and control over growth in the money supply. When these two elements of the stabilization policy were threatened after mid-1990, high inflation rates and economic distortions returned. The concern that economic reforms might be stalled in Vietnam reflects the balance between those forces pushing for continued macroeconomic stability—and the government retrenchment that stability would require—and those arguing for continued support of state enterprises through provision of credits from the Central Bank. These credits are the main source of inflation.

Issues of health, population, and gender in Vietnam are discussed by Joan Kaufman and Gita Sen in Chapter 9. In common with social sectors in other countries undergoing radical economic restructuring, the health and education sectors in Vietnam have been starved for funds since 1990. Along with the breakup of village-level assistance with child care, the sharp decline in quality and availability of social services, especially for women, threatens to undermine the significant investments in human capital made by the Vietnamese regime after 1976. Kaufman and Sen document the basic trends in declining services and demonstrate the similarity of the pattern to that of rural China after the People's Communes were disbanded. No quick or easy solution appears to be available.

How life in a North Vietnamese village changed during a decade of reform efforts in the 1980s is the topic of Chapter 10. Hy Van Luong undertook anthropological fieldwork in the summers of 1990 and 1991 and wrote a vivid account of the effects of reform, one of which Vietnam's political leaders might not have foreseen. There has been a resurgence of pre-1945 traditions and a greater observance of rituals, both of which were made possible by the increasing economic surplus and the shift from collectivized agriculture to household production in the multi-sector economy. The change in political economy has given a major impetus to the old traditions.

The dynamics and political economy of Vietnam's reform efforts are analyzed by Adam Fforde in Chapter 11. He attempts to identify the forces that have led, in his judgment, to what is essentially a market economy. Fforde has participated more directly in the reform process for a longer period than any other author represented in this volume, and his analysis amounts to an insider's view of how the debates have been framed.

William Turley widens the perspective, in Chapter 12, to include the political sphere. Is there any political reform, and if so, what does the new Vietnam look like? Vietnam's "renovation" is perceived by many to be driven by the economy, with political reform suspended. Turley takes issue with this perception and argues that the political system *is* being reformed, though not into the multi-party system the West would prefer. He analyzes six aspects of reform: bureaucracy, party, media, elections, representative assemblies, and mass organizations. Turley discusses the crises the party faces and suggests how Vietnam, abandoning former ideological models, might proceed.

Naturally, many people, in addition to the authors, are involved in producing a volume such as this. Not everyone can be thanked personally, but several individuals were essential to the process. Erin Sands, my assistant in the fall of 1991, managed the logistics of each seminar, provided administrative support for Börje Ljunggren, and kept in touch with authors in the early stages of manuscript revision. In taking over this role, Deborah McCarthy juggled all the complicated pieces of the publication process and coordinated the effort with Vukani Magubane, head of HIID's own publications office.

While the MacArthur Foundation provided much of the support for the seminar series, HIID made available substantial resources to publish this volume as the second in its new series devoted to fostering debate and discussion of topics in economic development. Thanks are due to Tim Blodgett for editing early drafts of the manuscripts. Carol F. Timmer was jack-of-all-trades for my own written effort in this book and for Börje's early contributions. The staff of Editorial Services of New England, Inc., under the direction of Constance Devanthéry-Lewis, substantially edited the final drafts and provided excellent copy editing and publication assistance.

Lastly, I would like to thank our friends and colleagues in Indochina whose names do not appear on any chapters, but whose knowledge and dedication to the process of reform are reflected on each page. I sincerely hope that the next volume on reform in Indochina will be written not only by their actions, but by their pens as well.

C. Peter Timmer
July 4, 1992
Cambridge, Massachusetts

*The Challenge of Reform
in Indochina*

1

Reforming the Economic Systems of Vietnam and Laos

Dwight H. Perkins

The Asian pattern of reform of socialist economic systems differs markedly from the path of change in Eastern Europe and the former Soviet Union. There are three distinctive features of the Asian pattern, as follows:

1. Economic reform precedes political reform. Although there has been some political reform in Indochina and elsewhere in Asia (with the exception of North Korea), communist parties in the region show no signs of surrendering their monopoly of power.

2. The Asian socialist states are much poorer than their counterparts in Eastern Europe and the former Soviet Union. The Indochinese states are the poorest of these Asian socialist nations. There is considerable controversy over how to measure the per capita gross national product (GNP) of Eastern Europe and the former U.S.S.R., but there is little doubt that per capita GNP in places like Hungary and Poland is at least 10 times the levels of Vietnam, Laos, and Cambodia.[1] Even China has at least double the per capita GNP of Indochina.[2]

3. Most of the population in Indochina, and to a lesser degree in China, is in agriculture, and much of the industrial output comes from small-scale units. In Eastern Europe, in contrast, most people live and work in cities, where large-scale units dominate industrial production.

These three characteristics of the Asian pattern of reform are related. The dominance of agriculture and small producing units is, in part, a reflection of Asia's poverty. The continued prevalence of authoritarian political systems is also, to some degree, a result of the region's low income levels.

---

[1]The *World Bank Atlas 1990* (1990, pp. 6–9), for example, gives the per capita GNP of Hungary and Poland as $2,560 and $1,760 respectively, and that of Laos as $170. These figures are unreliable but show the general magnitude of the difference.

[2]*The World Bank Atlas 1990* (1990, p. 6) lists China's GNP as being $360 but gives no figure for Vietnam. China's official exchange rate severely distorts its GNP in a downward direction.

It is tempting to say that Vietnam and Laos are in earlier stages of the reform process that is occurring in Eastern Europe, but this is to see reform patterns as immutable across socialist systems. According to this argument, if Eastern Europe's economic-reform efforts of the 1970s and 1980s ran into serious obstacles in the absence of political reform, it follows that Asian economic-reform efforts will run into similar obstacles. But the special characteristics of the Asian socialist systems make it unlikely that their pattern of reform will proceed in stages identical to those of Hungary or Poland.

Vietnam, Laos, and Cambodia *do* have problems common to Eastern Europe, notably the cutback in Soviet aid (which, in Eastern Europe, is mainly a cutback in low-priced oil) and the collapse of Comecon, the East's trading bloc. But the differences, beginning with politics, are profound. The Communist party in Vietnam came to power as a result of both internal and external forces. In contrast, communism in Eastern Europe was externally imposed, riding in on the back of the Soviet Red Army. And while both Vietnam and Eastern Europe followed the pattern of Soviet central planning in establishing centralized bureaucracies to control the economy, this process went much further in Eastern Europe than in Vietnam—particularly South Vietnam. The political-economic apparatus is necessarily different in Vietnam than in Eastern Europe, as Vietnam is a largely agrarian society that has recently undergone two decades of civil war, followed by unification under a nationalist leadership. Eastern Europe, highly industrialized and with ties to Western Europe, required a political-economic structure of a different sort, imposed from the outside by what was in essence a colonial regime.

How do these differences between Asia and Europe affect the prospects for and sequencing of economic reform in Vietnam and Laos? This essay will address that question, exploring the nature and direction of reform in Vietnam with occasional references to Laos. Laos is interesting for students of reform as an example of the limitations of the Soviet-style bureaucratic command system in a country that has barely entered the modern era. Vietnam, in contrast to Laos and like China, had the organizational capacity to make a Soviet-style system work adequately, at least for some purposes. I will not analyze Cambodia here, largely because its civil war has yet to end. The role of economic reform in the context of civil war is a separate subject that is outside the scope of this essay.

The Motivation for Reform

Why did Vietnam and Laos decide to undertake reform of their economic systems? The answer is not immediately obvious.

The Soviet system had served the U.S.S.R. reasonably well for half a century before an increasingly complex economy rendered the system more and more inefficient and economic growth tailed off. Eastern Europe, despite starting from a higher economic base, did not fare as well, but still got over two decades of growth out of the command system. Toward the end of this period of growth, countries such as Hungary and Poland resorted increasingly to borrowing from the West to sustain their development. When borrowing was no longer possible, those economies ran into serious trouble. China managed a quarter century of sustained economic development despite gross mismanagement of the economy in the late 1950s (The Great Leap Forward) and the late 1960s (the early stages of the Cultural Revolution). In Vietnam's case, only 11 years after the end of the Second Indochina War and the reunification of the country, the nation's leadership decided to jettison many essential features of Soviet central planning. Laos followed a course similar to that of Vietnam.

Did some crisis in the Vietnamese economy spur the policy changes introduced in December 1986 at the Sixth Party Congress? Certainly the national income (net material product) statistics of the early 1980s do not suggest a crisis. Industrial output in the 1981–85 period grew at an average annual rate of 9.5 percent, although some of this growth represented recovery after two years of economic crisis in 1978 and 1979 (Thanh Son, 1990, p. 39). Agricultural production in general and food production in particular rose at 5 percent a year during this same period (Chu Van Lam, 1990, p. 22). The increase in agricultural production resulted, in part, from renewed support for certain household-based production activities (what was called the "contract system"), but the early 1980s were hardly a period of sweeping rural reforms such as those that eliminated collective farming in China in the years 1981–83. In the period 1983–85, Vietnam's leadership still had the ambition to complete, not eliminate, the collectivization process in the southern part of the country.

Since the announcement of reforms in 1986, the performance of Vietnam's economy has not vindicated the reforms. Industry grew only modestly in 1987 and 1988 before declining slightly in 1989 (*SEVY 2000*, 1991, p. 28). Agriculture had a very poor year in 1987 and did not pick up until land-tenure reform, or decollectivization, had created household-based farming, and improved pricing and marketing policies had led to a sharp recovery, particularly in rice production, in 1989 and 1990.

This performance pattern contrasts with what happened in China when it began a reform effort in December 1978. In China, radical reform began with agriculture. Freeing up rural markets, followed by decollectivization, led to a big spurt in agricultural output and farmers' incentives. The obvious success of these rural reforms quieted those opposed to radical reforms and laid the groundwork for the introduction of the urban-industrial reform program in 1984. Not until inflation accelerated in China in 1988 and government corruption became increasingly conspicuous did the conservative opposition to reform find its voice again.

In Vietnam, prices, which had already been rising at a Latin American-style pace of 50 to 90 percent a year, jumped still further following the 1986 reforms to nearly 500 percent in 1986 and by similar amounts right through 1988. Only in 1989 did the government, probably only temporarily, bring prices under control (*SEVY 2000*, 1991, pp. 46–47).

The question then remains, what was the impetus for the 1986 reforms and why, despite disappointing results, have they continued? The industrial and agricultural performance of 1981–85 does not suggest a crisis or other rationale for reform. And clearly, the actual economic results of the 1986 reforms did not provide the rationale for continued reform in Vietnam. What then was it? The political economy behind the reform decisions of 1986 has not yet been analyzed in print, so I can only speculate. The year 1986 predates the more radical Eastern European and Soviet reforms, but significant change in those societies was already under way. Tens of thousands of Vietnamese were also living, studying, and working in Eastern Europe and the Soviet Union. In addition, Vietnam's economic policies have always been heavily influenced by China, even during periods of openly hostile relations between the two countries.[3] By 1986, China's economic reforms were recognized worldwide as a great success story. Also, the performance of Vietnam's East Asian nonsocialist neighbors could hardly have gone unnoticed by Vietnam. By 1986, Thailand was well into the kind of economic boom that South Korea and Taiwan had been enjoying for more than two decades. These events elsewhere certainly could have and probably did influence Vietnam's reform decisions.

By 1986, had Vietnam's economic planners become aware of the inherent shortcomings of Soviet-style central planning, in spite of a respectable level of real output growth? Did the leadership foresee, to some degree, the difficult years that lay ahead? By 1980, Vietnamese economists, disturbed by the extreme poverty they witnessed around them, had already begun to raise questions in Vietnamese economic journals about the viability of the Soviet model for Vietnam. Under Le Duan and until his death in 1986, however, active dissent against the Soviet model was stifled.[4] Further research is

---

[3]This is a major theme in Vo Nhan Tri's *Vietnam's Economic Policy Since 1975* (1990).

[4]I am indebted to Alexander Woodside for pointing out these earlier writings of economists such as Phung The Truong and Vu Tuan Anh.

required before we will have a clearer picture of the nature and depth of dissent over economic policies in the early 1980s.

By 1990, there were even more reasons to carry on with reform, regardless of its impact in the preceding few years. The imminent decline in Soviet aid and the breakup of Comecon meant that Vietnam would have to find new markets in the quality- and style-conscious environment of capitalist market economies. And as the Eastern Europeans had discovered when they tried to expand their manufactured exports to the West, the bureaucratic command system is poorly suited to providing market-oriented incentives to business enterprises.

The decision to abandon most elements of Soviet-style central planning and bureaucratic control of the economy is easier to understand in the case of Laos. Laos quite simply lacked the trained and experienced manpower needed to operate under a Soviet-style arrangement. Although a decentralized market structure also requires skilled manpower, the requirements are not as stringent and inflexible as in a system where distant bureaucrats give detailed orders to producers on what to produce and which inputs to use. Compounding the problem, Laos, largely a rural society, has only the most limited communications infrastructure. An attempt to run this kind of society along Soviet-style economic principles was bound to fail—and it did. (See Chapter 4 in this volume.)

Whatever the reasons for pursuing reform in Vietnam and Laos, once the process was under way, the economic leadership had few options. The principal choices were the following:

1. Whether to pursue an across-the-board move to a market economy or to expand the role of the market in a more limited manner, say, in only one sector. There are two fundamental ways to coordinate national economic activities: either through bureaucratic (hierarchical) commands or through the market. There is no third way, although some have tried to find one. In China in 1958–59, Mao Zedong thought that somehow his brand of ideology, if properly inculcated in party cadres, could circumvent the need for either market or central planning in coordinating the nation's economic activities. Instead, he allowed enterprises to produce whatever they pleased, which resulted in chaos and a massive waste of resources.

2. Whether to push through reforms quickly or gradually. The quick path is sometimes referred to as the "big bang" approach. Do everything at once, it is argued, or forces will build and eventually push the system back toward bureaucratic commands and central planning, or bureaucratic commands without central planning. The alternative, of course, is gradual, or step-by-step, reform. Which approach is more likely to succeed has much to do with

people's expectations about whether they will (or won't) gain from the reforms. These expectations in turn generate individual or group political action that is intended to advance or undermine the reform effort. Simply stated, the choice between rapid or gradual reform is mainly a question of politics.

The remainder of this essay deals with how these choices were made in Vietnam and Laos from 1986 to 1990.

Expanding the Role of the Market

Macroeconomic Stability: The First Requirement

For a market system to work, first of all, a country must have macroeconomic stability. If money were truly just a veil with no impact on production, it would be possible to have rampant inflation and still operate well-functioning markets. But rapid price increases, such as the triple-digit rates experienced by Vietnam in the late 1980s, distort the real economy both directly and indirectly. Directly, hyperinflation leads investors away from long-term, productive investments and into activities like excessive construction as a hedge against inflation, or into short-term financial speculation that often reaps larger profits than can be found in more useful activities. Indirectly, high inflation levels create political problems for the government. Often, the government will respond to these political pressures by introducing price controls.

Rather than just resorting to price controls, the government should respond by eliminating the sources of inflationary pressure. But it is not always in a position to do so, largely for political reasons. Price controls combined with continuing inflationary pressure lead to shortages of controlled goods. Instead of rationing by price as before, the society has turned to rationing by queuing (waiting in line), which is a waste of people's time. To get around wasting time, the government may reintroduce centralized allocation of goods; once again, the society is mired in a bureaucratic command system.

Balance-of-payments disequilibria operate in a similar manner. A shortage of foreign exchange often leads a government to impose quantitative controls over imports in an effort to stem the flow. On economic grounds, an exchange-rate devaluation, or even tariffs, is preferable to quantitative restrictions, but governments, out of ignorance or for political reasons, often don't see it that way. Quantitative restrictions are really just another name for the bureaucratic command approach to the allocation of goods.

What constitutes stabilization is a political question. The government and people of Vietnam have become used to high rates of inflation, so price increases of 50 percent a year and more do not necessarily create political difficulties. In China, in contrast, rates above 10 percent a year cause extreme political concern. But China, prior to the 1980s, had experienced two decades when the average annual rate of increase in prices was under 2 percent and in the 1940s, the Communist party had come to power in part because of the hyperinflation generated by *Guomindang* fiscal policies. Vietnam, on the other hand, had suffered from regular bouts of high inflation throughout the war period of the 1960s and 1970s and after. While Vietnam, unlike China, may tolerate inflation rates of 50 percent or more, rates this high certainly make the proper functioning of markets more difficult.

After Stabilization: The Other Four Components of a Functioning Market

Once an adequate level of stabilization prevails, a market system must have four additional elements in place before it can function well. Of these elements, described below, three are conceptually straightforward, while the fourth is not well understood.

1. Goods must be available for purchase and sale on the market. Goods that are allocated through bureaucratic channels are, by definition, not available on the market. In a *pure* Soviet-type system of central planning and bureaucratic commands, there are no goods available on the market. However, in the real world, there is no example of such a pure system—although China, during certain ascendant periods of Mao Zedong's thought, came close.

2. If goods are available on the market but are not priced to reflect their true relative scarcity, goods will end up in lower priority uses, and the economy will suffer. Pricing goods to reflect true relative scarcity, therefore, is an essential element in making markets work. Economists sometimes treat accurate relative pricing as if it were the only element that mattered, but this is clearly not the only issue when moving away from a bureaucratic command system.

3. Markets must be competitive. A functioning market system with monopoly control of most markets is possible, but there is little point in market-oriented reforms if monopoly prevails. A central objective of reform is to raise the rate of growth of total factor productivity. Competition among enterprises, foreign and domestic, is one of the main forces—probably the main force—putting pressure on firms to raise productivity. Markets are by far the most effective vehicles for promoting competition. Central planners, in contrast, prefer that enterprises have monopolies over particular markets. Competition makes planning more difficult as enterprises switch from one supplier to another.

4. Producing units, firms in particular, must maximize profits by cutting costs or boosting sales. This element is not only poorly understood but is also the most difficult to implement in a system long used to central planning and bureaucratic controls. Raising profits by extracting larger subsidies from the government, either through outright grants or protection from competition, is typical of a system dominated by bureaucratic controls, but is inconsistent with what well-functioning markets require.

The issue today is not whether market socialism is theoretically possible but whether it can be realized in practice. Oskar Lange demonstrated to most economists' satisfaction that a well-functioning market is possible with state ownership of enterprises, provided that those enterprises follow the profit-maximization rule. The key question is whether enterprise managers can be induced to follow this rule. To some analysts, this question hinges on "property rights." Will the state allow managers or boards of directors a sufficient personal stake in the enterprise so that they will follow the rule? Simpler versions of the discussion of property rights equate them with "privatization." If the government can just make the ownership of enterprises private, managers' (profit-maximizing) behavior will follow more or less automatically.

But privatization is not the cure-all that some advocates believe it is. Much depends on the kind of privatization implemented. A state firm turned over to the president's cronies with its subsidies intact isn't likely to change its behavior much. Similarly, an enterprise that is sold off to thousands of small shareholders, none of whom has any experience with share ownership, may well end up with management working in its own interest, not in the interest of the shareholders. Boards of directors that are the captives of management are rather common even in mature capitalist economies. These and related problems of principals and their agents are found in all economic systems, but they can be particularly serious in Soviet-type socialist systems.

Privatization, therefore, is not a sufficient condition for eliciting the appropriate enterprise behavior. Something else is required, but what? Privatization may not even be a *necessary* condition. Certainly, it is unnecessary on theoretical grounds, as Oskar Lange has demonstrated. But is it necessary on practical grounds, as many Eastern Europeans now argue? What will happen to nations like Vietnam (and China) that reject across-the-board privatization on political or value grounds? Are these nations doomed to retain the heavy hand of the bureaucratic command system until they change their minds? Even if the Eastern Europeans were right about the situation they faced, does it follow that the Asian socialist states face identical or similar problems?

Enterprises Must Be Autonomous for Success

It is easier to define the *requirements* for efficient operation of a state (or private) enterprise in a market environment than it is to determine whether what is required is *feasible*. The key is that the enterprise must be completely autonomous. More concretely, the enterprise must be allowed to fail. But failure does not necessarily have to mean bankruptcy, followed by shutting down the firm and laying off all its workers. Conceivably, only management need bear the brunt of the penalties for failure. If new management can turn the company around, it is also conceivable that the old labor force could remain. On the other hand, an enterprise that is a permanent money loser will—and should—fold in any society, not just a capitalist one.

If an enterprise is to be allowed to fail, it must not be free to get regular bailouts via government grants or subsidized loans from the banking system. It follows, too, that the banking and financial system should also not be able to get government bailouts. If the government won't bail out the banks, the banks can't afford to bail out their client enterprises. The client enterprises will thus face hard budget constraints and will be forced to make prudent cost-containment decisions unless the state is willing to step in with direct subsidies from its budget.

Recent Indochina Reforms: The Big Bang Approach

How far have Vietnam and Laos progressed in their efforts to introduce market systems? Have they achieved stabilization, and are the other four elements of a well-functioning market system in place?

Both Vietnam and Laos have chosen what amounts to an across-the-board, big-bang approach. The more radical reforms began at the Sixth Party Congress in 1986 in Vietnam and the Fourth Party Congress of 1986 in Laos, although party leaders had tried in the early 1980s to modify the command system. Within three years after the congresses, both countries had reintroduced market mechanisms into their entire economies, with the exception of their large-scale enterprises.

The Dominance of Small-Scale Enterprises in Asia

To economists studying Eastern Europe or the Soviet Union, rapid and comprehensive market reform that excludes large state enterprises will sound strange. What else is there but large state enterprises in a Soviet-type economic system? The answer in the context of Asia is, a great deal: large-scale state enterprises form only a small part of Asian national economies. Precise figures are not available, but in the case of Laos, the agriculture and services sectors together constitute 82 to 84 percent of GNP. Of the remaining 16 to 18 percent, probably no more than a few percent of value-added is produced by enterprises that are even a modest approximation of what economists call large-scale state enterprises.

State industry plays a larger role in Vietnam but is still a small fraction of the economy. Industry in 1989 constituted 24 percent of net material product, or 28.7 percent, depending on whether current or 1982 prices are used. Of total industrial output, state enterprises produced something over half, but many of those were not large. Only 700 of the 2,300 total government-controlled enterprises were under the control of the central government, while the remainder, producing mostly consumer goods, were under provincial or municipal authorities (*SEVY 2000*, 1991, pp. 29–30). Many of this latter group were quite small, as were all the considerable number of cooperative and private establishments. State enterprises under central control employed only 15 percent of all industrial workers, although the share of value-added would be much higher (*SEVY 2000*, 1991, p. 128). If large, state commercial and financial enterprises were added to those in industry, it would be surprising if together they constituted more than 15 percent of Vietnam's GNP. In China, by way of comparison, large enterprises account for 20 to 25 percent of GNP.[5] In Eastern Europe and the Soviet Union, the share of GNP of large-scale enterprise output is far higher than in Asia.

The implications of the dominance of small-scale units for the functioning of markets are straightforward. It is virtually impossible to run tens of thousands of small units through bureaucratic commands—or at least to do it efficiently. Central planning requires a body of reliable information, and personnel working in small units in a developing country lack the training required to produce such information on a timely basis. Small production units also use widely varying equipment and techniques (even within a single industry), which make it impossible to establish similar input norms. This is obviously true in agriculture, where weather and soil conditions vary, but it is also true in industry. In addition, the failure of a small firm does not have the same implications for the government as the failure of a large firm. A large firm going bankrupt can throw thousands of people out of work, which would have serious political implications even in highly authoritarian regimes. Closing down a large firm, therefore, is much more difficult than letting a small firm go out of business.

---

[5]This is a crude estimate taken from Dwight H. Perkins, "The Transition from Central Planning: East Asia's Experience," presented at the Korean Development Institute Twentieth Anniversary Symposium (1991).

Small-Scale Enterprises Lend Themselves to the Market System

Where small units prevail, therefore, it is both easier and more necessary to make the market system work. It is necessary because small units cannot meet the information requirements of efficient central planning. It is easier mainly because getting producing units to behave according to the rules of the market (the fourth required element), is not complicated. To begin with, as I have pointed out, small firms or farm households face hard budget constraints. No state will regularly bail out farm families or handicraft workers when they make mistakes. At the same time, farm households and small industrial enterprises can adjust their methods of operation to market forces much more easily. There is no need to retrain top management to focus on costs and marketing rather than plan targets. Farm households are natural profit or net-income maximizers. Small cooperatives, even in a Soviet-type system, must also be more market oriented on a day-to-day basis than large enterprises; hence, they have less to learn when the overall economic system converts to market principles.

The Process of Market Reform in Vietnam and Laos

Given the advantages of converting to a market system in an economy dominated by small units, how did Vietnam and Laos fare in speedily introducing market systems? The first three elements of a market system—making goods available on the market, freeing up prices, and enabling competition—were certainly established quickly enough. The Vietnamese made most goods available to the market and freed up all but three categories of prices (electricity, petroleum, and transport). By 1989, Vietnam had also unified the exchange rate, the most important price of all, and, by the latter half of 1990, had brought it more or less into line with the parallel market rate (*SEVY 2000*, 1991, p. 63). Laos followed a similar path, eliminating the dual-price system, where there was both an official price and a parallel market price for each commodity, in favor of a single, market-determined price. By July 1988, the Laotian government had eliminated multiple exchange rates, and the single rate is now adjusted in line with parallel market developments.

Accompanying the freeing up of prices in Vietnam was a loosening of state control over the distribution of goods and services. In many cases, state firms still handled distribution, but goods went to those who could pay, not to those designated in the plan to receive particular items. Not all barriers to competition disappeared in Vietnam; some barriers to trade remained, but many internal trade restrictions were eliminated. Private merchants were also legally let back into the internal distribution system. (Illegally, they had been there all along.)

The unified market-price system distinguishes Indochina's economic reforms from China's. In the 1980s, China greatly expanded the scope of goods distributed through the market at market-determined prices, but China retained below-market, officially set prices for many goods distributed by state organs. The power of the many large enterprises receiving subsidized state prices was too great to eliminate those prices altogether. The dual-price system solved one political problem for the Chinese leadership, but it created another. Individuals with access to goods allocated at official prices soon discovered they could make easy profits by reselling those goods at much higher market prices. The resulting corruption was one element of the discontent of China's urban population in the months leading up to the tragedy in Tiananmen Square on June 4, 1989.

With the unified market-price systems adopted in Vietnam and Laos, these countries came close to introducing full-blown market systems. Were they socialist market systems? Agriculture in both Vietnam and Laos was decollectivized, although decollectivization was more complete in the southern part of Vietnam than in the North. Outside of agriculture, the Vietnamese government was active in promoting collective enterprises and even private firms. These firms were predominantly in Ho Chi Minh City, where they accounted for a quarter of all manufacturing (Do Duc Dinh, 1991, p. 5). In the latter half of the 1980s, those collective and private firms grew much faster than the state-owned sector in Vietnam. The government also promoted foreign private investment, mostly in the form of joint ventures; however, the amount of direct foreign investment realized by the end of 1990 was still very small.

In Vietnam, the one sector that remained socialist by any definition of the term—the large state-owned enterprises—was also the one sector that remained, at best, only partially transformed into market-oriented entities. In Vietnam, these enterprises must operate in the market, but by no means do they operate in accordance with market principles. By one recent estimate, only 30 percent of state enterprises are well managed and profitable. Of the remaining 70 percent, 40 percent are deemed capable of being made viable, while the other 30 percent are probably irredeemable (Do Duc Dinh, 1991, p. 4). Comparable figures for Laos would probably show an even less favorable picture, although Laos has begun privatizing state enterprises.

The Task Still Ahead

Will the Vietnamese and Laotian governments succeed in reforming these state-owned enterprises so that they truly operate in accordance with market principles? Many economists and politicians in Vietnam and Laos recognize the need for these reforms.

In the case of Laos, privatization has already begun, and most state firms are destined to be privatized if they cannot be made efficient under state ownership. In Laos, the political costs of greatly reducing or eliminating state ownership of enterprises are not very great, largely because the state-owned sector is so small; conversely, the rewards for reform, mainly enhanced support from the international aid community, are attractive.

Vietnam will probably not follow a similar path. In comparison with Eastern Europe, the Soviet Union, or even China, Vietnam's state-enterprise sector is very small, employing only 844,000 people in industry in 1988 in contrast to more than 60 million in China (*SEVY 2000*, 1991, p. 128). But small as it is, it is still apparently politically powerful enough to make Vietnamese reformers hesitate. When the government bureaucracies were downsized and many ministries eliminated in 1986, at least some of the laid-off personnel were transferred to state enterprises. Retired military personnel may also have been given jobs with these companies. These individuals, in many cases, would have retained close ties to their former ministry and party colleagues. On the other hand, the political base of the Vietnamese Communist party is more in the army and perhaps the countryside than it is in the bureaucracy. It is unlikely, therefore, that the party relies on ownership of industrial enterprises to maintain its power.

In Eastern Europe, the Communist party, the bureaucracy, and the enterprise managers were one and the same. That is hardly the case in Vietnam. It is not the case in China either, and in China, the size of the bureaucracy controlling and managing the state-enterprise sector is far larger than in Vietnam, even on a per capita basis.

If Vietnam cannot orient its large-scale, state-owned sector toward the market, what are the likely consequences? One answer can be obtained by looking at the consequences of the failure to reform these enterprises. The biggest, immediate cost has been continued inflation. In the long run, the government will face extra costs in slower growth as state enterprises assume a larger part of the overall economy.

Addressing the Decline in State Revenue

Macro instability, however, is the most immediate problem for the coming few years. A common phenomenon in Soviet-type economies moving toward a market system is a fall in state revenues. Before the changeover, much state revenue was, in effect, generated by distorted prices that created state-enterprise profits that were then turned over to the government budget. When prices begin adjusting to market forces, much of this artificial income disappears. New forms of taxation, which will eventually replace these revenue sources, take some time to design and even a longer time to implement. Thus, revenues fall while subsidies to state enterprises are rising, also as a result of price reforms. The result is inflation.

The fiscal situation in Vietnam and Laos was even worse in the late 1980s than the typical news story would lead one to expect. To begin with, the Vietnamese and Laotian governments started from an unusually low tax base, around 10 to 12 percent of GNP in both cases. (See Chapters 4 and 8.) The Laotian tax base eroded further during the early phases of reform; Vietnam's base did not erode, largely because of a windfall from the start-up of the White Tiger oil field. Partly offsetting this gain, however, was a decline in Soviet foreign aid that had made modest contributions to budget revenues.

The lesson here is that the state cannot keep pumping large amounts of money into public enterprises unless it dramatically raises revenue from taxes. Even if it raises taxes, it is unlikely to be able to do so sufficiently to finance losses from state-owned enterprises as well as desperately needed increases in investment in the infrastructure. Vietnam's infrastructure, particularly in the north, is woefully inadequate, and that in Laos hardly exists. All the talk of privatization often obscures the fact that government investment typically makes up half the total gross capital formation in the early decades of development—even in the more resolutely capitalist nations (Perkins, 1991b). Most of this investment goes into infrastructure, without which growth of private industry could be seriously impeded.

If increases in revenue in Vietnam and Laos were directly or indirectly used to finance state enterprise, it is difficult to see how either country could build enough infrastructure to achieve sustained growth in either industry or agriculture. Infrastructure investments in Indochina will require sums equivalent to around 10 percent of GNP for decades to come. Even if a renewed flow of foreign aid begins in a year or two, it would cover only a fraction of this amount. The choices facing Vietnam, therefore, are straightforward. The first would be to eliminate losing enterprises, raise taxes, and invest in infrastructure. The second is to cut out investment in infrastructure. A third choice would be to continue investing in state-enterprise subsidies and infrastructure and let prices rise to hyperinflation levels. The last course is not really a choice at all but simply the consequence of a failure to choose. In the case of Vietnam, only the first option will lead to sustained growth. The situation in Laos is less stark, mainly because state enterprises are such a small part of the economy.

Reform of State Enterprises Needed to Achieve Fiscal Stability
Reform of state enterprises, therefore, is needed, especially in Vietnam, to achieve fiscal stability and sustained growth. Reform means either eliminating

those enterprises suffering large losses or making them profitable in a market context. Reform of state enterprises in Vietnam is also necessary over the long run if the country is to achieve balance-of-payments equilibrium. The balance-of-payments reasoning, however, is different from that for fiscal stabilization.

Vietnam's severe balance-of-payments problems in the late 1980s had little to do with the introduction of market-oriented reform. The problems had everything to do with the collapse of the Comecon trading bloc and the resulting chaos in the Soviet Union's economy. In the mid-1980s, almost two-thirds of Vietnam's imports from the nonconvertible currency area were financed by Soviet loans; these loans were reduced and then cut off in the late 1980s and early 1990s (*SEVY 2000*, 1991, pp. 60–63). In addition, the U.S.S.R. stopped selling petroleum and fertilizer at subsidized prices. Therefore, to sustain growth, Vietnam desperately needed alternative sources of foreign exchange.

The Need for Foreign Exchange

For Laos, access to aid from the international and nonEastern-bloc aid agencies has helped fill the gap. But Vietnam has been cut off from most such sources. Even if aid from the World Bank and others is forthcoming in the near future, the sums will cover only a part of Vietnam's needs. (Larger countries generally get less aid per capita than smaller countries.) Vietnam needs sustained increases in foreign exchange earnings from exports. But where are these exports to come from, and what are the implications of an export drive for market-oriented reforms?

China, it is worth noting, had to adjust to a similar balance-of-payments crisis brought about by the breakup of relations with the Soviet Union. But in China's case, this breakup occurred two decades before the country's decision to introduce market-oriented reforms. By cutting back imports in the early 1960s and expanding exports, mainly textiles, China achieved a balance in its external account and even repaid its debt to the Soviet Union. By the time China began introducing market-oriented reforms in the 1980s, it already had a stable source of foreign exchange on which to build.

Vietnam depended far more on Soviet loans than China ever did. In 1990, Vietnam, like China in the 1960s, faced an American embargo on trade, making the promotion of exports far more difficult. The American embargo will presumably end soon. Its main effect by 1990 was to undermine Vietnam's efforts to liberalize and open up its economy to the outside world, and that effect can hardly be a rational long-term goal for the United States.

Vietnam's Potential Exports. But if the markets are likely to become accessible, what does Vietnam have to sell? Like China in the 1970s, Vietnam has high hopes for earnings from newly discovered petroleum fields, and it is, in fact, already earning significant foreign exchange from the White Tiger field. As in the case of China, however, finding and developing additional oil fields will take time. If Vietnam's economy grows steadily in the meantime, the domestic demand for petroleum will grow, leaving a lower surplus for export. Much the same can be said for other minerals that Vietnam has in abundance. Perhaps Vietnam will achieve an export bonanza from these sources, but to rely on them would be unwise.

Can agricultural exports meet Vietnam's needs? Rice exports have already played a role in this regard. There is potential in other sectors as well, although tree crops take years to reach maturity. In the short run, agricultural products are probably Vietnam's best export opportunity if market incentives begin to generate surpluses of various cash crops. But over the longer run, Vietnam is unlikely to be able to rely on agricultural exports any more than its East Asian neighbors. Vietnam's endowment of arable land is one of the worst in the world; it is similar in that respect to Korea, Japan, and China. As incomes have risen in those countries, they have all become net *importers* of agricultural products, particularly grain.[6]

That leaves manufactured exports as the most likely long-term solution to Vietnam's balance-of-payments needs. Vietnam has the educated man-power needed for a manufactured-export drive. As the other East Asian states have demonstrated, however, successful export drives in industry also require style-and-quality-conscious firms. Put differently, the firms must be market oriented. In Vietnam's case, many small firms that are growing under the current reformed system will become export oriented. But it is hard to imagine a successful manufactured-export drive that is based on small firms alone (although Taiwan is one model for this kind of development). Even if the large firms are not themselves exporters, they still must be able to supply the smaller enterprises with low-cost high-quality inputs. Therefore, export of manufactured goods will require a market-oriented industrial sector, which would not be as crucial if Vietnam could rely solely on the export of minerals.

China has demonstrated that a partially reformed state and collectively owned industrial sector can increase the export of manufactures at a rapid pace.[7] Hong Kong was central to this process, supplying the marketing

---

[6]The difference between this statement and Peter Timmer's statements in Chapter 7 is more apparent than real. If there is a difference, it is over the number of years that agriculture could meet Vietnam's export needs before manufacturing exports took over. There is no dispute that manufacturing exports will have to take over, probably becoming dominant within a decade if overall growth proceeds rapidly.

[7]Chinese exports grew in nominal terms at 17 percent a year between the end of 1978 and 1990, faster than in either South Korea or Taiwan over the same period.

know-how that was missing in many mainland industries (Sung Yun Wing, 1991). Bangkok and Hong Kong conceivably could play a similar role in Vietnam.

Vietnam, like China, also has overseas communities in the United States and Europe. Conceivably, these communities could also play a role in opening up trade opportunities, as overseas Chinese did for China. None of this is likely to occur, however, if Vietnamese enterprises remain unreformed. Outsiders will have little economic incentive to invest if the state bureaucracy still dominates the manufacturing sector. Or perhaps outsiders will invest only in the South, where their main contacts are located. Such an investment pattern would eventually pose great difficulties for the North, where income levels are already low in comparison with the South.

Will Market-Oriented Reform of State Enterprises Take Place?

If this line of reasoning is essentially correct, sustained rapid growth will be impossible in Vietnam unless the country completes the process it started in 1986 by marketizing state-owned industrial enterprises. In the short run, agricultural growth and the exploitation of petroleum may sustain development, but probably not even for as long as a decade. In Laos, agriculture is probably the main alternative for some time to come, principally because manufacturing is barely in its infancy (although hydropower is a significant export). Laos, however, probably lacks the capacity, at present, to achieve East Asian–style growth rates of 7 or 8 percent of GNP a year. Laos simply lacks the human capital, the trained and experienced workers and managers, necessary for the achievement of such high rates of growth.

If Vietnam, to realize its full economic potential, requires further market-oriented reform, is that reform likely to be realized? That question brings us back to politics.

As stated at the beginning of this essay, Vietnam is unlike Eastern Europe, in part because the Communist party is still very much in control of the government. Can such a party take the steps required either to privatize state-owned industry or make state firms genuinely autonomous and subject to hard budget constraints? As I suggested, the Vietnamese Communist party's political base is very different from that of the communist parties of Eastern Europe in the 1980s and earlier. It is hard to believe, for this reason, that its interests are linked to the maintenance of a noncompetitive state industrial sector. Over the long run, market-oriented reforms probably will radically change the party's monopoly of power. But failure to achieve sustained growth through reform will also radically change the party's position, with consequences that may well resemble what happened in Eastern Europe in the 1980s.

References

Chu Van Lam. 1990. "Forty Five Years of Vietnam's Industry." *Economic Problems.* Hanoi: Institute of World Economy.

Do Duc Dinh. 1991. "Economic Renovation in Vietnam—A Process of Changes." Paper presented at Nineteenth Pacific Trade and Development Conference, Beijing, May 27-30.

Perkins, Dwight H. 1991a. "The Transition from Central Planning: East Asia's Experience." Paper presented at Korean Development Institute Twentieth Anniversary Symposium, Seoul, July 1-3.

————. 1991b. "Reforming Economic Systems." In Dwight H. Perkins and Michael Roemer, eds., *Reforming Economic Systems in Developing Countries.* Cambridge: Harvard Institute for International Development.

State Planning Committee, Stockholm School of Economics and Swedish International Development Authority. 1991. "The Socio-Economic Strategy for Vietnam up to the Year 2000" (SEVY 2000). (Background document.) Hanoi: Vietnam State Planning Committee.

Sung Yun Wing. Forthcoming. "The Economic Integration of Hong Kong, Taiwan, South Korea, and Mainland China." In Ross Garnaut and Liu Guoguang, eds., *Economic Reform and Internationalization: China and the Pacific Region.*

Thanh Son. 1990. "Forty Five Years of Vietnam's Industry." *Economic Problems.* Hanoi: Institute of World Economy.

Vo Nhan Tri. 1990. *Vietnam's Economic Policy Since 1975.* Singapore: Institute of Southeast Asian Studies.

World Bank. 1990. *The World Bank Atlas 1990.* Washington, D.C.: World Bank.

2

Indochina beyond the Cold War: The Chill from Eastern Europe

Nayan Chanda

On April 30, 1975, when the last American helicopter lifted off the helipad at the U.S. embassy in Saigon, Hanoi rejoiced. For the Vietnamese leaders, it was not only a victory in an epic struggle, but it also signaled the beginning of yet another "glorious" era in which Vietnam would rebuild the shattered country and emerge as the outpost of socialism in Southeast Asia. That new era would culminate, the Vietnamese leaders believed, with the triumph of socialism and an end to the Cold War. But the reality has turned out to be very different.

Fourteen years later, with the fall of the Berlin Wall, the East-West struggle in Europe was over, but for the ruling communist parties in Hanoi, Vientiane, and Phnom Penh, the Cold War had merely taken a more dangerous turn. Without the bulwark of the Soviet bloc, communists in Indochina were now left to fend for themselves. In addition to the unremitting pressure from their historical adversary, China, and the Chinese-backed Khmer Rouge, the Vietnamese were faced with a more fundamental challenge to their system from the antisocialist wave released by the turmoil in Eastern Europe. However, the fact that the Chinese themselves faced the same challenge to their system proved to be an incentive, pushing them to a begin a reconciliation with the Vietnamese.

The collapse of communism in Eastern Europe and dissolution of the Soviet Union had a traumatic impact on Vietnam. The events of 1989 in Eastern Europe and the collapse of the Soviet Union two years later brought about a fundamental reordering of the external balance at a time when the Vietnamese and Cambodian regimes had the least ability to maneuver. For the first time since the birth of the Indochinese Communist Party in 1930, the leaders in Indochina are virtually on their own, steering their leaky ships of state in uncharted waters. While the Vietnamese and Lao communist parties dug in their heels into the one-party system, Cambodia was forced to accept the idea of a multi-party system to be introduced under a United Nations-led plan. Ironically, though, the disappearance of the Soviet Union has-tened economic liberalization in all three countries. This essay attempts an analysis of the external changes around Indochina and their impact on the domestic and foreign policy developments of the three countries of Indochina.

When the Vietnam War ended in 1975, the leaders in Hanoi faced no external threat for the first time in decades. The time had finally come to settle down to the business of repairing the damage of war and building socialism. The external environment looked favorable. Hanoi saw the Soviet Union and a somewhat unenthusiastic China as the principal foreign backers, while also counting on billions of dollars secretly promised by President Richard Nixon. In addition, many Western and third-world nations seemed likely to offer sympathy and support.

However, within three years, those hopes were dashed. Hanoi's burgeon-ing conflict with the xenophobic Khmer Rouge and their supporter China forced a change in domestic priorities and led Vietnam to scrap its Five-Year Plan (1976–80). The Vietnamese invasion of Cambodia in December 1978 and China's punitive raid against Vietnam in February 1979 dramatically trans-formed the international landscape around Indochina. Although Soviet mil-itary and economic aid poured into Vietnam and Soviet naval bases were set up in Cam Ranh Bay, the Vietnamese were bogged down in a costly guerrilla war against the Khmer Rouge in Cambodia. Eventually, a stringent economic embargo and diplomatic condemnation turned Vietnam and its protégé regime in Phnom Penh into international pariahs.

Ironically, it was this international isolation against the backdrop of a deteriorating economic situation that forced Vietnam to take the first tenta-tive steps toward economic reform. Deprived of foreign assistance other than Soviet bloc aid, the Vietnamese had to seek ways of better using their domestic resources and skills. The beginning of Soviet *perestroika* in 1985 provided an additional impetus to liberalize the economy. An estimated $1 billion a year in assistance from CMEA countries (Englund, 1988, p. 227) sustained the Vietnamese effort to reform the economy. The Lao economic reform and Cambodian economic liberalization also were, in varying degrees, underwritten by assistance from the Soviet bloc countries.

It is thus not surprising that dramatic changes in Soviet foreign policy toward its friends, its growing détente with Washington and Beijing, and the collapse of communism in Eastern Europe created a whole new environment. While the threat the Vietnamese perceived from China and other hostile neighbors remained virtually unchanged, the external support that helped them cope with the threat was suddenly in doubt. And the blow suffered by communist parties in Eastern Europe raised an even more profound challenge to the communist regime in Vietnam. In the winter of 1989 when the Berlin Wall collapsed and Romanian president Nicolae Ceaucescu crumpled before a firing squad, not only was Vietnam's national security and its reforms threatened but its very raison d'être was in jeopardy.

It is useful to recall briefly the previous turning points in Indochina's external environment. Since the late 1970s, the foreign policy of Vietnam, in particular, had been predicated on obdurate hostility from China and Hanoi's reliance on a de facto alliance with the Soviet Union and other countries who were worried by China's regional power ambition. Vietnam signed a treaty of friendship with Moscow in November 1978, which was followed by the installation of a Soviet naval contingent at base facilities at Cam Ranh Bay. Relying on a distant Moscow to confront the immediate threat to the north was in many ways a reversion to a more traditional pattern. As a Vietnamese diplomat explained at the time, "In all of history, we have been secure from China under only two conditions. One is when China is weak and internally divided. The other is when she has been threatened by barbarians from the north. In the present era, the Russians are our barbarians" (Chanda, 1986, p. 135).

The sight of the same "barbarians" courting the rulers of the Middle Kingdom (China) was unnerving to the Vietnamese leaders. Following Mikhail Gorbachev's July 1986 Vladivostok speech calling for normalization of relations with China, Moscow steadily pressured Vietnam to follow the Soviet example in Afghanistan and withdraw its forces from Cambodia. Moscow argued that only then could Vietnam pay more attention to putting its own economic house in order. The ulterior motive for the pressure from Moscow, however, was Moscow's interest in improving relations with China. In July 1988, under Soviet prodding, the Vietnamese announced their plan—a joint communique between Gorbachev and Nguyen Van Linh—to withdraw all troops from Cambodia by the end of 1989. Cambodia had emerged as a major bargaining chip in Moscow's drive to normalize relations with Beijing.

A Sino-Soviet Détente Isolates Vietnam

The Soviets were sympathetic to China's security interest in Cambodia and a role for the Khmer Rouge. That coupled with the pressure they exerted on Vietnam to pull out its troops from Cambodia paved the way for the Sino-Soviet summit meeting in April 1989. Soviet pressure also went some way to make Vietnam and its allies in Phnom Penh accept the Khmer Rouge as a negotiating partner for a Cambodian political settlement brokered by the

United Nations (U.N.). Hanoi and Phnom Penh had long opposed a U.N.-based solution because the Khmer Rouge occupied the Cambodian seat at the U.N. Phnom Penh also resisted the idea of handing over its authority to a U.N. interim administration. Ultimately, however, both Hanoi and Phnom Penh relented under Soviet pressure. Soviet cooperation with the United States and China provided the diplomatic underpinning for the International Conference on Cambodia that assembled in Paris in July 1989, and following the failure of the Paris meeting, it formed the basis for a U.N. Security Council effort to devise a peace plan. Negotiations among the permanent five members of the Security Council—the U.S., Great Britain, France, the Soviet Union, and China—led to the signing of the Paris Peace Accords in October 1991.

The negative consequences of the improving Sino-Soviet relations on Vietnam's security were brought home to the Vietnamese in the spring of 1988 when Chinese gunboats attacked Vietnamese vessels in the South China Sea and the Soviet navy, based in Cam Ranh Bay, looked the other way. Moscow finally broke its deafening week-long silence on the incident to appeal for "self-restraint." "Our people are angry," a Vietnamese official told the author at the time, "Many are asking what is the use of letting the Soviets use Cam Ranh Bay?" (Bui Tin, 1988). The Soviet reaction was doubly ironic as the Vietnamese originally allowed them base facilities in the hope that they would be a deterrent to China. In December 1989, the Soviets quietly withdrew their air assets stationed in Cam Ranh Bay and announced that their presence there would end by 1992.

Although China's post-Tiananmen leaders, shocked by the events in Eastern Europe and the unrest developing in the Soviet Union, became critical of Gorbachev, Sino-Soviet relations at the state level nevertheless continued to improve. (In March 1991, China even offered the Soviet Union a $715 million loan in food, textiles, and consumer goods.) In 1990, China, stricken by Western sanctions on military transfers, began exploring the possibility of buying Soviet SU-27 jet fighters, and in May 1991, normalization between the two countries was completed when the Chinese party secretary-general Jiang Zemin visited Moscow—the first such visit in 34 years. While China remained critical of certain aspects of Soviet perestroika, the communique issued by Jiang and Gorbachev pledged to develop bilateral relations. However concerned the Vietnamese party may have been about Moscow-Beijing détente, it could fully endorse one part of the joint communique, which said that "to realize the potential of socialism, reforms are needed, and the important condition for them is to maintain stability of the state and in the society"(UPI, May 19, 1991).

While the warming Sino-Soviet ties underscored Vietnam's strategic isolation, a sharp decline in Soviet aid to Vietnam in 1990 also worsened the climate for the Vietnamese attempt at economic recovery. Political turmoil and weakening central authority in the Soviet Union meant a decline in the delivery of goods to Vietnam and also made Moscow unable to make any commitment for the future. On its own admission, Moscow failed to deliver 15 to 20 percent of the goods (such as cotton and fertilizer) it agreed to deliver in 1990. Of course, Moscow pointed out that Vietnam's delivery of rice also had fallen 50 percent short of target (Agence France Presse, December 27, 1990). The annual trade protocol that Vietnam and the Soviet Union signed in January 1991 called for $1 billion in two-way barter trade, although the price would be calculated in hard currency at the world price. The International Monetary Fund (IMF) has estimated that the change from ruble to hard currency accounting would cost Vietnam a terms-of-trade loss of $250 to 300 million or 4 to 5 percent of gross domestic product (GDP). In his half-yearly report to the National Assembly, Deputy Premier Vo Van Kiet said that the country's overall trade dropped "mainly because of the reduction in trade with the Soviet Union and Eastern Europe, which fell to only 15 percent of the level of the first six months of 1990" (Vietnam News Agency, August 6, 1991).

There was also a drastic cut in aid. Compared to the $4.3 billion in aid that Moscow pledged to provide Vietnam for the 1986–90 plan period, the Soviets offered only $100 million in technical-assistance credits and $10 million in grants for 1991 (Reuter, Feb. 6, 1991). The two sides also could not reach agreement on Vietnamese repayment of Soviet debt worth 9 billion rubles, which Vietnam is expected to settle in hard currency.

The changes in the Soviet bloc also meant the loss of remittances by Vietnamese workers in Eastern Europe and the Soviet Union. This export of labor not only helped cash-starved Hanoi repay its debt to the socialist countries—a percentage of the workers' salaries was deducted by the host countries for that purpose—but also trained many workers in factories far more modern than any in Vietnam. According to a senior Vietnamese official, the guest workers sent an average of $93 million a year back to Vietnam (interview with Senior Vietnamese Officials April 26, 1990). Of the 200,000 Vietnamese workers in Eastern Europe at the beginning of 1990, over 90,000 would have returned home by the end of 1991. In addition, 16,000 Vietnamese workers were repatriated from Iraq before the outbreak of the Gulf War.

Impact of Perestroika on Vietnam

While Soviet aid and the East European market have fallen off, the Vietnamese continue to be barred from international financial institutions due to U.S. opposition. Repeated attempts by France, Sweden, and other European countries to provide a bridge loan to Vietnam to enable it to repay its arrears and obtain fresh IMF credit have been blocked by the U.S. Although Sweden has provided an average of $50 million in aid and France has given a small amount of assistance, a move by some countries in the European Economic Community (EEC) to provide Vietnam with a soft loan has been foiled by Vietnam's irregular status at the IMF. The fact that Vietnam is not eligible for IMF loans has also discouraged commercial banks from lending to Hanoi.

How have the changes in the socialist world, conflict with China, and boycott by the U.S. and other Western countries affected Vietnam's domestic and foreign policy? Although Gorbachev's foreign-policy switch was a cause for concern, the Vietnamese had no option but to accept Moscow's assurance that its normalization with China would not be at the expense of Vietnam. Soviet perestroika gave an additional impetus to Vietnam's program of *doi moi* (renovation). Although the initial steps toward reforming the economy had begun in 1979, it was not until the Sixth Congress of the Vietnamese party in December 1986—a year after the emergence of Gorbachev as party general secretary in Moscow—that the reform program was formally launched. Vietnamese party secretary Nguyen Van Linh began encouraging openness by criticizing the failings of the government. Although private ownership of the press was not allowed, the Vietnamese media, for a while, displayed remarkable candor in exposing graft and mismanagement. By early 1988, the campaign against corruption had resulted in the replacement of almost all of the country's 40 province secretaries and 80 percent of the approximately 400 district party chiefs (Cima, 1989, p. 1). Another striking development was the emergence of a loyal opposition in the form of a club of resistance veterans in Ho Chi Minh City. The publications of the club made trenchant critiques of the party for its narrow-minded and outmoded policy, which, as one article noted, turned proud Vietnam into one of the poorest countries in the world.

The Vietnamese party, which has always attached the highest priority to security through armed defense, seemed impressed by the new Soviet thinking on the importance of economic renovation for national security. In a 1988 year-end interview in the party daily *Nhan Dan*, Foreign Minister Nguyen Co Thach said, "Nowadays a first class power might become a second class power if it is bogged down in a limited war for 5 to 10 years . . . In the era of this technological revolution the challenge to countries is mainly economic, not military and political. The very widening economic gap is becoming a threat to the security and national defense of each country . . . Military adventures, especially military quagmires abroad, will pose a monumental danger to any country in the global economic and technological race" (Foreign Broadcast Information Service—East Asia (FBIS-EAS), Jan 19, 1989, p. 53). Although this view does not appear to have been unchallenged inside the party (FBIS-EAS, February 10, 1989, pp. 54–58), the 1989 withdrawal of Vietnamese troops from Cambodia and the demobilization of half-a-million men from the army indicated Hanoi's willingness to shift its priority from defense to economy. Convinced that the development of the country would have to be financed by nonsocialist resources, Hanoi turned its full attention to courting private Western investment. In 1988, Vietnam adopted a very liberal foreign-investment code and undertook financial-sector reform. In fact, one unintended favorable consequence of the cutback in Soviet aid has been to shake the Vietnamese planners out of their complacence. The end of grant aid and subsidy- and dollar-based accounting of trade and aid forced the Vietnamese to seek improved management, quality control, and diversification of their markets.

However, in the summer of 1989, growing unrest in Eastern Europe and the Tiananmen upheaval raised warning flags to Vietnam about the political fallout from reform. Although Hanoi maintained public silence about the Tiananmen killings, in private some of the leaders expressed sympathy for the predicament of Chinese leaders in dealing with public challenges to their authority. Hanoi condemned Solidarity in Poland as "counter-revolutionaries" and even organized protest demonstrations against changes in Poland. Although Vietnam quickly had to relegate its ideological concerns behind the pragmatic needs of maintaining economic ties with Poland and other former East-bloc countries, it was worried. As the communist parties in Eastern Europe tumbled from power, the Vietnamese party began tightening its own control. The Vietnamese press was reined in, the Club of Former Resistance Fighters was disbanded, and some of the club's leaders were put under house arrest. Behind closed doors in Hanoi in early 1990, the eighth plenum of the Central Committee condemned Gorbachev's "deviationist" policies for the collapse of communism in Eastern Europe and called for heightened vigilance against imperialist attempts to overthrow the socialist regime in Vietnam. Although the Vietnamese leaders swiftly and quietly redressed grievances of students and farmers when they held demonstrations, the leaders nevertheless began bracing for worse. The eighth plenum authorized the creation of special forces equipped with automatic weapons and armored cars to deal with public demonstrations.

Interior Minister Mai Chi Tho sounded a warning that the U.S. and other intelligence organizations were sending spies "in the guise of tourists or members of economic, charity or religious institutions, cultural and scientific cooperation teams, journalists," with the object of overthrowing the Communist party and bringing about "a multi-party system and bourgeois-type democracy" (UPI, Aug 14, 1990). The Vietnamese leadership's concern over the threat to the party rose sharply. As the date for the Seventh Party Congress approached, an intense political debate was unleashed, and a number of influential voices in Vietnam publicly condemned the party. In November Colonel Bui Tin, deputy editor of the party daily *Nhan Dan*, left Vietnam to take up residence in France and launch a campaign for democratization in Vietnam. He was soon joined by other respected intellectuals such as historian Nguyen Khac Vien, veteran ideologue Hoang Minh Chinh, mathematician Phan Dinh Dieu, and leading novelist Duong Thu Huong.

In an open letter, Nguyen Khac Vien said that the Vietnamese people and low-level party members have "lost all faith" in the Politburo and other leading organs of the party, which are "all comprised of comrades who are either too aged, of ill health . . . or whose thinking and working style are too outmoded. . . . " Nguyen Khac Vien condemned the party for refusing to allow such democratic freedoms as freedom of the press, freedom of thought, and freedom of association to organize activities outside the administrative system (letter to Nguyen Huu Tho from Nguyen Khac Vien, 1991). Concerning the forthcoming Seventh Party Congress, he urged that the top leaders resign and the party "return all authority to popularly elected organs and the State."

In a commentary on the party's draft platform for the Seventh Congress Meeting, Hoang Minh Chinh rejected the charge that changes in Eastern Europe were the result of the "peaceful evolution" strategy of imperialism, the Chinese Communist party's theory that the United States had a strategy of bringing about the collapse of socialist systems through peaceful political and cultural penetration. "We must bravely and alertly acknowledge, no matter how painfully, that it was caused by a hidden cancer in the body of socialism that grew and exploded," he wrote. Hoang Minh Chinh ridiculed the party's objective of "making the transition to socialism . . . by skipping the phase of capitalist development." He argued that such a path is unscientific, nonhistoric, and illusory. "Thus there remains only one solution: to rely on the developed capitalist countries to help us skip the phase of capitalist development and advance directly to socialism. It is indeed a true paradox that we want to achieve" (Hoang Minh Chinh, 1991).

Noted mathematician Phan Dinh Dieu wrote a petition blaming centralized control over all aspects of life as the source of Vietnamese difficulties and calling for "an advanced market economy with macroeconomic state control in conjunction with a democratic political regime with unity and reconciliation" (Phan Dinh Dieu, 1991, p. 1).

The Rise of Dissent in Vietnam

In the political effervescence created since East European upheaval, Vietnamese writers have shown greater courage. Author Duong Thu Huong, who has been an avant-garde novelist, attacked the Vietnamese pretense of a proletarian dictatorship. She argued that factories cannot tell workers they will be paid in wages and pay them in goods instead—goods that the workers find hard to sell. "I have met other members of the proletariat who, because they are poor, have had to steal cement, iron and timber from work sites and who have been imprisoned for this. The number of prisons filled with these people has increased. Do they, the proletariat, have dictatorial rights over anyone? No! Those are fine but immoral words. In reality there is only the dictatorship of the bureaucracy with respect to the proletariat and other classes of people" (Duong Thu Huong, 1991).

The government responded by expelling Colonel Bui Tin from the party, arresting Duong Thu Huong and a number of other intellectuals and religious figures, and launching a campaign of denunciation against "agents of impe-rialism and reaction." In an unusual press conference, the Vietnamese min-istry of interior charged that "hostile forces" have exploited "eventful changes in East Europe and the Soviet Union as well as the present economic difficulties of the Vietnamese people to attack and whip up skepticism about the socialist orientation of Vietnam . . ."(FBIS-EAS, April 30, 1991, p. 70).

The Vietnamese party's Seventh Congress was held in late June 1991 against this backdrop of anxiety. Deep division within the leadership on the pace of economic and political reform and concern about the party's political hegemony led to near paralysis. The members of the party congress spent a great deal of time discussing fine points of Marxist-Leninist ideology and characteristics of socialist Vietnam, but they could not agree on the draft of the political program or economic strategy (*Far Eastern Economic Review,* July 11, 1991, p. 10). Most of the important documents were left to be "perfected" by the next Central Committee plenum.

However, the speeches by senior party leaders and the composition of the new Central Committee and Politburo made it clear that reform and renovation would have to be subjugated to the overriding need to maintain political stability and the party's monopoly of power. Political inertia was visible in the small turnover in the Central Committee, where only one-third of the members were new. Although the 13-member Politburo had eight new members, they were specialists in ideology and organization, with the excep-tion of pragmatic economists Phan Van Khai, Vo Tran Chi, and Le Phuoc Tho.

The Seventh Congress also reacted to the events in Eastern Europe by backing away from the prevailing liberal policy toward compatriots abroad.

From the time of the Sixth Party Congress held in 1986, Vietnam had stepped up its efforts to win the support of *viet kieu* (overseas Vietnamese) and encourage them to contribute to the economic development of the country. By the end of 1990, about 100 enterprises were operated by overseas Vietnamese (FBIS-EAS, July 5, 1991). Cash remittances to relatives (estimated at $60 million a year) or gift packages were encouraged and regularized. Taking advantage of the liberal investment code, overseas Vietnamese also began investing in manufacturing and service activities (Wain, 1991). But at the Seventh Congress, appeals for overseas Vietnamese investment were conspicuously absent. The reason is that in the wake of Eastern European upheavals, overseas Vietnamese opinion turned critical of Hanoi. A number of prominent Vietnamese abroad, who had supported the Vietnamese party during the war and encouraged the economic reforms, wrote an open letter calling for political pluralism (Lettre aux dirigeants . . . , 1990). Not only have many overseas Vietnamese been denied reentry into the country for signing that letter but in 1990–91 a number of overseas Vietnamese visitors were arrested on charges of promoting so-called "peaceful evolution"—transforming socialist Vietnam into a capitalist country (*Indochina Digest*, July 26, 1991, p. 1). Such an atmosphere of suspicion toward overseas Vietnamese cannot be very conducive to attracting their capital and skills.

Vietnam's dire need for external resources to sustain its viable economic reforms and the threat to its political stability from botched reforms have put the Vietnamese leaders on the horns of a dilemma. As its dwindling circle of socialist friends are unable to provide any significant assistance, Vietnam has had to cope with the political consequences of rising unemployment and inflation resulting from reform. And that dilemma has been accentuated by the problems Vietnam has faced in normalizing relations with its adversaries, such as China and the U.S., who could help Vietnam out of its economic crisis. A resolution of the dilemma was found in a compromise with Beijing.

After several years of unsuccessful efforts to woo the U.S. into accepting a Cambodia settlement that would freeze out China's ally, the Khmer Rouge, Hanoi was apparently persuaded by growing economic troubles, political isolation, and ideological worries to seek a deal with the Chinese. When asked, Vietnamese party secretary-general Nguyen Van Linh and Premier Do Muoi quickly responded to a Chinese proposal for a summit meeting with the Chinese party secretary-general Jiang Zemin and Premier Li Peng. The summit was held mainly to resolve bilateral differences over Cambodia. At the unpublicized September 1990 meeting in the Chinese city of Chengdu, Chinese leaders are said to have warned the Vietnamese against counting on United States cooperation in resolving their economic and diplomatic problems. According to the Chinese, the U.S. was seeking to overthrow socialism in Asian countries, and it was in the interest of the Vietnamese party to strengthen its collaboration with China. Beijing also held up the prospect of economic aid to Vietnam (Chanda, 1991a). Although no public comments were made, Chinese diplomats later charged that the Vietnamese failed to respect the summit agreement over Cambodia and accused Foreign Minister Nguyen Co Thach of being the principal obstacle.

Mr. Nguyen Co Thach has indeed been known for his advocacy of reform and closer ties with the West, and despite the effort of the Vietnamese party to woo China, he has made no bones about his dislike for Beijing's conservatives. In an unusually candid interview with the Czechoslovakian news agency a few months before the summit, Nguyen Co Thach said that Vietnam does not intend to normalize relations with China in exchange for its interference in the internal affairs of Cambodia and other countries and does not intend to "support the Chinese policy criticizing the restructuring in the Soviet Union" (CTK, Feb. 5, 1990). In an interview with the author in October 1990, Nguyen Co Thach said that the Chinese invitation for a summit was an attempt to sabotage Vietnam's improving ties with the U.S. (Chanda, 1990).

Nguyen Co Thach's removal from the Politburo and Central Committee during the Seventh Party Congress (although resulting partly from his domestic troubles) was seen as a friendly gesture by Beijing. The Vietnamese party had also come to embrace the Chinese theory about the Western strategy of so-called peaceful evolution. Not only is China a giant neighbor but it is also the only major communist power seeking to liberalize the economy while maintaining party control. China took the first step toward restoration of party ties with Vietnam when the Chinese Secretary General Jiang Zemin sent a congratulatory message to his Vietnamese counterpart on assuming the leadership position at the party congress—the first party-to-party message since 1978.

While conservatives in the Vietnamese party were disturbed by the Tiananmen affair, liberals like Nguyen Co Thach saw the resulting isolation of China as positive for Vietnam. Liberals hoped a disillusioned U.S. would see Vietnam as a balance against the instability of China. Hence, they were elated when, in July 1990, United States Secretary of State James Baker announced the opening of dialogue with Vietnam and also liberalized rules governing humanitarian aid from private U.S. agencies. The U.S. move, however, did not stem from strategic rethinking regarding China. It was designed to defuse congressional pressure for change on the U.S. Indochina policy.

Before his removal from the foreign minister's job Nguyen Co Thach made one last attempt to improve relations with the U.S. Three weeks after the Chinese-Vietnam summit at Chengdu in September 1990, Baker met Nguyen Co Thach in New York and told him of the economic benefits that could follow a resolution of the Cambodian problem. Nguyen Co Thach also made his maiden visit to Washington to discuss the issue of Americans missing in action in Vietnam. On his way home he made an official visit to Japan—the first since 1979—during which he received a promise of Japanese aid and investment after resolution of the Cambodian problem.

In early April 1991, the U.S. formally presented to Vietnam what has been termed a "road map," which outlined the steps Washington and Hanoi would need to take to lift the U.S. trade embargo against Vietnam, open international credit, and bring full normalization of relations, including granting of most-favored-nation status. Vietnamese cooperation on the missing-in-action (MIA) question and its support for a U.N. Security Council peace plan on Cambodia were the two important conditions for normalization. In the weeks following the presentation of the "road map," the U.S. announced the opening of a "temporary office" in Hanoi to resolve the MIA issue and granted the first official U.S. aid of $1 million to Vietnam's war invalids (Chanda, 1991b). The U.S. officials also pointed out that some $4.3 million in private U.S. aid had gone to Vietnam following the Baker announcement in July 1990, and Washington had contributed $11 million to evacuate Vietnamese workers from Iraq (Solomon, 1991b).

As a senior adviser to the Vietnamese party secretary put it to the author several months before the Seventh Party Congress, "It is a turning point for Vietnam. The U.S.S.R. is facing a very deep economic and political crisis. Indeed, the U.S.S.R. is a former superpower. There is no counterbalance to the U.S. And China is very keen to take advantage of the situation to surpass the U.S.S.R." (Chanda, 1991a, p. 14). He said that the first priority for Vietnam was to rearrange its international relations and find out how to succeed in maintaining independence in this totally changed world. "The way to do it," said the adviser, "is to balance interdependence with many—normalize relations with the U.S. and China and develop relations with others" (Chanda, 1991a, p. 14).

Hanoi's Cambodian Dilemma

The Seventh Party Congress indeed adopted the line of diversifying its foreign relations and announced its goal of seeking improved relations with both the U.S. and China. However, Washington's continued insistence on preconditions for normalization of relations and China's more friendly approach brought about a faster improvement of ties with China than the U.S.

China's softening stance on Cambodia made the Vietnamese dilemma of choosing between Washington and Beijing, both of whom had made Cambodia settlement a precondition for normal relations, somewhat easier. Against the backdrop of communist collapse in Europe, Beijing was now less interested in pushing Vietnam to the wall by demanding a free and fair election in Cambodia in the same way the United States was. Although China is a signatory to the U.N.-drafted Cambodia peace plan calling for such elections, it is less than enthusiastic about general elections as a litmust test for political legitimacy. China preferred to have a settlement in which former head of state and old friend of China Prince Norodom Sihanouk returned to Cambodia to head a coalition between the Khmer Rouge and the Vietnamese-backed People's Revolutionary Party of Kampuchea. The U.S. was firmly opposed to such a deal between the two communist factions in Cambodia.

By moving away from the U.N. plan, China facilitated a compromise that took shape in Beijing in mid-July of 1991. China hosted a meeting of the Cambodian factions—including the Vietnamese-backed Hun Sen regime—that decided to set up a de facto coalition led by Prince Sihanouk (Chanda, 1991c, p. 1). Speaking before the Cambodian faction leaders, Chinese premier Li Peng pointedly said that "the international community can provide some help but it is the SNC led by Sihanouk that will play the decisive role" (Xinhua, 1991).

Shortly after the historic Beijing meeting, senior Vietnamese party leader General Le Duc Anh led a delegation to China to discuss Cambodia and other issues of bilateral concern. The visit was never announced, but privately Hanoi officials acknowledged that it had taken place. That visit by the commander who had led the Vietnamese invasion of Cambodia was to offer personal apology for the "error" in attacking one of China's friends.

Soon after Le Duc Anh's visit, China announced that a Vietnamese deputy foreign minister would be visiting Beijing on August 8, 1991, to discuss political settlement of the Cambodian issue and Sino-Vietnamese relations. While the China-Vietnam minuet developed, China's moderating influence on the Khmer Rouge could be seen; they abandoned their long-standing objections to agree to set up a Supreme National Council (SNC) without significant U.N. presence.

Because the developing Sino-Vietnamese détente was surrounded in secrecy, one can only speculate that Vietnam's conservatives decided to bury the historical hatchet to remove a major handicap in foreign relations and, at the same time, protect the Vietnamese party's control. A deal with the Chinese that did not require Hanoi to abandon its friends in Phnom Penh had the potential to remove the most important barrier to Vietnam's economic cooperation with the West and paradoxically strengthen the Vietnamese party's hand in dealing with the challenge of pluralism. Like China, Vietnam could hope to carry on economic reform without making concessions to the multiparty system and the free press. With China backing away from the U.N.-based formula, Hanoi and Phnom Penh felt even less pressure to accept the U.S. demand for a comprehensive settlement involving the disarmament of all troops and a U.N.-monitored free election. Additionally, the conservative Hanoi leaders feared that the example of self-determination through free elections in neighboring Cambodia could have a destabilizing effect on Vietnam.

The Effects of Eastern European Communist Collapse on Laos

Like the Vietnamese party, the ruling parties in Laos and Cambodia were also distressed by the developments in Eastern Europe. According to some reports, the Lao party leader Kaysone Phomvihane, who had personally known Romanian president Ceaucescu, was stunned by his overthrow. A direct consequence of the East European events was a shift in the course of liberalism in Laos. Several party officials were arrested for publicly criticizing the government, which put an end to the open airing of grievances. The Lao party congress, held in April 1991, reaffirmed its commitment to continued economic liberalization but made it clear that the party would maintain its monopoly of power. Differences over the future political course of the party seem to have been an important reason why only two new faces were brought into the septuagenarian Laotian Politburo. Notable among the rising stars in the Central Committee were the children of senior Politburo members. As far as the economy is concerned, the Lao seem to have made socialism a very distant objective.

However, Laos did not face the foreign policy dilemmas encountered by Vietnam. With the exception of a brief period of Sino-Vietnamese border war, Laos had successfully hewn a neutral course between the two communist rivals. In a bid to separate Laos from the Vietnamese embrace, the Chinese too have adopted a lenient attitude toward Laos and encouraged closer Lao-Thai relations. The withdrawal of Vietnamese troops from Laos in 1987 gave Laos greater leeway in developing ties with its neighbors. While Laos remains a desperately poor country, the decline in Soviet aid to the country had a less dramatic impact than on Vietnam because of a wide range of relations with foreign countries and help from international financial institutions. An indicator of Lao diplomatic success came in 1989 when the Lao leader Kaysone made state visits to China, Japan, and France. Chinese premier Li Peng paid a return visit to Laos in 1990. In addition, China has opened its border for trade with Laos and offered to sell Chinese transport aircraft to Laos.

Cambodia's Economic Crisis

Phnom Penh's economic crisis has grown against the backdrop of Vietnamese troop withdrawal and East European turmoil. The fate of the Cambodian regime has been intimately bound up with that of its principal protector, Vietnam. Since the Vietnamese withdrawal in September 1989, the government has had to double its military expenditure to 30 percent of the national budget. Because of inflation and jittery confidence, the value of the riel has plummeted from 150 riel to 800 riel per dollar.

Meanwhile the price Phnom Penh has paid for protection from the Vietnamese against the Khmer Rouge for nearly a decade is its international isolation. And, as the Vietnamese umbrella disappears, the international embargo of Cambodia has become an even more serious problem. In 1991, Soviet aid to Cambodia was variously estimated to be between $100 and 200 million a year in economic aid and a roughly similar amount in military aid (Solomon, 1991a). Phnom Penh's principal opponent, the Khmer Rouge, is estimated by U.S. intelligence to have received Chinese economic and military aid worth $100 million a year since 1979 (*New York Times*, July 19, 1990). Some reports said that the Khmer Rouge was earning $5 million a month from leasing quarries of precious stones in the areas they control (*FEER*, February 7, 1991, p. 29).

Cambodia's economic recovery, including the reemergence of capitalism, has been made possible by the incredible resilience and ingenuity of the Cambodian people, who were left largely to their own devices by a weak government. Although, since 1983, the government has been collecting some taxes from private business, state-run enterprises, peasants, and city-dwellers, almost 80 percent of the Cambodian government's budget is believed to come from aid and long-term loans from socialist countries. Industrial and consumer goods supplied by the Soviet bloc countries have generated revenue to pay for governmental expenditures, ranging from defense to social expenditures and salaries.

Under the 1990 national budget, drawn up before the East European upheaval, the expected government revenue was 25 billion riel ($166 million) and expenditures were targeted at 30 billion riel ($200 million). But at the end of the year, the deficit had reached five times the planned amount. In 1991 the revenue more than doubled but so did the expenditure. It raised the deficit to a whopping 59 billion riel—or 50 percent of the expenditure (World Bank, annex 14). An important reason for the massive deficit was the demise of the Soviet Union. In practical terms it meant a sudden disappearance of some $100 million in annual aid that Cambodia had received from Moscow since the mid-80s. The Soviet aid, Cambodian Prime Minister Hun Sen said in a speech, has "completely dried up at a time when our needs are great" (Chanda, ASWJW, January 6, 1992). Phnom Penh suddenly had to find alternative resources to pay for the import of fuel, fertilizer and other essentials that came as part of the Soviet aid package. This loss of aid seems to have given a direct boost to economic liberalization. In a bid to raise funds the government launched a privatization program. Not only were state-controlled enterprises leased to private domestic and foreign investors, but land and buildings belonging to the government were put up for sale. By the time the United Nations Transitional Authority in Cambodia took charge of Cambodia in November 1991, other than the socialist-leaning People's Party of Cambodia, there was little that was socialist in Cambodia.

China's Cambodia Gambit

Cambodia's diplomatic options brightened briefly in early 1989 when the Thai government under Chatichai Choonhavan accorded de facto recognition to the Heng Samrin regime and invited Premier Hun Sen to visit Bangkok. Some moderate leaders under China's premier Zhao Zhiyang also showed tantalizing signs of increasing flexibility toward Phnom Penh. In May 1989, three Chinese officials joined a Thai trade delegation to secretly visit Cambodia. Ostensibly, the Chinese team was there to explore the possibility of repairing a Chinese-built cement mill. But from all the evidence, the Chinese were interested in exploring the possibility of establishing indirect business connections. However, the emergence of hard-line leaders in Beijing seems to have put an end to that initiative (interview with Cambodian vice-premier Kong Samol, June 27, 1989).

The Chinese search for a political compromise was resumed a year later against the backdrop of a disappointing performance by the Khmer Rouge on the battlefield and a new international context. Prince Sihanouk's desire to return home and reach an accommodation with Hun Sen provided the Chinese with a perfect vehicle to discreetly resume feelers toward Phnom Penh and advise the Khmer Rouge to switch their strategy from armed struggle to political struggle. Following the meeting of the Cambodian factions in Jakarta in November 1990, which set up a Supreme National Council for Cambodia, Beijing accorded implicit recognition to Phnom Penh by sending a Chinese diplomat to Jakarta to meet with his Cambodian counter-part. The United States decision to establish contact with Phnom Penh led to a meeting between Hun Sen and the U.S. ambassador in Jakarta and to several meetings between American and Cambodian diplomats in Vientiane. How-ever, the Cambodian refusal to accept the detailed U.N. plan, required by the U.S., led to a stalemate.

By the middle of May 1991, China appeared to have decided not to insist on the full acceptance of the detailed draft peace agreement drawn up by the so-called Perm Five—the permanent members of the U.N. Security Council, which included China. In the joint communique signed by the Chinese party secretary-general and Gorbachev in Moscow, the Chinese leader agreed with Gorbachev that the Cambodian peace settlement should be based on the U.N. framework document of August 1990, but he conspicuously avoided any reference to the later, detailed draft agreement that permitted a more intrusive U.N. role in Cambodia. With that change of position, the stage was set for two important meetings of the Cambodian factions in Pattaya and in Beijing. The June 24–26, 1991, meeting in Pattaya, where Pol Pot directed the negotiations from behind the scene, resulted in an agreement on an indefi-nite cease-fire, the elimination of foreign-arms supplies, and the set up of the Supreme National Council, or SNC, in Phnom Penh (Chanda, 1991d, p. 3). For Phnom Penh, this agreement signaled an end to its demand that the top leadership of the Khmer Rouge be excluded from the settlement and brought to trial. Not only did the SNC include Khieu Samphan and Son Sen—two of the notorious eight leaders of the Khmer Rouge—but these men were allowed to come to Phnom Penh—a major political concession. For the Khmer Rouge, the move opened the road to political rehabilitation and legitimacy, but at the cost of accepting the Hun Sen regime's control of the capital.

During the Beijing meeting in mid-July 1991, the factions elected Prince Sihanouk as president of the SNC, and agreed to invite the U.N. to send a survey team to prepare for its observer role. The SNC was to hold to its first full-fledged meeting in Bangkok in late August of 1991 and set up its headquarters in Phnom Penh in November.

In July 1991 during a visit to North Korea as a guest of Prince Sihanouk, Hun Sen agreed with Prince Sihanouk to set up the Commission in Search of Aid headed by Prince Sihanouk. Since it was only a biparty agreement, Hun Sen and Prince Sihanouk decided only to seek foreign aid for the economic and social rehabilitation and development of Cambodia. If the international community turns out to be generous, the formation of this committee could mean the beginning of much-needed rehabilitation for Cambodia.

Despite initial, hopeful signs, peace in Cambodia was still uncertain. Some members of the U.N. Security Council, especially the U.S., were now concerned that a deal between the Chinese and the Vietnamese centered on Sihanouk would shelve plans for open elections. Secretary of State James Baker warned: "Our view is that there has to be and should be ... a comprehensive settlement to this problem of Cambodia. We in the United States are not interested in any shortcuts that would result in only a partial settlement" (*Washington Post*, July 25, 1991). While the Cambodian parties may agree to a limited U.N. presence, the members of the Security Council would have to approve whatever role the U.N. would play.

Although by the middle of 1991 the U.S. was publicly acknowledging Vietnam's greater cooperation in accounting for MIAs, the U.S. was still far from accepting the issue as closed. It also continued to demand, as another precondition to normalization, that Vietnam exercise its influence over Phnom Penh to reach a "comprehensive settlement"—a demand that Vietnam refused to accept. The continued absence of U.S.-Vietnamese relations and the imposition of the trade embargo only helped to confirm the suspicion of conservatives in Vietnam that Washington is only interested in weakening and destabilizing Vietnam. Even if the embargo is lifted "at certain times," the central military commission of the Vietnamese party (a stronghold of conservatives) said that the imperialist enemy "will step up measures to provoke socio-economic crisis that would lead to a political crisis, thus step by step bourgeoisifying our society and compelling us to depend on imperialism and do away with socialism and national independence."

Vietnamese economic reform has gone far enough to beat any retreat from it, and even the conservatives acknowledge that without liberalization of the economy the dangers of instability would be greater. But the leadership's fear of losing political control while opening up the economy is likely to make Vietnam's road to reform bumpy and its process of democratization slow and painful.

References

Agence France Presse. 1990. December 27.

Beresford, Melanie. 1988. *Vietnam: Politics, Economics, and Society*. London: F. Pinter.

Brown, Frederick Z. 1989. *Second Chance: The United States and Indochina in the 1990s*. New York: Council on Foreign Relations Press.

Brown, MacAlister and Joseph J. Zaslof. 1987. *Apprentice Revolutionaries: The Communist Movement in Laos, 1930–1985*. Stanford: Hoover Institution Press.

Chanda, Nayan. 1986. *Brother Enemy: The War After the War*. San Diego: Harcourt Brace Jovanovich, p. 135.

———. 1989. "Civil War in Cambodia." *Foreign Policy*, no. 76 (Fall).

———. 1990. "Vietnam's Vice Premier Sees Progress Toward Normalizing Relations with U.S." *The Asian Wall Street Journal Weekly* October 15, p. 24.

———. 1991a. "Vietnam Hits Crossroad On Path to a New Order." *The Asian Wall Street Journal Weekly* February 11, p. 1.

———. 1991b. "End to Sanctions?: U.S. Unveils Timetable for Links to Vietnam." *The Asian Wall Street Journal Weekly* April 15, p. 1.

———. 1991c. "China Plays Key Role in Cambodia Settlement." *The Asian Wall Street Journal Weekly* July 22, p. 1.

———. 1991d. "Pol Pot directs Cambodia Peace Talks Sparking Concerns About Future Role." *The Asian Wall Street Journal Weekly* August 5, p. 3.

———. 1992. "Cambodian Peace Accord May Be in Jeopardy As Economy Unravels Amid Government Crisis." *The Asian Wall Street Journal Weekly* January 6, p. 1.

Cima, Ronald, ed. 1989. *Vietnam: A Country Study*. Washington, D.C.: Department of the Army.

Clark, Dick. 1991. *The American Vietnamese Dialogue, February 11–14*. Queenstown, MD: The Aspen Institute.

CTK (Czechoslovak News Agency). 1990. February 5.

Curtis, Grant. 1989. *Cambodia: A Country Profile*. Stockholm: SIDA.

Duong Thu Huong. 1991. Interview with *Doan Ket*, a Vietnamese magazine published from Paris. Reprinted in *The Asian Wall Street Journal Weekly* May 6, p. 10.

Elliott, David, ed. 1981. *Third Indochina Conflict*. Boulder: Westview Press.

Englund, Karl. 1988. "External Assistance in the Context of Vietnam's Development Effort." In David G. Marr and Christine P. White, eds., *Postwar Vietnam: Dilemmas in Socialist Development*. New York: Southeast Asia Program, Cornell University.

———. 1991a. Hong Kong. February 7, p. 29.

Far Eastern Economic Review. (FEER). 1991b. Hong Kong. July 11, p. 10.

Foreign Broadcast Information Service—East Asia (FBIS-EAS). 1989a. Washington, D.C. January 19, p. 53.

———. 1989b. February 10, pp. 54–58.

———. 1991a. April 30, p. 70.

———. 1991b. July 5.

Hoang Minh Chinh. 1991. "Contributing Opinions on the Draft Program." Hanoi, January 22. Mimeo.

Indochina Digest. 1991. Washington, D.C. July 26, p. 1.

Interview with Bui Tin, Deputy Editor, *Nhan Dan*. 1988. Sydney, May 15.

Interview with Cambodian Vice-Premier Kong Samol. 1989. Phnom Penh, June 27.

Interview with a Senior Vietnamese Official. 1990. Hanoi, April 26.

"Lettre aux dirigeants du Vietnam et aux vietnamiens de l'intérieur et d'outre-mer sur la restructuration du système politique." 1990. An open letter to Vietnamese leaders, Paris, January 22.

Muscat, Robert J. and Jonathan Stromseth. 1989. *Cambodia: Post-Settlement Reconstruction and Development*. New York: East Asia Institute, Columbia University.

New York Times. 1990. July 19.

Nguyen Khac Vien. 1991. Letter to Nguyen Huu Tho, president of the Vietnam Fatherland Front, January 6.

Reuter. 1991. February 6.

Solomon, Richard H., U.S. Assistant Secretary of State for East Asian and Pacific Affairs. 1991a. Testimony before the Senate Foreign Relations Committee, April 11.

———. 1991b. Testimony before the Senate Foreign Relations Committee's East Asian and Pacific Affairs Subcommittee, April 25.

Stuart-Fox, Martin. 1986. *Laos: Politics, Economics, and Society.* London: F. Pinter.

United Press International (UPI). 1990. August 14.

Vickery, Michael. 1988. *Kampuchea: Politics, Economics, and Society.* London: F. Pinter.

Vietnam News Agency. 1991. August 6.

Wain, Barry. 1991. "Hanoi Courts Overseas Vietnamese to Tap Savings and Skills, but Ambivalence Remains." *The Asian Wall Street Journal Weekly* May 20, p. 1.

Washington Post. 1991. July 25.

World Bank. 1992. *Cambodia: Agenda for Rehabilitation and Reconstruction*. Washington, D.C.

3

Market Economies under Communist Regimes: Reform in Vietnam, Laos, and Cambodia

Börje Ljunggren

Personal Perspective

My first contacts with Indochina date back almost 20 years. The Second Indochina War was still going on. Sweden was providing humanitarian aid to Indochina and had begun to discuss assistance for the reconstruction of the region. As an official of the Swedish International Development Authority (SIDA), I participated in planning the assistance. Later, in 1978, I was posted as the first Swedish chargé d'affaires to Laos, primarily to coordinate Swedish assistance in the reconstruction and development of that war-torn country. While in Vientiane, I saw the Lao revolution turn "reformist," as the Lao leaders began to realize that central planning and radical changes in the relations of production were not the hoped-for vehicles to rapid moderniza-tion. The search began for what would work under the prevailing conditions of deep underdevelopment in Laos. In 1985, the Lao People's Democratic Republic embarked upon the New Economic Mechanism (NEM), a major program of economic reform.

Initially, Vietnam's growing economic difficulties following the reunifica-tion of the country in 1976 were seen as transitional. However, it slowly became clear that increasingly unorthodox methods had to be instituted. The Third Indochina War and the isolation of Vietnam and Cambodia had dra-matically tightened resource constraints. During the next decade, reforms in Vietnam grew increasingly comprehensive. In 1986, the government initiated *doi moi*, a program of renovation and renewal, and, in early 1989, it launched a comprehensive reform of its planned economic system. In the process, the "foreign aid relationship," of which I was a part, was redefined.

Cambodia, although still at war, would begin to undergo similar changes. When visiting the country for the first time in 1988, I found the horrors of the Pol Pot years present everywhere, in every village, in the stories told by every family. Still, despite the war and the isolation of Cambodia by the international community, the country had been able to recreate rudimentary social systems; peasant families were again tilling land to which they had tenure; and the economy was undergoing visible changes, more or less spontaneously that produced an ambiguous blend of total absence of state control and remnants of central planning. What then could the international community do to help when changing political conditions finally opened up the avenues for reconstruction of the country?

My experiences prompted my interest in conducting a current analysis of the origins, scope, sequencing, effects, dilemmas, and future direction of reforms in Vietnam, Laos, and Cambodia. Because the reforms have received little recognition, even though they are far reaching, and because so little international support has been forthcoming from the nonsocialist world, I regarded such an analysis as an urgent task. The dramatic changes that have taken place in China, the Soviet Union, and Eastern Europe have captured the world's attention, while very little notice has been paid to the economic reforms undertaken in Vietnam, and even less to the parallel reforms in Laos and Cambodia. The international debate is still often based on stereotyped notions of the conditions prevailing in the countries. Since they are ruled by communist parties they are assumed to behave in certain ways.

I have very vivid memories of discussions on development cooperation held in Stockholm in 1972 with a delegation from Vietnam. A main theme in the statements made by the head of the Vietnamese delegation was that Vietnam wanted Sweden to participate in the industrialization and modernization of Vietnam, and that pulp and paper were deemed to be Sweden's most valuable potential contribution. The Vietnamese educational system was crying for text and exercise books, and paper was in very short supply. Vietnam wanted a large plant with modern technology. SIDA presented some preliminary data from a feasibility study that raised many questions that would have to be addressed before any decisions could be made, and that also showed an alarmingly low rate of return on investment, based on the economic assessments at that time. In the meantime, available Swedish funds could be used for other urgent needs in Vietnam.

The Vietnamese delegation found Sweden's response highly unsatisfactory, and SIDA's suggestion to use available funds for other purposes downright imperialistic. How could anyone doubt Vietnam's need or the feasibility of establishing a paper mill? The Vietnamese government was determined to develop the country in bold strides. Certainly, if it was able to win the war, it should be able to mobilize equally efficiently for reconstruction and development, given international support. Feasibility studies should not be allowed to interfere with the important objective of supplying at least a couple of kilos of paper per capita.

The issue became a political one, and the Vinh Phu pulp and paper mill was built, albeit on a smaller scale than originally envisioned by the Vietnamese government. The project never became the scandal that Swedish critics of Vietnam claimed it to be, but would remain a major issue in the Swedish debate on development cooperation for the next 20 years.

The attitude of the Vietnamese government at that time—around 1972— reflected many of the elements of what later was to become known as the DRV model, DRV standing for the Democratic Republic of Vietnam. This model was characterized by a strong belief in central planning and quantitative targets, in the state as the pivotal engine for development, in industrialization as the main vehicle, and—not least—by a lack of openness that stemmed from the war experience and the prevailing view that the socialist development model was "correct."

It is easy to forget that the Vietnamese government was not alone in embracing this mode of thought. The view prevalent in many developing countries at the time was that colonialism and exploitation could be overcome only through the planned use of scarce resources. The private sector and the world market were seen as part of the cause of underdevelopment rather than part of the solution. Markets meant inequity and an indefensible waste of human resources. The United States' war against Vietnam had made the country a symbol of the aspirations for justice of third-world countries, and Vietnam saw itself as a vanguard country.

In the early 1980s, a new attitude began emerging in Vietnam—a desire to discuss alternative ways of doing things. Management models, decentralization, incentives, and cost effectiveness became key concepts. The DRV model had revealed shortcomings that inevitably pushed thinking beyond conventional boundaries and into the realm of an increasingly open, pragmatic debate about what worked and what did not.

I recall a conversation with then Prime Minister Pham Van Dong in early 1987. What did he see as the most important objective of doi moi, the major reform effort that the Sixth Party Congress had launched a few months earlier? He answered in a single word: efficiency.

In February 1991, I attended an international symposium in Hanoi on the draft of the nation's socioeconomic strategy for the 1990s. The symposium, attended by economists from all over the world, was one step in the process of preparing a strategy document for the Seventh Party Congress, held in June

1991. The government and the party wanted to learn from the experiences of economists from South Korea, France, the United States, the World Bank, and other countries and institutions before submitting its proposals to the party congress. Prime Minister Do Muoi, who was elected party leader later in 1991 by the Seventh Party Congress, was also asked to define the objectives of reform. His answer was as straightforward as Pham Van Dong's had been: the main objective was to generate rapid growth, while preserving important social gains, and catch up with neighboring countries. The foremost question on his mind was not *whether* to pursue reform, but *how* to do it.

During a conversation I had with (the new) Prime Minister Vo Van Kiet in January 1992, he spoke with self-confidence, in virtually a new language, about the results of the reform program. He sounded like a person who had jumped into an unknown ocean of reform without knowing whether he would ever reach the shore, and who now, finally, felt certain that he would make it. In 1991, Vietnam had managed to export one million tons of rice, in spite of a bad monsoon, while facing famine when the monsoon failed in 1988. Exports to the convertible area had almost tripled, and all this had been accomplished in spite of the fact that the old life-line, assistance from the former Soviet Union, had vanished.

As a consequence of the reform process, Vietnam's aid relationship with other countries changed from being project focused and restrained to encompassing the whole range of reform issues, on both a macro and micro level. Vietnam wanted to learn about the management of enterprises, about banking, about taxation, and about other elements of a market economy. It sought the experiences of Sweden and other countries.

Vietnam was discarding the old model as "voluntaristic," finding it had been a grave mistake to assume that reality could be transformed as a function of sheer will. What now mattered to the government were concrete measures that would create conditions for rapid development. In its draft political report to the Seventh Party Congress, Vietnam's Communist party, while referring to "socialist ideals," recognized the open nature of the process of change: ". . . our Party, State, and people have been searching for and blazing an untrodden path of renewal that is devoid of any present model" (Vietnam, Communist Party of, 1990b, p. 3). The attitude of the international community toward Vietnam's "search" is of great importance. International aid provided in an open dialogue could accelerate and broaden the process. As of November 1992, Vietnam is still denied crucial support from the International Monetary Fund (IMF), the World Bank, and the Asian Development ment Bank because of continued U.S. opposition stemming from the legacy of the Vietnam War. However, France, Italy, Germany, Canada, and Japan, are increasingly finding this attitude obsolete, and during the last year, Vietnam's bilateral relations have expanded considerably.

At the regional level the situation has changed beyond recognition. The question of Cambodia has not been resolved in the sense that a clearly viable internal solution can be seen. However, an international agreement was reached in Paris in October of 1991, and Cambodia has ceased to be a deeply divisive international issue. During 1992, the United Nations deployed 20,000 troops and civilian administrators to Cambodia, in accordance with Security Council Resolution 745/92 (February 28, 1992).

Cambodia was not a major topic on the agenda of the fourth summit of the Association of Southeast Asian Nations (ASEAN) held in Singapore on January 27–28, 1992. Instead of forming two deeply antagonistic blocks in a global confrontation the three Indochinese countries have begun to discuss regional cooperation. At the summit the ASEAN leaders pledged to "forge a closer relationship with Indochinese countries, following the settlement of Cambodia." (*Asiaweek*, February 7, 1992). At the next ASEAN meeting, held in July 1992, Vietnam and Laos signed the 1976 Treaty of Amity and Cooperation in Southeast Asia (the so-called Bali Declaration), which binds signatories to resolve disputes peacefully (*Vietnam Investment Review,* 1992). It will take time before they can become members of ASEAN, but the accession to the 1976 treaty is an important first step. These developments amount to nothing less than a sea change. Regional cooperation is replacing ideologically based alliances, offering Vietnam and Laos a new "foothold" in the wake of the dissolution of the Soviet Union and international communism.

It will take a very long time for Cambodia's wounds to heal, and it is questionable whether healing can occur as long as the Khmer Rouge remains intact. Still, the two major developments we have seen unfolding—the profound domestic reform processes of the past decade and the transformation of the international climate from a highly confrontational atmosphere to one increasingly open and motivated toward economic development—make it reasonable to believe that the populations of Vietnam, Laos, and hopefully Cambodia (among the very poorest in the world, with incomes per capita of less than $200) will begin to see their lives improve. Whether such growth will be shared equitably—equity having been such a crucial element of the revolutionary vision of modernization—is much less certain. It is only in Vietnam that such a vision has deep roots.

The paths of Vietnam, Laos, and Cambodia are bound to diverge as they, as "inverted dominos," struggle for space within a Southeast Asia in search of an identity on the threshold of an economic *pax Nipponica*.

Socialist Reform—An Overview

A Conceptual Framework for Socialist Reform

Janos Kornai, the foremost Eastern-European reform economist, discusses four different periods, or stages, of socialism:[1]

- the revolutionary period
- classical socialism
- reform socialism
- postsocialism

Kornai's analysis encompasses all socialist countries—26 in all, according to Kornai's somewhat arbitrary selection.[2] The revolutionary period is the transitional phase leading to the establishment of a socialist society. Classical socialism is the "unreformed" stage of planning that the countries of Eastern Europe were living under until recently. Reform socialism is the period during which the ruling party institutes certain reforms, while trying to preserve its monopoly on power. Postsocialism is the stage during which fundamental political and economic reforms are undertaken, leading to a pluralistic political system, well-defined and substantially private property rights, and market-based allocation processes. The last stage is manifested when a market economic system is introduced after the ruling communist party has given up its monopoly on power. However, a country may not necessarily go through all four stages. For example, while Hungary may be said to have gone through all four, Czechoslovakia has virtually leaped from stage two to stage four. Kornai's experiences over the last decades of reform efforts in Eastern Europe have made him deeply skeptical that far-reaching economic reform can occur as long as the one-party political monopoly remains in place.

In Kornai's main line of causality, the undivided power of the Marxist-Leninist party and the dominant influence of the official ideology are the root impediments to reform (Kornai, 1992, p. 361). Changes in other blocks of his

---

[1] For a somewhat different, more political "basic sequence," see Ferdinand (1989, pp. 298–301): 1) a phase of reconciliation during which the regime attempts to get the country working again following the revolution; 2) a "revolution from above" in the shape of the first five-year plan; 3) a phase during which the countries begin "to diverge and pursue their own roads to socialism"; and 4) a phase during which the chief concerns are political democratization and market reform, even survival itself.

[2] The presentation of Janos Kornai's ideas is primarily based on my extensive notes from his course "The Political Economy of Socialism," taught at Harvard University in the fall of 1990. The course was given while he was finalizing his manuscript entitled "The Socialist System—The Political Economy of Communism" (1992). Also, see Kornai's book *The Road to a Free Economy: Shifting from a Socialist System: The Example of Hungary* (1990); his address to the World Bank (April 1990); and Fischer and Gelb's "Issues in Socialist Economic Reform" (1990).

chain of causality can only be very partial as long as fundamental political reform does not occur. The fact that a country may have progressed substantially in trying to create a market, allowing private-sector activities, would not change Kornai's assessment as long as the power of the party remains unbroken. As he sees it, a market economy cannot function within the political context of a Marxist-Leninist party monopoly. There can be no "comprehensive and consistently radical transformation in the other spheres while the key feature of the old classical structure, the Communist party's power, remains" (Kornai, 1992, p. 566).

A similar view is held by Peter Ferdinand who, in his comparative study of the evolution of the Soviet, Chinese, and Yugoslav models, has come to the conclusion that "at least in communist regimes, radical democratic reforms are a requirement for market reforms" (Ferdinand, 1989, p. 313). His conclusion is primarily based on his analysis of the *nomenklatura* system, on "the ability of party officials to determine the appointment of enterprise managers at even quite a low level . . . and to put pressure upon local banks to make extra credit available to loss-making local enterprises" (Ferdinand, 1989, p. 312). There is, as he sees it, a fundamental difference between communist and authoritarian regimes such as the one in South Korea "where attitudes and incentives are vital at the level of the micro-economy" (Ferdinand, 1989, p. 313). Ferdinand is, however, less definite than Kornai. The stifling effect of the power of local party officials could, as he sees it, possibly be curtailed if new sources of political or economic authority, such as privately controlled factories, were introduced as counteracting forces (Ferdinand, 1989, p. 313).

There is less emphasis on political reform as a prerequisite to establishing a market economy in other works. Hewitt says that reforming an economy means "to reform the institutional arrangements constituting the system by which resources are allocated"; that is, reforming "the set of institutions that somehow decide what will be produced, in what quantities, who will produce it, what techniques and factor combinations will be used, and who will receive the product" (Hewitt, 1988, p. 13). Economic reforms "alter the way those decisions are made in an effort to improve the performance in areas of importance to political leaders" (Hewitt, 1988, p. 13). Hewitt distinguishes between comprehensive and limited reform. The former ideally would affect all institutions simultaneously: the hierarchy, the information system, and the incentive mechanism. As a "practical matter," however, Hewitt chooses a less stringent definition of comprehensive reform: "a reform would be sufficiently comprehensive if it recognized vital interconnections and sought to deal with them in a way that seems a priori to have a chance of succeeding," for example, "a reform that seeks to give enterprises more autonomy and simultaneously limits the power of central administrators and planners . . ." (Hewitt, 1988, p. 16). Hewitt strongly emphasizes that economic reform is a *process*, normally started by debate of some kind, not an event. A reform can be comprehensive, according to Hewitt, but limited from Kornai's broader political-economic perspective.

A key question is what is required to make markets work better. Dwight Perkins identifies four major elements of a functioning market system: goods must be available on the market, prices must reflect true relative scarcities, decision makers on markets must behave according to the rules of the market, and these decision makers must pursue some approximation of profit maximization.[3] Perkins, at the same time, emphasizes that "increasing the role of the market and making markets work better is a much more complex process than is commonly supposed." A second major point of his is that "markets even in the most market-oriented economies determine only a fraction of the economic decisions that are made" since "hierarchical or bureaucratic decisions play a major role in deciding what is produced in all economies." He further notes that "the role of the state in most contemporary economies is pervasive" and that "the great majority of developing nations cluster at the highly regulated end of the spectrum" (Perkins, 1989). Hence, economic reform involves *both* increasing the scope of the market and better managing hierarchies (Perkins, 1991, p. 5).

Alec Nove's thinking on these matters differs considerably from that in today's mainstream, neoclassical economic literature. His main objective in *The Economics of Feasible Socialism Revisited* (1991) is to develop what he calls a model for "feasible socialism." Nove is critical of the liberal-capitalist model: several factors—such as scale and specialization—"are now working against the efficacy, or even the survival, of the liberal-capitalist model," and a system has to be developed that looks out more for the "general interest" than is possible in a liberal-capitalist system dominated by "enormous business corporations and conglomerates" in which the worker finds himself increasingly alienated (Nove, 1991, pp. 2–3). Nove emphasizes that the market should play a major role and points out the negative effects of "price controls, below market clearance levels" (Nove, 1991, p. 195). Even though he envisions a mixed economy, especially for developing countries, he nevertheless foresees an economy in which private enterprises play a limited role in comparison to state enterprises controlled and administered as "centralized state corporations," publicly owned enterprises with full autonomy and a management responsible to the work force ("socialized enterprises"), and

---

[3]Perkins's analysis is presented in Chapter 1.

enterprises owned and/or controlled by the work force (Nove, 1991, p. 213). Nove stresses that there would be freedom of entry, but it would be rather narrow as far as the private sector is concerned. Perkins's market conditions would hardly be fulfilled under Nove's model. "The motive of competitors would not primarily be monetary," and managers would not be trying to reach even an approximation of profit maximization (Nove, 1991, p. 217).

Can market forces, then, lead to an efficient allocation of resources without extensive private ownership of the means of production? In his essay on the introduction of market forces in Eastern Europe, Manuel Hinds's answer is no, because, he reasons, the socialist mode of organization eliminates the factor markets (Hinds, 1990).

In his major work, *Governing the Market—Economic Theory and the Role of Government in East Asian Industrialization* (1990), Robert Wade concludes that "the confidence with which the neoclassical school prescribes liberalization and privatization" cannot be grounded in either theory or the experiences of the East Asian Newly Industrialized Countries (NICs) (Wade, 1990, p. 348). In his article entitled "State and Market Revisited," Wade argues in favor of "new interventionism," which "seeks to guide, not replace markets. It uses price and non-price methods to channel investment away from unproductive uses, expand technological capacity, strengthen links with foreign firms and give a directional thrust to selected industries." As Wade sees it, Taiwan offers "an example for others to consider" (Wade, 1992, p. 77).

The complex question of the capacity of the state to manage reform and the role of bureaucracies in the reform process is a subject that many scholars consider to be of crucial importance. Fischer and Gelb (1990) note that the restructuring of the economy "also requires fundamental changes in the role of and the capabilities of the state" and that "political reform prior to economic reform may be needed to prevent the latter from being stalled by an entrenched bureaucracy." At the same time, they emphasize the importance of viewing reforms as a process of complex political-economic interaction where "successful partial economic reform can provide space for political reform" (Fischer and Gelb, 1990, p. 2). "In practice," they say, "any given country will face many choices concerning its reform path" (Fischer and Gelb, p. 35). In a more recent paper, they note that "the most strategic choices [in the process of reform] arise out of the interplay between economics and politics. System-wide reform is an intensely political process: indeed, the main differences among reform strategies largely reflect differing views of what will be politically sustainable" (Fischer and Gelb, 1991, p. 104).

An increasing number of scholars point to the risk of excessive ideological enthusiasm leading to "reaction too far" against the state as an economic agent. For example, Killick and Stevens note in their essay "Lessons from the

Third World" in *Reform in Eastern Europe and the Developing Country Dimension* that "experience suggests that the state needs to remain a large and active participant in the economic system" (Killick and Stevens, 1992, pp. 31–32). In his essay "Changing Perceptions of the Role of Government," Dahrendorf concludes that "different government" does not mean "a return to the functions of the 'night-watchman,' not even the referee." The role of "player-manager" must be retained to some degree, and "what is really needed . . . is government as the guardian of the entitlements of citizenship and as the 'facilitator' of economic growth" (Dahrendorf, 1987, p. 120).

The debate among economists on socialist reform is focused on two closely intertwined themes, which may be labeled "comprehensiveness" and "sequencing." The former primarily addresses one question: what are the necessary elements? The latter deals with the following questions: in what order, in what kind of packages, and at what speed should the various reform measures be launched? None of the questions is purely economic or technical. Indeed, the issues that these questions raise are interwoven with such crucial political issues as the government's social objectives and its ability to sustain public support. In addition, one must always take the specific nature of the initial political and economic conditions into account.

Oktay Yenal, the World Bank's former chief economist for Asia, notes in his paper, "Transition to the Market System," that there are "remarkable similarities in the nature of the problems that have surfaced, trends that have emerged and challenges that have sharpened."[4] There seems to be more agreement or, at least, more clarity on the *nature* of the necessary elements for reform than on the sequencing of events. Sequencing advice ranges from the "big bang" approach, as Jeffrey Sachs and David Lipton recommended for Poland, to considerably more "phased" approaches—particularly with regard to privatization and ownership issues. With passing time, however, the debate on sequencing has simmered down—differences of opinion have narrowed somewhat—as concern has grown for "real" private owners, institution building, and other necessary elements of successful system-wide reform. What is emerging is a book about how to cook rather than one standard recipe, with growing input from the real world of reform. The 1991 World Development Report, entitled *The Challenge of Development*, contributes to this learning process by broadening the discussion of the experiences gained so far (World Bank, 1991). The conclusion in the report is that there is "no single reform sequence [which] will fit all the transitional economies." The report emphasizes the need for a comprehensive,

---

[4]Paper presented at the World Bank's Development Strategy Symposium for senior Vietnamese officials in Malaysia (1991, p. 1).

longer-term approach to reform, with capacity and institution building as central elements.

The reform process is, however, not just a matter of conscious choices of elements and sequences, but a much more complex change process in which state and party only partly determine events. In his analysis of China's development strategy after Mao, Gordon White gives a picture of a "party-government apparatus," "the Leninist centre," in full command: "The centre defines the basic parameters which make or break individual leaders, structure policy agendas and establish the limits of reform, whether from the Left or the Right" (White, 1983, p. 181). In the cases of Vietnam, Laos, and Cambodia, however, the leaders are as much victims of the forces that be as they are strategic actors. They try to survive by going with the flow; that is, by developing their "adaptive survival" capacity. The image of a stationmaster standing on a platform, watching trains passing by at high speed, captures an element of the relationship between the leaders and the reform. Stopping the trains—by reintroducing central planning—has long ceased to be an alternative. The real task facing the station master is to learn how to manage the decentralized and seemingly chaotic world of the market, with its multitude of "trains" whizzing past each other and competing for space like the infinite number of bicycles—and the rapidly increasing number of motorbikes—taking people and goods through the busy streets of Hanoi.

The reform processes initiated in 1979 in Vietnam, Laos, and Cambodia (although a special case) do not qualify as stage four in Kornai's classification of socialist countries, since all three remained one-party states. Vietnam and Laos are also likely to remain so for the foreseeable future. From Kornai's analysis it follows that he does not place much faith in reforms undertaken by such regimes. Under Kornai's scheme, all three countries are in the socialist reform stage, which has proved largely unworkable in Eastern Europe (Kornai, 1992). The Vietnamese and Lao reforms are, however, comprehensive in the sense suggested by Hewitt (Hewitt, 1988). In a 1990 World Bank publication about the Vietnamese reform experiences, Zdenek Drabek, today an advisor to the Czechoslovakian government, concludes that "the package of measures adopted in the spring of 1989 was impressive. Together with measures adopted at the end of 1988, the package represented perhaps the most comprehensive and radical set of reform measures adopted by any socialist country at the time" (Drabek, 1990, p. 37). The Cambodian economy may, at this stage in the transition process following the Paris agreement, be one of the least regulated economies in the world.

Indeed, the literature on reform in China or Eastern Europe does not seem to represent the changes and processes we have been witnessing in Indochina. According to Kornai, a market economy cannot develop as long as a communist party monopoly remains in place (Kornai, 1992). But the move to a market economy is actually occurring in Vietnam, Laos, and Cambodia, even though the adjustment of state and party is slow, ambivalent, and incomplete, and even though these economies may remain inefficient. Reality does not seem to be obeying "Kornai's law." How have these rapid changes been possible? One often overlooked reason is that the economies of Vietnam, Laos, and Cambodia were always more different from the economies of the Soviet Union and Eastern Europe than conventional wisdom suggests. All three countries are basically agrarian economies, with Vietnam's large-scale industrial sector being rather small. And, certain markets—legal as well as black—and different "outlets" for entrepreneurial drive have always existed; peasants, traders, the multitude of small manufacturing units did not need to be told how to relate to them, as price controls and other elements of central planning were removed.

Premises

Today, the Vietnamese call their old system "the bureaucratic, centralized state-subsidy system," while the Laotian government refers to its original socialist model as "the centralized bureaucratic-management mechanism." The Hun Sen regime in Cambodia sometimes talks about a "socialist production model," but prefers not to give its old model any label. The main reason is that it would like to see itself as having been on the reform path ever since it got into power in 1979. On the whole, its former model was "mainstream" socialist, in the tradition of its Vietnamese mentors.

I want to analyze the development from these original Marxist-Leninist notions of how to accomplish modernization to today's increasingly market- and outward-oriented development models. What did the Vietnamese, Laotian, and Cambodian economies look like in 1979, the year the first changes took place? How did the reform processes start, in what sectors of the economies, and why? How have the processes developed? Are there any clear stages, any definite sequences? How do these processes compare with those of other countries in transition? How far have these countries come with regard to marketization, price reform, dismantling of central planning, agrarian and industrial reform, macromanagement of the economy, and a new financial system? What are the main difficulties they face today? Can these countries develop the state capacity needed to manage open-oriented, market-based economies, generate the resources necessary for sustained development, and safeguard their social achievements? What kind of political-economic model (or models) is emerging, and how soon can these countries become members of ASEAN and other regional initiatives, beyond the divisions that have riven Southeast Asia in the past? What role can international aid play in strengthening and accelerating the reform processes?

To assess the extent to which the old systems have changed and new systems have evolved, I will examine the following dimensions of reform:

- agrarian reform (decollectivization)
- state enterprise reform and privatization
- establishment of functioning markets for goods and services
- dismantling of central planning and establishment of macromanagement of the economy
- development of factor or asset markets (labor, land, capital)
- liberalization of foreign trade, foreign investments, and other external flows

Available space does not allow detailed analysis, nor does the limited database. My intent is rather to try to put the main issues of these reform processes in Indochina into the broader comparative framework of economic systems reform, and do so from an historical and political perspective. I will apply a regional perspective. However, one clearly cannot treat Vietnam, Laos, and Cambodia as identical entities, even though many important issues are intertwined. They shared a common ambition to build up socialist economies and Vietnam played a dominant role in the region during the last half-century. (Only the northern part of Vietnam became a planned economy in any meaningful sense.) The three countries not only have very different endowments; they also had very different points of departure when initiating their reform processes. In my discussion, Vietnam will dominate, while I will treat Cambodia to the extent possible, given the extreme lack of data and the uncertainty surrounding its future.

My analysis of the transformation occurring in the region is grounded in these *seven main premises*:

1. Modernization through "the building of a large-scale socialist production system" has been seen as the principal road to development (Duan, 1977, p. 244). Modernization is, however, increasingly viewed as a means of creating economic growth (increased per capita incomes and welfare) rather than as an a priori goal. To understand developments in Indochina, one has to abandon the idea that the ultimate goal remains that of building up a specific kind of socialism based on Marxist-Leninist principles. These socialist ideals were the response to colonialism, exploitation, and underdevelopment; they were considered to offer a convincing analysis of the prevailing situation, and, most important, a direct road to modernization. Central planning seemed to be the vehicle to independence, social justice, and national strength.

2. The economic reforms have gone far beyond "socialist renovation" or "personal plot socialism."[5] Looking back, one can see that what started in 1979 as limited inner-systemic reforms has developed into profound reform processes that include dismantling of planning, freeing up of prices, and other essential features of an outward, market-based development model. In the process, the definition of "socialism" has been modified beyond recognition.

3. A hostile international environment and the reduced flow of aid created resource constraints in these countries that drastically limited the scope within which the governments could operate. As a consequence, reforms that would stimulate economic efficiency were introduced by and accepted among the elite who set the agendas.

4. The reform processes have, in some important respects, been internally driven. Changes have come about because of peasant alienation and other discontent over the authoritarian and symbiotic nature of the party/state. Domestic pressure and bottom-up adaptations of the prevailing model through "fence-breaking" initiatives have played an important role in shaping reforms meant to break the "low productivity stalemate" (Woodside, 1989, p. 296).

5. Simultaneous world developments—such as *perestroika* and the economic crisis in the former Soviet Union, reform in China, and the successes of neighboring countries like South Korea and Thailand—have sanctioned and accelerated the reform process and led to an entirely new international situation for the countries of Indochina. The possibility of depending on aid from the former Soviet Union and the Comecon (CMEA, the Council for Mutual Economic Cooperation) has vanished, and international cooperation, trade and finance with the West have become of decisive importance for the stabilization, deepening, and success of their reform and development efforts. The Soviet-style "aid regime" based on central planning has been dismantled. Vietnam and Cambodia are facing a critical lull between the old regime and the IMF/World Bank–dominated market-oriented regime on which they must now depend. (Laos already receives substantial support from the World Bank and the IMF.)

6. Politically, the emphasis is on stability. Yet, the political system is also undergoing reform in a number of ways, albeit cautiously. Political reform in Vietnam and Laos is being undertaken within the framework of the one-party state. An important objective of their entire reform process is to strengthen

---

[5]The concept "personal plot socialism" is used by Steven L. Sampson in his paper "The Second Economy of the Soviet Union and Eastern Europe" to describe the "metaphorical private plots" from which East Europeans have been trying to squeeze "every last bit of value . . . whether it be legally or illegally" (Sampson, 1987, p. 137).

the credibility of party and state as legitimate forces of change. The model that is emerging—in Vietnam and Laos—appears to have a number of features in common with what has become known as the East Asian market-based one-party state model and, as in these countries, can be expected to become less monolithic over time, provided the economic "project" yields credible results. For Cambodia, the Paris agreement sets the stage for an exceptional experiment in multiparty politics in that country.

7. Indochina, which emerged as a consequence of French colonization, will enter a new era as each of the three economies sees its comparative advantages in new contexts. The anticolonial struggle gave birth to the idea of increasingly close cooperation after independence, and the states of Vietnam, Laos, and Cambodia are today linked by agreements of friendship and cooperation. However, while these agreements were seen as fundamental 10 years ago when the reform process got under way, they are clearly decreasing in importance as the relationships between each of these countries and the rest of the world are expanding. As this trend continues, the relationships among the three countries can be expected to become increasingly less "special," as their economies become integrated units of regional initiatives, such as ASEAN, and the world economy. The epoch that was born with French colonization may be approaching its end.

I have chosen for this chapter the somewhat provocative title "Market Economies under Communist Regimes" because I have come to the conclusion that these economies can be best understood if viewed as market economies, however poorly functioning. The countries themselves prefer to use concepts such as "managed market economies," hoping to build something different from the "brutal" form of the market system they have distrusted so deeply. However, even though they are one-party states, these states are weak, both institutionally and financially. Not only Cambodia but all three countries are unable to generate even a minimum of revenue, and they are heavily dependent on external resources for their public investment. The fact that the possibility of receiving Soviet aid has vanished has aggravated the situation further, making successful market reforms a prerequisite for the "renovation of the state."

Major tasks ahead will be to redefine the role of the state and develop the capacity to manage the emerging market economy with increasing efficiency, develop the necessary infrastructure, provide social services, create conditions for agricultural and industrial development, and protect the environment. The crucial question is not whether Vietnam, Laos, and Cambodia will become market economies. Rather, the crucial questions are whether they can build the capacity to manage such economies with any efficiency so that total factor productivity can increase significantly, and whether their political systems will develop the adaptability required to achieve the necessary degree of legitimacy domestically and internationally. Prudent international support can accelerate the pace of both developments.

Before we address these reform issues, we have to reconstruct the prereform world from which the reform process emerged. Why did Vietnam, Laos, and Cambodia turn communist in the first place?

The Prereform World

The Historical Setting

The concept of Indochina emerged as a consequence of the French colonization of Vietnam, Cambodia, and what was left of Laos, during the latter part of the nineteenth century. Until then, there was no common name for this part of Southeast Asia and nothing that gave it any sense of unity. Conflict, annihilation, and incorporation rather than cooperation and voluntary integration had characterized the relationships among the entities occupying the area all through its recorded history. There was no common language, and different areas had been under profoundly different cultural influences. The Vietnamese had been thoroughly Sinicized by a millennium of Chinese rule, while Cambodia and Laos had been Buddhist and Indian in cultural orientation.[6] The French colonization of the region as a whole would have profound consequences during the entire century that would follow.

France created the concept of Indochina in its effort to bring its Asian conquests under "a unified administration, without insisting on uniformity of its disparate elements," with Hanoi as the administrative and cultural center (Cady, 1976, p. 428). The colonization created its antithesis—the struggle for independence. The struggle, as so often has been the case, was dominated by young people whose analysis of the colonial situation found its inspiration in Marxism-Leninism, and whose vision of the future was one of rapid modernization based on scientific socialism. The founding of the Indochinese Communist Party (ICP) in 1930 was a key element in the history of the

---

[6]Lucien Pye notes in his book *Asian Power and Politics—the Cultural Dimensions of Authority* that "more than any of the other non-Chinese cultures, the Vietnamese took to the ideals of power of traditional Confucianism" (Pye, 1985, p. 236). He does, however, also say, "None of the Asian colonial countries matched Vietnam in the extent to which its people assimilated the imperial European culture" (Pye, 1985, p. 237). SarDesai suggests that "the Sinicization of Vietnam affected mainly the upper classes of society, while the villagers were left to themselves." The effects of the French administration went deeper: "The French administration in Vietnam destroyed the peasants' traditional civilization . . . .The French broke the village autonomy and its corporate character" (SarDesai, 1989, p. 177).

struggle, which, quite naturally, came to be dominated by the Vietnamese.[7] The struggle for independence would—like the colonization—encompass the whole of Indochina.

At the eighth plenum of the ICP Central Committee in May, 1941, the Indochinese communists decided to launch the Viet Minh as their organizational vehicle. This decision was, as David Marr and, most recently, Stein Tonnesson have emphasized, "a fundamental event in the history of Vietnamese nation-building. By limiting party activities to a minimum and subordinating themselves to the charismatic leadership of Ho Chi Minh, the communists managed to establish an organization which . . . achieved a status as unchallenged leadership of a national liberation struggle" (Tonnesson, 1991, p. 417). When Japan surrendered to the Allies on August 14, 1945, the Viet Minh "emerged from the sidelines to the center of politics" (SarDesai, 1989, p. 182) to fill the "power vacuum of August 1945" (Tonnesson, 1991, p. 416). Three weeks later, on September 2, "a crowd of a half a million in Hanoi heard Ho Chi Minh proclaim the birth of the Democratic Republic of Vietnam (DRV)" (SarDesai, 1989, p. 182).

President Roosevelt showed a strong interest in Indochina and pursued the idea of placing it under an international trusteeship (Tonnesson, 1991, pp. 13–19). The Allies, however, decided to reestablish the status quo ante. Chinese troops entered from the north, and British troops from the south. The British immediately released the French (Vichy) from prison and "contrary to instructions, gave them arms" (SarDesai, 1989, p. 182). The circle was closed when Charles de Gaulle's liberated France declared itself determined to reassert its colonial rights in Indochina, despite an impassioned appeal for independence to de Gaulle from abdicated Vietnamese Emperor Bao Dai.

France's decision to try to reestablish its colonial empire after the Second World War (and the U.S. decision to give France the necessary financial support)[8] led to eight years of war—the First Indochina War—and brought

---

[7]Ho Chi Minh fused the three prominent communist groups in Vietnam into a single party and named it the Indochinese Communist Party (ICP), "although there were few communists then in Laos and Cambodia. By 1931, the ICP claimed 1,500 members besides 100,000 peasants affiliated in peasant organizations" (SarDesai, 1989, p. 180). On November 11, 1945, the central executive committee of the ICP declared that, "ready to put the interests of the nation above all class interests," the party had decided to dissolve itself (quoted in Huynh Kim Kha'nh, 1982, p. 329). This self-dissolution was carried out for tactical reasons to ensure the party's survival as a political force as Chiang Kai-shek's forces threatened its existence. In January, 1950, the ICP was reconstituted as the Vietnam Workers' Party, which, in 1951, publicly affirmed its leadership of DRV. Separate communist parties were subsequently formed in both Laos and Cambodia.

[8]George McT. Kahin notes that "a badly ravaged postwar France possessed neither the military equipment nor the financial resources to mount a major military effort in Vietnam. It was thanks to the United States that she was able to marshal the crucial elements of power which she began to apply there within a few months of the war's end" (Kahin, 1987, p. 7–8).

the Cold War to Indochina. Following the Geneva Conference (1954), which put an end to the French era, the U.S. government declared that its central objective was to "build a dike around the present loss," the "loss" being the northern half of the divided Vietnam (quoting John Foster Dulles in Hess, 1990, p. 52). The communist movements would, however, grow in strength.

Already in 1953, the DRV had begun to undertake a land reform in its liberated areas. Between 1953 and 1956, the reform was extended to the whole area north of the 17th parallel, and in 1959, the government embarked upon the collectivization of agriculture. Rapid industrialization was another important feature of the socialist reform, especially from 1959 to 1964 (Beresford, 1988, pp. 129–134).

It would, however, take a Second Indochina War to turn the whole of Indochina into a region ruled by Marxist-Leninist regimes, and a Cold War to cause the tremendous destruction and division that still is plaguing the three countries of Indochina. The nature of Indochinese communism was deeply influenced by the fact that it evolved under war conditions.

The Second Indochina War ended in the spring of 1975, when communist forces entered Saigon and Phnom Penh, and the U.S. presence exited. Toward the end of the year, Laos also would become a "people's republic." The following years, however, would not be characterized by reconstruction and normalization. Political developments would make security matters a main concern.

The United States fought the Second Indochina War in the name of anticommunism. The economic development since 1975, however, has shown that communism was much less of a uniting force than the believers in the Domino theory claimed, and that nationalism was a much stronger force than most observers had understood.

The conflict between Vietnam and the Pol Pot regime in Phnom Penh came out into the open only in March, 1978, but serious border fighting took place much earlier with several hundred thousand Vietnamese and Cambodians crossing the border to become refugees in Vietnam (Chanda, 1986, pp. 219–225; Ablin and Hood, 1990, pp. xxxviii–xxxix). China's decision to give military and economic support to the Khmer Rouge accelerated a polarization process through which Vietnam and Laos moved increasingly close to the Soviet Union and to Comecon (CMEA). Vietnam became a member of Comecon in the summer of 1978. China retaliated immediately by "terminating all its economic, military and technical assistance to Vietnam and withdrawing Chinese experts" (SarDesai, 1989, p. 291).

Vietnam's installation of the Heng Samrin regime in Phnom Penh in January 1979 incited China to attack northern Vietnam and created a deeply hostile relationship between the countries of Indochina, (united under Vietnam's leadership) and ASEAN. The United States supported China and ASEAN, making the isolation of Vietnam a key element of its policy toward the region.

The Cold War, the Sino-Soviet conflict, and the Cambodian conflict reinforced each other, putting socialist transformation and security considerations on a par in the strategies of Vietnam, Laos, and Cambodia. Vietnam and Laos signed a 25-year treaty of friendship in 1977, and Vietnam and Cambodia entered into a similar treaty in March, 1979. What Hanoi sought was not only the security of a political bloc but also the creation of an economically integrated unit in which to achieve "gradual implementation of labor distribution, ensuring an effective use of labor and land potentials of the three countries."[9] All three countries based their security on Soviet support, and Vietnam became Comecon's largest recipient of aid, receiving around 40 percent of total Comecon aid to developing countries (United Nations, 1990b, p. 221).

By 1979, Vietnam found itself closely tied to the Soviet Union and the economic mechanisms of the Eastern bloc. Its efforts to normalize its relationship with the United States had been in vain, although it had given up all claims on U.S. assistance for the reconstruction of the nation. Most assistance from Western countries ceased, including support from the World Bank and the IMF. Laos never became as isolated, but only a few Western countries provided bilateral aid. The new government in Phnom Penh received substantial support through the United Nations during 1979 when the country was threatened by a major famine, but most of this aid ceased the moment the immediate threat was over. Many times more aid would go to refugees in Thailand, grouped in camps controlled by the Khmer Rouge and the other two factions that the world chose to recognize (see Shawcross, 1984). The world undoubtedly looked deeply divided as seen from the capitals of the three Indochinese countries. Socialism had to be built in a hostile environment.

The Indochinese governments took it for granted that socialism would continue to expand globally; this was a scientific necessity given the wasteful and disorderly nature of capitalism, which was ridden by increasingly deep cycles of unemployment and unable to manage its inevitable contradictions. In an address to the Lao Supreme National Assembly in February, 1979, the Lao party leader and then Prime Minister Kaysone Phomvihane voiced the prevailing Indochinese interpretation of history: "The Soviet Union and its socialist brother countries have obtained glorious successes in their effort to build socialism, and the material and technical basis of Communism. At this

---

[9]Quote cited by Chanda from speech by Vo Van Kiet at the First Indochinese Planning Conference in February, 1984 (Chanda, 1986, p. 375).

moment, Soviet industry is capable of producing a larger volume of goods than that of the whole of Western Europe. The economies of the socialist countries have developed at a rapid pace . . . " (Phomvihane, 1979, p. 2).

Modernization through central planning, however, revealed itself to be a considerably rougher journey than the leadership in Hanoi, Vientiane, and Phnom Penh envisaged. Very few among them had seen the actual conditions in other parts of the world beyond the socialist part. Experience gained in the struggle for independence defined their vision. They were convinced that "collective mastery" could be attained through the so-called three revolutions: in production relations, in science and technology, and in ideology and culture. What they, in their self-criticism, have called "voluntarism" played a major role in shaping their vision: ". . . it [the Party] has committed errors originating from subjectivism and voluntarism and violating objective laws; haste in socialist transformation, willingness to promptly abolish the mixed economy . . . many erroneous decisions related to price, monetary and salary reforms . . . " (Vietnam, Communist Party of, 1991, p. 46). "Ideological will," in effect, drove economics.

Vietnam

At the time of unification in 1976, the northern part of Vietnam had many characteristics of a centrally planned economy. But it was also different in important respects. It was not an Eastern European-type socialist economy in which nearly everything belonged to the state sector, and it was not an economy entirely without private market activities with all prices set by decree. Furthermore, it was largely rural. It had the following characteristics:

- Enterprises were run by either the state, local government, or cooperatives, and agriculture (except for family plots) was collectivized.
- Management of the economy was based on a comprehensive plan, and all planning was made in real magnitudes (material balances), supported by central controls on financial magnitudes.
- All key prices and wages were set administratively, with prices playing only a marginal role in decisions about resource allocation.
- Large subsidies in the budget went to commodities and state enterprises, the latter enjoying a so-called soft-budget constraint (i.e., any losses would be covered, and no company was ever declared bankrupt).
- There were hardly any capital, labor, or other factor markets; interest rates were maintained at artificially low or negative real levels; and the return on investments mattered very little.
- All foreign trade was monopolized and administered by the Ministry of Foreign Trade through specialized state trading corporations.

- Official exchange rates were of accounting significance only, with administered prices bearing hardly any relation to world market prices; macromanagement of money supply, aggregate demand, and other economic variables had very little scope.

The nature of the Vietnamese economy was, to a significant degree, a result of the fact that its socialist transformation took place largely during war time and under the extreme conditions that the war against the United States imposed. The *via dolorosa* of the Vietnamese leaders as struggling revolutionaries and the war itself created a mentality of sacrifice to which economic incentives and the variety of a market economy mattered very little. The term "war communism" effectively conveys the spirit that emerged in North Vietnam.

This spirit stood in sharp contrast to that of the South, where the state had failed to mobilize the people, where almost anything was sold on open markets, and where consumption had been kept at artificially high levels through American subsidies. The two parts of the country had grown widely apart during two decades of separation, and their reunification became a considerably more difficult task with much more serious and long-term consequences than the leaders in Hanoi imagined.

The decision to impose the northern model on the South had its focus on agriculture, industry, and trade. Initially, the emphasis was on economic restoration rather than transition, but in 1976, enterprises were pressured to enter into joint ventures with the state, and in early 1977, the government turned to collectivization of agriculture (preceded by compulsory quota sales). The government took measures to regulate the predominantly Chinese private businessmen, and in early 1978, a campaign was launched against large-scale traders.[10] The whole country had entered a new stage—a transitional period to socialism in which, according to Party Secretary Le Duan, "the whole country fulfills a *single* strategic task of carrying out socialist revolution" (quoting Le Duan in Vo Nhan Tri, 1990, p. 62). National defense became the other strategic task after China destroyed vast border areas in northern Vietnam in February, 1979, following Vietnam's installation of the Heng Samrin government in Phnom Penh a month earlier.

A grave economic crisis was one consequence of these developments. Agricultural production and procurement fell, and in 1978, Vietnam had to import 1.4 million tons of food grains, worsening the balance-of-payments situation and the budgetary position and causing prices on the free market to

---

[10]Main sources: Melanie Beresford, 1988; Marr and White, (eds.), 1988; Vo Nhan Tri, 1990.

increase by 50 percent. Peasant alienation and resistance grew, as Alexander Woodside notes, and the government inflicted on itself what Christine White has called a "procurement crisis" (Woodside, 1989, p. 286; White, 1985, p. 111). Vietnam's limited domestic and financial resources were diverted to defense. The exodus of boat people began.

Problems in the management and planning of the economy came to the surface. The economy grew annually by only 2 percent in 1977 and 1978, instead of the 14 percent envisaged in the Five-Year Plan. The situation became untenable when Chinese aid stopped and Western aid began to decrease, the latter as a consequence of the world's changing perception of Vietnam in the wake of boat refugees and Vietnam's invasion of Cambodia. Vietnam was becoming increasingly isolated. It had to try new measures—more pragmatic measures such as those Prime Minister Pham Van Dong had favored, rather than the "highly centralized, managerial, and statist" measures advocated and pushed forward by Le Duan, which Woodside has called "Southeast Asia's most extravagant recent ventures in state-sponsored managerial utopism" (Marr and White, 1988, p. 140; Woodside, 1989, p. 293).[11] "The severe economic difficulties experienced in Vietnam at the end of the 1970s had prevented the consolidation of the centrally planned system" (Van Arkadie and Boi, 1992, p. 10).

External developments, in particular the critical resource constraints, played a crucial role in provoking Vietnam's search for workable solutions. But the original development of that process was—as Melanie Beresford and Adam Fforde have noted—in important respects driven by domestic economic and social pressures and local initiatives, that is, forces working from the bottom up (Beresford, 1988; Fforde, 1991). The authorities reacted by attempting to use market-type measures "as a limited tool within the context of a continuing effort to centrally plan the state sector" (Van Arkadie and Boi, 1992, pp. 12–13). There were clear limits to what the party could digest. In 1982, Nguyen Van Linh, who would become the chief architect of doi moi, would be removed from the Politburo for advocating liberal economic measures that had been successfully tried in the South.

---

[11]For an illustration of Le Duan's thinking, see his *Selected Writings* (1977), and especially "Toward Large Scale Socialist Agriculture," a conference speech delivered in 1973. Le Duan regards "organization of production and management on the district scale" as necessary: "The problem to solve is, from what standpoint can we re-organize production and proceed with a new division of labor . . ? It is obviously impossible within the framework of a cooperative covering some hundred hectares of land and employing a few hundred people as is common at present . . . I think that in the present conditions of mechanization it is possible for a locality handling about ten thousand hectares of agricultural land and employing about forty thousand people, that is the scale of a district, to carry out such a division of labor and organization of production in a better and a more rational manner" (Le Duan, 1977, p. 514).

Laos

The revolutionary Lao leaders, who, in December of 1975, turned their country into a people's democratic republic, had had very little opportunity to gain experience in running a national economy; they had spent most of their lives in the remote northern border areas launching their struggle. They took charge of a capital—and a bureaucracy—that epitomized the very kind of neocolonial economy and culture they regarded as a root cause of the national crisis. The economy was one of the world's least developed, with 80 percent of the population engaged in agriculture. Many practiced shifting cultivation. The war had not wreaked the same amount of destruction as in Vietnam, but some 700,000 persons had fled Pathet Lao areas "largely to escape American bombing" (Stuart-Fox, 1986, p. 36). The termination of the largely United States-financed Foreign Exchange Operations Fund, which upheld the value of the Lao currency, coupled with a Thai economic blockade undermined the artificial urban economy. A large portion of the nation's trained people left the country during the first few years after the revolution, and thousands spent many years in forced reeducation.

The Lao revolution took place at a time when the socialist world regarded revolutionary change through radical transformation of the relations of production as possible at quite different conditions. The Lao leadership concluded that there was no reason, given its underdevelopment, to go through the stage of capitalist development. Laos would "advance step by step, to socialism" and do so directly (quoting FBIS, March 24, 1976, in Stuart-Fox, 1986). A number of steps were taken during 1976; then, during 1977, the scope of the reform expanded to include the collectivization of agriculture, as the pace of transformation quickened (Evans, 1990, p. 47). Expanded reform brought the following changes:

- A rudimentary, highly centralized planning system was established. State-owned enterprises were run directly by the ministries, which hardly granted these enterprises any authority; provinces did, however, take initiatives of their own.
- The banking system and major industrial enterprises were nationalized.
- State trading organizations were created and given a monopoly on all foreign trade and domestic trade in essential goods.
- A public internal-distribution system, with the mandate to provide the population with basic goods at low and stable prices, was being created; no transport by private haulers was allowed.
- Government employees received a large share of their salaries in the form of coupons to be used in state stores; the salary hardly sufficed

to buy anything in the free market. Peasants who sold paddy to the state also received coupons, which they could use to buy inputs and goods in state stores.

- Exchange rates (multiple) were highly artificial. A black-market rate became increasingly important, determining the price level in the free market (which never actually disappeared completely, although it was seriously suppressed at times).

- State finances became burdened with heavy subsidies to state enterprises and the distribution system.

The existing conditions faced by the new government were exceedingly difficult; the transformation measures it undertook further aggravated the situation and created grave imbalances. Self-sufficiency in rice was the government's highest priority, but rice production fell, necessitating substantial food imports. As a consequence of this dependence on imports and a very poor export performance (partly due to Thai policies toward Laos), the balance-of-payments situation grew increasingly weak. Money expansion caused the rate of inflation to rise to three-digit levels.

During 1978, certain improvements were noticeable. Macro imbalances such as the budget deficit and aggregate supply and demand became somewhat less serious as the government, with advice from international financial institutions, gained some experience in using exchange rate, monetary, fiscal, and pricing tools.

Nevertheless, in the spring of 1978, the government decided to go ahead with the collectivization of agriculture. This step was, as Stuart-Fox has noted, "taken both for ideological reasons and in order to increase both production and government control over what was produced" (Stuart-Fox, 1986, p. 100). In a major speech on collectivization in November, 1978, the Secretary-General of the party and then Prime Minister Kaysone Phomvihane declared that "the re-organization of agriculture and forestry, having the peasants advance gradually toward the collective, socialist way of working" was "a most important and most urgent problem" (translation from the French, Phomvihane, 1978, p. 1). If this could be accomplished, "conditions would have been created which would make the transformation and consolidation in other areas easy," such as administration, defense, and security (translation from the French, Phomvihane, 1978). The transformation of the relations of production were given highest priority. The reform was supposed to be voluntary, but, in reality, the government pushed hard to reach its objectives by 1980.

Less than one year later, the collectivization program came to an abrupt halt. In a circular issued on July 14, 1979, by the Central Committee of the party, the party called for the "immediate and absolute suspension" of the program.[12]

The decision to suspend the program was clearly because of the crisis situation and not a conscious ideological shift. Acute problems demanded immediate action. The collectivization drive had not only hampered rice production but it had also worsened the internal security situation and led to an increase in insurgency. Many peasants who were not in the areas governed by the Pathet Lao, the Lao Patriotic Front (Neo Lao Hak Sat), during the war were unprepared for the kind of changes mandated by the party cadres. These changes had not been a part of the programs adopted by Pathet Lao in 1967 or 1968, programs which had gained wide acceptance in the country.

Actually, collectivization did not become an explicit objective, except inside the Lao People's Revolutionary Party (LPRP), until 1975.[13] It is openly stated for the first time in the December 1-2, 1975, program of action of the Government of Lao People's Democratic Republic that an objective is "to favor and assist the peasants to move towards collective living in order to improve production and to better their living conditions" (quoting documents in Brown and Zasloff, 1986).

But peasant discontent and falling production created a situation in which the government had to choose between collectivization through repression and a less ideological approach. It chose the latter; if it had chosen the former, the number of peasant families crossing over to Thailand would most probably have increased considerably.[14] Agrarian change entered a new era of pragmatism, and Laos entered an era of cautious reform through trial and error. Socialism would no longer be realized in rapid leaps but would remain a goal to be reached gradually. Different forms of ownership would come into play. A first reform package was launched in November, 1979, by the seventh plenary session of the Central Committee of the Lao PRP.

---

[12]For detailed accounts of this process see Stuart-Fox (1986) and Evans (1990).

[13]LPRP was the dominating force within the Pathet Lao. At the time, not much was known about the party.

[14]At the time, those who "crossed the river" stood a good chance of being granted asylum in the United States or, to a lesser extent, other Western countries. In its analysis, the United Nations High Commissioner for Refugees (UNHCR) noted that the fact that it was relatively easy to be accepted by a third country had a "pull effect" on those considering fleeing.

Cambodia

What happened to Cambodia during the Second Indochina War and especially during the Pol Pot years cannot be repeated too often. Quoting an
authoritative source, Grant Curtis:

> In 1979 Kampuchea was a ruined country. Much of the previously urban-
> based population had been obliterated, including most educated individu-
> als. Fewer than 50 doctors and only 5,000 of the former 20,000 teachers
> survived the Kampuchean holocaust. The horrors of the Khmer Rouge
> regime, the scope of the physical and psychological destruction, the social
> dislocation caused by the death of millions, and the flight across the border of
> the surviving population were such that the first Western observers to reach
> Kampuchea in 1979 questioned the very survival of the Kampuchean people.
> Kampuchea's resurrection demanded the creation of a normal economic
> and social life out of an almost complete void. (Curtis, 1990, p. 17).[15]

In its first effort to assess the needs of the Cambodian economy, the
United Nations Development Program (UNDP) sketched this picture: "[the
new regime] inherited a country close to chaos, with physical infrastructure
and industrial plants destroyed, crops in ruin, draft animals halved in numbers, and no central administration" (UNDP, 1989, p. vi). "There had been no
currency or markets for four years, no taxes had been collected for at least
nine . . . " (Vickery, 1986, p. 128). The gross national product may have been
equal to a couple of percent of that of neighboring Thailand.

"Pol Pot saw," as Ablin and Hood have noted, "enemies everywhere—not
only within the communist party, but also among the professional and
educated elite, ethnic and religious minorities, and urban dwellers. The nearly
four years of Democratic Kampuchean rule is in large part the story of his
effort to eliminate perceived and real sources of opposition" (Ablin and Hood,
1990, p. xxxvii).

The new regime, called the People's Republic of Kampuchea (PRK) was
put into power by Vietnam, and the structure that emerged in 1979 was
naturally strongly influenced by the large number of Vietnamese advisors and
administrators who helped the very inexperienced new leadership start
rebuilding the country. The most important task was to organize agriculture
and avoid a famine. The government announced that agricultural producers
would be organized in "solidarity groups" (*krom sammaki*) of ideally 10 to
15 families who would cooperatively produce and share in the rewards
(Vickery, 1986, p. 139). All communal living and other extremes of the Pol Pot
era were abandoned, but the objective remained to build up a society along

---

[15]For a recent detailed account, see David P. Chandler's *The Tragedy of Cambodian History—
Politics, War and Revolution Since 1945* (1992).

socialist lines. The new solidarity system was motivated both by ideology and by the need to solve the serious problems caused by shortages of able-bodied males, tools, and draft animals. Collectives were the longer-term goal, but this goal was not pursued in any zealous way. To have done so, after what the people had gone through under Khmer Rouge, would have caused further alienation.

The new constitution, adopted in April 1979, recognized three types of economic organization: state, cooperative, and family (private). Industries and transport would be in the public sector, which also had a major role in the distribution of rice and other necessities. But private markets were allowed and soon became of some importance. The same was true for foreign trade. A state monopoly was introduced, but private traders were allowed to operate. A system of central planning, with physical production targets and administrative controls, was built up, and the government set about determining key prices and wages. In 1980, the new central bank cum commercial bank introduced a Cambodian currency.

The task of the new government was further impeded by the decision of the Western world to isolate the new regime and recognize the factions trying to topple it with military means. Survival rather than experiments became a necessity. It was natural that the mainstream model of the time, the one that Vietnam had instituted in its own country, was what the new Cambodian regime, highly dependent on Vietnamese advisors, would inherit as its basic model. However, there was some latitude for family and private activities. Later on, as its interest in market-oriented solutions grew, the regime would be able to build on these activities.

Model and Reality

Vietnam, Laos, and Cambodia found themselves at quite different stages of socialist development in 1979, although all of them were extremely poor countries. Vietnam was far ahead in many respects, having advanced further in transforming the relationships of production. It was the dominant country economically, militarily, and ideologically. And only Vietnam had institutions of higher learning and an intellectual class formed under socialism.

All three countries, however, followed a development model based on the notion of the leading role of the party and the idea of development through central planning and the state. In this model, the objective was to transform society, going from small- to large-scale production through rapid growth and under highly egalitarian conditions. Economic incentives were designed to encourage behavior consistent with the socialist ideal.

Such was the model. Reality was different. The party and the state never fully implemented a centrally planned system, not even in North Vietnam. Markets always existed (except in Cambodia during the Pol Pot years). Local markets were allowed, and they played an important role in the rural economy. Not only vegetables but also rice was being marketed privately in North Vietnam as early as 1968 (Fforde, 1989). Also in 1968, experiments with an agricultural contract system took place in certain parts of the North.

Because of existing markets, the price system had a dual-track character. Private trading included some border trade, and a foreign currency market flourished at rates many times higher than the official rate. Inflation was not supposed to exist in these planned economies, but in reality, it was a serious problem, as were large budget and current-account deficits. Salaries and wages did not cover even the bare minimum for survival; this caused corruption to spread.

Such problems were not confined only to countries trying to build socialism. But, if socialism were going to work in these states, the imbalances and deficits would have to be addressed—either through all-out efforts to establish central planning as the sole coordination mechanism (which would require even larger volumes of Soviet aid) or through adjustments and reform. The former course would aggravate an already serious situation of scarcities by further weakening the incentive structure in the economy. The latter course would mean an opening up of the prevailing socialist model. What would unfold during the decade to come was, as Woodside put it, "poorly disguised withdrawals from ideologically blind alleys" (Woodside, 1989, p. 286).

From Limited to Comprehensive Reform

Beginning in 1979, two developments set in motion Vietnam's internal reform process: (1) the movement away from collectivization in the agricultural sector, and (2) so-called "fence breaking" by state-owned enterprises (SOEs) that went beyond the delivery targets of the plan and started operating on the market. Both developments arose not because the party and government wanted to abandon central planning but because the ruling elite, facing a crisis situation, realized that the position of the state and the party would only be further weakened by pursuing statist and collectivist policies. Originally, the idea was to supplement the socialist model by incorporating spontaneous developments that had proven viable. The party did so in a reactive manner, trying to get out of a crisis situation. At the time, nobody understood that the reforms might grow like cuckoo eggs inevitably altering the orderly life of the nest where they were put.[16] It would take another seven years before doi moi would emerge as a strategy of renovation.

---

[16]The dynamics of these processes are a main theme in Chapter 11 of this book.

Similar developments took place in Laos and Cambodia. Agrarian change began in 1979 in all three countries. And although "fence breaking" did not emerge as an equally important factor of change in Laos or Cambodia, questions concerning the autonomy of state enterprises and the role of the private sector were among the first to be addressed in the reform processes of these countries. In the case of Laos, "authorized reforms" were tried in a few southern provinces.

Cooperatives, Peasant Families, and Markets

The changes that began to occur in Vietnam, Laos, and Cambodia in 1979 had one important element in common: they would all affect the relationship between peasants and land, initiating a process of "peasantization" that would lead to an increasingly direct relationship among peasant families, production, and markets.

Vietnam. Vietnam was facing severe economic difficulties and a crisis in the relationship between its two alienated parts. The Central Committee, at an August 1979, meeting "held in a mounting atmosphere of crisis," decided to try a number of unorthodox measures, which since have become key elements of its "renovation" (Beresford, 1988, p. 160). Beresford describes the Vietnamese reform, as it affected most of the Mekong River delta peasants, in this way:

> The reforms . . . involved the introduction of *direct contracting* between individual farmers and the state in which the state undertook to supply inputs in return for a proportion of the harvest over and above obligatory quota sales. These above-quota sales can be made at *a negotiated price* which is close to (but still below) the price obtainable on the free market. Agricultural taxes and obligatory sales (at state prices) were fixed for a five-year period. One of the major features of the reforms was a change in the price structure in mid- to late 1981, the purpose being to *bring prices closer to those prevailing in the free market*, to bring prices in the North closer to the prices in the South and to offset the effects of a devaluation of the Dong. (quoting Beresford in Lundahl, 1985, p. 388, italics added)

The Vietnamese peasants, including those in collectivized North Vietnam, had always been able to sell products grown on their own plots of land (the household economy) in the local market. So, the private market was well known to them. Although the government-sponsored output contract system was limited in scope and in intent (the purpose being to strengthen and, ultimately, "recollectivize" the system), it set in motion increasingly independent decision making on the part of peasants operating in a market (Fforde, 1989, p. 204–5). The beneficial effects on production were immediate, which is why the idea prevailed in spite of its heretical nature. The eventual result was the deconstruction of one pillar of the prevailing model.

The preceding conclusions can be drawn today with the advantage of hindsight. But, at the time, these developments were not part of a longer-term plan, and peasants could not count on them. In fact, as Ngo Vinh Long and others have shown, cooperativization or collectivization remained on the party agenda, subjecting peasants to substantial "system risks," as in China. In December 1982, the third plenum of the Fifth Party Congress declared, for example, that the cooperativization of the southern region should be "basically completed" by the end of 1985 (Ngo Vinh Long, 1988, p. 164), and in 1984, an effort to renew "the collectivization drive, in abeyance since 1979," was made by the fourth plenum (Beresford, 1988, p. 165). Professor Vo-Tong Xuan, Chancellor of the Agricultural University in Can Tho in the Mekong Delta, recalls that in October 1980, his television program on the experiment with the contract systems in his province was stopped and condemned by the most senior party functionary in charge of land reform in the South (conversation with Vo-Tong Xuan, April, 1991). The notion of collective agriculture constituted a key element of the revolutionary ideology, and the new orientation put the party's ability to change—and preserve its unity—to a severe test.

At the same time, it is worth noting that the idea of a contract system was not a new one when introduced in 1979–80. It had been tried 11 years earlier in the North Vietnamese province of Vinh Phu.[17] At the time, it was initially reported to be a success in a series of articles in the district newspaper, but was ultimately rejected as bourgeois by Maoist-oriented leaders like Truong Chinh. In a debate about reunification in 1975, Truong Chinh argued that the Vietnamese people "must go direct to the socialist revolution by-passing the stage of capitalist development." In 1986, he retrospectively acknowledged, with reference to the failed effort to collectivize the South, that "had our policies [toward the peasants]—especially . . . pricing, circulation, and distribution policies—been rational, the peasants would certainly not have given up tilling, would not have pulled up tobacco plants, would not have destroyed sugar cane, and would not have given up hog raising: on the contrary they would have enthusiastically produced more" (quoting Truong Chinh in Vo Nhan Tri, 1990, p. 80). In 1986, however, results mattered more than ideology, and the forthcoming party congress would lay the foundation for more comprehensive changes. Through doi moi the state started its uphill task of bridging the gaps between state-controlled prices, domestic market prices, and world market prices.

---

[17]See Hy Van Luong's *Tradition and Revolution in a North Vietnamese Village (1925–1988)* (forthcoming, 1992).

The Sixth Party Congress, held in December, 1986, was of great importance in every field, including agriculture. It endorsed the move toward a market economy. But, it was only after the adoption of Politburo Decree No. 10 in April 1988 that the peasant family was clearly understood to be the basic unit in the agrarian structure. The legal basis for Decree No. 10 was a decision of the Council of Ministers (Fforde and de Vylder, 1991, p. B-V-150). Through Decree No. 10, the contract system became the basis of a long-term tenure system granting user rights. The peasant family gained security on its land and freedom to sell its produce on the open market. A tenure period of 15 to 20 years is common today. Leases can even be inherited and transferred. There is, however, as yet, no uniform system with regard to inheritance and transfers.

In the Communist party's *Strategy for Socio-Economic Stabilization and Development of our Country up to the Year 2000*, prepared for the Seventh Party Congress in June, 1991, the reform received a clear endorsement. According to the document, "Peasant holdings are to be granted long-term land leases with proper licenses. The law is to provide specifically for the inheritance and tranfer of the right to lease land" (Vietnam, Communist Party of, 1991, p. 161).

However, the *Political Report*, approved by the Seventh Congress, reflects a more ambivalent attitude, as it attempts to reconcile the ideas of family-based agriculture and cooperative management. A main task is said to be:

> to continue renovating the management system of agricultural cooperatives toward ensuring autonomy for the members' households while enhancing the role of management boards in managing and regulating production, ensuring necessary services, and carrying out, together with the administration and the people's organizations, social policies and the building of the new countryside. (Vietnam, Communist Party of, 1991, p. 115)

This is no small order, and far from a clear one. It combines functions normally performed by service cooperatives with functions within the realm of local government, and shows that sufficiently influential groups within the party still would like to see the cooperative play a role in "managing and regulating production."

During the Seventh Congress, the questions of land ownership and the relationship between the household economy and the cooperative caused considerable debate. Private ownership of land as distinguished from user rights—was, not surprisingly, rejected. More surprising, it was agreed that the household, although important, "will not be able to exist as a separate entity in the way that the state, collective, individual, private capitalist and state-capitalist sectors may" (*Nhan Dan*, 1991). The implications of this resolution, which appears to be a reaction to recent changes in the agrarian structure, are not clear. The views were articulated by delegates from the North, who wanted the cooperatives to play a larger role in managing common matters and assuring equity. The guidelines for socioeconomic stability and development in the period from 1992 to 1995, which were adopted by the Central Committee at its second plenum (November 25–December 4, 1991), contain the same notion, saying that "cooperatives will be reformed in such a way as can ensure members' mastery while making collective management more effective" (*Vietnam Courier*, 1992, p. 5).

In the *1992 Constitution of the Socialist Republic of Vietnam*, it is clearly stated that "land is allocated by the State to organizations and individuals for stable long-term use . . . .They are also entitled by law to transfer the right to use the land allocated by the state" (Vietnam, Socialist Republic of, *1992 Constitution,* Article 18). The process that began somewhat more than a decade ago when the contract system was sanctioned as a way of countering a growing food deficit, and that, after the Sixth Party Congress (1986), was developed into a long-term tenure system (Decree No. 10, 1988), has, hence, received a clear constitutional endorsement. The issue caused a heated debate in the National Assembly.

The role of collectives, or cooperatives, is treated in very general terms in the new constitution. The article does not convey ambivalence in the way that the political resolution approved by the Seventh Congress did:

> Economic collectives set up through the contribution of funds and manpower by citizens for a cooperation in production and business will be organized under different forms on the basis of voluntarism, democracy and mutual benefit. The State shall facilitate the consolidation and expansion of efficient economic collectives. (Vietnam, Socialist Republic of, 1992, Article 20)

Nothing is said in the new constitution about a role for the cooperatives in managing or regulating production.

In practice, government and cooperatives have steadily reduced their control over the peasant economy. The cooperatives have not been abandoned, and will not be, but their role has changed from the omnipotent one of administrative responsibility over production to one of nonmonopolistic distribution of inputs, provision of irrigation and other services, collection of taxes and fees, and procurement of outputs. The cooperative also continues to own capital equipment, such as tractors and trucks, but management has been contracted to individual operators, and private ownership is permitted. Most livestock and fish production has been fully privatized. Forest land can be leased for 30 years, and sometimes longer. The number of cooperative officers has been reduced by 50 percent, easing the financial burden on its members.

The actual role of the cooperative is often considerably more limited than that suggested above, especially in the south. The cooperatives remain, however, powerful in some respects, having decisive influence over certain crucial matters such as the leasing of land. Whether there continues to be a strong link between party and cooperative leadership is not clear. How is the "patriarchalism" of the system (as Woodside describes it) affected by the strengthened position of peasants and markets? Do "cadre families" get particularly good land or other advantages, or is their power weakening as state and party become less omnipresent? Does the patriarchy shift toward the newly rich peasant? While Hy Van Luong's recent fieldwork in a village 17 miles north of Hanoi conveys an impression of reduced party-cadre patriarchalism, the power structure is likely to vary considerably (Luong, 1991b). No broader studies exist yet on this important question. It is, however, often said that political cadres reserve good land for themselves, thus becoming part of yet another elite, that is, the new elite of better-off peasant families.

An important underlying question is how the base of the party is affected by the de facto privatization of agriculture. Will the party be able to strengthen its base among the vast number of peasants who, no doubt, have seen their livelihood improve as a consequence of tenancy and price reforms?

And what should be the "correct" governmental attitude toward the surplus farmer, who may acquire increasingly large areas to cultivate? The answer will, no doubt, evolve through continuous dialogue between party and peasantry. What does efficiency demand? How can social justice be served in ways that do not hamper production? A dialectical tension will continue to exist between the drive for growth and the concern for equity. Emerging "capitalist peasants" will raise different demands than the peasant families who remain poor. The poorer families, who have a greater need for a social safety net, may want the cooperatives to play a more comprehensive role by, for example, continuing to provide certain entitlements. The prevailing trend is clearly toward household-based, market-oriented farming, limiting the role of the cooperative to services rather than management or regulation.

The changes since 1979, and especially since 1988, have greatly affected production. Once a chronic rice importer, Vietnam today is exporting huge quantities of rice. During 1989 and 1990, Vietnam exported approximately 1.5 million tons per year, making it the world's third largest rice exporter. The figure for 1991 was lower (approximately 1 million tons), due to unfavorable weather conditions and pests that affected the winter crop in the North, but the country seems to have been able to break the "low productivity stalemate" that emerged from peasant resistance to the old extracting system

(Woodside, 1989, p. 286).[18] Average per capita consumption remains, however, very low; malnutrition remains widespread, as the surplus is concentrated in the Mekong Delta; and economic and social differences are growing within villages and among regions. All these tendencies are bound to remain very real issues in the country's continuous debate on how to shape its future.

In Chapter 7, Peter Timmer argues that, at least for the decade of the 1990s, Vietnam's economy must be "agriculture driven." He shows the role agriculture could play in setting the stage for Vietnam's general economic transformation. The agricultural sector could hardly play such a role, however, if the party weakened the incentive structures created in recent years. In the final analysis, that insight is likely to be of decisive importance in Vietnam's choice of a strategy. In the meantime, the countryside will not stand still. It will continue to undergo change, including the revival of old traditions and rituals, as illustrated by Hy Van Luong in his study of a North Vietnamese village (Luong, 1991b).

Laos. In Laos, the intensification of the drive toward collectivization created the first real crisis of confidence between the masses of people and their new leaders. While half of the peasant families in prerevolutionary Vietnam had been landless or nearly landless, the majority of Lao peasant families, in contrast, suffered no scarcity of land and either cultivated their own land or practiced shifting cultivation, often combining the two. These families did not want to give up their land or make their draft animals part of a collective. Some Lao peasant families chose to become refugees in Thailand rather than accept the kind of change the LPRP had in store.

In July 1979, the decision to stop collectivization shifted the emphasis from expansion to consolidation. At the time, some 2,500 cooperatives had been formed, most of which were in the early stage of a "mutual aid team" and others hardly started (Stuart-Fox, 1986, p. 115). As in the case of Vietnam, we can see, in retrospect, that this decision signified the beginning of a qualitative change in the LPRP's strategy toward peasants and land. Collectivization continued to be the ostensible long-term goal. Hence, in his 1986 political report, Kaysone Phomvihane saw the creation of cooperatives as "a most important strategic task" during the transition period. The party was, as Grant Evans notes, in search of a class on which to base itself, and establishing cooperatives appeared to offer the only possible approach, given the

---

[18]According to the *Far Eastern Economic Review*, Vietnam may actually be facing a surplus problem in 1992 as "the farmers in the Mekong River delta are sitting on a surplus of about 2.5–3.0 million tons," which they are finding impossible to sell (Hiebert, 1992e, p. 57).

agrarian nature of the Lao society (Evans, 1988, p. 85). Nevertheless, despite rhetoric to the contrary, cooperativization gradually ceased to be part of the increasingly pragmatic "real" agenda.[19]

At the Fifth Party Congress held in March 1991, the recognition of the "household economy" was formalized. In its political report to the congress, the executive committee of the Central Committee repeatedly underscored the importance of "the farmers household economy." It said, "Our Party's basic policy in this field [agriculture] is to strongly promote the farmers household economy aiming at gradually shifting from subsistence production to commodity production" (Lao People's Revolutionary Party, 1991, p. 18). The peasant family is, and clearly will remain, the basic unit in Lao agriculture. Now, once again, peasant families are left to themselves. Laos is, again, a more typical developing country, characterized by weak institutions and in clear need of improved credit and extension services.

Legally speaking, all land still belongs to the state. Current land legislation focuses on user rights rather than formal ownership. In its political report to the Fifth Party Congress, the Central Committee's executive committee said that "land is the national community's property that each of its members has a right to use . . ." However, it also said, "So, we shall accelerate land registration and issue land certificates to those who have the legal right to use it so that each plot of land will have a legal owner (Lao People's Revolutionary Party, 1991, p. 18). The forthcoming law, expected to be adopted during 1992, will clarify and codify the development toward peasant land tenure and a market in land-user rights. The peasants already treat the land as theirs. Their children can inherit the right to use the land, and they are allowed to lease or sell their right. The market for user rights is, however, limited and is likely to remain so for quite some time, except in densely populated, irrigated areas with a high cropping intensity.

The cautious reform package endorsed in November 1979 by the Central Committee of the LPRP caused considerable internal disagreement. By 1985, however, the party was ready to confirm a wider concept of reform launched as "the new economic mechanism." Today, domestic prices of most goods and services are determined by the market. Prices are negotiated freely, and administrative bodies are forbidden to interfere in the market mechanism. Procurement prices, used by state trading corporations in agriculture, have been aligned with market prices. Subsidies for agricultural inputs, such as fertilizer, were eliminated as part of price rationalization. Markets are however, highly fragmented due to the lack of communication systems and

---

[19]For a detailed account of how the relationship between the Lao peasant and the cooperative has developed, see Evans, *The Lao Peasant under Socialism* (1990).

infrastructure. For these and other reasons (weak support services, shortages of fertilizer, etc.), the improved price signals have had only limited impact on producers.

In 1980, for the first time, rice production (paddy) surpassed 1 million tons, confirming the prudence of the new, pragmatic policies. This production increase, however, has not been consistent or steady in the years since 1980. Even though the best rice crops in recent years have been twice as large as the crops harvested in the late 1970s (reaching 1.4 million tons in 1986 and 1.5 million tons in 1990), drought reduced the crop to 1 million tons in 1988 and 1.2 million tons in 1991. Nevertheless, production has risen sufficiently so that no rice is imported in years with normal weather conditions. And further production increases are likely with the improved security of land tenure, market liberalizations, price stability, and increased supply of fertilizer.

Cambodia. In Cambodia, the situation facing the Heng Samrin government, when it came to power in January 1979, was one of extreme internal dislocations and the imminent threat of starvation. (Starvation was averted eventually through international relief.) The area cultivated in 1979 was one-third of that worked in the late 1960s, and the number of draft animals that remained was one-fourth of the number in 1969. The extreme collectivism practiced by the Khmer Rouge was replaced by solidarity groups consisting of a number of peasant families, krom sammakis. Each family was also allocated a private plot for a house and allowed to carry on private farming for family consumption or private sale. Producers were free to sell their own produce in the market without "anyone having the right or authority to forbid them" (quoting decree in Vickery, 1986, p. 139). What in fact emerged in the 1979 planting season had elements of family production (Vickery, 1986, p. 139).

The declared objective, as expressed in a circular issued in August 1980, was the development of a collective economy (Curtis, 1990, passim). The strategy incorporated a three-tiered structure of collectivized groups. The most advanced, Level One, consisted of "groups where all means of production were collectivized and yields shared on a work-point basis after payment of collective debts and taxes" (Curtis, 1990, p. 61). Level Two, which would become the most common level, was considerably less collective in nature. Land and equipment were divided among families, with family units working the land and keeping after-tax production for their own use. Tasks such as plowing, transplanting, or harvesting were performed collectively, as had been the actual, traditional practice in Cambodia. Level Three was, as Vickery describes it, "little more than family economy on allotments of land made at the beginning of the season; . . . ideally, contracts with the state purchasing agencies should be made for the disposition of surplus" (Vickery, 1986, p. 143).

Farming tended to be of a subsistence nature, and production developed slowly. The market had little to offer in return for agricultural products, and the state at first demanded no taxes. The state would, however, start to demand "voluntary contributions," and by 1984, it explicitly required that "the peasants . . . deliver part of their produce to the state" (quoting decree in Vickery, 1986, p. 144). The state also traded industrial products for paddy and certain other basic agricultural products. Other products farmers could sell freely on the market. At this stage, the ambition of the state to establish a state distribution system clashed with the emerging private market. At the organizational level, there was a corresponding tension between the declared goal of collectivism and the lack of any genuine development toward collective Level One. According to the French agronomist François Grünewald, Level One collectives comprised only 10 percent of total krom sammakis in 1983 (quoting Grünewald in Vickery, 1986, p. 143).

As in the case of Vietnam and Laos, these tensions have been resolved in favor of the market and the family unit. Curtis notes that:

> The krom sammaki agricultural system has undergone important changes since its introduction in 1979, particularly regarding the degree of collectivization. Whereas full agricultural collectivization initially was promoted, the trend over the last six or seven years has been towards private agriculture . . . so that by 1987 Level Three krom sammakis were the dominant form of agricultural organization—and production—throughout rural Cambodia. (Curtis, 1990, p. 62)

In 1989, collectivization was formally abandoned as state policy. Recent reports indicate that the krom sammaki has all but disappeared in a formal or organized sense.

The move toward an economy with different kinds of ownership was reinforced in 1985, when the Fifth Party Congress explicitly recognized not only the state, collective, and family economies but also the private economy. And an amendment to the constitution in April 1989 granted land-ownership rights with three tenure regimes: private property around the house, usufruct rights to state-owned land, and grants of surplus land or land to be brought into cultivation by farmers who are in a position to expand their cropping activities. In 1991, these new concepts were slowly being put into practice (information provided orally by Grant Curtis in the spring of 1991.)

Since 1989, farmers have been required to sell only a portion (10 percent or less) of their harvest to the state. Farmers have to sell to the state at a price lower than the market price. Hence, they are being taxed through public procurement. In addition to quantities procured by the state, the peasants are supposed to deliver a certain quantity to the state as a "patriotic contribution," or tax. The quantities have been reduced over time, with the 1989 assessments ranging from 60 kg per hectare for land with good yields to less than half that quantity for low-yielding land. (It is unclear whether the peasants are taxed at all today.) Farmers may sell all that remains of their production in the free market. The vast majority of peasant families are, however, selling only limited quantities, as they practice subsistence farming.

Available data do not allow any analysis of the country's level and structure of production over time. A United Nations' fact-finding mission that visited Cambodia in the spring of 1990 concluded that there is "evidence that the productive capacity in agriculture has approached the levels prevailing in the late 1960s" (United Nations, 1990a, p. 146). Other observers have come to the same conclusion.

The recovery, however, is not evenly spread. While paddy production and the size of the herds of draft animals have bounced back, the production of rubber, an important cash crop, remains at half the level of the 1960s. Moreover, in the beginning of 1991, concerned United Nations' agencies began to fear that drought, hostilities, and the rapidly decreasing Soviet supply of fertilizers could lead to a serious shortage of food. In a January 1991 report on Cambodia's food situation, the World Food Program (WFP) concludes that "it is abundantly clear that, compared to last year, there has been a reduction in both the area planted as well as the average yield" (Statement by the World Food Program at the Cambodia Donor's Meeting in Bangkok, January 22, 1991.) A United Nations Food and Agriculture Organization (FAO) mission that visited Cambodia in March through April of 1991 pointed to the serious consequence of the discontinuation of Soviet aid: "The interruption in the provision of most forms of agricultural aid by Cambodia's traditional donors has resulted in a severe shortage of production means. This critical situation cannot be met through government resources due to serious constraints on foreign exchange availabilities" (Communication FAO-UNDP, April 17, 1991). The measure of food security that Cambodia had managed to obtain during the past decade appeared threatened unless the country could again increase the area under cultivation, and unless the international community could provide fertilizers and other inputs. However, 1991 did pass without a famine, even though food aid covered only a small part of the deficit. "Many went hungry," as noted by *The Economist*, but no famine occurred (*The Economist*, 1992, p. 50).

The major conclusion that emerges from this analysis is that the conditions for agriculture in Vietnam, Laos, and Cambodia have changed dramatically since the late 1970s. Today, peasant families in all three countries have direct access to land through some kind of constitutionally guaranteed long-term tenure with elements of ownership. In addition to tenure, the peasants have an entirely new relationship to the market. They may, by and large, grow what they choose to subsist or to sell in the market, with prices negotiated between the parties. However, while obstacles to development have been removed, institutions and strategies have yet to be developed that will make appropriate technology, better seeds, credits, and so on, available to peasants, who now suffer from the more traditional lack of inputs and institutional support rather than from collective regimentation. Only with such support can the potential of market reforms be efficiently used.

Industry and Decentralization

The Vietnamese reform initiated in 1979 also included the industrial sector, although the original intentions were even more limited for industry than for agriculture, and the effects less significant. There were four issues the state wanted to address: (1) how to create growth and surpluses through improved efficiency and better use of installed capacity in existing state enterprises; (2) whether state-owned enterprises should be allowed to trade directly and outside the plan, with other state-owned enterprises; (3) whether state-owned enterprises should be allowed to relate to the market; and (4) whether private activities should be permitted wider scope.

As in the case of agrarian change, the process did not start as a top-down reform but as spontaneous fence breaking by a number of state-owned enterprises. These enterprises started to become "commercialized" as they developed an appetite for the more profitable opportunities of the "non-planned" world.

The conditions faced by Laos and Cambodia, with their very limited industrial sectors, were different in significant respects. However, they also had to address issues such as the low efficiency of state enterprises and their disappointing contributions to the budget; the harmful consequences of centralization and the lack of incentives; and how to relate to the private sector and the dual-price structure that had emerged. The new government in Phnom Penh tried, however, to rehabilitate mainly the little that was left of industries of any size within a framework of traditional central planning.

Vietnam. Rapid industrialization in the form of large-scale modern industry has been a key element of the socialist development model. The DRV model in Vietnam was no exception. State capital was committed to industrialization, the priority task of national construction. The focus was almost entirely on production for domestic needs, and especially on basic heavy industry. The state supplied the inputs and capital requirements of enterprises and set quantitative output targets, and the enterprises, through the system of price controls, accounted for the bulk of domestic budget revenues. Although the five-year plan, in theory, was a centralized one, its implementation was, in fact, not centralized. The local and provincial governments had actual authority over the majority of state-owned enterprises, and they often followed their own agenda.

North Vietnam's First Five-Year Plan (1961–65) emphasized basic heavy industries, which continued to be the focus in industrial policy until about 1980. Yet, in the late 1970s, heavy industry accounted for less that 40 percent of industrial production in reunited Vietnam, while light industry, dominated by textiles and food processing, accounted for more than 60 percent. Only a small percentage of the industrial labor force was actually engaged in heavy industry. At official accounting prices, which tended to overestimate industry, the industrial sector generated one-fourth of Gross Domestic Product (GDP).

Even though the nonstate sector was not given priority, and even though many of the larger industrial units in the South were nationalized after reunification, the private sector did not disappear. Small-scale industries and handicraft, especially those that were organized as cooperatives, remained important.

The fate of the ceramics industry in the Tan Van ward of Bien Hoa city, the second-largest industrial center in the South, gives an accurate picture of what happened. After the political changes in 1975, five large kilns were "donated" to the state, nine other large kilns remained outside the state sector until 1984, and the remaining seven kilns were pressured to become cooperatives. The manager and part owner of three very large ceramics businesses contributed one to the state, offered the second as a joint state-private enterprise, and was able to keep the third as private until 1982. Enterprises in Bien Hoa became nationalized or cooperativized to a much greater extent than those in neighboring Song Be Province.

The transformation from private to cooperative ownership could, however, be rather nominal.[20] Prices of products produced by cooperative enterprises were not fixed through central planning. While the prices of products manufactured by state enterprises changed infrequently, the prices of products manufactured in cooperative and private enterprises did. As a consequence a dual-price structure emerged, causing considerable inflationary pressure.

The government initiated reform measures to abate the crisis faced by the industrial sector in 1979 and 1980. While the target growth rate in the Second Five-Year Plan was 16 to 18 percent, the actual outcome was a growth

---

[20]Information provided orally by Hy Van Luong. Also, see Hy Van Luong's chapter "The Political Economy of Vietnamese Reforms: A Microscopic Perspective from Two Ceramics Manufacturing Centers" in Turley and Selden, 1992.

rate of 0.6 percent. Food and consumer goods shortages grew, and so did the scarcity of inputs to the agricultural and industrial sectors (UNDP, 1990, pp. 124–42).

In a sense, the reform process in Vietnam started well before 1979. In 1977, the government issued new guidelines for state-owned industrial enterprises, which, after testing in 40 enterprises, were implemented in 1979. The guidelines, summarized in a May 1979 IMF report, are representative of the then prevailing approach to industrial efficiency.[21] The application of these guidelines had some effect, but they failed to boost the economy enough to keep the reform efforts within the socialist framework of central planning. More unorthodox recipes had to be introduced.

The new measures launched in the crisis year of 1979 would build on the more dynamic tendency of enterprises to do fence breaking, the spontaneous bottom-up adaptation of the DRV model through which state enterprises "swapped or sold goods on the open market in order to raise cash to buy materials or pay bonuses to workers. Deals were done with other factories, or with agricultural cooperatives to supply materials" (de Vylder and Fforde, 1988, p. 68). These activities absorbed some of the slack in the economy and placed traditional customers of the enterprises under considerable pressure, creating an element of competition between the planned way and the open market. Fforde and de Vylder note that the subsidized sectors of the economy were put under considerable pressure, since higher costs had to be passed on to the traditional customers. Most important, state enterprises started to operate on a market. The foundation for an entirely new way of looking at economic activities was being laid.

This development also was not primarily the result of government policy. It generated policy change because it showed a vigor that the government could not disregard in the critical situation it faced in 1979. The sixth plenum of the Central Committee, which met in August 1979, not only endorsed experiments with the contract system in agriculture but also sanctioned the development of fence breaking.

Under the Three Plan system that emerged two years later, enterprises, in addition to using inputs supplied by the state to produce for the state (Plan A), were legally permitted to acquire resources through their own efforts and dispose of the outputs as they wished to acquire additional inputs (Plan B), as well as diversify their production by turning out minor products for state trading organs and the open market (Plan C) (UNDP, 1990, p. 130).

---

[21]The guidelines had many similarities with those the Soviet leaders tried to introduce to arrest the deterioration of the Soviet economy (Hewitt, 1988, Chapter 5).

Simultaneously, the party started to shift its emphasis from heavy industry to light industry and exports. The initiation of the latter, very cumbersome reorientation, was approved in 1982 by the Fifth Party Congress. At least partly through these measures, the downward trend of the period 1975–80, during which the annual output of state enterprises fell by 2.7 percent, was reversed. A growth rate of 7.8 percent was reached during the period 1980–85 (quoting from *Statistics 1976–1989*, Vietnam's General Statistical Office, in UNDP, 1990). This was not a remarkable result in view of the fact that only about 40 to 50 percent of productive capacity had been used prior to the changes, but nevertheless a detrimental downward trend was reversed.

The reversal of the slide produced pressure for further reform as fence breaking became increasingly common. However, the government resisted the pressure, actually reversing the reform process in 1982–83 by reasserting centralization and reimposing restrictions on the private sector. Only after it had become clear that this policy would not be effective did the government again take steps toward reform.

Actually, state-owned enterprises that had begun to operate commercially, trading with each other and/or trading on the market, were unwilling to return to the world of material balances. Ideally, they wanted to have one foot in each camp, receiving raw materials, and so on, under the plan at subsidized prices (often provided by the then Soviet Union or other donors), while selling the final product in the open market at market prices. Such a double-life would allow them to pay market-related wages and provide bonuses and other fringe benefits to their workers. The spontaneous commercialization of state-owned enterprises became a major force behind the development of activities outside the plan, that is, of markets.

A parallel development took place with regard to family and private enterprises. Frequent shifts in policy, lack of access to inputs and credit, lack of a legal framework, and so on, continued to hamper the development of the private sector. In December 1986, however, the Sixth Party Congress recognized the role of the private sector, although halfheartedly: "We have not fully recognized the fact that the multi-sector economic structure in our country will still continue to exist for a long period," being "a characteristic feature of the transitional period" (Vietnam, Communist Party of, 1987, pp. 22, 64).

A number of important decrees, resolutions, and laws affecting the industrial sector were adopted during the next few years, hardening the budget constraints on state-owned enterprises, laying the legal framework for foreign investments, and giving more explicit recognition to the nonstate sector. In the beginning of 1991, a law allowing for limited-liability companies and share-holding companies was passed; other laws, such as a bankruptcy law, are under way. Gradually, Vietnam will be establishing the legal framework for a market-based economy.

The budget constraints hardened significantly in the major reform package that the government introduced in early 1989, and many enterprises faced severe problems as the government tightened control over credit expansion, increased the interest rates to positive real levels, and expected greater financial autonomy from state-owned enterprises.

However, during 1990, the constraints softened through the expansion of subsidized bank lending. The expansion was less dramatic than some critics have suggested, but large enough to cause increased inflation (around 70 percent per year). The new lending policies allowed the continued, substantial subsidizing of loss-making enterprises. At the same time, private enterprises continued to lack access to the financial system, even at market terms.

The Seventh Party Congress, while emphasizing the leading role of the state economy, recognized that loss-making SOEs would have to close down and endorsed the possibility of selective privatization: "As for units for whom State-run status is no longer necessary, it is necessary either to change their form of business and ownership or to dissolve them" (Vietnam, Communist Party of, 1991, p. 14). Judging from the guidelines for socioeconomic stability and development adopted by the Central Committee at its second plenum in December 1991, the attitudes toward loss-making SOEs would harden during 1992. Curbing inflation was given a high priority, and it was said that "subsidies to business will be entirely scrapped, and credit banks will have to operate on a purely commercial basis" (*Vietnam Courier*, January 1992, p. 5). A rather large number of state-owned enterprises have now been forced to close down, and a few hundred thousand workers have been let go and given severance grants. In February 1992, the government decided to proceed with privatization of SOEs on a trial basis, and in May 1992, it decided to go ahead with privatizing some 20 units. Profit-making enterprises would also be included. The state, however, would keep a share, remaining the largest, single shareholder.[22]

The effects of adjustment and reform on the structure of the industrial sector are now becoming visible. According to recent Vietnamese statistics, the nonstate sector produces almost one-half of total manufacturing output, divided roughly equally between collectives and private firms, most of which are small (Vietnam, Socialist Republic of, 1991, pp. 41–49). In Ho Chi Minh

---

[22]Information received during a visit to Hanoi in May 1992. A seminar organized by Vietnam's State Planning Committee and the World Bank on the restructuring of public-sector enterprises took place in Hanoi at the time.

City, the country's economic hub, the private sector, in 1991, produced 51 percent of the city's industrial output. The most successful private companies manufacture for export (Hiebert, 1992b, pp. 51–52).[23]

In employment, the share of the nonstate sector is considerably larger than 50 percent. According to the 1989 census, 62.7 percent of manufacturing employment is in the nonstate sector, 18.8 percent in the cooperative sector, and 44.3 percent in the private sector. However, only a handful of private companies employ more than 1,000 workers, and less than 1,200 private companies have an invested capital of more than the equivalent of U.S. $20,000 (Vietnam, Socialist Republic of, 1991, p. 51). The only comprehensive empirical study of the emerging private sector in Vietnam confirms this picture: "... the private sector is a much more important source of employment (43.7 percent) than the state sector (36.3 percent)" (Ronnas, 1992, p. 167). The average number of workers in the urban nonstate sector varied from 4.8 in the household enterprises to 35 in the cooperatives. The number of private and partnership enterprises fell inbetween with 13.7 and 14.8 workers (Ronnas, 1992, p. 133). The increase in the establishment of rural enterprises has been very dramatic. No less than 58.6 percent of the enterprises surveyed had been established in the years 1988–90 (Ronnas, 1992, p. 70).

Light industry contributes around 70 percent of manufactured output, and heavy industry around 30 percent—proportions that are very different from those prevailing in Eastern Europe, the former Soviet Union, and China. The latter figure would have been even lower if only enterprises classified as large by Eastern European standards had been included.

Industry has been negatively affected by the adjustment and stabilization program. Production fell in 1989 (−2.3 percent). However, there was some recovery in 1990. In 1991, state enterprises and household units in the Red River Delta, which had been exporting to the Soviet Union, lost their market. This caused severe problems for the northern economy. Still, industry, helped by oil and a recovery in small-scale family and individual production, showed a total gross-output growth for the year of over 5 percent. Oil production rose by over 40 percent, and small-scale individual production by over 12 percent (Fforde, 1992, p. 1).

The consequence of the new attitude toward private industry can be seen in the ceramics industry in Tan Van ward of Bien Hoa city, the example that was cited earlier. Some units have been returned to their former

---

[23]The Hiebert (1992b) article gives a good picture of the situation, including many of the uncertainties and obstacles facing private businesses.

owners. In June 1989, the state privatized a pottery and eleven kilns (Luong, 1991a, p. 1).

Significant changes have taken place during the last three years. The Communist party has been showing the strains of dealing with such a profound adjustment process, formulating compromise positions required to build consensus rather than policies fully recognizing the realities on which future developments may build. As in the case of many previous dilemmas of this kind, the more pragmatic line is likely to prevail, continued subsidies being clearly incompatible with the urgent task of curtailing inflation. Those who favor preserving the SOE sector will be unable to raise the financial means required to support their favored position, without resorting to inflationary methods. Heightened competition from abroad; the need to increase exports; the preference of the growing number of foreign investors for the private sector; and, not least, the shift from Soviet aid to support from international financial institutions such as the World Bank, the International Monetary Fund, and Western donors—all are factors that will continue to undermine the position of those who want a large SOE sector.

In spite of the ambivalence existing within the party, major changes have also taken place in the attitude toward the private sector. "The private sector was," Ronnas notes:

> tolerated as a temporary necessity rather than appreciated for its true worth. The past few years have seen fundamental changes in the official attitude toward the private sector. It has officially been put on an equal footing with the other economic sectors, its vital role in the economy is recognized, and it is no longer seen as a transitory phenomenon. (Ronnas, 1992, p. 167)

While a declared objective is to put state-owned and private enterprises on an equal footing, that is not the reality today. Private enterprises, for example, have hardly any access to bank credit; 95 percent of credit goes to the public sector. Loss-making state-owned enterprises are still receiving loans—at rates that, at times, are clearly below the rate of inflation to which such lending is contributing and below the rate that banks are paying on deposits. Many enterprises—one-third is a common estimate—would have to be liquidated if their subsidies were removed. A clear problem is that the labor market would only be able to absorb a fraction of those who would have to leave their jobs.

Among the many pressing development issues that Vietnam faces, the reform of public-sector enterprises is probably the most urgent—and the most difficult. How could SOEs be managed more efficiently? What role should the state play as owner? Which legal form should the ownership take?

Who should appoint managers? Who should make larger investment decisions? How fast should one proceed with divesture?[24] A new policy is clearly emerging, based on the principle that enterprises should be able to manage on their own, without subsidies, as autonomous economic entities. The biggest qualitative difference in comparison with the past is that the enterprises operate on an increasingly competitive commodity market where prices give increasingly meaningful information about economic efficiency and the cost of the absence thereof.

Laos. At the time of the Laotian revolution, the Lao industrial sector was still at an early stage of development, accounting for less than 5 percent of GDP and employing less than 1 percent of the labor force. The sector had always been constrained by the country's landlocked position, its small and fragmented domestic market, and competition from Thai imports. After the revolution, the sector, which was largely but not entirely nationalized, faced grave problems. The shortage of spare parts and raw materials became acute; technical and managerial staff were among those who left the country; to open lines of credit with foreign banks became all but impossible; and the centralized management system did not permit price and wage incentives. Centrally owned entities were granted no autonomy, in reality being run by the ministries. Their products were marketed at artificially low prices through the public distribution system, while goods brought in from Thailand by traders were sold at entirely different prices that reflected the exchange rate prevailing on the parallel foreign-exchange market. The Lao leaders soon realized that the widely divergent, dualistic price structure, caused by the uncontrollable—and actually indispensable—inflow of Thai goods, had to be addressed by reforms rather than by isolation and bureaucratic controls.

The government began to look closely at the issue of reform of state-owned enterprises in the early 1980s. At that time, public enterprises were still under a strict central planning process. The investment, employment, import, output, and export of each enterprise were all to be determined through constant reviews by provincial authorities, central ministries, and the state planning committee. However, in actuality, lack of information made reviews very difficult. The government began to discuss what to do about the SOE system given its poor contributions to the budget and its often very low level of capacity utilization. What became increasingly clear was that to effectively build socialism a more efficient way of running enterprises had to be found.

---

[24]For a recent assessment of management development needs, see Wallroth et al., "A Strategy for the Development of Management in Vietnamese Enterprises," (1990), a consulting study undertaken at the request of SIDA.

The debate focused on the questions of autonomy, responsibility, and incentives. From 1981 to 1985, eight state-owned enterprises were given somewhat greater management autonomy on a trial basis (Thepsimuong, 1992, p. 7).

Enterprise reform gained momentum after the Fourth Party Congress in November 1986, when it was launched as a key element of the new economic mechanism (NEM). This was followed by a party resolution in January 1988 that presented the objectives of enterprise autonomy in the context of decentralized decision making and stressed the importance of greater reliance on market signals (Thepsimuong, 1992, passim). Simultaneously, the scope for private enterprises was widened.

Until 1986–87, the Lao reform lagged behind that of Vietnam. Since then, however, the Lao government has taken a number of more far-reaching steps toward disengagement. The task has not been as large as the task facing Vietnam, and in addition, Laos has had the significant advantage of substantial external support. Seven of the steps the government has taken are of particular significance:

- leasing, privatization, and shutdown of state-owned enterprises
- management reform within the public sector
- control of credit to publicly owned entities generating losses
- grant of full autonomy to SOEs (except public utilities) to set prices
- encouragement of private enterprise
- liberal foreign investment legislation
- development of a legislative framework

So far, the vast majority of private enterprises are very small, usually artisans employing three to six people. Some of the 153 foreign investments that had been approved by September 1991, such as textile and garment factories, are of medium size (Pham Chi Do, 1991, p. 94).

More than half of the public enterprises supervised by the Prefecture of Vientiane, where a large share of the SOEs are located, have been made autonomous, leased, or partially or fully sold. Large companies, like Lao Plywood, have been leased to foreign companies. Additional disengagements and liquidations are planned, while the management of those that remain in the public sector will be strengthened. Simultaneously, a standard accounting system is being introduced.

Privatization will continue to be the centerpiece of the reform strategy, and the government has decided upon a major expansion and acceleration of the process with assistance from the World Bank. Under the 1991 initiative, only a small number of public enterprises (the electric company, the postal service, and three Ministry of Defense enterprises) will be retained in the public sector (Thepsimuong, 1992; Pham Chi Do, 1991). Some observers have expressed concern that the disengagement process may be a bit too hasty, given the country's very limited knowledge of the alternatives at hand. From now on, a two-track policy will be followed. First, all small enterprises (with up to 30 employees) will be auctioned off within the next three years. Second, about 25 larger enterprises will be divested annually through direct sales, joint ventures, or public-share issues. So far, somewhat more than 100 out of 640 public enterprises have been fully or partially sold or leased. A big headache for the government is what to do with state-owned enterprises that do not interest the private sector and that remain unprofitable.

The tightening up on credit to loss-making enterprises is a significant accomplishment. Until 1990, credit given to public enterprises was a major source of monetary expansion and inflation. The credit volume increased by 70 percent between March 1989 and March 1990. Since then, there has been no expansion whatsoever; state-owned enterprises do, however, still borrow at a subsidized interest rate. If continued, this stricter credit policy will, in itself, lead to a number of closures of unprofitable state-owned enterprises. To the extent that subsidies continue, they should be in the form of explicit budget subsidies rather than banking system abuses.

Until recently (1989), Laos had no actual laws enacted by a legislature, only different forms of decrees. The reform process has brought on a frenetic effort to introduce legislation, especially in the commercial, economic, and financial fields. Contract, property, ownership, accounting, labor, and inheritance laws have been enacted, while a company law and laws on arbitration, negotiable instruments, bankruptcy, and secured transactions have been drafted. Approval of these laws by the Supreme People's Assembly is expected during 1992. Harvard Law School is providing assistance under a UNDP-World Bank contract.[25]

It will clearly take considerable time before the weak Laotian legal system is capable of applying this body of legislation, and before it is recognized as a system of legally binding principles for business conduct and transactions. Until there is a history of enforcement and compliance, these new laws are just so many words on a sheet of paper. The government's ambition to create a legal framework conducive to private-sector development is, however, very clear.

Gradually, a foundation for market-based industrialization is being put in place. Many of the same issues that need to be addressed in Vietnam need to be addressed in Laos. It will take many years before Lao industry gains

---

[25]For a complete listing of recent Laotian economic legislation, see Pham Chi Do 1991, pp. 96–104.

efficiency and before it can contribute much to bridging the country's exceptionally large trade deficit. Industry's share of GDP remains low (manufacturing contributed only 9 percent in 1989), but recent growth rates suggest that this share will increase as domestic demand increases and foreign investments expand. After a strong recovery in 1990, industry may actually have grown by 24.7 percent in 1991 (Pham Chi Do, 1991, p. 27).

The pragmatism reflected in the ongoing reform efforts give reason for optimism. The *Draft Policy Framework for the Public Investment Program, 1991–1995* says that the Third Five-Year Plan "calls for the private sector to be the main engine of growth in the manufacturing sector," and that "the Government role will increasingly be restricted to maintaining an economic environment to promote private sector growth, ensuring that appropriate infrastructure is constructed, and ensuring that skilled labor is available . . ." while continuing to improve the efficiency of state-owned enterprises until they can be privatized (Lao People's Democratic Republic, 1990, p. 42).[26]

Cambodia. Almost nothing of Cambodia's industrial sector, which, in 1969, accounted for about 12 percent of GDP, survived the Pol Pot years and its immediate aftermath. Industries considered essential were retained by the Khmer Rouge, but they fell into disuse because of inadequate maintenance, lack of spare parts, and shortage of trained staff. Much important machinery was destroyed either during Khmer Rouge rule or in the tumultuous period following their departure (Curtis, 1990, p. 93).

A centralized system was established in 1979. State enterprises that could be restored relatively quickly, even if only partially, were treated as full "budgetary units." Hence, "all expenses and revenues were ventilated through the central budget. All profits automatically accrued to the central budget and all losses were automatically covered through central funds. All investments were financed through the budget, actual funding being provided through the National Bank, beginning in March 1980 when the National Bank was re-created" (United Nations, 1990a, p. 160). Enterprises under the authority of provincial and local authorities were treated in much the same way. In addition to publicly owned enterprises, there were small handicraft and artisan units, private units, and units organized by the krom sammakis. However, the total value of industrial production was estimated at far less than $10 million. As markets emerged, a growing stream of Thai goods found their way to market through border trade. The market value of the Cambodian riel (reflected in market prices) contrasted sharply with the local price structure.

---

[26]The draft has been prepared by consultants, therefore the language is that of consultants rather than the Lao goverment. It has never been formally approved by the government. It does, however, form the basis for planning.

For a long time, state-owned enterprises continued to be managed in a highly centralized fashion, having no authority of their own, while the nonstate sector was allowed to operate outside the plan and determine its own prices. In 1985, the private sector was explicitly recognized as a fourth sector, in addition to state, collective, and family sectors, and in 1989, a foreign-investment law was established (Cheriyan and Fitzgerald, 1989, p. 15).

In recent years, the state has made efforts to devolve control of state-owned enterprises, in a manner similar to that of Vietnam (under whose advice the reforms have taken shape) and Laos. Much development has taken place spontaneously rather than as a result of state-mandated reform, as the government has recognized the limits of state capacity and allowed more latitude for private initiative. With the increasingly liberal mood, in 1990, some state-owned enterprises were allowed to fix their own prices under a "self-financing system," with the proviso that they pay profit taxes on these earnings. According to a decree on state control, SOEs were divided into three categories based on the extent to which they were controlled by the state. Enterprises in the first category remained subject to central planning, with the state providing inputs and determining production and prices, while those in the noncontrolled third category were to receive no inputs from the state (Coady and Desai, 1990, p. 10). The Ministry of Industry began to introduce the "self-accounting management system" into all its industries and factories.

During 1991, a dozen SOE industries were leased to the private sector, including major ones like a brewery (personal correspondence, by Grant Curtis). An additional number of SOEs were handed over to the private sector as the government tried to rescue the cash-strapped state sector, which had been hit hard by the dramatic reduction in aid from the former Soviet Union (*Far Eastern Economic Review*, 1991). Toward the end of 1991, the disinvestment process accelerated. At the same time, it assumed some rather chaotic forms, a development caused by the increasingly severe budget situation and rapidly spreading corruption. The increase in corruption seemed to stem from widespread uncertainty among civil servants in the aftermath of the Paris agreement, as well as extremely low civil service salaries. Nayan Chanda conveyed an image of the dramatic changes in an article entitled "Cambodian Peace Accord May Be in Jeopardy as Economy Unravels Amid Government Crisis." Everything, including the ministry of finance, seemed to be for sale (Chanda, 1992, pp. 6–8). The situation has been further aggravated by government efforts to extract liquidity from the enterprises.

Industry still accounts for a very low share of Cambodia's total GDP. In 1991, the total industrial sector, including construction, electricity, gas, and water, represented 15.6 percent of GDP, out of which manufacturing was 54 percent. In 1991, manufacturing grew by approximately 7 percent and continues to be dominated by food processing and other consumer industries. A portion of the industrial sector has remained inoperative, and hardly any units of any size have been added. New investments have been either of the artisan type or very small scale in nature. Some impressive rehabilitation has, however, taken place, such as the OXFAM-assisted Battambang jute-sack factory. But, generally, shortages of raw materials, spare parts, electricity, and management and technical skills have imposed severe constraints. According to estimates dating back to 1989, Cambodia has approximately 70 state-owned enterprises with 14,000 employees, of whom 4,000 work in artisanal units and some 10,000 in small private and collective (krom sammaki) units. In 1988, the total value of production of all industrial and handicraft units throughout the country was estimated as $19.8 million (in U.S. dollars), out of which $7 million was generated by cigarette factories (Curtis, 1990, pp. 93–110). The actual value must, however, be larger unless industry's share of GDP is considerably lower than suggested in the limited literature available on Cambodia.

The general picture that can be drawn from the foregoing analysis of industrial change and reform in Vietnam, Laos, and Cambodia is that the state is assuming a qualitatively redefined role vis-à-vis industry. The new role has the following main characteristics:

- disengagement from individual enterprises
- efforts to make state-owned enterprises autonomous and financially independent of government
- deregulation of prices and increased reliance on markets
- widening the scope significantly for the private sector
- active pursuit of foreign investment

These processes have not occurred simultaneously, but the general direction has been the same in all three countries. Laos has gone further than the others in disengaging the state from direct involvement in industrial undertakings, while Vietnam only recently has shown readiness to privatize state-owned enterprises (still intent on preserving a larger role for the state). In Cambodia, crisis appears to play an increasingly large role in determining events. The nonstate sector is still disadvantaged in all three countries when it comes to access to bank credit and imported raw materials. No reliable data is available, but it seems safe to say that the nonstate sector is generating half or more of the value added by industry in all three countries, and that the private sector is likely to grow faster than the state sector.

Markets and Planning

In an essay on economic systems reform in developing countries, Dwight Perkins notes that the question of how to make markets work is central not only to reforming socialist countries: "Most developing countries are quite a long way toward the bureaucratic command end of the spectrum" (Perkins, 1988, p. 41). He identifies four components necessary to a well-functioning market system (Perkins, 1989, pp. 41–43):[27]

- goods must be available for purchase and sale on the market
- prices must reflect true relative scarcities
- the markets must be competitive
- decision makers in markets, notably producers, must behave according to the rules of the market and pursue some approximation of profit maximization

As a prerequisite, Perkins adds that there must be a reasonable measure of macroeconomic stability.

Have Vietnam, Laos, and Cambodia come anywhere close to what is required for functioning markets? We have seen how price controls have been removed and how peasants in all three countries have become free to sell their products on the open market. State procurement agencies still procure for the public distribution system and for export (Vietnam), but in both Vietnam and Laos, the state procures at market prices or prices very close to that price. It is unclear whether certain remnants of a dual structure remain in Cambodia. Peasants can sell the bulk of their products, including rice, on the open market, but the state might continue to procure certain quantities at lower prices or by trading in kind (fertilizer) at similarly low prices. National markets have just begun to emerge. Private wholesalers are rare, but even grain can be moved across provincial boundaries with traders operating as intermediaries between producers and markets. Still, the prevailing form of trade is that of producers selling their own goods on local markets.

In the case of Vietnam, public trading organizations are likely to continue playing an important role, especially with regard to export crops. The *Political Report to the Seventh Party Congress* states that one should "restructure and renovate the State-run trade system to increase its efficiency and develop its positive role in stabilizing and regulating market price. To concentrate efforts on whole-sale trade, combined with retail sale of essential goods . . . " (Vietnam, Communist Party of, 1991, p. 117). However, the report

---

[27]See also Perkins's "Reforming China's Economic System" (1988, pp. 6–10).

also stresses the importance of "the formation of nation-wide unified markets linked in with the world market . . . " (Vietnam, Communist Party of, 1991, p. 73).[28] Recent World Bank studies of the state grain-trading organizations show that these organizations operate as commercial enterprises. Still, while the state ought to have a crucial role in ensuring food security and price stability, the quoted passages reflect a state role that goes further and encompasses elements that could be left to the market.

In Laos, the role of state trading organizations is clearly intended to be limited to what is required to maintain a food security system and (which is more questionable) trade in export crops such as coffee. In the recent *Political Report to the Fifth Party Congress*, the role of trade in the development process is stressed in a way that sharply contrasts with the traditional party notion (Lao People's Revolutionary Party, 1991, p. 22).

The Cambodian situation is too uncertain for an assessment of how the system may develop. In recent years, the role of the private sector in the circulation and distribution of goods has become predominant.

No price controls exist in either Vietnam, Laos, or Cambodia, except de facto controls for certain export crops, like rubber or coffee, which only the state can procure. The price the state pays for some of these crops is still below the world-market price. The price paid by the Vietnamese state trading organizations for paddy is lower relative to the export price than in comparable countries, largely indicating high transaction costs. As small and increasingly open economies, all three countries function, however, as price takers on the world market, and important prices are already well in line with world-market prices. Monopolies are breaking down as direct links are established between suppliers and foreign trading organizations.

The overall picture is incomplete in many ways, but available evidence suggests that prices on agricultural products today are determined in markets, albeit imperfect ones, and that these markets increasingly function in the same way that they do in the majority of market-oriented developing countries. Goods are available for purchase and sale on the market.

Whether prices reflect relative scarcities is more uncertain. It will take time before producers get sufficiently accustomed to the market for price signals to have full impact on their decisions. The markets are still too scattered to permit effective interregional competition, but the number of

---

[28]In 1992, the government of Vietnam actually intervened by providing loans directly to food-processing companies to prevent the price of unhusked rice from falling to levels that would hurt production, as peasants in the South were "sitting on a surplus of about 2.3–3.0 million tons" (Hiebert, 1992e, p. 57).

sellers and buyers in the typical local market indicates that a fair amount of competition does exist.

Peasants are, as yet, not likely to maximize their profits even under existing limitations on access to technology, inputs, credit, and so on. There is, however, every reason to assume that present-day peasant households with land tenure will be pursuing profit maximization with increasing vigor as they learn more about the market situation for different products.

Many of our notions about how markets work in developing countries come from studies of the agricultural sector with its small household-based units. The lessons gained from agriculture, however, may lead, as Perkins notes, to an oversimplified reading of the dynamics of introducing market forces into an industrial sector, especially one with large-scale SOE units (Perkins, 1989, p. 1). Dismantling planning in the form of material balances and price controls is hard enough. Developing a market is a considerably more complex matter. However, Perkins does not mean that the existence of such large-scale units makes market development under communist rule impossible—although he sees the persistence of "bureaucratic forces" as a serious obstacle. In his study of reform in China, he assumes the continued existence of a large number of state-owned enterprises and focuses his analysis on measures that may harden the budget constraints, increase the extent to which enterprises pursue profit maximization, and create competition (Perkins, 1988).

Kornai's position is more absolute. He believes that an end to communist monopoly of power is a prerequisite before enterprises can genuinely pursue profit maximization. As long as the party monopoly remains in place, bureaucratic coordination and party loyalties will prevail over market forces. State ownership will, as he sees it, mean that there will be no effective ownership and result in inevitable inefficiency.

How then do the reforms undertaken in Vietnam, Laos, and Cambodia come out in light of such analyses? The markets for industrial products appear less developed than the markets for agricultural products. The absence of functioning factor markets causes distortions. State-owned enterprises still enjoy advantages over nonstate enterprises in the form of subsidized credit, preferential allocation of imported raw materials, aid flows, and negotiable taxes. However, all but a few price controls have been removed in both Vietnam and Laos, and state-owned enterprises are now struggling as best they can to survive in markets where domestic competition, as well as import competition, plays an increasingly important role. The new tax laws are, at least in principle, neutral with regard to the types of ownership. Loss-making enterprises, especially in Vietnam, are kept alive by cheap credit, but the loss makers have been identified, and those who do not improve their results will find additional credit increasingly difficult to obtain. The governments have seen the serious inflationary effects of such lending, and Vietnam is aware of the incompatibility of such lending policies with the structural-adjustment support it hopes to obtain from the IMF and the World Bank. Time is therefore running out for the chronic loss makers. A number of such enterprises have been closed down, and a bankruptcy law will harden the edge.

Maximization of profit is obviously not the sole objective of management, but cost consciousness is clearly higher than it was a few years ago. It is becoming increasingly clear to managers that the future of their companies depends on the decisions they make. Management more often addresses questions of how to reduce costs and how to succeed in domestic and international markets. Redundant workers are laid off. Larger SOEs will be turned into joint stock companies, a development that will clarify the role of the state as owner with regard to, for example, appointment of managers and responsibility for investment decisions.

According to Hinds and a number of other students of socialist reform, market forces cannot lead to an efficient allocation of resources without extensive privatization of the means of production (Hinds, 1990, p. 100). So far, Vietnam has leased or privatized very few companies. Laos has gone considerably further in this respect, and Cambodia has also disengaged itself from a considerable number of enterprises. Vietnam, however, already has a private sector, offering state-owned enterprises growing competition. Indeed, the fact that Vietnam's nonstate sector already contributes close to half the gross value of manufacturing production means that the market situation is qualitatively different from one where state-owned units dominate. The state will have to disengage itself further before proper markets can flourish (a prerequisite to the necessary "sanitation" of the financial sector), but market forces are already pushing forward a more efficient allocation of resources. Hinds appears to be too rigidly focused on privatization, especially as the SOEs may gradually shrink into a rather insignificant portion of a growing industrial sector.

Enterprises must, as Perkins emphasizes, "cut loose from government if markets are to function properly" (Perkins, 1991, p. 9). How have the developments described above, and other measures that the governments have taken, affected the role of the party and the degree of party intervention in the life of enterprises? We have seen the decisively "subversive" role that state-owned enterprises, especially in Vietnam, have played in commercializing industry and creating markets. Today, their role is more ambivalent (especially at the provincial level), as management and party cadres within the enterprises use their influence to obtain subsidized credit, often succeeding despite their obvious inability to carry their loans.

Still, the behavior of both the state and enterprises is undoubtedly changing in Vietnam and Laos. Managers of state-owned enterprises no longer can be said to be mere extensions of bureaucracy and the party, that is, mere nomenklatura. They are under heavy pressure to become autonomous, and they know that ultimately they will not survive unless they can handle the market. Hence, managers are showing a growing concern for costs, including labor costs.

In Laos, banks have received instructions not to lend to loss-making enterprises, and the total credit volume has, as we have seen, not increased since 1990. Party cadres with interests in a certain enterprise continue to try to keep the budget constraints soft, but they are likely to find it increasingly difficult to mobilize the financial resources required to maintain nonviable remnants of central planning.

Available information does not allow review of the situation in Cambodia. The exceptionally severe financial situation there makes it increasingly difficult to keep nonviable enterprises alive. The Cambodian process, as noted earlier, has shown increasingly chaotic tendencies.

The sector for services, other than public utilities, is traditionally very small in socialist countries, because of the way this sector has been perceived in the Marxist-Leninist tradition and the many obstacles surrounding private-service activities. This has been the case in Vietnam, Laos, and Cambodia. But, in recent years, the service sector has grown rapidly in all three countries, and today, the informal sector and small private enterprises provide a large variety of services. Life in cities and towns has changed greatly as this development has gained momentum. In the past, periods of expansion were often followed by government efforts to control and tax. Recently, the authorities seem to have become more benign, as the policy of allowing all sectors to grow becomes more firmly established, and as the attitude of the government becomes less ideological and paternalistic and more focused on revenue. A crucial question is whether the tax system will stabilize at tax levels that encourage enterprises to invest.

Public utilities and housing still remain highly subsidized and are likely to remain so for a long time to come. Both Vietnam and Laos, however, have raised electricity prices significantly and are planning further measures. Reforming the method of pricing housing will be a gigantic task, especially in Vietnam where public-sector employment is large and the rents are nominal, amounting to just a fraction of 1 percent of salary. Nevertheless, certain rent increases have been introduced. In Cambodia, those who occupy individual houses have been granted ownership rights at nominal prices.

Developing factor markets will require considerable change in both mentality and institutions. In its draft *Socio-Economic Strategy*, the Communist

Party of Vietnam states that "commodity markets" should comprise "all the factors of the production process: goods and services, labor force, capital, money and property" (Vietnam, Communist Party of, 1990b). A move in this direction has begun. Earlier, we discussed land usufruct rights. Next, we will look at how labor and financial markets are changing.

Even though certain formal restrictions on movement of labor remain, a number of developments are undermining this administrative approach to allocating labor. Private employers can, for example, hire as many workers as they need, and wages are determined between the two parties. The service and informal sectors are expanding rapidly without much government control. A qualified worker may still have difficulty switching from a state-owned enterprise to a private one, but there are instances where it has happened. Another thorny question is how to reduce the considerable difference in employment conditions that exists between the public and private sectors. The former includes a large number of benefits, such as housing, free health care, paid maternity leave, pension, and so on. The latter is devoid of such rights, often being small, family-centered; or cooperative units.

Yet another crucial question is whether workers can be laid off. Today, this is happening. Relatively large numbers have been laid off in Vietnam and Laos and these workers given a lump-sum distribution as severance pay. In Vietnam, total public-sector employment—including civil service, state enterprises, and the military—declined by 1.5 million between 1988 and 1991. During 1992, further substantial reductions will occur. At the same time, state-owned enterprises are under considerable pressure to keep their workers and find ways of providing alternative employment within the enterprise because unemployment is already a serious problem (especially in Vietnam).

The Financial Sector

In the past, the governments mobilized most investment resources through the budget. The role of the financial sector was extremely limited. Reliance on financial intermediation is still very low, but a number of significant steps are being taken to reform the financial sector to serve the needs of a multisector economy. This process is in its beginning stages, and it will take a long time before banks make independent assessments of creditworthiness and risks, before public and private enterprises are treated equally, and before the public develops enough confidence in banks to regard them as the natural repository for their savings. The risk of political interference will remain. In Vietnam, for example, the party continues to have considerable influence over the decisions made by commercial banks, especially at the provincial level.

Financial-sector reform has focused on the development of a two-tier banking system through the separation of central banking from commercial banking. This formal step has been taken in Vietnam and Laos, but, in Cambodia, the National Bank of Cambodia still acts as the monetary authority, the government's depository bank, a development bank, and a commercial bank. The Cambodian system, however, has begun to change.

So far, none of the central banks can be said to play an independent role vis-a-vis the government. It is the ministry of finance, the council of ministers, and the party—rather than the central bank—that have the final say when it comes to monetary policy. The central banks also remain much too directly involved with the government-owned commercial banks.

Nonetheless, gradual separation of roles is taking place. In Laos, a number of measures have been introduced to broaden the central bank's instruments of monetary control. The government has established reserve requirements, and the central bank has begun to issue interest-bearing securities for open-market purposes and has opened a formal credit window for commercial banks. Foreign reserves have been transferred to the central bank, and a centralized system of reserve management has been installed.

In the past, interest rates in all three countries have been very low and highly negative in real terms. State-owned enterprises have been obliged to deposit their money in designated banks, but the public have not deposited— nor have they been expected to deposit—savings in the banks. Since 1989, the governments in both Vietnam and Laos have tried to introduce greater flexibility into the determination of interest rates, while maintaining rates that are positive in real terms. In Vietnam, household deposits increased very significantly following interest-rate reform in early 1989 when real interest rates temporarily became positive. In Laos, where this process has advanced further, commercial banks now have autonomy to set their own interest rates within the central bank's guidelines on minimum rates. According to a recent estimate by the IMF representative in Laos, financial savings through the banking system may have actually increased significantly during 1990–91 (Pham, 1991, p. 50). However, it may be too early to talk about a trend in Laos.[29] A positive development in this area may be expected in Vietnam, provided that a reasonable measure of price stability can be established. In Cambodia, the real interest rates remain highly negative. It is likely to take a long time before private savings in the society, which probably are already of some size, in the society find their way to the Cambodian banks.

---

[29]The nominal rate of interest on deposits in Laotian commercial banks has remained as high as 24 percent, even though the rate of inflation has been brought down to around 10 percent—a clearly untenable difference.

Traditionally, none of the countries had a foreign-currency market, except for the free, or parallel, market. Foreign currency was allocated administratively, according to government regulations. The differences between the official and the free-market rates were dramatic. In recent years, however, large volumes have been traded on the parallel markets, at rates that normally have been less than 10 percent higher than the official rates. Today, all three countries have unified exchange-rate systems. The governments are making efforts to establish full-fledged currency markets by developing the role of commercial banks in foreign-exchange transactions, by allowing bank accounts in foreign currency, and by allowing nonbank foreign-exchange dealers to do business. Two foreign-exchange centers have been opened in Ho Chi Minh City and Hanoi. By the end of January 1992, the foreign-exchange center in Ho Chi Minh City had 62 members who traded a daily average of $800,000–1 million (in U.S. dollars) two days a week (Hiebert, 1992c, p. 62). The bulk of Vietnam's foreign currency is still transacted through the parallel market.

A key issue for commercial banks is how to proceed with their recapitalization, considering their large volumes of bad and doubtful debts. They may actually have been insolvent at the time of their formation, considering that the transfer of liabilities from the central banks was based on the book value of the assets. The recapitalization operation has to be based on critical assessments of the debt, and, to be successful, the bank must be allowed to operate without traditional interference from the moment the operation has been completed. Nothing less than a cultural revolution, including very ambitious training programs, will be required.

The governments have recognized the importance of competition among commercial banks. Vietnam's two major state-owned commercial banks, the Industrial and Commercial Bank of Vietnam (ICBV) and the Agricultural Bank of Vietnam (ABV), are being turned into general-purpose commercial banks, and private-sector share-holding banks are being formed. The latter provide only limited banking services but play an important role as testing grounds for new ideas that may ultimately be adopted by the major banks.

The poor quality of domestic and international payment mechanisms constitutes a serious obstacle to economic development as these mechanisms are unable to accommodate the growing need for normal commercial payments. Not uncommon are delays of two to six months in processing payments between provinces. The Bank for Foreign Trade of Vietnam (BFTV), until recently the only institution allowed to finance foreign trade, cannot, without providing cash collateral, obtain the foreign-bank confirmations of letters of credit required by suppliers because of its poor track record.

Foreign banks can play an important role in facilitating international trade and promoting the general development of the banking systems. During the last two years, foreign banks have begun to operate in a limited way in all three countries. In 1990, Laos and Vietnam entered into their first agreements with foreign banks. Laos entered into a joint venture with a Thai bank and Vietnam with an Indonesian bank, both with an operational focus on foreign trade. A number of other foreign banks are beginning to operate in Vietnam; recently, six foreign banks have been granted the right to have a representative. In June 1991, Cambodia entered into its first collaboration with a foreign bank by signing a joint venture agreement with Siam Commercial Bank (*Indochina Digest*, 1991). At present, two joint-venture foreign banks operate in Cambodia, but many more have been approved for entry into the banking system. This rapid increase is not grounded in any plan or overall design, and there is an obvious risk of "overbanking" and banking abuse in the absence of regulatory and supervisory structures.

No studies exist on the informal financial sector, but it appears safe to say that money lending is playing an increasingly important role in all three countries in the absence of a functioning banking system. The private sector is almost completely dependent on informal money markets.

In the case of Vietnam, serious large-scale fraud has occurred as urban cooperative banks have mushroomed without the necessary regulations and controls. The *Political Report of the Central Committee at the 7th National Congress* said that "a big mistake was committed when we let urban credit organizations mushroom without proper guidance and control, leading to fairly widespread bankruptcies which involved quite a few cases of fraud" (Vietnam, Communist Party of, 1991, p. 78). An effective system of bank supervision is needed in all three countries.

The financial system is also moving into entirely new spheres. Laos, for example, has begun to issue short-term bonds, and Vietnam has introduced bonds on an experimental basis in the city of Hai Phong. Even a stock exchange is on the Vietnamese agenda, though such an institution will become significant only at a later stage of market economic development.

Banking is an area in which long-term technical assistance will be of vital importance. Until 1989, no such assistance had been forthcoming, but today, Vietnam and Laos are receiving significant technical assistance from a number of countries, as well as from UNDP and the World Bank. The overall impression shared by those who are involved in technical assistance to the financial sectors in Vietnam and Laos is that both governments are firmly committed to financial reform.

The Role of Foreign Trade, Foreign Investments, and International Aid

Foreign trade played a very limited role in the traditional socialist model. The emphasis was on development of trade on a barter basis with other socialist countries. Foreign investments were not excluded, but there was no foreign-investment legislation, and almost none of the joint ventures that were discussed ever materialized. Development assistance from the Soviet Union and other socialist countries played a major role in financing imports and investments.

During the last few years, the situation has changed dramatically in all three respects. Foreign trade has been recognized as a crucial growth factor, the composition of trade has swung sharply in the direction of the convertible area, and all three countries have adopted liberal foreign-investment laws. Aid from the former Soviet Union and Eastern Europe has all but ceased. Laos is receiving substantial aid from the West. Development in Vietnam is looking toward the normalization of relationships with international financial institutions and Western donors. Western (especially Japanese) aid can be expected to play a leading role in the eventual reconstruction of Cambodia. In June 1992, Japan hosted a large ministerial-level international conference on the reconstruction of Cambodia.

Vietnam. In 1980, Vietnam's total exports amounted to only 3.9 percent of its gross national product (GNP), out of which three-fourths went to the Comecon (CMEA) area under barter arrangements. Imports amounted to approximately 10 percent of GNP, the difference financed largely by grants and credits from the Soviet Union. Vietnam has not received any new loans from the IMF, the World Bank, or the Asian Development Bank since the late 1970s, and the flows from Western donors have been very limited.

As a consequence of the large deficits, Vietnam's international debt grew rapidly. In 1991, the debt amounted to approximately 9.7 billion rubles and approximately US $3.5 billion in convertible currencies. A large share of the debt to the convertible area consisted of arrears on payments that had fallen due. This is a large debt in comparison to the country's GNP (estimated at around $11 billion), but nevertheless manageable, considering that the convertible part amounts to only $3.5 billion (provided there is a comprehensive debt rescheduling). The servicing of the debt to the former Soviet Union is likely to remain very limited, considering the insignificant flow of new aid that the Russian Federation is likely to extend. In spite of its precarious balance-of-payments situation, Vietnam has, since the late 1980s, met new payments falling due to the IMF.

The Vietnamese attitude toward foreign trade started to change in the mid-1980s, when export was made one of three priorities (the other two being agriculture and consumer goods). However, significant activity in this area was evident until 1989. In that year, exports to the convertible area doubled, in spite of the continuing U.S. embargo, from $490 million to $968 million. In fact, Vietnam gained a small surplus in its trade with the convertible area. A large devaluation of the Vietnamese currency in the beginning of 1989 was a major factor triggering this change, and so was the decision of the government to allow the export of rice. The emergence of crude oil as a major export product was a third factor of critical importance to nascent foreign trade.

Today, exports amount to more than 15 percent of Vietnam's GNP. Export earnings have increased greatly since 1988. In 1991, exports, in spite of reduced rice export, reached approximately U.S. $1.9 billion, which is two-and-a-half times the figure for 1988. In 1992, exports are expected to reach $2.3 billion. While the trade account in 1988 showed a deficit of close to $0.7 billion, it has been balanced for the last two years. The foreign-trade structure has changed equally significantly, with more than 90 percent of total foreign trade today in the convertible area. In 1991, Singapore ($868 million), Japan ($709 million), and Hong Kong ($502 million) accounted for half of Vietnam's two-way trade (Hiebert, 1992d, p. 56).

The importance Vietnam attaches to trade is clearly shown by the fact that it is aiming for an export increase of 500 percent during the 1990s. If that happens, and if overall growth is as high as envisaged in the socioeconomic strategy of the Communist party, export would be equal to 25 percent of the GNP by the year 2000 (Vietnam, Communist Party of, 1992, p. 181). An economy like that would have very little in common with the autarchic barter trade economy that Vietnam had when the reform process began (even though a large share of the exports would consist of crude oil).

Soviet aid was fundamental to upholding the old model. As recently as 1989, Soviet aid in the form of crucial commodities such as gasoline, fertilizer, steel, and cotton equalled at least 5 percent of Vietnam's GNP. The sale of these commodities did not generate the budget support (in the form of counterpart funds) that it could have, because they were sold to state-owned enterprises at very low prices. Thanks to Soviet supplies, however, some of these enterprises did make significant transfers to the budget. Hence, even if not visible in the budget, Soviet commodity assistance also constituted an important source of revenue. The mechanism of cooperation presumed a bureaucratically managed economy.

In less than two years, this important aid program has been reduced to marginal levels, the relationship being transformed to one based on trade in convertible currencies. According to a transitional agreement for 1991, certain projects would be completed and a limited volume of technical assistance continued, while the debt would be converted into a hard-currency obligation under terms still to be agreed upon. For 1991, the trade targets were set at U.S. $500 million in each direction. The actual figure that was achieved was only a fraction of the targeted. Border trade with China did, on the other hand, increase very significantly and is likely to continue to do so, even though strained relations between the two countries are likely to continue because of unresolved territorial issues.[30]

Any economy would find it very hard to absorb such a drastic reduction in aid flows, and to do so at a critical stage in an adjustment process, while being denied support from international financial institutions, is a truly herculean task. Although this deprivation has further aggravated Vietnam's current account deficit, put the budget under further strain, and fueled inflation, Vietnam's export performance has made it possible to survive this critical juncture between the Soviet and the Western aid regimes.

The question is how long this period without aid from the former Soviet Union or substantial aid from the West will last. So far, other major Western donors have accepted the United States' veto, although with growing uneasiness. No other developing country has had to go through a fundamental adjustment and reform process without support from the international financial institutions and, in addition, face a U.S. embargo. During 1991, the total aid flow may have been as low as $150 million, less than 2 percent of Vietnam's GDP and less than one-third of what the World Bank recommends as a minimum. The figure for 1992 can be expected to be somewhat better, as bilateral cooperation has begun to grow.

Vietnam, as well as Laos and Cambodia, has adopted liberal foreign-investment legislation, also allowing joint ventures with domestic private companies. In the case of Vietnam, this legislation, which was originally enacted in 1988, has led to approximately 400 signed contracts valued at $2.9 billion. Less than 25 percent, however, has been spent. A number of contracts for oil exploration dominate the portfolio. More than 60 percent of all investment capital comes from Asian countries. Taiwan is leading the way with $670 million, followed by Hong Kong with $410 million (*The Nation*, 1991; *Vietnam Investment Review*, 1992, p. 2).

Laos. Also, since the mid-1980s, Laos has given priority to exports. However, its account deficit (excluding official transfers) has since then risen further and today equals 15 percent of GDP. Exports, as a share, had fallen back to 8.2 percent of GDP by 1990, while imports were at 26 percent. Such deficits clearly make the Lao economy very vulnerable, especially since two

---

[30]In March of 1992, Vietnam and China signed an agreement "preparing the way for the resumption of direct rail, air, postal and shipping links that were cut . . . in 1979. The normalization of transport links is expected to result in rapid increases in trade between the neighbors . . . " (*Far Eastern Economic Review*, 1992, p. 53). On May 16, 1992, Vietnam issued a statement protesting an "agreement between Chinese and US oil companies for the exploitation of oil and gas on the continental shelf of Vietnam" in the southwestern part of the South China Sea (statement by the Ministry of Foreign Affairs of the Socialist Republic of Vietnam, May 16, 1992, Hanoi).

items, hydroelectricity and timber, dominate exports. Moreover, public savings are negative, so aid finances not only the public investment program but part of public consumption as well. A crucial test will be whether trade can grow at a faster rate than the economy at large so that the objective of "gradually erasing the trade balance" may be met (Lao People's Revolutionary Party, 1991, p. 22).

Laos has accumulated an external debt (U.S. $0.636 billion) that is large in comparison to its GDP (approximately U.S. $0.8 billion), but it is mainly public and provided on soft terms. Furthermore, only 0.36 is to the convertible area. Thus, the debt-service ratio is likely to remain rather low (below 15 percent). In spite of its exceptionally high current account deficits, Laos has, thanks to increasingly substantial aid flows, been able to build up reserves equivalent to a few months imports—an entirely new phenomenon for the country.

The effects of the drastic decline in aid from the former Soviet Union and Eastern European have been considerably less dramatic for Laos than for Vietnam. One reason is that the aid levels were not as high in recent years. The more important reason is that Laos never was totally denied support from the IMF, the World Bank, or the Asian Development Bank. In recent years, the support from these institutions has been substantial. The group of bilateral Western donors has all along included Australia and Japan, as well as Sweden.

Initially, the relationship between Laos and the international financial institutions (IFIs) was strained. However, these institutions have gradually assumed a central role in the Lao reform process, providing crucial adjustment loans and important advisory services. So, while Vietnam had to undertake its reform without Western support (with the exception of crucial advisory services from the IMF and the World Bank), Laos has enjoyed increasingly solid support, facilitating its transformation from a rudimentary planned economy to an emerging market economy.

Laos' liberal investment law had, as of April 1991, yielded 109 foreign-investment contracts worth $231 million. However, only five were priced at more than $5 million. Nearly half are with Thai companies interested in trading, forestry, hotels, and tourism. However, major Australian and U.S. companies have also come to explore mining possibilities, and one British and one American company have begun searching for oil and natural gas (Hiebert, 1991). Only a fraction of the contracts signed have led to investments, but a steady increase in the number of contracts appears likely. While Laos eagerly seeks Thai investors, it also fears that it might end up on the losing end in its dealings with its economically superior neighbor.

Cambodia. In 1980, the government of Cambodia instituted a state monopoly on foreign trade and payments along traditional socialist lines, separating domestic economic activities from foreign ones so as to preserve a substantial degree of price and policy autonomy. The bulk of its few exports (rubber, soybeans, and timber) went to the Soviet Union, other Eastern European countries, and Vietnam. Approximately 15 percent of Cambodia's imports from these countries were paid for in this way.

During the last few years, recorded trade has been liberalized through decentralization and wider recognition of the private sector, although the export monopoly on commodities such as rubber, soybeans, and timber (smuggled in great quantities) remains. Private trade has increased rapidly since 1987, when the private sector was allowed to start exporting, while border trade has continued to expand. According to some estimates, unrecorded trade may be as large as recorded trade, while Coady and Desai suggest that only around 20 percent goes unrecorded (Coady and Desai, 1990). In 1990, the last year for which any figures exist, exports were worth 42 million rubles and U.S. $17 million, while imports amounted to 132 million rubles and U.S. $38 million (Coady and Desai, 1990, table 7). The picture for 1991 is bound to be different, considering the sharp fall in flows from the former Soviet Union and Eastern Europe. Cambodia will be unable to find alternative sources to finance the large trade deficits that it has maintained during the past decade unless international aid is forthcoming.

The international community provided emergency assistance to Cambodia in the critical year of 1979, but by 1982 had ceased to extend any help to activities inside Cambodia. There were important exceptions like UNICEF, primarily funded by Australia and Sweden, and a number of important nongovernmental organizations (NGOs), but the Soviet Union and, to a lesser extent, countries in Eastern Europe soon became the only bilateral donors. In addition, Vietnam played an important role in Cambodia's initial reconstruction, especially in building a rudimentary administrative system and repairing basic infrastructure. The Soviet Union and other Comecon (CMEA) countries provided an annual aid flow estimated at U.S. $100 million per year (probably less in world-market terms) throughout the 1980s (Curtis, 1990, pp. 173–74; Mysliwiec, 1988). In addition to technical assistance and certain rehabilitation projects, the Soviet Union also supplied much needed quantities of fuel and fertilizer.

In the last two years, the aid picture has changed dramatically. Aid from the former Soviet Union has been reduced to marginal levels, leaving Cambodia with an acute shortage of both fertilizer and fuel, commodities on which its fragile self-sufficiency in rice as well as its transport and urban water supply are based. This aid loss has also further weakened Cambodia's already critical fiscal situation. In addition, a great number of technical assistance personnel were withdrawn, with potentially dire consequences for infrastructure such as electrical generation, water purification, and civil aviation.

The question of Western aid to Cambodia returned to the agenda at the Paris Conference in August 1989. Before that, United Nations' contacts with the Phnom Penh government were defined in a way that did not allow even a needs assessment study to be undertaken in the country. A UNDP-recruited team had to limit itself to a desk study made in Bangkok (UNDP, 1989). In the spring of 1990, a large United Nations fact-finding mission was sent to Cambodia to gather information about the country that would be required if and when a United Nations operation could be launched (United Nations, 1990a). Other studies followed, and, in 1990, UNDP opened a liaison office in Phnom Penh.

An entirely new situation was created by the signing, in October, 1991, of the Paris Agreements on a Comprehensive Political Settlement of the Cambodia Conflict. So far, the concrete results in terms of aid have been, however, limited because the United Nations needs time for preparatory work before operations of any size can begin. In July 1992, 9 months after the signing of the Paris agreement, the United Nations Transitional Authority in Cambodia (UNTAC) was still not fully in place. Furthermore, according to the Declaration on Rehabilitation and Reconstruction (Annex IV) of the Agreements, the scope of what the United Nations could do was limited to rehabilitation; reconstruction would have to wait until after the elections scheduled for 1993. A rigid application of this approach would have had serious long-term repercussions, considering the comprehensive nature of current needs. The whole public sector of the Phnom Penh regime is in need of financial as well as technical support if it is to maintain any administrative capacity, provide education and health services, and so on. Ultimately, no external assistance can be provided to the country unless a rudimentary local administration is there to handle it.

Studies undertaken by the Asian Development Bank, UNDP, and, in particular, the World Bank were indications of a gradual move in the direction of such a comprehensive analysis. Also, the appeal issued by the Secretary-General of the United Nations in May 1992 furthered this objective (United Nations Transitional Authority in Cambodia, 1992). The Secretary-General's appeal sought U.S. $112 million in commodity aid and balance-of-payment support "in order to avert runaway inflation and the disintegration of the civil service" and in order "to help stabilize the economic and social situation in the country" (UNTAC, 1992, p. 1). The appeal, which was launched in spite of Khmer Rouge protests, constituted an important step away from a narrowly focused rehabilitation approach (*Bangkok Post*, May 9, 1992, p. 9).

In June of 1992 Japan hosted a large ministerial-level international conference on the reconstruction of Cambodia. Total aid commitments exceeded the amount requested in the Secretary-General's consolidated appeal, and a consultative group under the chairmanship of Japan (the International Committee on Reconstruction of Cambodia) was established (Ministerial Conference on Rehabilitation and Reconstruction of Cambodia, 1992). Due to Khmer Rouge protests, the conference did not result, however, in any workable consensus with regard to how to actually achieve "economic and social stabilization." The Khmer Rouge had made it clear (by threatening not to attend the conference) that it was against commodity aid and balance-of-payment support—the types of aid that would be required for such a comprehensive approach to succeed—and the conference did not want to jeopardize the current peace process by further alienating the Khmer Rouge. The latter has refused to let its troops be cantoned and disarmed (Sanger, 1992, p. A2; Thayer, 1992, p. 12; Chanda, 1992, pp. 8–9).

Hence, nine months after the signing of the Paris agreement only limited increases in aid disbursements can actually be seen, even though certain countries, such as Australia, France, and Sweden, have increased their contributions through UN agencies or begun to prepare bilateral projects. Thailand has begun to provide critically needed infrastructure. As a result of the Tokyo conference, Cambodia can expect to begin receiving substantial amounts of aid—probably more aid than it can possibly absorb. But the country will continue to face a destabilizing vacuum, in spite of the "holding operation" recommended in the appeal issued by the Secretary-General to keep the productive capacity at its current level and to restore and maintain macroeconomic stability. No such operation has been put in place, and the economy is rapidly drifting toward hyper-inflation.

In July 1989 the government promulgated a liberal but somewhat deficient foreign investment code. Full details were presented for the Council of Ministers in April 1991. The government also set up a National Investment Council, with the task of reviewing all foreign investment decisions. So far, there have been few concrete decisions, but some state-private companies (primarily export and import) have been formed through investments from foreign and Cambodian businessmen. And by June 1991, the government had received more than 200 investment applications, 30 percent of which had come from overseas Khmers (*Far Eastern Economic Review*, June 20, 1991). In the wake of the war, the country's natural resources, especially its forests and ore deposits, were being depleted through often corrupt arrangements with Thai and other groups; not least the Khmer Rouge, for whom such trade had become the principal source of finance.

Where Do Vietnam, Laos, and Cambodia Stand?
In the World Bank's *World Development Report 1991* (World Bank, 1991) entitled "The Challenge of Development," the elements of a "preferred

sequence" of reform, spanning a ten-year period, are presented in a box figure (World Bank, 1991, p. 146). The figure provides a useful basis for an assessment of how Vietnam, Laos, and Cambodia have taken the path of reform.

None of the countries started the process in the way that the figure suggests; that is, by trying to stabilize the macroeconomy through fiscal and monetary means, liberalize prices, remove quantitative restrictions, and develop and privatize small companies. Looking at 1979 as the year when the processes that would develop into today's comprehensive reforms de facto began, then the reforms in Indochina—as in China—were of two kinds: agrarian change and various efforts to increase the efficiency of state-owned enterprises. It was not until 1987 in Laos, 1989 in Vietnam, and the last few years in Cambodia, that prices were freed and the question of macrostability was addressed in a comprehensive way.

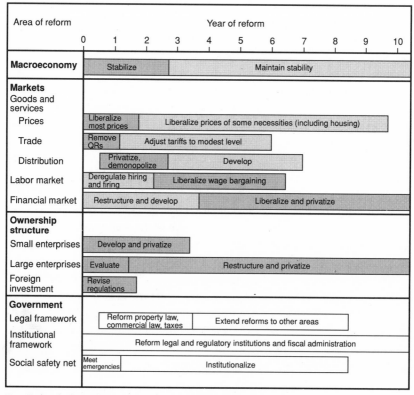

Note: Darker shading indicates intensive action. QRs, quantitative restrictions.

Figure 3-1. *The Phasing of Reform. Source:* World Development Report 1991. *The World Bank. Reprinted with permission.*

The Vietnamese reform process can be divided into four distinct stages. The first one was initiated in 1979. Its most important elements were the contract system in agriculture, the reform of state-owned enterprises, and the half-hearted recognition of the private sector. Steps taken by the government were reactive, but in the process, markets developed and a dual-track price structure emerged.

The second stage, introduced in 1985, widened the scope of reform to include wages, prices, and subsidies, but stopped short of removing price controls. The government tried to solve the problem of dual price structures by raising official prices to levels close to the market price level, by devaluing, and by allowing more room for the private sector.

The foundation for the third stage was laid at the Sixth Party Congress in December 1986 with the launching of doi moi. However, it was not until the first quarter of 1989 that the crucial step—the freeing of most prices—was taken (van Brabant, 1990, pp. 209–29).

It was only when the government took this very bold step, thereby entering the fourth stage, that the reform meant a truly qualitative change. As noted by D.M. Leipziger, "socialist economic thinking" in the form of central planning and price administration was abandoned (Leipziger, 1992, p. 2).

The same stages can be identified in the Lao reform, while the Cambodian reform process is less distinct and less developed.

Today Vietnam, Laos, and, in some respects, Cambodia have begun to address all the dimensions suggested in the World Development Report model. Earlier, a number of characteristics of the prereform model were identified. The emerging model looks qualitatively different, and is rife with challenges:

- Central planning has been all but dismantled (only remnants are left).
- The economies are increasingly managed by indirect, macroeconomic means, such as monetary and fiscal policies. (The Lao economy has reached the most stable stage, while the necessary conditions for any kind of macromanagement are absent in Cambodia.)
- Prices of goods and most services are no longer determined by the state, and, because of trade links, important prices are already in line with world-market prices.
- Investment decisions have been decentralized to enterprises and farmers; investments, however, remain low (Laos), very low (Vietnam), or exceptionally low (Cambodia).
- Agriculture is household based, and user rights have been written into the constitutions, with Vietnam searching for a new balance between

individual farm households and cooperatives; there is hardly any collective farming left. The role of agriculture in the economy has been redefined, upgraded from the vehicle for "socialist industrialization" to a sector that should play a leading role in the transformation of the economy. The traditional terms of trade bias against agriculture have been greatly reduced.

- Industry has been decentralized, and the private sector has become significant. The state has begun to disengage itself through leasing, joint ventures, and privatizations (especially in Laos and Cambodia but also, more recently, in Vietnam). Light industry, like consumer-goods manufacture, gets priority.

- The state fixes government employees' salaries (at exceedingly low levels), but a labor market in which wages are negotiated is rapidly developing. Increased real income as well as increased disparities are emerging.

- The banking systems are being reformed through separation of central from commercial banking. This process has just begun, and banks do not play an independent role, still lending almost exclusively to the public sector (95 percent in Vietnam). Real interest rates are often still negative, and there are hardly any private savings through the banking system.

- Foreign currency is still allocated administratively, but the banks, as well as nonbank foreign-exchange dealers, have begun to sell foreign currency. Large volumes are sold in parallel markets at rates that are only slightly higher than the official ones. In reality, the currency markets are free, although in urgent need of development.

- A land market is emerging through the right to transfer the usufruct rights.

- High priority is attached to exports, which, in the old autarchic model, played a marginal role. (If Vietnam's optimistic objectives were to materialize, its export earnings, by the turn of the century, would be at least one-fourth of the envisaged GDP or eight times the share in 1980.) Foreign trade has ceased to be a state monopoly, and individual enterprises can enter into contracts with foreign companies.

- The private sector is playing an important role in the economies, contributing considerably more than half of GNP (63 to 70 percent in Vietnam) through agriculture, manufacturing, construction, trade, and other services.

- All three countries have adopted liberal foreign-investment legislation, and, especially in the case of Vietnam, foreign investments have begun to be of significance.

- The tax systems are being adjusted to the requirements of a market economy through the introduction of profit taxes, sales taxes, and income taxes, thereby replacing the fading system of transfers from state enterprises. This process will, however, take considerable time. In the meantime, the revenue situation will remain critical with revenue/ GDP ratios that are exceptionally low (Vietnam and Laos) or exceptionally low (4 percent/GDP in Cambodia). There are hardly any public savings in any of the economies.
- A rudimentary legal framework in the form of company law, bankruptcy law, and so on, is coming into being; Vietnam and Laos are attaching very high priority to legislation.
- Social services have been negatively affected by the public-sector crisis, as the real value of salaries and the provision of textbooks, medical supplies, and so on, has fallen off (or simply remained poor, as in Laos). New ways of financing social services, such as fees and privatizations, have been sought. Social safety nets are deemed largely unaffordable in the present fiscal situation.

What were minor, "reactive" adjustments within the socialist model in 1979 have, over the last decade, clearly developed into profound reform programs that make the transition to socialism as an economic system appear increasingly distant. The internal debate is no longer about whether the prices of goods and services should be determined administratively or by the market. The market predominates. What is referred to in Vietnam as "the old mechanism based on bureaucratic centralism and State subsidies" has been permanently discarded.

Some observers argue that the changes taking place, especially in Vietnam, are tactical and, hence, could be reversed at any time. However, a number of studies of the reforms in these countries show that these economies are today actually low-productivity market economies rather than planned economies. Both the IMF and the World Bank have come to this conclusion in their analyses of the Vietnamese and Lao economies. Government—and party—interventions remain widespread and ad hoc, but that does not alter the fact that commodity supply and demand, rather than central planning, determines most prices. (The Cambodian economy may actually be one of the most liberal in the world, the government largely having ceased to exercise control over the economy.) Much remains to be done before markets can function well, but these tasks fall in the realm of reforming market economies rather than the socialist one of making an entire economy function like one single well-greased factory.

Increasingly mixed economies are emerging. No reliable figures are available, but institutions such as the World Bank have estimated the nonstate share of Vietnam's GDP to be as high as 63 percent (somewhat higher estimates are found in Vietnamese documents).[31] Such a nonstate share is typical for developing market economies and dramatically different from economies in the reform socialist countries with which Vietnam, Laos, and Cambodia are often grouped. There is no reason to believe that the Lao or Cambodian share would be higher, or that the share of any one of the countries will increase during years to come. None of the governments deems what Nove calls "feasible socialism" to offer a sufficiently realistic alternative (Nove, 1991).

Obviously, Perkins's four conditions for a functioning market are not completely fulfilled in these countries. Could one then argue that these three economies are examples of "neither plan nor market" or "socialism without planning," considering what remains to be done before markets can function well? Such a characterization would, clearly, not give due credit to the significant developments that have already taken place since prices were decontrolled. The question is, rather, how regulated these markets will be in a few years. Elaborate systems of regulation, as Perkins notes, are the rule rather than the exception in developing market economies (Perkins, 1989).

The reform processes taking place in the three countries are not uniform ones. Laos has, in some respects, gone further than the others—and done so with considerable international support. Not only has Laos advanced further in actual reform measures but also, and this is equally important, when it comes to stabilization, the Achilles' heel of Vietnamese reform. Vietnam has, however, been able to bring down its rate of inflation during 1992 because it has addressed the underlying causes with increased determination. The same cannot be said for Cambodia where macroeconomic instability is an acute problem and the capacity to manage the economy by macroeconomic means remains to be developed. Also, there are grave signs of widening macroeconomic imbalances due to monetary expansion.

Stabilization will remain a critical issue for all three countries, including Laos, considering the size of the country's domestic and external deficits and its very low levels of domestic financial savings. The country needs to deepen its enterprise reform, strengthen its fiscal resource mobilization, adapt expenditure management to the new role of the state, and strengthen

---

[31]According to a recent World Bank study, the nonstate sector produces 63 percent of GDP. In Vietnamese documents, the nonstate share has been estimated to be as high as 73 percent.

government administration, that is, develop the state and human capacity required to manage reform.

Will the reforms then set the economies on more rapid growth paths? It is too early to tell, especially for war-torn Cambodia in search of a government. What we can tell is that all three economies would have plunged into deep economic crises following the dramatic decrease of aid from the former Soviet Union if they had remained "unreformed."

The Laotian GDP grew by 13.5 percent in 1989, 6.6 percent in 1990, and 4.0 percent in 1991. The GDP performance in 1991 was affected by floods that reduced rice production by 20 percent (Funck, 1991, Table 1).

Vietnam's figures are better than envisaged when the 1989 reform package was introduced, primarily because of significant increases in rice production. Its GDP grew by 7.1 percent in 1989, 5.1 percent in 1990, and 3.0 percent in 1991 (Dollar, 1991, p. 2; and more recent information received from the international financial institutions).

No official figures are available for Cambodia, but recent accounts indicate considerable economic activity despite innumerable signs of growing difficulties facing the state in the fragile transition process inherent in the Paris agreement. Cambodia's annual growth in net national product, according to the best available sources (World Bank), averaged 9 percent between 1987 and 1989; fell by 0.1 percent in 1990 due to poor agricultural-sector performance; and expanded by 13.5 percent in 1991. The fact that, in the process, Cambodia's income distribution, is becoming increasingly skewed is a cause for grave concern.

None of the three countries have, as yet, created conditions for steady and rapid growth (Cambodia's situation again being exceptional). Still, as Vietnam, Laos—and Cambodia—become increasingly integrated parts of the economic life of the Southeast Asian region, rather rapid growth—although predictably unbalanced—rather than stagnation is the most likely scenario. Necessary state capacity will be in short supply. Even under the best of circumstances, all three countries have years of reform and institution building ahead of them before they become "developmental states" (Sorensen, 1992, p. 20). A fundamental difference between now and the past is that the "voluntarist" approach to development, that is, "the belief that history could be accelerated through the application of (collective) will power," has been discarded (Ferdinand, 1989, p. 14). They have concluded that change cannot be controlled through central planning and that the market cannot develop if treated like a bird in a cage, with the plan functioning as the cage.[32] Instead,

---

[32]Chen Yun, one of the oldest of the old guard of China's leadership, is supposed to have said that China wants "the market to play the role of a bird in a cage, with the plan performing the

one has to develop capacity and statecraft to manage increasingly open, mixed economic systems as one steers through uncharted territory.

References

Ablin, David A. and Marlow Hood, eds. 1990. *The Cambodian Agony*. Armonk, N.Y.: M. E. Sharpe, Inc.

Amor, Moncef Hadj. 1992. "A Report on the Experience of the Democratic Popular Republic of Laos." Paper presented at the UNDP/MDP-ODI Colloquium on Management Development of Centrally Planned Economies in a New Global Environment, London, April 1–3.

Asia Development Bank, International Monetary Fund, United Nations Development Program, World Bank. 1992. *Cambodia Socio-economic Situation and its Immediate Needs.* Document prepared for the Ministerial Conference on the Rehabilitation and Reconstruction of Cambodia. May.

Asian Development Bank, economic reports.

Australia, Ministry for Foreign Affairs of. 1990. *Cambodia: An Australian Peace Proposal*. Canberra: Australian Government Publishing Service.

Awanahara, Sasumu. 1989. "Japan and East Asia: Toward a New Division of Labour." *The Pacific Review* 2, no. 3: 198–208.

Balassa, Bela. 1989. "China's Economic Reforms in a Comparative Perspective." In Morris Bornstein, ed., *Comparative Economic Systems—Models and Cases*. Boston: Irwin.

Bangkok Post. 1991. "Kiet Vows Closer Ties with ASEAN." October 21.

———. 1992. "Khmer Rouge object to UN money appeal." May 9.

Becker, Elisabeth. 1986. *When the War Was Over—the Voices of Cambodia's Revolution and its People*. New York: Simon and Schuster.

Beresford, Melanie. 1985. "Agriculture in the Transition to Socialism: The Case of South Vietnam." In Mat Lundahl, ed., *The Primary Sector in Economic Development*. London and Sydney: Croom Helm.

———. 1988. *Vietnam—Politics, Economics, and Society*. London and New York: Pinter Publishers.

Berggren, Hakan. 1990. *En Okand Varld—Malay-kulturen och ASEAN-landerna*. Stockholm: Wahlstrom and Widstrand.

Blejer, Mario, David Burton, Dunaway Steven, and Gyorgy Szapary. 1991. *"China: Economic Reform and Macroeconomic Management."* Occasional Paper, no. 76. Washington D.C.: International Monetary Fund.

---

role of the cage" (quoting Yun in Ferdinand, 1989, p. 301). Nove's version of the same story focuses on the manager: "Our managers are in too small a cage. They cannot spread their wings. We must build them a bigger cage. But we must keep them in the cage, otherwise they will fly away" (Nove, 1991, p. 160).

Bourdet, Yves. 1990. "Macro-Economic Stabilization with Trade Liberalization and Deregulation." Institute of Economic Research, University of Lund, and Department of International Economics, Stockholm School of Economics.

———. 1992a. "Reforming Laos Economic System." *Economic Systems* 16, no. 1, April 1992.

———. 1992b. "Perestroika au Laos—Performances et Perspectives de l'Economie Laotienne." Reprint Series No. 160. Department of Economics, University of Lund, Sweden.

Brown, MacAlister and Joseph J. Zasloff. 1986. *Apprentice Revolutionaries: The Communist Movement in Laos, 1930–85*. Stanford: Hoover Institution Press.

Cady, John F. 1976. *Southeast Asia—Its Historical Development*. T M H edition. New Delhi: Tata McGraw-Hill Publishing Company, Ltd.

Chan, Steve. 1988. "Puff, the Magic Dragons: Reflections on the Political Economy of Japan, South Korea, and Taiwan." *Journal of Developing Societies*, IV (July-October): 208–25.

Chanda, Nayan. 1980. "Vietnam Uber Alles." *Far Eastern Economic Review* (June): 28–29.

———. 1986. *Brother Enemy—the War After the War, A History of Indochina Since the Fall of Saigon*. New York: Macmillan Publishing Company.

———. 1991a. "Indochina." In Anthony Lake, ed., *After the Wars—Reconstruction in Afghanistan, Indochina, Central America, Southern Africa, and the Horn of Africa*. U.S.-Third World Policy Perspectives, no. 16, Overseas Development Council. New Brunswick (U.S.A.) and Cambridge (U.K.): Transaction Publishers.

———. 1991b. "Indochina Beyond the Cold War: The Chill from Eastern Europe." Draft paper presented in HIID's seminar series on Indochina, Cambridge, MA, October.

———. 1992a. "Cambodian Peace Accord May Be in Jeopardy as Economy Unravels Amid Government Crisis." *The Asian Wall Street Journal Weekly* January 6, p. 2.

———. 1992b. "Cambodia: Ghost at the Feast." *Far Eastern Economic Review* July 2.

Chandler, David P. 1992. *The Tragedy of Cambodian History—Politics, War and Revolution Since 1945*. New Haven and London: Yale University Press.

Cheriyan, K.C. and E. V. K. Fitzgerald. 1989. "Development Planning in the State of Cambodia." Report of a mission by the NGO Forum on Cambodia. Phnom Penh and The Hague: NGO Forum.

Coady, David and Meghnad Desai: 1990. "Fiscal Reform in Cambodia." Second draft of a consulting paper undertaken for the Cambodia Trust.

Csaba, Laszlo. 1990. "The Bumpy Road to the Free Market in Eastern Europe." *Acta Economica* 42, nos. 3–4: 197–216.

———. 1991. "New Perspectives on Systemic Change and Stabilization in Central Europe: An Overview." In Laszlo Csaba, ed., *Systemic Change and Stabilization in Eastern Europe*. Dartmouth, MA.: Aldershot Press.

Curtis, Grant. 1990. *Cambodia—A Country Profile*. Stockholm: Swedish International Development Authority (SIDA).

Dahrendorf, Ralf. 1987. "Changing Perceptions of the Role of Government." In *Interdependence and Co-operation in Tomorrow's World*, a symposium marking the twenty-fifth anniversary of OECD. Paris: OECD.

Dapice, David and David Coady. 1992. "Cambodia's Priority Needs in Economic Policy Analysis." Paper prepared for the Cambodia Development Resource Institute. Cambridge, MA.: Harvard Institute for International Development.

Dollar, David. 1991. "Vietnam: Successes and Failures of Macroeconomic Stabilization." Draft paper prepared for HIID's seminar series on Indochina, Cambridge, MA, February.

Drabek, Zdenek. 1990. "A Case Study of a Gradual Approach to Economic Reform: The Viet Nam Experience of 1985–88." The World Bank Asia Regional Series, Report No. IDP 74. Washington, D.C.: World Bank.

Ebihara, May. 1990. "Return to a Khmer Village." *Cultural Survival Quarterly* 14, no. 3: 67–70.

The *Economist.* 1991. January 11–17, p. 50.

Eriksson, Gun. 1992. "Market Oriented Reforms in Tanzania: An Economic System in Transition." Stockholm: Stockholm School of Economics.

Evans, Grant. 1988. "Agrarian Change in Communist Laos." Occasional Paper No. 85. Singapore: Institute of Southeast Asian Studies.

———. 1990. *Lao Peasants under Socialism*. New Haven: Yale University Press.

Far Eastern Economic Review. 1992. Hong Kong. March 19, p. 53.

Ferdinand, Peter. 1989. *Communist Regimes in Comparative Perspective—The Evolution of the Soviet, Chinese and Yugoslav Models*. London and Savage, MD.: Harvester Wheatsheaf and Barnes & Noble Books.

———. "The Process of Socialist Economic Transformation." *Journal of Economic Perspective* 5 (Fall): 91–105.

Fforde, Adam. 1989. *The Agrarian Question in North Vietnam 1974-79—A Study of Cooperator Resistance to State Policy*. Armonk, N.Y.: M. E. Sharpe, Inc.

———. 1991a. "The Political Economy in Vietnam—Some Reflections." Draft paper presented in HIID's seminar series on Indochina, Cambridge, MA, April 1991.

———. 1991b. *Country Report—Vietnam*. Report for SIDA. Stockholm: SIDA.

Fforde, Adam and Stefan de Vylder. 1991. "Study of Economic Reforms in Selected Planned Asian Developing Countries—Vietnam." Draft report prepared for the Asian Development Bank.

———. 1992. "Vietnam: Economic Commentary and Analysis—A Bi-Annual Appraisal of the Vietnamese Economy." Introductory issue. London and Canberra: Aduki Ltd.

Fischer, Stanley and Alan Gelb. 1990. "Issues in Socialist Economic Reform" (draft). Washington, D.C.: World Bank.

Funck, Bernard. 1991. "Laos: Decentralization and Economic Management." Draft paper presented in HIID's seminar series on Indochina, Cambridge, MA, April 1991.

Genberg, Hans. 1991. "On the Sequencing of Reforms in Eastern Europe." IMF Working Paper. Washington, D.C.: International Monetary Fund.

Goll, Sally. 1992. "Art in the Time of *doi moi*." *Far Eastern Economic Review* May 7, 36–37.

Gonzales Casanova, Pablo. 1990. "The Third World and the Socialist Project Today." In William K. Tabb, ed., *The Future of Socialism—Perspectives from the Left*. New York: Monthly Review Press.

Gorbachev, Mikhail. 1988. *Perestroika—New Thinking for our Country and the World*. (Updated version of the original edition published in 1987.) London: Fontana/Collins.

Grindle, Merilee and John Thomas. 1991. *Public Choices and Public Policy—the Political Economy of Reform in Developing Countries*. Baltimore and London: Johns Hopkins University Press.

Grunewald, Francois. 1990. "Le Cambodge agricole du début des années 1990." Paris: Group de Recherche et d'Echanges Technologiques (GRET).

Gunn, Geoffrey C. 1988. *Political Struggles In Laos (1930-1954)*. Bangkok: D.K. Publishers.

Hall, D. G. E. 1968. *A History of Southeast Asia*. Third edition. New York: St. Martin's Press.

Hess, Gary H. 1990. *Vietnam and the United States—Origins and Legacy of War*. Boston: Twayne Publishers.

Hewitt, Ed A. 1988. *Reforming the Soviet Economy—Equity vs. Efficiency*. Washington, D. C.: The Brookings Institution.

Hiebert, Murray. 1991a. "The Long Haul—Laos Aims to Reverse Years of Fiscal Neglect." *Far Eastern Economic Review* April 25.

————. 1991b. "Exit Heng Samrin." *Far Eastern Economic Review* October 31.

————. 1992a. "New Directions—Press Takes Bolder Stand on Corruption." *Far Eastern Economic Review* February 20, 21-22.

————. 1992b. "Red Capitalists—Private Enterprise Flourishes Despite Hurdles." *Far Eastern Economic Review* February 20.

————. 1992c. "Out of the Black—Vietnam Moves Closer to Genuine Currency Markets," *Far Eastern Economic Review* February 27.

————. 1992d. "Sea-saw Fortunes—Vietnam Looks to Asia after Soviet Collapse." *Far Eastern Economic Review* May 14, 56-57.

————. 1992e. "The Tilling Fields—Rice Glut Worries Vietnamese Farmers." *Far Eastern Economic Review* May 14, 57.

————. 1992f. "Election Strategy No Threat to Communist Party Rule in July Polls" July 9, 21.

Hinds, Manuel. 1990. "Issues in the Introduction of Market Forces in Eastern European Socialist Economies." Internal discussion paper Report No JOP-0057. Washington, D.C.: World Bank.

Ho Chi Minh. 1979. *Patriotism and Proletarian Internationalism*. Hanoi: Foreign Language Publishing House.

Houtard, Francois, and Genevieve Lemercinier. *Hai Van—Life in a Vietnamese Commune*. London: Zed Books, Ltd.

Huntington, Samuel P. 1992. *The Third Wave. Democratization in the late Twentieth Century.* Norman: University of Oklahoma Press.

Indochina Digest. 1991. (Weekly publication by the Indochina Project, Washington, D.C.) June 7, 1991.

International Monetary Fund (IMF). Reports on recent economic developments in Laos and Vietnam.

Kahin, George McT. 1987. *Intervention: How America Became Involved in Vietnam.* New York: Anchor Books.

Khanh, Huynh Kim. 1982. *Vietnamese Communism 1925–1945.* Ithaca and London: Cornell University Press.

Kiernan, Ben and Chantaou Boua, eds., 1982. *Peasants and Politics in Kampuchea, 1942–81.* London: Zed Press.

Killick, Tony, and Christopher Stevens. 1992. "Lessons from the Third World." In Stevens and Kennan, eds., *Reform in Eastern Europe and the Developing Country Dimension.* ODI Development Policy Studies. London: Overseas Development Institute.

Kornai, Janos. 1983. *Contradictions and Dilemmas.* Budapest: Corvina.

———. 1990a. *Vision and Reality, Market and State.* New York: Routledge.

———. 1990b. Address to World Bank Executive Directors Colloquium, Washington, D.C., April.

———. 1990c. *The Road to a Free Economy: Shifting from a Socialist System: The Example of Hungary.* New York: Norton.

———. 1992. *The Socialist System—The Political Economy of Communism.* Princeton, N.J.: Princeton University Press.

Lao People's Democratic Republic (P.D.R.), Ministry of Economy, Planning, and Finance, State Statistical Center. 1990a. *Basic Statistics about the Socio-Economic Development in the Lao People's Democratic Republic for 15 years (1975–1990).* Vientiane: Lao People's Democratic Republic.

———. "Policy Framework for Public Investment Program—Lao PDR" 1990b. Draft document prepared by a consultant team (PDP Australia Pty Ltd) financed by UNDP, November.

———. 1992. "Socio-Economic Development Strategies," vol. I. Document prepared for the Round Table Meeting (UNDP), Geneva, February.

Lao People's Revolutionary Party (L P R P). 1991. "Political Report of the Executive Committee of the Central Committee of the Lao People's Revolutionary Party." Report presented at the Fifth Party Congress, Vientiane, March.

Le Duan. 1977. *Selected Writings.* Hanoi: Foreign Language Publishing House.

Leipziger, D. M. 1992. "Awakening the Market—Vietnam's Economic Transition." World Bank Development Discussion Paper No. 157. Washington, D.C.: World Bank.

Li, Bob and Adrian Wood. 1989. "Economic Management Capabilities in Vietnam: An Evaluation and Assessment of Needs, with a Suggested Priority Project for UNDP's Management Development Program." Draft paper prepared for UNDP.

Lindbeck, Assar. 1986. "Public Finance for Market-Oriented Developing Countries," quoted from Wade 1990. Stockholm: Institute for International Economics.

Lundahl, Mats, ed., 1985. *The Primary Sector in Economic Development.* London and Sydney: Croom Helm.

Luong, Hy Van. Forthcoming 1992. *Tradition and Revolutionary Process in a North Vietnamese Village (1925–1988).* Honolulu: University of Hawaii Press.

———. 1991a. "The Political Economy of Vietnamese Reforms: A Microscopic Perspective from Two Ceramics Manufacturing Centers." Draft paper. Toronto: University of Toronto.

————. 1991b. "Economic Reform and the Intensification of Rituals in a North Vietnamese Village." Draft paper presented at the Fairbank Center for East Asian Research, Harvard University, Cambridge.

Makarov, N., S. Malyguine, and D. Bogatova. 1989. *Countries of Indochina on the Threshold of the 21st Century.* Moscow: Institute of International Economic and Political Studies, Center for Asian Studies, Indochina Division.

Marr, David G. 1981. *Vietnamese Tradition on Trial 1920-1945.* Berkeley, CA.: California University Press.

Marr, David G. and Christine P. White, eds. 1988. *Postwar Vietnam: Dilemmas in Socialist Development.* Ithaca, N.Y.: Cornell University Press, Southeast Asia Program.

Marx, Karl. 1887. *Capital.* Preface to Vol. I.

Migdal, Joel S. 1988. *Strong Societies and Weak States.* Princeton, N.J.: Princeton University Press.

Ministerial Conference on the Rehabilitation and Reconstruction of Cambodia. 1992. Tokyo Declaration on Rehabilitation and Reconstruction of Cambodia. Tokyo, June.

Mirsky, Jonathan. 1991. "Reconsidering Vietnam." *The New York Review of Books* October 10, 44-52.

Moise, Edwin. 1976. "Land Reform and Land Reform Errors." *Pacific Affairs* 46.

Muscat, Robert J. 1989. *Cambodia: Post-Settlement Reconstruction and Development.*

Myrdal, Gunnar. 1968. *Asian Drama—An Enquiry into the Poverty of Nations.* Vols. 1, 2, and 3. New York: Pantheon.

Mysliwiec, Eva. 1988. *Punishing the Poor—the International Isolation of Cambodia.* Oxford: Oxfam.

Ngo Vinh Long. 1988. "Some Aspects of Cooperativization in the Mekong Delta." In Marr and White, eds., *Postwar Vietnam: Dilemmas in Socialist Development.* Ithaca, N.Y.: Cornell University Southeast Asia Program.

Nguyen Van Linh. 1989. *Answers by General Secretary of the CPVCC Nguyen Van Linh.* Hanoi: Foreign Language Publishing House.

Nhan Dan. 1991. Hanoi. June 29, 1991.

The Nation. 1992a. Bangkok. January 16, 1992.

————. 1992b. Bangkok. June 27, 1992.

Nixson, Fredric. 1992. "Enterprise Reform and Economic Restructuring in Transitional Economies: Mongolia, Vietnam and North Korea." Paper presented to a conference entitled "Post Privatization Policy and Performance: International Perspective," University of Bradford, March.

Nordhaus, William. 1990. *The Longest Road: From Hegel to Haggle.* New Haven: Yale University.

Norlund, Irene. 1990. "Vietnamese Industry in Transition—a Case Study of Some Recent Changes in the Vietnamese Textile Industry." Paper presented at the annual conference of the Nordic Association of Southeast Asian Studies: "Asian Societies in Comparative Perspective," September 30–October 3.

Nove, Alec. 1986. *Socialism, Economics and Development*. London: Allen and Unwin.

———. 1991. *The Economics of Feasible Socialism Revisited.* Second edition. London: Harper Collins Academics.

Okita, Saburo. 1989. *Japan in the World Economy of the 1980s*. Tokyo: University of Tokyo Press.

Perkins, Dwight. 1988. "Reforming China's Economic System." Development Discussion Paper No. 261. Cambridge: Harvard Institute for International Development.

———. 1989. "Economic Systems Reform in Developing Countries." Development Discussion Paper No. 307. Cambridge: Harvard Institute for International Development.

———. 1991. "The Transition from Central Planning, East Asia's Experience." Paper presented at the Twentieth Anniversary Symposium of the Korean Development Institute, Seuol, July.

Pham Chi Do. 1991. "Economic Reform in the Laos P.D.R.: Trends and Perspectives." IMF Representative Office in Vientiane, December.

Phomvihane, Kaysone. 1978. "Points de vue de Camarade Kaysone Phomvihane concernant les problèmes de Transformation en coopératives agricoles et l'introduction des zones rurales dans le socialisme." Vientiane, November 16.

———. 1979. "Rapport sur l'état de l'édification du régime Democratic Populaire Lao au cours des 3 années écoulées et sur les orientations et taches de l'année 1979." Report to the National Assembly and the Council of Ministers, Vientiane.

———. 1980. *La Révolution Lao*. Moscow: Editions du Progrés.

Pierce, David W. 1986. *The MIT Dictionary of Modern Economics.* Third edition. Cambridge, MA: The MIT Press.

Pike, Douglas. 1992. "Vietnam in 1991—the Turning Point." *Asian Survey* XXXII, no. 1: 75–96.

Porter, Gareth. 1972. "The Myth of the Blood Bath." Cornell University Studies of the International Relations of East Asia, Interim Report No. 2, September. Ithaca: Cornell University.

Pura, Raphael. 1992. "ASEAN Leaders Set Course for Integrated Market." *The Asian Wall Street Journal Weekly* February 3, 1992, p. 1.

Pye, Lucien W. 1985. *Asian Power and Politics—the Cultural Dimensions of Authority*. Cambridge MA.: The Belknap Press of Harvard University Press.

Ronnas, Per and Orjan Sjoberg, eds. 1989. "DOI MOI Economic Reforms and Development Policies in Vietnam." Papers and proceedings from a SIDA, SSE/CIEM international symposium in Hanoi, December.

Ronnas, Per. 1992. "Private Entrepreneurship in Vietnam." Draft paper prepared for the International Labor Organization (ILO).

Sampson, Steven L. 1987. "The Second Economy of the Soviet Union and Eastern Europe." *ANNALS, AAPSS* 493 (September): 120–36.

Sanger, David. 1992. "880 Million Pledge to Cambodia But Kmer Rouge Pose a Threat." *International Herald Tribune,* June 23, A2.

SarDesai, D.R. 1989. *Southeast Asia—Past and Present*. Second edition. London: Macmillan (Westview Press).

Sesser, Stan. 1992. "A Reporter at Large (Singapore)—a Nation of Contradictions." *The New Yorker* January 13, 37–68.

Shapiro, Helen, and Lance Taylor. 1990. "The State and the Industrial Strategy." *World Development* 18, no. 6: 861–78.

Shawcross, William. 1984. *The Quality of Mercy—Cambodia, Holocaust and Modern Conscience*. Fontana/Collins.

Sheehan, Neil and Susan. 1991. "A Reporter at Large in Vietnam." *The New Yorker* November 18, 54–119.

Skocpol, Theda. 1985. "Bringing the State Back in: Strategies of Analysis in Current Research." In Evans, eds., *Bringing the State Back In*. London: Cambridge University Press.

Sorensen, Georg. 1991. *Democracy, Dictatorship and Development—Economic Development in Selected Regimes in Third World Countries*. Macmillan.

———. 1992. *Democracy and the Developmental State*. Aarhus, Germany: Institute of Political Science, University of Aarhus.

Stuart-Fox, Martin. 1986. *Laos—Politics, Economics and Society*. London: Francis Pinter.

———. 1991. "Laos at the Crossroads." *Indochina Issues 92* March.

Ta V Tai. 1991. "Vietnam's Accelerated Law Reform." Draft memorandum on the current state of legislation in Vietnam. Harvard Law School, Cambridge, MA.

Taylor, Lance. 1988. *Varieties of Stabilization Experience—Towards Sensible Macroeconomics in the Third World*. Wider Studies in Development Economics. Oxford: Clarendon Paperbacks.

Thayer, Nate. 1992. "The War Party—Khmer Rouge Intransigence Threatens Peace." *Far Eastern Economic Review,* June 25, 12.

Thepsimuong, Bounmy. 1992. "Economic Reform in Lao PDR: The Transformation from a Centrally-planned Economy." Paper presented at the UNDP/MDP-ODI Colloquium on Management Development of Centrally Planned Economies in a New Global Environment, London, April 1–3.

Timmer, C. Peter. 1991. "Food Policy and Economic Reform in Vietnam." Draft paper presented in HIID's seminar series on Indochina.

Tonnesson, Stein. 1991. *The Vietnamese Revolution of 1945—Roosevelt, Ho Chi Minh and de Gaulle in a World at War*. London: Sage Publications; Oslo: International Peace Research Institute (PRIO).

Turley, William. 1986. *The Second Indochina War—A Short Political and Military History, 1954-1975*. Boulder, CO.: Westview Press.

———. 1991. "The Effects of Vietnam's Economic 'Renovation' on the American-Vietnamese relationship." Paper presented at the second annual American-Vietnamese dialogue, sponsored by the Aspen Institute, Jamaica, February 10–15.

———. 1991. "Political Renovation in Vietnam." Draft paper presented in HIID's seminar series on Indochina.

Turley, William and Mark Selden. 1992a. *Reinventing Vietnamese Socialism: Doi moi in Comparative Perspective*. Boulder, CO.: Westview Press.

————. 1992b. "More Friends, Fewer Enemies—Vietnam's Policy Toward Indochina-ASEAN Reconciliation." In Simon Sheldon ed., *Reinventing Vietnamese Socialism: Doi Moi in Comparative Perspective,* Armonk, N.Y.: E. M. Sharpe 1992.

UNICEF. 1989. "Kampuchea—Project Proposals for Supplementary Funds." Phnom Penh.

United Nations. 1990a. "Report of the United Nations Fact-Finding Mission on Present Structures and Practices of Administration in Cambodia." April 24–May 9. New York: United Nations.

————. 1990b. "Economic Reforms in Centrally Planned Economies and their Impact on the Global Economy." *Journal of Development Planning* no. 20.

United Nations Security Council. 1992. "Report of the Secretary General on Cambodia. S/23613. February, 19.

United Nations Development Program (UNDP). 1989. "Report of the Kampuchea Needs Assessment Study—Executive Summary." New York: UNDP.

————. 1990. "Macro Economic Report, Vietnam." Draft report. New York: UNDP.

————. 1991. Human Development Report. New York: Oxford University Press.

————. 1992. Human Development Report. New York: Oxford University Press.

United Nations Food and Agriculture Organization (FAO). 1991. Communication to the UNDP concerning Cambodia's food situation. April 17.

United Nations Transitional Authority in Cambodia (UNTAC). 1992. "Secretary General's Consolidated Appeal for Cambodia's Immediate Needs and National Rehabilitation." May.

United Nations World Food Program (WFP). 1991. Statement of the Cambodia Donor's Conference in Bangkok, January 22.

Van Arkadie, Brian, and Vu Tat Boi. 1992. "Managing the Renewal Process: The Case of Vietnam." Paper presented at the UNDP/MDP-ODI Colloquium on Management Development of Centrally Planned Economies in a New Global Environment, London, April 1–3.

Van Brabant, Joseph. 1990. "Reforming a Socialist Development Country—The Case of Vietnam." *Economics of Planning* 23: 209–229.

Vickery, Michael. 1986. *Kampuchea—Politics, Economics and Society*. Boston: Allen and Unwin.

————. 1990. "Notes on the Political Economy of the People's Republic of Kampuchea (PRK)." *Journal of Contemporary Asia* 20, no. 4: 435–464.

————. 1991. *Cambodia after the Peace*. Penang: Samidzat.

Vietnam, Communist Party of. 1987. *Sixth National Congress of the Communist Party of Vietnam—Documents*. Hanoi: Foreign Languages Publishing House.

————. 1990a. *Draft Platform for the Building of Socialism in the Transitional Period*. Hanoi.

————. 1990b. *Draft Strategy for the Socio-Economic Stabilization and Development of our Country up to the Year 2000*. Hanoi.

————. 1991. *Seventh National Congress—Documents*. Hanoi: Vietnam Foreign Languages Publishing House.

Vietnam Investment Review. 1992. 2, no. 30, May 4–10.

Vietnam, Socialist Republic of. 1981. *Constitution of the Socialist Republic of Vietnam (1980)*. Hanoi.

———. 1991. *Economy and Trade of Vietnam 1986–90*. Hanoi.

———. 1992a. *1992 Constitution of the Socialist Republic of Vietnam*. Hanoi.

———. 1992b. Statements by the Ministry of Foreign Affairs. Hanoi, May 16.

Vietnam Courier. 1992. "The Second Plenum of the Central Committee of the Communist Party of Vietnam." no. 27, January.

Vo Nhan Tri. 1990. *Vietnam's Economic Policy Since 1975*. Singapore: ASEAN Economic Research Unit, Institute of Southeast Asian Studies.

de Vylder, Stefan and Adam Fforde. 1988. *Vietnam—An Economy in Transition*. Stockholm: Swedish International Development Authority (SIDA).

Wade, Robert. 1990. *Governing the Market—Economic Theory and the Role of Government in East Asian Industrialization*. Princeton: Princeton University Press.

———. 1992. "State and Market Revisited." *The Economist*, April 4, 1992, 77.

Wallroth, Christer et al. 1990. "A Strategy for the Development of Management in Vietnamese Enterprises." Draft report prepared for SIDA , dated November 1990. Stockholm: The Swedish Management Group/SIDA.

Walsh, James. 1992. "Home Alone: A New Era." *Time Magazine* January 27, 31–36.

White, Christine. 1985. "Agricultural Planning, Pricing Policy, and Cooperatives in Vietnam." *World Development* 13, no. 1.

White, Gordon. 1983. "Chinese Development Strategy of Mao: Revolutionary Socialist Development in the Third World." Brighton, Sussex.

———. 1984. "Developmental States and Socialist Industrialization in the Third World." *The Journal of Development Studies* 21, no. 1.

Williams, Michael. 1992. *Vietnam at the Crossroads.* London: The Royal Institute of International Affairs, Pinter Publishers.

Woodside, Alexander. 1989. "Peasants and the State in the Aftermath of the Vietnamese Revolution." *Journal of Peasant Studies* 16, no. 4: 283–97.

World Bank. Country Economic Reports on Vietnam and Laos.

———. 1991. "The Challenge of Development." *World Development Report 1991*. Washington, D.C.: World Bank.

Xuan, Vo-Tong and C. Peter Timmer. 1990. "A Food Policy for Vietnam." Development Discussion Paper. Cambridge: Harvard Institute for International Development.

Yenal, Oktay. 1989. "Chinese Reforms, Inflation and the Allocation of Investment in a Socialist Economy." *Asia Regional Series*, Report No. IDP 52. Washington, D.C.: World Bank.

———. 1991. "Transition to the Market System." Paper presented at a World Bank Development Strategy Symposium, Kuala Lumpur. Washington, D.C.: World Bank.

4

Laos: Decentralization and Economic Control

Bernard Funck

After occupying a top position on French and then American strategic agendas in the 1950s, Laos returned to its previous obscurity. In a way, the Lao themselves may not be displeased with this situation, for history has shown that foreign interest in their domestic affairs has more often than not meant trouble.

However, Laos, now the Lao People's Democratic Republic (Lao PDR), does have some legitimate claim to fame. While other countries struggled for years to try to implement a gradualist approach to the reform of their socialist economies—with mixed results—Laos was probably the first country to attempt the "big bang" approach to market transformation—as early as 1987. In this effort, the country has been rather successful, especially when compared with similar endeavors in Eastern Europe. The thrust of this "New Economic Mechanism" was to free markets and decentralize administrative and economic decision making "to the grassroots" (that is, to autonomous administrative bodies and enterprises) as a remedy for the obvious failures of the previous command economy.

The main lesson that can be learned from the Laotian experience—which is similar in some ways to Yugoslavia's (but with a happier ending)—is that market socialism cum decentralization is difficult to combine with economic stability. In Laos, a framework of autonomy without accountability very rapidly led to a deterioration of public-sector savings—the main instrument of resource mobilization under a socialist regime—and to difficulties in curtailing credit expansion. In 1989, the country underwent a severe bout of inflation. The government repressed this flare-up by fiscal reforms and a drastic tightening in monetary policy. A lasting solution will however require (1) a move away from market socialism toward state and private capitalism and (2) a recentralization of government administration. This appears to be the approach taken by the Fifth Party Congress (March 1991), as reflected in its resolutions.

The People and the Nation

Understanding the reform process in Laos is impossible without considering Laos's culture and topography. The features of the country's geography and ethnography conspire toward fragmentation of public actions.

Two physical factors have a particular bearing on the political situation of Laos: its landlocked position and its mountainous terrain. The former has made the country vulnerable to continual foreign meddling in its domestic affairs, while the latter, along with low population density, has resulted in a patchwork of often inaccessible local communities. Laos's population of about 4 million is sparse for a territory of 91,000 square miles. And a poor communication network has prevented a national economy from emerging. Only the alluvial plain of the Mekong River and its main tributaries has been propitious for irrigated agriculture and for trade and communication with the outside world. The high country is dominated by the Annamite chain of mountains, which marks Laos's northern and eastern borders with China and Vietnam and defines the line dividing the two major Asian cultures: the Indian and the Chinese (Dommen, 1985, p. 4).

While Laos's political relations with Vietnam undoubtedly became very close after 1975, cultural affinities remain very close with the Thai.[1] The ethnic Lao share the same religion with the Thai (Theravada Buddhism) and similar languages. Family ties, even among the current leadership, extend across the borders, especially into northeast Thailand, which was part of Laos in the heyday of the Kingdom of Lane Xang. The ethnic Lao and the other Lao Lum groups are part of the larger T'ai ethnic group, which includes, among others, the T'ai Lu from southern China, the T'ai Syam from Thailand, the Hill T'ai from North Vietnam (and northern Laos), the Shan from Burma, and some hill tribes of Assam (India). T'ai groups apparently migrated south from southern China during the first millennium under the pressure of the expansion of the Han Chinese. The T'ai Lao branch settled in the upper Mekong valley and rolled back the aboriginal inhabitants of Indochina to the inhospitable mountains of the Annamite chain.

Today, however, the Lao Lum constitute only about 55 percent of the population. Descendants of the original inhabitants of Laos, the Lao Theung groups, represent another 27 percent of the population. They sometimes are called *kha* (slaves) in reference to their precolonization status, and are animist in their beliefs. The balance is made up of the various Lao Soung groups, which migrated from southern China after the violent suppression of their

---

[1]The word "T'ai" designates the T'ai ethnic group, while "Thai" designates the inhabitants of the Kingdom of Thailand.

uprising in Yunnan in the mid-eighteenth century. Also primarily animist, they settled mainly on the mountain tops.

The concept of a nation state is not part of the (ethnic) Lao tradition. As among other T'ai groups, the basic form of Lao political organization was the *muong* (principality) to which semiautonomous villages gravitated and paid tribute. Larger state entities traditionally took the form of leagues or loose confederations of muongs, like the Sip Song Chau T'ai (in what is northern Vietnam today) and Sip Song Panna (which encompassed regions now in northern Burma and southern China). State forms appeared only when one muong managed to bring surrounding ones into its orbit, often with foreign support. Such arrangements were a breeding ground for irredentism and tended to last as long as the central muong had the power to generate centripetal force and command the allegiance of the peripheral muongs.

In fact, only once before 1975 was the country independent and unified. The country emerged as a nation in the middle of the fourteenth century with the ascendancy of Fa Ngum of the Kingdom of Lane Xang (Kingdom of the Million Elephants), which covered today's Lao PDR and northeast Thailand (Isan). For 350 years, the territories unified by King Fa Ngum constituted a powerful kingdom in Indochina, ruled by a theocratic monarchy. Until the contemporary period, Lao society remained a caste system, consisting of the Lao elite (the royal family and the major urban families), the ethnic Lao peasantry, and the Lao Theung slaves. In addition to its religious and cultural role, the Sangha (Buddhist clergy) was the guardian of the social order; by accumulating "merit," the faithful could hope to move from one caste to another in the cycle of reincarnation.

This construction collapsed at the end of the seventeenth century into three kingdoms (Luang Prabang, Vientiane, and Champassak), which were often no more than a collection of principalities open to the influence and rivalries of Siam, Burma, and Annam. By the beginning of the nineteenth century, the whole country had passed under Siamese rule, despite competing claims from Annam.

This situation was to be challenged at the end of the century by the advance of French colonialism. In Laos, as in Cambodia, the French moved in to support the Vietnamese claim against the Siamese, who were considered too close to the British. The French reestablished the nominal authority of the king of Luang Prabang over his kingdom but maintained direct administration of Vientiane and the southern provinces under the governorship of the prince of Champassak. The French rulers delineated the country's contemporary borders, leaving Isan to Siam. As a consequence, about 15 million ethnic Lao currently live in Thailand, while only 2 million live in Laos. The French political influence remained very superficial. While Laos continued to be divided into small baronies, what little administration there was was largely staffed by Vietnamese.

Lao nationalism emerged during the Second World War. It was, in fact, promoted by the French who sought to counteract the reassertion of Thai influence in the country. Benefiting from the growing power of their Japanese allies in East Asia, the Thai launched a pan-T'ai propaganda campaign to raise the T'ai groups against their colonial rulers. To underscore this policy, the Thai changed the name of their country in 1938 from Siam to Thailand. However, the promotion of nationalist feelings was to ultimately backfire on the French.

At the end of the Second World War, France determined to restore its rule over Indochina. As in Vietnam, the French lit a fire that devoured the country for 30 years. The royal family of Luang Prabang and the Lao elite split over the attitude to adopt vis-à-vis the French.[2] The Kuomingtang, which would disarm the Japanese occupation force in northern and central Laos, favored the short-lived Lao Issara (Free Lao) government, but the French moved swiftly from the southern British zone to restore their rule.

The French then created the Kingdom of Laos and incorporated it into the French union. It encompassed, for the first time in two-and-a-half centuries, all the Lao territories on the east bank of the Mekong River, under the nominal authority of the new king of Laos (the previous king of Luang Prabang). This arrangement did not last. Although the country received a semblance of independence from the French in 1947, the conflict persisted. One part of the Lao Issara, led by Prince Souphanouvong, sided with the nascent communist movement in a complete rejection of the colonial system.

This coalition between the Lao Issara and the communist movement led to the creation of the Pathet Lao (the Lao Nation), so named in an appeal to nationalist feelings.[3] Sponsored by the Vietminh, the Pathet Lao moved to establish revolutionary bases in the northeastern provinces of Laos, which historically have been under strong Vietnamese influence. During the ensuing civil war, the Pathet Lao found its principal support among the Lao Theung

---

[2]The Luang Prabang monarchy was in fact composed of two branches: one branch provided the reigning kings and a collateral one provided the governing Maha Ouphahat, the prime ministers or viceroy. The split after World War II was, by and large, between these two dynasties.

[3]The depth of nationalist feeling should not, however, be overestimated. The following remark about China applies even more accurately to Laos: "It happened that nationalism, great as was the stir which it made, loudly as it raised its voice, often had to compromise. Too often it came off second best in China at this time in a struggle with the quiet voice of family obligations. It was seldom that the claims of the nation would totally prevail over the more ancient social ties. . . . Society was simply a federation of families. To keep this in mind is to understand many things about the modern history of Asia" (Calvocoressi et al., 1989, p. 676).

(and, to a lesser extent, among some Lao Soung groups), who the French had antagonized by trying to submit them to forced labor.

The country became, in effect, partitioned into two zones under separate administrations: the Mekong valley and adjacent areas ruled by the royal government, and the region from Sam Neua at the northern Vietnamese border to most of the highland subsumed by the Pathet Lao as it gradually extended its administration. A national reconciliation was agreed to at the Geneva Conference of 1954, which put an end to French rule over Indochina, but the reconciliation never materialized. Despite the declaration of Laos's neutrality, the emergence of a neutralist faction, and several attempts to build coalition governments under Prince Souvanna Phouma, the conflict became internationalized in the wake of the Cold War and then of the Second Indochina War. There followed two decades of intermittent ground war, rigged elections, ephemeral coalitions, and widespread corruption and hardship, during which foreign influence increasingly came to pull the strings on both sides of the frontline.

Toward Centralism and Back

After winning the civil war and proclaiming the establishment of the Lao People's Democratic Republic on December 2, 1975, the Pathet Lao leadership confronted two questions: How can we rule this country? How can we establish socialism in a subsistence economy? Events since 1975 can be seen as a series of attempts to answer these twin questions. In these attempts, the problems of administering the country and managing its economy have always been intertwined; each new policy course has implied administrative as well as economic reforms. Quoting the secretary-general of the party and Prime Minister, Kaysone Phomvihane, Grant Evans correctly pointed to the heart of the dilemma: "Laos, he frankly admitted, did not possess a unified national economy. It had only a combination of what he called a central economy and local economies: 'The local level is a constant objective structure of the Lao society.' Kaysone's references to the local level is oddly reminiscent of the Asian mode of production concept, whose object was societies where despotic dynasties rose and fell against the background of an unchanging village society" (Evans, 1988, pp. 31–32).

The evolution of the Lao communists' economic doctrine can be characterized by backtracking through the history of Soviet Marxism-Leninism: from war communism (advocated by Trotsky and implemented by Stalin) to the cooperative movement (put forward by Lenin in his last writings) to the New Economic Policy of 1922–24 and, finally, to capitalism (briefly surfacing in Russia in early 1918). Conveniently enough, each phase offered a separate body of doctrinal justification for the official policy course. The Fifth Lao Party Congress of March 1991 represented the logical outcome of this ideological evolution: socialism was hardly mentioned, and only in a distant perspective.

During its first years, the regime put in place a highly centralized war economy based on forced procurement at administered prices, in an attempt to overcome the devastations of the civil war and reestablish an administration after the massive departure of the Lao elite to exile or to "reeducation" camps. Each province was to become self-sufficient in food, and interprovincial trade was banned or severely restricted. In the modern sector, most enterprises were de facto nationalized. The government did not forget to make appeals to patriotic feelings, which it assumed were shared by the population. The regime accompanied economic measures with a series of jacobin-like measures such as the abolition of the monarchy, adoption of Lao as the country's official language, elimination of the Laotian honorific mode, simplification of the alphabet (to make it easier to spread to the non-Lao-speaking ethnic groups), and abolition of the system of village autonomy. The government also made attempts to reorganize lowland rural life, traditionally centered around semiautonomous villages, to conform to the popular commune system. The scope of the latter policy reportedly remained limited for lack of administrative capabilities.

In the context of growing regional tensions, caused by the mounting hostilities between Vietnam, and Kampuchea and Vietnam and China, on the other, as well as severe food shortages arising from the disruption of rural production patterns, the leadership, in May 1978, launched a desperate bid to force the modernization of agriculture through the generalization of production cooperatives. (A similar policy was initiated at the same time in South Vietnam.) As Kaysone set it out in a progress report in August of the same year: "The process of integration of state and society was to build down by establishing the provincial level as an all-round and complete strategic center which would concentrate on building an integrated provincial economy and government; and to build up from the villages, integrating them into the national level through the formation of cooperatives . . . (and) transforming the district into the direct leading level for the *tasseng* and agricultural cooperatives" (quoting Kaysone in Evans, 1988, p. 32).

The extent of the cooperative movement of 1978–79 is hard to assess. It apparently encountered widespread passive resistance from farmers, who were already on the brink of subsistence and therefore in no mood for another experiment. Facing a disaster, the government abruptly canceled the movement in July 1979.

This failure led to a reassessment that paved the way for the current reforms. The party acknowledged the necessity of slowing the pace of the transition to socialism and adopted the New Economic Policy (NEP) as the official policy inspiration. "This is Lenin's main principle applied to the true situation in Laos" (quoting Kaysone, April 1982, in Evans, 1988, p. 51). From 1979, the government stressed market-oriented reforms and placed emphasis on restoring the role of the villages. The number of cooperatives declined steadily. Unfortunately, this first trial ended in 1982–83 with a bout of inflation and a crackdown on the reformers. Again, the government shifted policy, this time focusing on strengthening planning mechanisms and, once again, generalizing cooperatives. By 1985, however, it was clear that the forceful enrollment of farmers in cooperatives was a mistake, as were the repeated attempts to implement a central planning system. Furthermore, these failures, along with political repression, had caused a mass exodus, mainly among the educated: between 1975 and 1985, the country lost about 10 percent to 15 percent of its population.

The New Economic Mechanism

Reforms took a new tack in 1985, initially on an experimental basis. The party congress of 1986 sanctioned this new direction, and the leadership adopted a new policy program known as the New Economic Mechanism (NEM).

The party recognized its failures and attributed them to two causes. The first was an excess of centralization. In a country with virtually no communication infrastructure to serve a population scattered in small valleys or even to link the main alluvial plains, the idea of establishing a centrally planned system had always been a fantasy. The development policy pursued during the first decade of the regime further aggravated obstacles to centralization. With most public resources devoted to creating and keeping afloat state enterprises and similar bodies, what little infrastructure that remained after decades of war had fallen into decay. More than half the road network, for example, is impassable in the rainy season. There is also no telecommunication between the capital and most provincial centers, and the main mode of interprovincial passenger transportation is the airplane.

The second cause of failure was voluntarism or leftism in the construction of socialism. The party had to admit that there was no scope for building socialism in a subsistence economy. The prerequisites for such an advance were the generation of a marketable surplus in agriculture and a sustained improvement in productivity through a deeper division of labor and an initial accumulation of capital.

From this assessment of the causes of failure, the party drew two conclusions. One was that there was a need for decentralization of administration and for economic management from the grassroots up. This concept encompassed the notions of self-reliance (each administrative or economic unit fending for itself, without subsidies) as well as self-management (each unit handling its own business without central instructions). Following these precepts led to a massive devolution of government prerogatives to the provinces, introduction of self-management into state enterprises, and abolition of subsidies to enterprises and local governments.

The second conclusion the party reached was that for the economy to move beyond subsistence activities, it had to undergo a capitalist phase. At least in official parlance, this move was seen merely as a means to give a more solid foundation to the construction of socialism. Party cadres saw the need to maintain and strengthen, if possible, the party's political control and preserve the final objective after opening the Pandora's box of reform. In the words of Kaysone, "Lenin stressed that under conditions in which administrative power is in the hands of the people, we are not afraid that free trading will develop. On the contrary, we can prevent capitalism from developing along the path of state capitalism and create necessary, firm conditions for turning state capitalism into socialism in the future. The capitalist economy is still useful to production and social life. . . . We are fully capable of using its positive characteristics in our production and social life, and of checking and limiting its negative sides without being afraid that when capitalism is fully developed it will override socialism" (Kaysone, 1982).

Thus, the party gave priority to "strengthening popular democracy" over "moving toward socialism." The ambitious nature of the reforms can be viewed in this way: once the party made the decision to go through a capitalist transition, procrastination could only delay access to the socialist age. Political factors aided this sweeping move, whose main beneficiaries were the small farmers. While the Pathet Lao formed a coalition of both urban nationalists and rural communists, its dominant sectors represented the rural areas, where private activities had continued under the veneer of collective organizations. Conversely, the marginal role of the industrial sector limited the support for proindustry regulations. Also, in implementing the reforms, the leadership could rely on the liberal-minded scions of the former bourgeoisie, who still occupied middle-level positions in the administration.

Perhaps the most far-reaching step the government took was its adoption in 1987 of the "one market, one price" principle, which called for the elimination of the dual-price system (official and parallel prices) for goods and foreign exchange and the determination of all prices by the market.

Unification of the multiple official rates started in 1986 when authorities devalued the commercial exchange rate of the kip, one of the seven official rates, from 35 to 95 kip per dollar. Then, in September 1987, the government reduced the number of rates from seven to four, with ranges from 10 to 350 kip per dollar. The latter rate, which applied to commercial transactions, was set in line with the parallel market. In mid-1988, the government resolved to establish a unified, market-related exchange rate. It eliminated multiple exchange rates and announced a single rate at 400 kip per dollar. The government since then has periodically adjusted the exchange rate, following parallel market developments, in an effort to maintain a slight premium between the official and the parallel market rate. Since the beginning of 1990, the exchange rate has been about 700 kip per dollar.

Domestic prices of most goods and services are now market determined. This fundamental policy reform took effect in June 1987. Parties freely negotiate prices, and administrative bodies are strictly forbidden from interfering with the market mechanism. Procurement prices used by state trading corporations in agriculture have been aligned with market prices. The government eliminated subsidies for agricultural inputs like fertilizer as part of the price rationalization. At the same time, it abolished the system of forced procurement of wage goods by the public sector at below-market prices for payment of salaries in kind. Starting in January 1988, these goods were procured at market prices. Authorities gradually adjusted selling prices and nominal wages to reflect the market value of wage goods.

The government complemented price liberalization with measures to stimulate domestic and foreign competition through private-sector promotion and import liberalization. These reforms allowed private-sector participation in all areas of production. Formation of any kind of economic association, including mixed and private enterprises, became legal in 1987. Private businesses and farmers gained access to imported raw materials, machinery, transport, and fertilizers and could borrow from the banking system. Small ventures have flourished since then, particularly those in trade, handicrafts, and other services, as well as some light industries. In agriculture, the government made participation in cooperatives a voluntary matter and eliminated preferential treatment of cooperatives and state farms. Production cooperatives have now virtually vanished.

Recently, the government has begun to disengage from state enterprises in a variety of ways, ranging from outright sale of assets to management contracts and leasing arrangements. Finally, to attract foreign investors, the government issued a Foreign Investment Code in July 1988. This liberal code has sparked some interest abroad, in particular in the wood-processing, garment, and mining sectors, and some joint ventures are already in operation. But an underdeveloped legal framework for companies, poor infrastructure and the country's remoteness from world markets have limited this interest, falling short of translating into substantial foreign involvement.

Reform came to the domestic trade sector in 1987 when the government abandoned the objective of self-sufficiency at the provincial level. Before then, the policy was to limit the movement of goods between provinces, primarily to state companies. This policy aggravated the impact of natural barriers and poor infrastructure, which, in themselves, hamper national economic integration. The abolition of this restriction in 1987 opened domestic trade to private and cooperative traders. At the same time, abolition of the payment of wages in kind resulted in the dismantling of government rice-procurement companies.

Important steps have also been taken toward foreign trade liberalization. On the import side, all economic agents, private or public, now have access to imported goods through licensed traders. A new import tariff, introduced in March 1988 in the context of overall tax reform, streamlined tariffs and extended coverage. Under the tax reform, the tariff range was narrowed from 0 to 200 percent to 0 to 70 percent. The state monopoly on exports has also largely disappeared.

However, while economic reforms were furthering the integration of the country into a single market, the political system was moving away from centralism, and Laos was transformed into a quasi confederation of local entities. There are three tiers of government in the Lao PDR: (1) The central government, (2) 16 provincial governments *kheung* and a prefecture that covers Vientiane and its environs, and (3) provinces are divided into as many as 15 district *muong*, which are further divided into subdistricts *tasseng*, which cover from five to 10 village *ban*.[4]

There is no functional specialization within these various levels. Government at each of these levels is organized like a sovereign government. Provincial and district governments have approximately 12 departments that mirror the central government ministries (that is, agriculture, finance, industry, foreign affairs, defense, interior, and so on). There are, however, no functional or hierarchical relations between central and local administrations in the same areas. The local administration is under the sole authority of the president of its administrative committee. The president of a province has a

---

[4]This paper reflects the administrative organization of the country until the promulgation of the constitution in September 1991. This constitution and related legislation seek to address some of the issues raised herein.

cabinet-level status and therefore reports only to the prime minister. In most cases, the secretary of the party and the president are the same person, and since 1982, the secretary of the provincial party committee has been almost automatically a member of the Central Committee.

The tradition of autonomy enjoyed by the provinces reached its culmination in 1986 with a decision by the Fourth Party Congress to make local governments completely self-sufficient financially. Thus, provincial and district tax administrations work under provincial governors and have no direct communication with the central tax administration. Local and central tax administrations divide up the taxpayers among themselves but not the taxes. Each level of government applies the same taxes (income tax, turnover tax, custom duties, and export taxes) to different taxpayer groups and retains the full proceeds; enterprises under the jurisdiction of the central government are taxed by the central tax administration, and enterprises under local jurisdiction, as well as all the local private enterprises, are taxed by the provincial or district government of their location.

The central government receives less than 50 percent of fiscal revenues. No scheme or formula exists to correct the consequent revenue inequality that emerges among provinces. Conversely, the central government has no control over the spending of local administrations.

To add to the fragmentation, each sectoral administration at each level of government supervises those state enterprises located on its territory and in its sector. Moreover, until 1990, each province had authority over the branch of the State Bank of Lao PDR (which is both a central and commercial bank) sited in its territory.

At the same time, the government sought to decentralize business management. The concept of self-management had long been held in disrepute by Marxists and most mainstream socialists because it divides the working class and distorts the distribution of income in favor of capital-intensive activities. However, the concept had emerged in the 1980s as the only solution to the reform of socialist economies along market lines, while maintaining collective ownership of the means of production. Following Yugoslavia, Hungary, and Poland, Laos has traveled along that road in the past decade. In the case of Laos, this system, whereby the usufruct[5] of state enterprise was granted exclusively to its managers and workers, fit well with rural traditions of land allocation. In traditional Lao society, the land belonged to the king, but its disposal rested with the village. Land was given in usufruct to village members only insofar as they actually exploited it.

---

[5]That is the right to run enterprises and enjoy the benefits from their assets without owning them.

Decree No. 19 of March 1988 formally established this principle: state enterprises "are the property of the people, granted by the State for the management and use of workers to develop the business" (free translation of Decree 19 Article 1, Lao PDR, 1988). In other words, the decree introduced a distinction between the *ownership* of state enterprises, which rests with the people at large—thus with government—and the *usufruct* of these enterprises, which is granted to workers.

The operational freedom conferred on autonomous state enterprises is quite extensive. State enterprises set their own product prices in accordance with market conditions. In domestic procurement, public enterprises are entirely free. Autonomous enterprises also have the authority to determine their borrowing and investment policies, although certain practical restrictions apply. Nonetheless, they are not required to get approval to borrow from domestic banks in spite of the possibility that the state, as owner of the enterprises, would become liable in case of default. State enterprises are free also to hire and fire labor as long as they respect internal procedures. They are similarly able to fix and adjust wages freely as long as they respect minimum-wage levels.

Public enterprises are autonomous not only in operational, borrowing, and investment decisions but also with regard to profit distribution. Decree No. 19 grants enterprises the right to "use their profit as decided by the Assembly of Workers and Employees" (free translation of Decree 19, Lao PDR, 1988). Not surprisingly, the bulk of profits in many autonomous public enterprises has recently gone into bonuses. In addition, management can raise salaries and wages to let the staff participate in the company's surplus even before it shows a profit. This practice had apparently become so widespread, and raises so high, that from 1987 to 1989, state-enterprise salaries reportedly rose from approximate parity with civil-service salaries to three to four times that level.

Managers and workers of enterprises share the return on enterprise assets but bear no risks associated with running them. Weak performance accountability is aggravated by the fragmentation of the system of public-enterprise supervision. As noted, each state enterprise is assigned to one particular government level to which it then "belongs." It reports and pays all its taxes (direct and indirect) only to this level. While interference from supervisory agencies in managerial affairs remains widespread, the financial supervision of autonomous enterprise is quite limited. Apart from administrative deficiencies, this weakness reflects the absence of clarity as to the role of the state vis-à-vis its enterprises.

The adoption of broad reforms has also necessitated a complete revamping of the instruments of fiscal resource mobilization. Under centralized economic management, the government budget benefited from the forced procurement of goods and services at administered prices and from the funneling of any state-enterprise operating surpluses into it. The former source vanished with price reform, while the second conflicted with market reforms. Pooling state-enterprise savings and channeling them to the state was consistent with central planning. Under such a system, in which prices are set according to the planners' view of social values, savings usually are not generated in sectors where they are needed for capital accumulation. Savings would, for instance, be low in a sector where, according to planners' objectives, prices are set at a low level to encourage consumption but where investable funds are needed to develop productive capacity. The government, under this scenario, would therefore use the budget to channel resources from surplus sectors to deficit sectors. The result would be a pattern of fiscal levies, varying from one sector to another.

The rationale for such a system disappears once the economy switches to a market system. In a market system, the market generates a sectoral distribution of profits that reflects its preference and provides the necessary signals for the allocation of resources. Therefore, the tax system must be neutral so as not to disrupt the allocation of resources.

The reform of 1988 introduced a profit tax in lieu of the system of transfers of operating surpluses. The tax rates, however, continued to vary from one sector to another (and between profits on domestic sales and profits on exports). In June 1989, the government abandoned this approach in favor of a single-profit tax rate and increased reliance on indirect taxes. The tax system took on a neutral character.

Once it had jettisoned microeconomic planning as well as operating and investment subsidies to state enterprise, the government had to transform the role of the banking sector. That sector used to be a passive cashier of the Plan, but now it needed to take an active role in the allocation of credit according to market signals. Furthermore, in the absence of price controls, credit policy had become crucial for macroeconomic stability. Hence, in March 1988, the government decided to separate the central and commercial banking functions of the state bank and convert its provincial branches into autonomous commercial units. By early 1991, this process was virtually completed.

Results and Difficulties of the Economic Reforms

After the 1987 economic decline, growth revived in 1988, accelerated in 1989 (see Table 4-1), and continued at a sustained pace in 1990. In view of

Table 4-1. GDP by Industrial Origin, 1986–1990 (in constant 1988 prices).

	1986		1987		1988		1989		1990	
	(% GDP)	Growth Rate	(% GDP)	Growth Rate	(% GDP)	Growth Rate	(% GDP)	Growth Rate	(% GDP)	Growth Rate
Agriculture	(59.8)	9.7	(59.3)	−5.2	(59.6)	3.7	(56.1)	4.3	(56.6)	6.2
Paddy	(26.7)	3.9	(23.3)	−16.7	(18.7)	−16.9	(23.7)	39.9	(23.9)	6.1
Other crops	(10.1)	−23.5	(14.3)	35.3	(18.3)	32.4	(16.4)	−1.2	(16.5)	6.1
Livestock and fishery	(10.5)	6.2	(10.3)	−6.3	(10.4)	4.0	(10.3)	9.0	(9.9)	1.4
Forestry	(12.4)	119.7	(11.4)	−12.3	(12.1)	9.6	(5.8)	−46.7	(6.4)	15.4
Industry	(16.9)	15.2	(14.3)	−19.4	(13.6)	−1.7	(16.2)	31.8	(16.2)	5.5
Mining and quarrying	(0.4)	21.4	(0.3)	−22.3	(0.2)	−21.6	(0.3)	37.8	(0.3)	10.6
Manufacturing	(8.1)	14.4	(8.1)	−4.7	(7.3)	−6.4	(8.9)	35.4	(8.8)	3.8
Construction	(4.6)	40.0	(3.2)	−33.2	(3.6)	15.9	(4.1)	24.0	(4.0)	3.3
Electricity, gas and water	(3.8)	−4.3	(2.7)	−33.4	(2.4)	−6.6	(2.9)	32.1	(3.1)	13.3
Services	(21.3)	−0.8	(24.3)	9.0	(24.9)	5.8	(25.5)	13.6	(25.6)	5.7
Transportation, storage, and communication	(4.0)	32.2	(4.8)	14.8	(5.0)	7.1	(4.7)	5.3	(5.3)	17.9
Wholesale and retail trade	(8.8)	9.7	(9.8)	6.1	(8.4)	−11.0	(9.8)	28.4	(9.7)	5.0
Banking, insurance, and real estate	(0.1)	91.8	(0.4)	279.3	(0.2)	−41.1	(0.2)	3.1	(0.2)	1.9
Ownership of dwellings	(1.2)	3.0	(1.3)	3.0	(1.3)	3.0	(1.2)	2.9	(1.2)	2.1
Public administration and defense	(4.8)	3.9	(5.4)	7.9	(5.5)	4.3	(4.7)	−5.8	(4.4)	−0.1
Nonprofit institutions	(2.2)	−49.9	(2.4)	3.3	(4.3)	82.1	(4.8)	23.5	(4.6)	1.7
Other services	(0.1)	37.4	(0.1)	14.7	(0.2)	34.5	(0.2)	3.7	(0.2)	1.9
Import Duties	(2.0)	−8.6	(2.2)	4.8	(2.0)	−7.0	(2.2)	20.6	(1.6)	−23.8
GDP	(100.0)	7.7	(100.00)	−4.3	(100.0)	3.2	(100.0)	10.7	(100.0)	5.3

Source: World Bank estimates based on data provided by Lao PDR authorities.

the performance observed in other formerly planned economies taking the fast lane to the market, Laos's record is quite remarkable. Supporting the resumption of growth was a shift in the terms of trade between agriculture and industry in favor of the former, generated by the price and exchange-rate liberalization (see Table 4-2). This was by far the most important policy success achieved under the NEM: it established the appropriate price structure for the resumption of agricultural production—a critical factor because the agricultural sector has the best growth potential and employs the vast majority of the population.

The same phenomenon also contributed to a redistribution of national income away from the public sector (government and state enterprises), whose share in disposable income fell from 12.8 percent in 1986 to 6.4 percent in 1989 (see Table 4-3). The ensuing 29 percent cumulative increase, in real terms, in the disposable income of the private sector fueled a consumption spree and a housing boom (see Table 4-4) that transfigured the life of the country, especially in urban centers.

However, with an estimated income per capita of U.S. $180, Laos remains one of the poorest countries in the world, despite considerable resources in land, timber, and hydroelectric resources. Most of the country's 4 million people live in scattered villages, where they practice subsistence activities, and lack access to the market. Agriculture accounts for 57 percent of gross domestic product (GDP) and 80 percent of employment. The predominant crop is rice, which takes up more than 80 percent of the cultivated area. The small industrial sector, which contributes about 16 percent of GDP, consists mainly of electricity, rice and saw mills, small enterprises producing implements and consumer goods, and joint ventures in garments. Laos's landlocked position makes access to foreign markets difficult; it exports only about one-third as much as it imports. Despite a healthy expansion in nontraditional exports (thanks to the economic reforms), the export sector remains dominated by electricity and wood, which represents respectively 28 percent and 40 percent of the total.

The transition to a market economy has by no means been smooth. After years of low inflation, the country experienced a flare-up in 1989: prices

Table 4-2. Terms of Trade Between Agriculture and Industry, 1985–1989 (1988 = 100).

	1985	1986	1987	1988	1989
Agricultural Prices	35.6	53.5	69.1	100.0	150.3
Industrial Prices	61.1	72.9	85.4	100.0	145.9
Terms of Trade	58.3	73.4	80.9	100.0	103.0

Source: World Bank estimates based on data provided by Lao PDR authorities.

Table 4-3. Income Account of the Various Sectors, 1986–1990 (% of GDP).

	1986	1987	1988	1989	1990
1. Private Sector					
1.1 Gross primary income	85.5	86.7	82.6	87.8	85.3
1.2 Current transfer to (−) other sectors	0.2	0.7	2.4	3.4	3.1
1.3 Disposable income (1.1 + 1.2)	85.7	87.5	85.0	91.1	88.3
(p.m. percentage changes at constant prices)	(7.9)	(−1.0)	(7.7)	(13.6)	(4.9)
2. Public Enterprises					
2.1 Gross primary income	10.8	10.8	2.4	0.8	2.7
2.2 Current transfer to (−) general government	−10.0	−10.1	−3.3	−1.7	−1.7
2.3 Disposable income (2.1 + 2.2)	0.8	0.7	−0.9	−1.0	1.0
3. General Government					
3.1 Gross primary income	2.0	1.8	9.0	6.9	9.7
3.2 Current transfer from the other sectors	10.0	10.3	3.0	0.5	0.4
3.3 Disposable income (3.1 + 3.2)	12.0	12.1	12.0	7.4	10.1
4. Rest of the World					
4.1 Gross primary income	0.7	1.3	4.3	4.9	3.1
4.2 Current transfer from the economy	−0.2	−0.9	−2.0	−1.4	−1.2
4.3 Disposable income (4.1 + 4.2)	0.5	0.5	2.3	3.5	1.9
5. Statistical Discrepancy	0.9	−0.7	1.6	−0.3	−0.8
6. Gross Domestic Product (1.1 + 2.1 + 3.1 + 4.1 + 5 or 1.3 + 2.3 + 3.3 + 4.3 + 5)	100.0	100.0	100.0	100.0	100.0

Source: World Bank estimates based on data provided by Lao PDR authorities.

accelerated at a 68 percent rate over the year (see Figure 4-1). The economy was on the brink of hyperinflation in the summer of that year, when remedial fiscal and monetary measures, as well as a substantial inflow of balance-of-payments support, eased inflationary tensions. From December 1989 to December 1990, inflation declined to about a 20 percent annual rate. Following the same trend, it declined to 12 percent by August 1991. However, the initial bout of inflation made visible some fundamental problems of the Lao economy that still continue to stifle its development.

First, it must be recognized that the Lao economy is inherently unstable. With about 70 percent of its exports concentrated in two products and more than 75 percent of its imports financed by foreign aid, the economy is highly vulnerable to external shocks like changes in international prices and quantity restrictions. In addition, authorities have limited control over the liquidity of the economy. The wide circulation of foreign cash in the country affords great latitude for currency substitution, a phenomenon that magnifies underlying imbalances. Nominal factors amplify real shocks.

Table 4-4. GDP by Category of Expenditure 1986–1990 (in constant 1988 prices).

	1986		1987		1988		1989		1990	
	(% GDP)	Growth Rate	(% GDP)	Growth Rate	(% GDP)	Growth Rate	(% GDP)	Growth Rate	(% GDP)	Growth Rate
Private Expenditure	(78.0)	7.9	(80.7)	−1.0	(84.2)	7.7	(86.4)	13.6	(86.1)	4.9
Public Consumption	(18.1)	−4.1	(16.8)	−11.6	(16.8)	3.1	(14.1)	−7.1	(13.0)	−2.6
Government	(16.0)	8.6	(14.5)	−13.4	(12.4)	−11.5	(9.0)	−19.5	(10.1)	17.1
Non-profit institutions	(2.1)	−49.2	(2.3)	2.2	(4.3)	96.6	(5.0)	28.4	(2.9)	−38.0
Public Investment	(18.4)	0.0	(18.4)	−4.5	(15.2)	−14.7	(15.5)	12.8	(15.4)	4.7
Government	(17.9)	−0.2	(17.4)	−7.1	(13.7)	−18.7	(13.7)	10.6	(13.6)	4.7
Public enterprises	(0.5)	7.7	(1.0)	91.3	(1.5)	54.8	(1.8)	32.8	(1.8)	5.3
Total Domestic Demand	(114.5)	4.5	(115.9)	−3.3	(116.2)	3.5	(116.0)	10.5	(114.5)	4.0
Exports	(12.3)	1.4	(12.8)	−0.4	(12.5)	0.7	(13.3)	17.8	(14.8)	16.7
Total Final Demand	(126.9)	4.2	(128.7)	−3.0	(128.7)	3.2	(129.3)	11.2	(129.3)	5.3
(Less) Imports	(−26.9)	−7.1	(−28.7)	2.1	(−28.7)	3.2	(−29.3)	13.2	(−29.3)	5.3
Gross Domestic Product	(100.0)	7.7	(100.0)	−4.3	(100.0)	3.2	(100.0)	10.7	(100.0)	5.3

Source: World Bank estimates based on data provided by Lao PDR authorities.

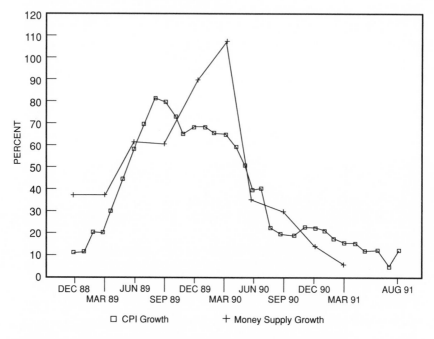

Figure 4-1. *Domestic Money and Inflation: Annual Rate of Growth.*

of GDP in 1986 to a negative 3.3 percent in 1989 (see Table 4-5). While the government endeavored to adapt its tax system to the new situation (with initial success in indirect taxes), the fall in state-enterprise profits was so deep that consolidated public-revenue mobilization dropped from 13.2 percent of GDP in 1986 to 7.8 percent in 1989. Government and state enterprises responded differently to the resulting resource squeeze: the government cut its expenditures; the state enterprises turned to the banking sector. Accommodation of the latter's financing requirements was the driving force behind the inflation flare-up. And its curtailment, by and large, explains the recent stabilization.

This poor revenue performance can be traced largely to previous inefficiencies in public-resource mobilization and heavy reliance on economic distortions benefiting state enterprises. Under the former system of central economic management, mobilization of public-sector resources depended primarily on: (1) the forced procurement of goods at below-market prices and exchange rates by government and state enterprises, and (2) the generation of gross operating surpluses in state enterprises, whose size was determined partly by these forced levies and partly by direct controls over public-sector wages. Price distortions therefore concealed the vast inefficiency of state enterprises. The economic rents so captured allowed state

Table 4-5. Public-Sector Consolidated Accounts, 1986–1990 (% of GDP).

Resources

	1986	1987	1988	1989	1990
A. Revenues	13.2	13.0	11.7	7.8	12.8
I. Fiscal Revenues	12.4	12.3	12.6	8.8	11.8
1. Taxes	1.2	1.3	10.4	7.4	7.9
1.1 Direct taxes	0.5	0.4	3.3	1.8	1.8
Companies	0.5	0.4	3.3	1.8	1.8
Individuals	—	—	—	—	—
1.2 Indirect Taxes	0.8	0.8	7.2	5.6	6.1
2. Nontax Revenues[1]	11.1	11.0	2.1	1.4	3.9
II. Public-Enterprise Gross Savings	0.8	0.7	-0.9	-1.0	1.0
B. Financing (net)	5.7	9.5	16.6	17.8	17.1
2.1 Foreign (net)	5.5	10.7	17.6	17.8	17.6
Official	5.2	10.3	15.9	15.8	15.6
Private	0.2	0.4	1.7	1.9	2.0
2.2 Domestic (net)	0.2	-1.2	-1.0	0.1	-0.5
C. Total	18.9	22.5	28.3	25.6	29.9
Memo item: Public-Sector Gross savings	2.5	2.7	-1.4	-3.3	-1.8

Uses

	1986	1987	1988	1989	1990
A. Current Expenditures	10.7	10.3	13.0	11.1	14.6
1.1 Wages	3.4	3.3	5.5	5.4	7.5
1.2 Goods and services	7.0	6.8	6.9	4.3	5.5
1.3 Pensions	0.0	0.0	0.1	0.7	1.0
1.4 Interest	0.3	0.1	0.5	0.7	0.7
B. Capital Expenditures	8.2	12.2	15.2	14.6	15.3
2.1 Government	7.7	11.2	13.7	12.8	13.5
2.2 Public enterprises	0.5	1.0	1.5	1.8	1.8
C. Total	18.9	22.5	28.3	25.6	29.9

[1] excluding depreciation transfers

Source: World Bank estimates based on data provided by Lao PDR authorities.

enterprises to hide operational inefficiencies, like poor quality, and transfer their costs to the rest of the economy (through suboptimal growth performance) and to future generations (through deferral of rehabilitation and modernization of productive capacities and infrastructure or overexploitation of natural resources—for example, overlogging).

State-enterprise profitability was the necessary victim of the pricing-policy and trade reforms. The liberalizing of prices and floating of the exchange rate, combined with trade liberalization, produced a reduction of gross margins; most state enterprises could not adjust their selling prices enough to recoup the higher cost of their inputs and wage payments. Industrial enterprises, handicapped by obsolete equipment and techniques, lacked the cost- and quality-competitiveness to match the stepped-up competition from abroad. And state enterprises in the service sector were faced with more dynamic private enterprises.

In addition, the policy of freeing wages and leaving the disposition of after-tax profits to the workers caused a decline in the distributive share of profits. Price and exchange-rate liberalization was bound to produce a one-shot adjustment in the level of gross profits, corresponding to the transfer of rents back to the private sector. Liberalization does not explain the further decline in state-enterprise profitability in 1989. The culprit was state-enterprise wages, which started to accelerate and absorb an increasing share of the remaining gross income, once the corset of central regulation had disappeared. With no external claim on their profits, decentralized state enterprises sought to maximize their workers' income rather than ensure an adequate return on the assets entrusted to them by the nation.

The shrinking profitability ricocheted on the budget: state-enterprise transfers to the budget declined by an estimated 7.3 percent of GDP from 1986 to 1989. In addition, the abolition of forced procurement at administered prices and exchange rates cost the current budget an amount that equaled 4.9 percent of GDP over the same period. Furthermore, the fiscal and administrative decentralization made the squeeze even worse on the central government. While rich provinces were keeping the best part of their revenues for themselves, Vientiane, notwithstanding the autonomy principle, had to come to the rescue of the poorer provinces to maintain a minimum level of public services there. On the whole, however, in contrast to state enterprises, the government adjusted its expenditures to meet its constrained resources. The result was a reduction in all categories of expenditure by a cumulative 27 percent in real terms from 1986 to 1990.

The financing of this growing public-sector deficit led initially to an unsustainable monetary expansion; broad money grew by as much as 90 percent in 1989. Major weaknesses of decentralization became evident. Like the rest of the country, the banking sector was organized on a provincial basis. Each province had its own branch of the state bank, and the provincial authorities nominated the bank's management. Provincial banks were pursuing their credit policies without orders from the central authorities; the authorities controlled the banks mainly by rationing the delivery of currency.

Experience in China shows how the decentralization of a banking system complicates credit policy. Since regulated interest rates do not reflect the scarcity of savings, credit has to be rationed, mainly by informal means. In a decentralized system, this creates a cooperation dilemma. Economic control is a national issue, but for local governments, it is someone else's problem. Each province tries to maximize its own income but hopes that other provinces will reduce their credit demand to prevent inflation. In addition, in Lao PDR, the autonomy of banks vis-à-vis state-enterprise supervisory agencies was very limited: the agencies could compel the banks to finance state enterprises, irrespective of their financial performance.

In China and in Lao PDR, central authorities have historically been weak—in both cases for geographical reasons (the large size of the country or difficult terrain) and because consensus building between the central and provincial levels of government is the main form of political decision making. The ensuing bargaining process tends to lead to excessive credit expansion if central authorities lack the clout to resist provincial demands or the instruments to curb them.

Furthermore, this institutional setting severely hinders the buildup of savings. The physical restriction to the issuance of currency has created a deep-rooted mistrust of the banks, arising from the fact that sight deposits cannot be turned into cash when currency rationing becomes binding. The population therefore prefers to hold onto any other form of savings instrument, like foreign notes, precious metals, and real assets.

The authorities fortunately moved quickly to suppress the inflation flare-up in 1989. Traditional instruments initially brought about the stabilization of the economy after the summer of 1989. The June 1989 tax reform reversed the deterioration of the fiscal situation, while the decision in August of that year to keep interest rates positive in real terms curtailed the demand for credit. The disposable income of the public sector thus regained about 4.7 percent of GDP in 1990, making room for some improvement in civil servants' salaries and permitting some recovery in public savings (from − 3.3 percent of GDP in 1989 to − 1.8 percent in 1990). Furthermore, the inflow of external balance-of-payments support, combined with a recovery in electricity and log exports, stabilized the exchange rate, thereby reducing the incentive for currency substitution.

A decisive, albeit atypical, action was the rationing of currency issuance. Inflation plunged almost immediately. Unfortunately, this success came at a very high cost: a dramatic erosion in the (already low) public confidence in the banks. Local currency deposits had declined at the end of 1990 to only 18 percent (1.8 percent of GDP) from 31 percent of broad money (3 percent of GDP) at the end of 1987.[6]

The Prospects for Laos

Thanks to the country's rich endowment of fertile land and its extremely low population density, Laos has the potential for sustained growth. However, it will materialize only with a determined effort to advance the education, enhance the health, and raise the productivity of the population, all of which are among the worst in Asia. This will require sustained investment in social as well as physical infrastructure. The effort will require domestic savings, private or public. But despite the rapid increase in private disposable income since the initiation of reforms, the mobilization of private financial savings is hampered by the public's deep mistrust of the banks and the burgeoning private demand in consumption and housing, long pent up during the years when conspicuous spending could mean political trouble. The public sector is thus the logical source for the needed savings. While 1990 saw a slight improvement in public savings, thanks principally to the credit squeeze put on state enterprises, the road to recovery is still long.

Just as important, serious regional disparities that have emerged from decentralization policies threaten national integrity and would probably already have caused irredentism to resurface were it not for the integrating role of the only two national institutions: the party and the army. These regional disparities could even become a crippling obstacle to any political opening. Since the civil war, the army, and to a lesser extent the Laotian Communist party, has found its main backing among the ethnic minorities, mainly Lao Theung, disgruntled by the neglect shown to them by ethnic Lao. The reform process has recreated a situation where the ethnic Lao are getting richer while the minorities, who dominate the outlying provinces, are being left behind.

The New Economic Mechanism is therefore incomplete. Three issues need to be revisited: the country's territorial organization, the status of enterprises, and the restoration of public finances. Recent policy actions and the

---

[6]Broad money is currency in circulation and bank deposits.

outcome of the Fifth Party Congress indicate that the leadership understands the issues that require attention. The rejuvenation of the leadership at the Fifth Party Congress, after about 40 years of no change, may give it fresh political stamina to carry out the ambitious endeavors necessary to complete economic reform.

The congress strongly reaffirmed the party's commitment to a market economy: ". . . Our country's economic structure is that of a market economy bearing many forms of ownership and organizations with different levels and sizes, all enjoying equality before the Law. . . . Another basic approach of our Party towards the economy is to continue to renovate economic policies and economic management mechanisms. First of all, it is to continue to eradicate the remnants of the centralized bureaucratic management mechanism using market-oriented policies and promoting the strong development of the market economy. . . . Within this mechanism, the State will not directly manage business units but will concentrate on playing its role in macroeconomic adjustment with economic instruments and on a firm legal basis" (free translation of the Political Report of the Executive Committee to the Fifth Party Congress, Lao PDR).

With respect to territorial organization, the process of restoring central control has started. It has moved fastest in banking. Over the last two years, the former State Bank of Lao PDR has been turned into a central bank—the Bank of the Lao PDR—and its provincial branches have been merged into multiprovince commercial banks. Putting these banks at an arm's length from the provincial governments and their enterprises undoubtedly helped drastically curtail credit to state enterprises.

With regard to state enterprises, remedial action to counter their disappointing performance under "market socialism" has been initiated: since mid-1989, the government has embarked on a state-enterprise privatization program, first on an experimental basis in the Prefecture of Vientiane and then as a national policy with the Privatization Decree of March 1990. Efforts are also under way to reassert the shareholder prerogatives of the state vis-à-vis its enterprises. With the benefit of hindsight, the "decentralized socialism" system may therefore one day appear as just a transition phase between central planning and (state and private) capitalism.

In the wake of a national conference on public finances held in July 1990, the government is trying to recentralize fiscal prerogatives. The undertaking is risky because it runs counter to well-entrenched provincial interests. Quite apart from the political implications of this process, its economic stakes are high: the provinces still collect and control about half the fiscal revenues. The government is therefore at the mercy of a tax strike that could rock the economy.

Given the already dismal situation in public services, the restoration of public finances will have to rely on revenue increases. The situation in public services, however, hinders revenue mobilization. In the absence of visible improvement, it would be hard to explain to taxpayers what they were paying for. Expenditure rationalization through administrative reforms and a drastic reduction in the bloated civil service, with a view to freeing resources for enhancing basic public services, is therefore a necessary complement to resource-mobilization efforts.

The task ahead is huge, but all indicators show that the country has benefited from the boldness of reforms. By proceeding swiftly, Laos avoided the sequencing dilemmas that have plagued more gradual approaches to liberalization. In these other cases, market mechanisms and administrative regulations led to market segmentation and aggravated prevailing economic imbalances. But a rapid transition has its drawbacks too: it strains financial structures and administrative capacities. A sudden price liberalization, for instance, forces an immediate reallocation of profits across sectors and causes a deterioration of bank portfolios for which banks are ill prepared. If the institutional framework cannot keep pace with reforms (due, for example, to an absence of foreclosure procedures or undercapitalization), the available options tend to be limited to two evils: large-scale defaults or bailouts. Moreover, some reforms, like tax reform, require careful analysis because of technical complexity or cross-sectoral implications. There is then a trade off between the speed with which reforms are undertaken and the quality of their design and consistency.

The expression "big bang," which I used to describe the Laotian approach early in this chapter, would be misleading if it pointed toward a sudden revelation instead of the climax of a gradual awakening. It would be unwise to believe that the reforms were prepared on the drawing board with a careful weighing of the design, the interconnection and sequencing of policy actions. These concepts, which are intellectually associated with adjustment policies, do not describe the way Laos has made system changes. Of course, it would be useful and/or desirable to follow such a rational approach; but events unfold in a way that leaves policy-makers little room for such an armchair exercise.

Once a critical stage is reached, economic reforms acquire their own momentum and policymakers find themselves overtaken by the logic they have unleashed. Difficulties emerge that require another set of changes that while perhaps not desired, must be implemented, otherwise the leadership may forfeit the whole process. Even forfeiture may not truly be possible, because when the embrace of the state loosens, a civil society quickly develops and starts evolving under its own momentum. The movement toward change even grabs hold of political institutions by offering fresh opportunities to members of the establishment to look after their private or family interests. Once the process has begun, even authoritarian institutions are left with few choices other than "riding the tiger."

The most obvious lesson to draw from the Lao reforms is that the fiscal situation is the weakest link in the chain. This is so because in a socialist system the government manipulates prices administratively to make them the main instrument of resource mobilization. Removal of price "distortions" implies abandoning this powerful instrument. While the efficiency gains from fiscal reforms are undoubtedly great, such reforms will inevitably cause economic imbalances if no effective substitute is in place. Unfortunately, well-administered tax systems and sound financial institutions are not created by the stroke of a pen.

This leads to a final consideration, which is that economic reforms necessitate government reforms. In tandem with the emergence of a "new" civil society, the country needs to create a modern state. The Lao leadership calls this replacing the rule of the party with the rule of law. It implies establishing of a secure environment for social transactions and also developing instruments to collect taxes, manage the budget, administer the civil service, supervise state enterprise and local governments, and implement program development policies. All these instruments are required to guide the economy through universal rules rather than through progressively weaker party fiat.

Acknowledgments

This paper is the fruit of an intense collaboration with my colleagues at the World Bank. I am particularly indebted to Klaus Lorch for his contribution on state enterprises and banking and to Su-Yong Song for the quantitative analysis. The views presented here are strictly my own and should not be interpreted as reflecting those of the World Bank.

References

Brown, MacAlister and Joseph J. Zasloff. 1985. *Apprentice Revolutionaries: The Communist Movement in Laos, 1930–1985*. Stanford: Hoover Institution Press.

Calvocoressi, Peter, Guy Wing, and John Pritchard. 1989. *Total War (Volume 2): The Greater East Asian and Pacific Conflict*. Revised second edition. New York: Pantheon Books.

Deuve, Jean. 1984. *Le Royaume du Laos, 1945-1965: histoire événementielle de l'indépendence à la guerre américaine.* Paris: Ecole Française d'Extrême Orient.

Dommen, Arthur J. 1985. *Laos: Keystone to Indochina.* Boulder: Westview Press.

Evans, Grant. 1988. "Agrarian Change in Communist Laos." Occasional Papers Series No. 85. Singapore: Institute of Southeast Asian Studies.

Gunn, Geoffrey C. 1988. *Political Struggles in Laos, 1930-1954.* Bangkok: Editions Duang Kamol.

Marx, Karl. 1965. *Pre-Capitalist Economic Formations.* From the "Grundisse" Manuscript, 1857-58. New York: International Publishers.

Stuart-Fox, Martin. 1982. *Laos: Studies in the Politics and Society of the Lao People's Democratic Republic.* St. Lucia: University of Queensland Press; New York: St. Martin's Press.

———. 1986. *Laos: Politics, Economics and Society.* London: Frances Pinter; Boulder: Linne Rienner.

Taillard, Christian. 1989. *Laos: Statégies d'un Etat-tampon.* Montpellier: G.I.P. Reclus.

Yenal, Oktay. 1989. *Chinese Reforms, Inflation and the Allocation of Investment in a Socialist Economy.* Washington, D.C.: The World Bank Asia Regional Series.

5

"Beyond Suffering": The Recent History of a Cambodian Village

May Ebihara

In 1989, I had the extraordinary experience of returning to a Khmer village that I had not seen since I conducted anthropological fieldwork there in 1959–60. To my astonishment, the village, as well as several dozen people I had known, had survived the turmoil of the intervening decades. I have already described elsewhere my first brief, intensely moving reunion with the village I call Sobay (Ebihara, 1990). During subsequent trips to Cambodia in the summers of 1990 and 1991, I reestablished bonds with the villagers, whose warmth and hospitality remained undiminished by the traumas they had endured.

Thirty years ago, Sobay, located southwest of Phnom Penh in Kandal province, had some 790 inhabitants living in three hamlets (called West, Middle, and East). My original fieldwork centered on West Hamlet with about 159 people in 32 households, and it is these villagers on whom I continue to focus in my current research. I have now seen almost all the hamlet's survivors who still live in the region or in Phnom Penh, and I have also conducted interviews with descendants of people I knew in 1959–60. West Sobay is the name now given to Middle and West Hamlets when they were merged under the People's Republic of Kampuchea shortly after the 1979 fall of Democratic Kampuchea—better known as the Khmer Rouge regime.

In 1959–60, virtually all of West Sobay's villagers were peasant wet-rice cultivators. They grew rice mostly for consumption rather than the market because they had only small landholdings averaging about one hectare per household. Men and women individually owned means of production (land, draft animals, tools, and so on), as well as other kinds of property. The family was the primary unit of production and consumption; each cultivated its fields using mainly its own labor, buttressed with mutual, cooperative aid from kin and neighbors during the busiest farming seasons. Although most families were largely subsistence cultivators, they were also part of a market economy insofar as they depended on purchasing various necessities and selling produce or labor. Most families were poor but not destitute; they kept themselves afloat with various part-time pursuits to earn cash.

The village formed a social unit as an aggregate of kinsmen, neighbors, and friends. Various bonds of affection, loyalty, and mutual aid also extended beyond the village to relatives on both sides of the family. Religion was an integral and critical part of village life. Sobay had its own Buddhist temple compound (*wat*), with resident monks, that served as a moral and social center. Politically, Sobay and its village chief formed the lowest rung of an administrative ladder that rose through various territorial levels to the central government in Phnom Penh and, ultimately, to Prince Norodom Sihanouk, who evoked considerable respect and loyalty from Sobay villagers in 1959–60.

The Late 1960s and Early 1970s

In Cambodia, the late 1960s were a time of increasing difficulties, including a deteriorating economy, mounting dissatisfaction with the Sihanouk government, emergence of the insurgent Khmer Rouge, and repercussions from the war in neighboring Vietnam. Sobay villagers, however, look back on the 1960s, in contrast to what followed, as something akin to a golden age when people had "enough" for survival and had peace. The Lon Nol coup, which appeared to Western observers to be a major political event, did not mean much to the villagers, despite their previous loyalty to Sihanouk. As one villager put it, "What does it matter who the leader [of the country] is? What matters is war."[1] And, indeed, the civil war between the rebel Khmer Rouge forces and the Lon Nol government was the first blow in the fracturing of Sobay.

One of the early Khmer Rouge strongholds was southwestern Cambodia (Vickery, 1984; Kiernan, 1985). Prior to 1970, however, the Khmer Rouge had not infiltrated into Sobay itself. Villagers said there were some rebels "in the wilderness (*prey*)"[2] to the south near the border between Kandal and Takeo provinces, but the Khmer Rouge were not yet firmly entrenched and would "come and go." The fact that some Lon Nol army troops were quartered near Sobay evidently kept the insurgents from visiting the village.

---

[1]This and subsequent quotations are translations from the Khmer. Some are virtually verbatim quotes, while others are close approximations or edited translations of what was said. To protect informant confidentiality, I do not give the names of informants who are quoted.

[2]The term *prey* can be variously translated as forest, jungle, wilderness, or uninhabited area. The Khmer Rouge initially came out of, and in some places still inhabit, forested mountain regions known as *prey*.

In the early 1970s, however, the Khmer Rouge began making forays into this region, and villagers were caught in crossfire between rebel and government troops. In 1970–71, two respected elders in West Hamlet were accidentally killed by gunshots, and several houses were demolished by artillery shells. The insurgents also captured some people and took them south to Khmer Rouge bases. Such incidents caused villagers to flee Sobay in the early 1970s. Most escaped to the relative security of Phnom Penh, although some 25 families in other hamlets elected to move to Khmer Rouge communities to the south because they thought they could not earn a living in the city. Therefore, Sobay was almost empty during the Nixon-Kissinger "strategic bombings" of the Cambodian countryside in the summer of 1973, during which the area around a nearby market town (hotly contested by Khmer Rouge and Lon Nol troops) was at one point bombed every day for an entire week. Although the bombs were intended to destroy rebel bases, in fact, the flight of villagers from this region left it open for the Khmer Rouge to enter and establish themselves there during 1974 and early 1975.

In Phnom Penh, the villagers scattered to different parts of the city (often settling near one another or otherwise maintaining contact) and eked out whatever existence was possible: pedaling bicycle-cabs, raising and vending vegetables, working as construction laborers, and the like. A number of able-bodied men became Lon Nol soldiers, whether through conscription or voluntary enlistment. Life in the capitol was not easy: it was bursting with other refugees from the countryside. Inflation soared, food became scarce, and artillery bombardments raked the city as the Khmer Rouge closed in on it. One former Sobay woman lost all of her four children when her house was shelled, and another elderly villager died from wounds suffered in an artillery attack. Finally, there was no more refuge when the Khmer Rouge marched into Phnom Penh on April 17, 1975.

Democratic Kampuchea

The Democratic Kampuchean (DK) regime instituted by the Khmer Rouge undertook radical transformations to create a new revolutionary society free from class exploitation and "colonialist-imperialist" foreign domination. In its attempt to establish an egalitarian social order, reconstruct a war-torn economy, and maximize agricultural production, DK evacuated urban centers and turned virtually the entire population into peasantry. It reorganized people into cooperatives with communal ownership, production, and distribution, and replaced the family/household with work teams as the basic socioeconomic unit. The DK declared Buddhism to be feudalistic and exploitive and crushed it, replacing it with a political ideology propounding new values and codes of behavior that extended to modes of proper dress and demeanor. The DK expected strict obedience and discipline in all aspects of life and punished infractions through criticism sessions, beatings, imprisonment, and even executions. From an ostensibly classless society, a new sociopolitical hierarchy emerged, dominated by DK cadre and "old people" or "base people"—that is, those who had come from DK base regions under Khmer Rouge control before 1975, or people from the "basic" classes of poor and lower-middle peasantry. These persons were given a superior status to "new people" from urban centers or areas "liberated" only as of 1975.

In talking to Sobay villagers, I did not expect to discover anything dramatically new about the DK regime under Pol Pot. Rather, I wanted to explore their reactions to conditions during DK, particularly in view of some suggestions (e.g., Vickery, 1984, p. 121; Twining, 1989, p. 131) that peasants would not have found DK as difficult as did urban upper- and middle-class evacuees because villagers were already familiar with agriculture and accustomed to manual labor, a spartan diet, and meager living conditions. Another question was whether Sobay villagers might have been treated less harshly than were urbanites from higher social classes because, under DK, lower and lower-middle level peasants were the politically correct strata. As Vickery (1984, p. 121) states, "peasants . . . should not have had trouble either due to class background or inability to do the work required." The accounts of Sobay villagers indicate, however, that they found life in DK to be as horrendous as did city people from more comfortable socioeconomic strata. In discussing the Pol Pot period, villagers constantly used such expressions as, "It was all suffering," and "It was beyond suffering."

The villagers' first taste of DK came shortly after April 17, 1975, when Khmer Rouge soldiers ordered people to leave Phnom Penh, ostensibly because Americans were coming to bomb the city. Virtually everyone from Sobay set out to return there, taking only bare necessities because they had been told they could return to the capitol in three days. Although Sobay was only 30 kilometers distant, the journey turned out to be circuitous, protracted (sometimes taking several weeks), and painful. Some experienced the anguish of seeing an aged mother, husband, or siblings suddenly swept away in a crowd of people who were arbitrarily ordered to go off in a different direction by Khmer Rouge soldiers. These villagers still do not know what happened to some of their relatives, only that they never saw them again.

When people eventually reached Sobay, they found a bombed-out landscape that was now largely wilderness—and a number of DK cadres. While the villagers had expected to resettle on their familial lands, the DK did not permit them to stay in Sobay but instead sent them to an uninhabited prey region to the south to clear the land and build shelters for themselves. Hundreds of evacuees spent several months there, camped on a barren landscape, with little water, under a blazing summer sun. Scarcity of food and medicine caused numerous deaths from starvation or illness.

When the villagers were permitted to return to Sobay, they found it had been (symbolically) renamed New Village. The cadre also labeled them "new people," "April 17 people," "Lon Nol people," or, more ominously, "the enemy." The villagers found themselves under suspicion because they had fled to Phnom Penh instead of joining the revolutionary forces. The Khmer Rouge tried continually to ferret out people's socioeconomic backgrounds by collecting written personal histories, questioning individuals (even children) about others, and sometimes exposing people to the bites of red ants. Although the villagers answered truthfully that they were peasants, they were suspected or accused of having been Lon Nol soldiers, urbanites from higher social classes, or even CIA. One villager related an exchange he had with DK cadre when he was ill:

> They said, "The reason you're sick is that you're used to living well." I replied, "How can you say that? I've been a farmer all my life." They said, "You're used to living in comfort and never worked hard. We fought all the battles and liberated you. You just came here with your two empty hands and your empty stomach. So *we* have the right to tell you what to do; what *we* say, goes."

People from 25 of the 32 households I had known in West Sobay managed to return. Former Sobay residents were mixed with other new people evacuees. The DK old people, cadre, and the soldiers now governed their lives. In late 1975 and 1976, however, about half the families originally from West Sobay were moved south to various communes near the border with Takeo province. Subsequently, a number of people (including some formerly from West Sobay) were sent to Pursat, a northwestern province where conditions were very harsh. Few people survived. There were similar relocations throughout Kampuchea as DK deployed labor power to various parts of the country (Vickery, 1984, pp. 82–83). Obviously, these moves ruptured people's ties to their home communities, familial lands, kin, and friends.

The DK divided the country as a whole into territorial-administrative units called zones. Sobay was located in the Southwest Zone, which had been a stronghold of the Pol Pot faction of the Kampuchean Communist party and a region in which conditions were severe compared with zones administered by more moderate factions (Kiernan, 1980, 1985; Vickery, 1984). At the local level, the DK regime enlarged and institutionalized the prerevolutionary tradition of mutual aid and labor exchange (whereby villagers formed temporary cooperative groups for the busiest cultivation periods) by organizing virtually the entire populace into permanent work teams. Organized on the basis of age and gender, these teams were made up of work groups of the elderly, mature adults, younger adults and adolescents, and children, with each work group divided in turn into male and female units. A military model underlay the organization, regimenting the work both literally and figuratively. Labor teams were designated "shock troops," "platoons," and the like; behavior was subject to extreme order, uniformity, and discipline (Carney, 1987; Vickery, 1984).

The restructuring of society obviously affected family life. While couples supposedly lived together (in tiny huts that contrasted unfavorably with larger family homes before 1975), they worked separately during the day and came together only at night. Young husbands and wives were sometimes placed in teams working in different locales, so that these couples met for only a few hours once every 10 days, when political meetings were held during the ostensible day of rest. Adolescents and young adults were organized into mobile teams sent to various parts of the country, wherever labor was needed, and hence seldom saw their parents. Youngsters past the age of six or seven were also separated from their families and put into children's teams that lived and worked together in the commune. Sometimes children were literally wrested away, as was the case with one woman and her daughter. The woman said:

> [When the DK cadre came to get my child,] they took her hand and pulled her away. I grabbed onto her other hand and cried out, "A child should stay with its mother!" But they said, "No!" and yanked her away.

This tug-of-war, with a terrified child in the middle, symbolizes not only the DK attempt to suppress the sentiments and bonds of what they called "family-ism" (Kiernan, 1983, pp. 182–83, although cf. Vickery, 1984, pp. 174ff.), but also their focus on youth as a special target for indoctrination into revolutionary ideology. As a corollary, the customary status of the old and young was reversed: parents and elders, who once were accorded respect, were now seen as survivors of the old reactionary regime, while youths were elevated as the bearers of a new revolutionary order.

Another manifestation of the state's replacement of parents was the phenomenon of forced marriages, in which DK cadre arbitrarily paired off men and women. Several young West Sobay couples were married in this manner. A woman wryly described one such instance:

> [People were gathered together and the DK cadre] said, "You're going to marry so-and-so." You'd just grab [each other's] hands, and that was it—you

were married. Afterward, you might forget whom you were married to because you'd seen the person only once.

In conversations with villagers about the DK regime, one of the most (possibly *the* most) frequent subjects was lack of food. With the collectivization of property and labor, the collection and distribution of produce became centralized. Rice and other food crops were sent to certain storehouses; from there, some produce (especially rice) went to the state, while other produce was supposed to feed commune members. In 1976–77, the government instituted communal dining halls and forbade cooking or keeping food at home. As Kiernan (1980) has noted, the state, by this means, could then control food distribution down to bedrock level and extract more produce. The state could also maintain greater control over the population by preventing food storage for escapes and by meting out daily rewards and punishment, in the form of food, for conduct. The state (and local cadre) gradually increased its appropriation of produce at the expense of ordinary people. Sobay villagers said repeatedly, with anger and bewilderment, that there *was* food, but not for them. The villagers recounted:

> They [the DK cadre] caught fish to eat; we'd see the fish, but they wouldn't even give us the fish bones. They said, "Why do you need fish? You've got some *trokuen* [an aquatic plant] in your soup. The fish swim by and brush against the *trokuen*, so you're getting the taste of fish." . . . We worked so hard planting and harvesting; there were piles of rice as big as this house, but they took it away in trucks. We raised chickens and ducks and vegetables and fruit, but they took it all. You'd be killed if you tried to take anything for yourself. You could *see* food, but you weren't allowed to eat it.

Villagers said that one commune to the south had adequate food at the beginning of the DK period, although Sobay seems to have had little food from the outset. After about 1977, people lived primarily on rice gruel (*boboo*) that was mostly water, soup made from foraged plants, and occasional handouts of beans or corn. Villagers spoke of being constantly famished, scavenging for anything edible, sometimes stealing food (although this was clearly dangerous), and being reduced to eating even rice husks that were once considered "food for pigs." In addition, food in the communal dining halls was doled out in small quantities and tied to meeting work requirements. No labor meant little or no food, so even the sick would drag themselves to work to get something to eat.

A second theme in villagers' accounts is unrelenting and arduous work. In its desire to restore and increase agricultural productivity after the ravages of war and to create a largely self-sufficient economy, the DK set people to work on intensive cultivation, on the construction of large-scale irrigation projects intended to reduce dependence on rainfall and produce several harvests a year,[3] and on rationalizing the layout of paddy fields (formerly broken up into parcels of varying size and shape) into huge rectangular plots of a hectare or more. The villagers thus found themselves driven to unceasing work: plowing, transplanting, and harvesting rice fields (particularly in areas where more than one crop a year could be grown); planting vegetables and fruit trees; digging irrigation canals; reshaping the paddy fields; tending cattle; collecting night soil for fertilizer; gathering palm leaves for thatching, and so on. As soon as people finished one task, they were dispatched to do something else. Work hours varied somewhat depending on the type of work team and activities, but labor often began at dawn and sometimes continued into the night, with brief stops for lunch and dinner but no other breaks. Some groups received one day off for every 10 days of work, but political meetings occupied several hours of the "rest" day. The work was difficult, even for peasants who had experienced hard labor. Some of them recounted the hardships:

> You'd [carry] heavy loads, fall down, get up and fall again. . . . Even when you were sick, you didn't dare stop working because they'd kill you. So you kept working until you collapsed. You'd come back at night, brush off your feet, and fall into bed. . . . [But sometimes there was little sleep. In the darkness, you might sneak out to search for food or bury people who had died, or,] you'd lie awake thinking of all the people who had died. . . . You lay there and wept.

It is not surprising that sickness and death also loom large in the villagers' accounts. While the Khmer Rouge demolished the village temple, they left standing the meeting hall (*salaa*) in the temple compound and turned it into a hospital. People did not trust the Khmer Rouge medicines, however, and would often discard medication or run away from the hospital. It is said that hundreds of people died in and are buried near the hospital. Physical ailments were endemic during DK. Children had swollen faces and feet, while their bodies were mere skin and bones. Scrapes and punctures acquired during the course of work became badly infected. Many women ceased to menstruate because of the hard labor and malnutrition, and several women said that their uteruses fell. One woman recalled that her uterus fell out when she was

---

[3]During DK, youth work teams, using no machinery, built a large dam about 6 kilometers to the northwest on the Prek Tnaot river, with some irrigation canals running into parts of Sobay. Thus, certain fields in this area (as well as in some communes to the south with other sources of water) did yield two or more rice crops a year. At present, the irrigation system is in disrepair and inoperative in Sobay, but the Mennonite Central Committee has been working with the Cambodian government to reconstruct it. Work is going slowly because of shortage of funds.

working in the fields. Afraid to cut it off, she pushed it back inside, plugged herself up with a piece of lime, and continued to work until she collapsed. Even now, people report that they suffer from constant exhaustion, difficulty in walking, faulty memory, impaired vision, and other physical problems that they attribute to the hard labor or beatings suffered during DK. They explained several deaths among villagers since 1979 as due to the lingering aftereffects of illnesses that developed during the DK regime.

In the villagers' discussions, death during the time of DK is a recurring topic. The Sobay villagers attributed many deaths to starvation, beginning in 1975 after the evacuation from Phnom Penh and continuing throughout the DK regime. People said that the elderly, in particular, could not endure the lack of food, and even hardier adults succumbed when malnutrition was combined with exhausting labor or illness. In other cases, people lost the will to live. One woman described her daughter's death this way: "She just gave up; she didn't want to struggle any more; she just gave up and died."

Even more frightening for the villagers were the deaths of people who were "taken away." These incidents increased during the widespread purges in 1977 and 1978: the Pol Pot faction of the Kampuchean Communist party not only eliminated rival DK cadre but also killed ordinary people who, for inexplicable reasons, became suspect. These seemingly arbitrary murders of common folk were perhaps a strategy of terrorism designed to suppress dissent. One man recalls:

> From 1977 on, people were taken away to be killed (*vay chaol*). Many died at a prison [to the south] that was a headquarters of the Pol Pot people. [After DK] they found lots of corpses in a ditch; some of them still had ropes on their hands and feet and blindfolds on their eyes. [One day in 1977, seven men in Sobay] were taken away. [The Khmer Rouge] said, "Come on, load up everything, you're being taken to build houses." They lied. They didn't tell you they were going to kill you; they said you're going to work. But I knew. C [one of the young men being taken] also knew. He cried and embraced his father. I went up to C, and he said to me, "We're about to be separated now; I'm going." When people were taken away, I knew in my heart they were going to die. I knew when they were taken away with their hands tied behind their backs, but also when they were called away to work. I kept thinking, when will *I* be taken away? But you couldn't ask, and you couldn't run away—or even kill yourself—because then they'd get your wife and children.

Villagers also spoke of how, at harvest time in late 1978, the Khmer Rouge had planned to invite people in the area to a big feast and serve them poisoned noodles, but were thwarted by Vietnamese troops coming into the region. They also spoke of how the Khmer Rouge called people in western provinces to political sessions and then blew them up with mines planted in the meeting grounds. Regardless of whether these stories are true or apocryphal, they express the common feelings that "The Khmer Rouge considered the April 17 people to be totally expendable. They said, 'You were on the Lon Nol/American side; we don't need you.' They used us without a thought as to whether we lived or died."

The death toll was high. In 1960, West Sobay had some 159 inhabitants. Of these, 16 died before 1970 of old age or illness, while four more died in the early 1970s because of the civil war. This left 139 remaining villagers, of whom 70 (50 percent) died during DK. Of these 70 deaths, 39 (56 percent) were male; men evidently suffered higher mortality because they were more likely to die from starvation and executions (Boua, 1982). Of the West Sobay families that lived in 1975, some perished completely, and others were left with only one or a few survivors. There is no one who did not experience the deaths of close family members—whether parents, grandparents, siblings, spouse or children—during DK.

After 1979

The nightmare of DK ended in early 1979 when the Vietnamese entered Cambodia, captured Phnom Penh, and pushed DK forces toward the Thai border. In the renewal of fighting and dislocation, people scattered to safe places or escaped Khmer Rouge efforts to force them to join the DK exodus. Villagers were grateful to be rescued by Vietnamese troops, whom they found to be protective and helpful. Calm was restored, and people returned to Sobay from places of temporary refuge. Over the ensuing months, other former residents, who had gone elsewhere during DK, gradually drifted back. (One woman took more than a month to walk back from Pursat province.) As one villager stated, "It was then, in 1979, that we found out who else was alive and who was dead."

Now, some 12 years later, it can be said that the villagers are "beyond suffering" in a different sense: having endured misery beyond normal reckoning, the survivors moved beyond it to reconstruct their community and their lives. At first glance, much of what I see in present-day Sobay resembles what I knew three decades ago, and in recent years, the government has been increasingly tolerant of the revival of prerevolutionary aspects of Khmer culture. But, of course, village existence has been inevitably altered by the upheavals and by the different sociopolitical and economic setting of contemporary Cambodia.

A New Government

The different sectors of Sobay still exist—or rather have been recreated in slightly different form. At the beginning of the new government, the People's Republic of Kampuchea (PRK), an administrative reorganization split Sobay into two separate villages: East Sobay and West Sobay. The latter merged what were formerly Middle and West Hamlets. In 1991, 59 persons from the 1960 population of West Hamlet were still alive (after some deaths in the 1980s). Thirty-three of these survivors remained in or returned to Sobay, while the others live in various parts of Cambodia (including in some nearby communities and Phnom Penh). Only one escaped Cambodia as a refugee and now resides in Tacoma, Washington.

According to 1990 census figures at the district (*srok*) office, West Sobay (in its current form) has 421 persons living in 108 households, of which 26 are families of former West Hamlet residents or their descendants. Such households are usually, as in prerevolutionary times, either nuclear or extended family units. The latter generally consist of elderly parents (or a widowed parent) with a married child and his or her family, but other kin may also be included.

West Sobay is no exception to a new and striking feature of contemporary Cambodia: a disproportionate number of widows in the adult population (Boua, 1982). Official figures on West Sobay list 421 persons: 339 females (80.5 percent of the population) and 82 males. Looking at a somewhat different and smaller universe of the 59 people from the original West Hamlet who were still alive in 1991, 36 (61 percent) were adult women. Of these, 19 were currently married (with some remarriages after deaths of first husbands); 12 were widows whose husbands died during DK; one was divorced; one was abandoned by her husband who took up with another woman;[4] and the current marital status of three other women (living elsewhere) is not known by the villagers.

A Semisocialist System. Mortality during DK also affected village economy. In 1979, the new PRK government faced the problem of rebuilding and reordering agricultural production that had been disrupted by the warfare and population movements accompanying the Vietnamese rout of DK forces. The government developed a semisocialist economy out of both design and necessity. Shortage of male labor, as well as draft animals and agricultural implements, led to the implementation of the *krom samaki* (solidarity group)

---

[4]While polygyny was permitted in prerevolutionary Cambodia, it was rare at the village level (Ebihara, 1974). Polygyny is no longer legal, but the preponderance of women has led to many instances of men taking "second wives" or mistresses (Boua, 1982). This practice does not appear to be widespread in the Sobay region, but villagers knew of several cases.

system for cooperative production and communal distribution. At the same time, the government permitted some private activities, including the "family economy," as a supplement to communal organization. Households received family plots to be used for private production and consumption (Boua, 1983; Vickery, 1986; Curtis, 1990).

There was evidently considerable regional and temporal variation in the operation of this system (Grunewald, 1990; Heder, 1980a, 1980b; Boua and Kiernan, 1987, 1989). In early 1979, when Sobay numbered about 105 families, authorities formed two large krom samaki of approximately 50 families each. These two units divided about equally the available resources and means of production: oxen, labor power (both male and female), plows, and different types of paddies. Labor contribution determined the distribution of communally grown food (rice and some vegetables). The able bodied were considered "#1 labor" and received the most produce, while proportionally less went to the elderly and disabled ("#2 labor") and children ("#3 labor"). While cattle were viewed as private property, their owners had to use them for cooperative production. They were compensated by receiving an additional share of produce. (A team of oxen was considered equal to one able-bodied human laborer.) Families were allowed to keep produce from kitchen gardens on private household plots, however, for home consumption, barter, or sale.

In 1980, authorities reduced the size of solidarity groups to 12 to 13 families because it had been difficult to organize labor and divide produce in the large *krom*. But as production revived in the village, as the number of cattle increased, and as possibilities for extra household income increased through such endeavors as raising pigs, people lost enthusiasm for krom labor and preferred to direct their energies to private activities. It is said that by 1984 krom existed only on paper, and there was de facto household production and consumption in Sobay.

In 1986, rice fields were distributed to households, with each family member receiving .16 to .18 hectare of rice paddies (about one-sixth of a hectare). Provincial, district, subdistrict, and village officials joined in planning an equitable division of land, an exceedingly difficult task given the fact that paddies vary in features like soil types and location. (There was no attempt to take pre-1975 holdings into account.)

The New State of Cambodia

In 1989, the reinstatement of private property was formalized in the new constitution of the State of Cambodia (SOC, as the PRK renamed itself). Private ownership was extended to house sites and trees as well. Some land is communal property, like groves of bamboo that are meant for everyone's use; some land remains state property, like land bordering an irrigation canal.

Land Redistribution. Land redistribution was intended to be egalitarian in giving a more or less equivalent amount of paddy land to every villager, but large families obviously ended up with more land. Holdings range from a low of about one-third of a hectare for a couple without children to 1.8 hectares for a fairly large extended family. By comparison, the average paddy holding in West Hamlet in 1960 was about 1 hectare per household, with a range from .06 to 4 hectares, while four families owned no rice fields. Hence, some former West Hamlet households are now poorer than they were before 1975, some have improved their lot, and some have remained economically about the same.

Social classes did not exist in the Sobay of 1960, but villagers did speak of four categories of wealth: rich people (*neak mean*), "people with enough" (*neak kuosom*), poor people (*neak kroo*), and people who were impoverished (*neak toal*). In the village context, prosperity was based primarily on the amount of rice fields that households owned, because those who could produce a surplus of rice to sell, beyond ordinary home consumption, would of course have money for nicer houses, more clothes, jewelry, and better food.[5] The DK regime tried to level socioeconomic differences by radical means, and the PRK made more moderate attempts at egalitarian distribution of resources. The restoration of private property and a thriving market economy, however, has led to the reemergence of economic differentiation in the village, as well as the country as a whole (Heder, 1980b; Grunewald, 1990). As one villager said, "After Pol Pot everyone had the same standard of living, but then some got better or worse."

Although no one in present-day Sobay is considered rich, households can once again be differentiated according to their means. Of the families of former West Hamlet residents, one is said to be impoverished—a couple with no children and just .32 of a hectare of paddies, who are sometimes driven to ask neighbors for money and food. Certain households of widows without male labor power or families with many young children to support are considered poor people with limited resources who may run out of rice before the next harvest. A larger number of households are said to have "enough" because they produce sufficient rice to last through the year and (possibly) some surplus to sell. In addition, they may possess cattle or receive

---

[5]In 1960, only the largest landholder in the entire village, with 4 hectares of paddies, was deemed a rich person. Several families owning 2 hectares of paddies were considered to be "people with enough," while the bulk of the households with about 1 hectare were said to be poor people. Some six families or couples with little or no paddy land were thought to be impoverished.

money from offspring with nonagricultural occupations, from prosperous kinsmen in Phnom Penh, or from refugee kin living abroad. Nonetheless, as one man (considered to have "enough") put it, "It's still a struggle to live; you still have to work hard to grow rice."

Cultivation and Production of Rice and Other Income Supplements. Cultivation is still carried out with traditional implements such as a wooden plow and harrow, and hand labor is the norm for transplanting, harvesting, and threshing. Some households with enough labor power can work their fields using family effort supplemented by traditional forms of reciprocal labor exchange and cooperative arrangements for the busiest seasons. Widows and elderly couples without able-bodied men to call on may have to hire labor for plowing (and possibly other tasks as well), paying in cash or with return labor. Another possibility is a sharecropping arrangement in which a family cultivates someone else's land in exchange for half the crop.

Rice yield is said to average somewhat more than 1 ton per hectare,[6] but production is chancy as landowners depend on the vagaries of rainfall. (In 1990, for example, a dry spell reduced the harvest by one-quarter to one-half, while a flood in 1991 cut the crop by a half.) As in the pre-1975 village economy, many households strive to make ends meet or earn supplementary income through such activities as raising pigs and chickens for sale, making sugar from lontar palm liquid, selling surplus fruits or vegetables, vending prepared foods, making cow collars and rope for sale, repairing bicycles or machinery, playing music at weddings, and working at odd jobs in the countryside or Phnom Penh.

Material Changes in Sobay—1991. My brief return to Sobay in 1989 gave me the impression that the village had become impoverished compared to what I had known in the past. I realize now that I was misled principally by the fact that most people live in rather small thatch houses on the ground rather than the wooden and/or thatch dwellings raised on piles that were typical of the Khmer before 1975. To build even a simple house on piles would cost the equivalent of about $500 (U.S.) nowadays, a sum that is beyond the reach of most Sobay villagers. After spending more time in Sobay, however, I now realize that almost all families have the essentials for living, and sometimes a bit (if not a whole lot) more. Bicycles, for instance, were few in 1960 but are commonplace now. And some households have possessions

---

[6]The PRK government introduced IR 36, a high-yield variety of rice that can produce as much as 4 tons per hectare and two crops a year if it gets sufficient water and fertilizer. While some households grow IR 36, others do not because their fields do not get enough water, they cannot afford to buy fertilizer, or they prefer the taste of traditional varieties of rice.

like radios and motorcycles that were rare or unknown in earlier times.[7] Villagers say they are managing and that their existence now is certainly preferable to conditions in the Pol Pot period.

The Revival of Buddhism. During DK, Theravada Buddhism, the country's chief religion, was forbidden. The central temple at the village wat compound was blown up with mines, and its remnants were carted away to serve as building material. While the early PRK government allowed religion to be revived, only men over the age of 50 could become Buddhist monks, and it took a year or two under PRK before local temples were functioning again. The State of Cambodia has espoused Buddhism as the state religion, and young men are permitted once more to become monks. Although Wat Sobay has not finished rebuilding the central temple (*vihia*) because of lack of funds, it has refurbished the salaa for religious observances, and there is a small contingent of four monks (including three young ones). Villagers once again celebrate the annual round of Buddhist ceremonies and other observances at the wat, as well as various rituals at home like blessing ceremonies, weddings, and funerals. Khmer religion includes not only Buddhism but also beliefs and rituals centered around various animistic spirits. These have also been revived, along with religious specialists (such as *kru*) who cure illness or prognosticate one's future.

Local Government Administration. At the local level, government administration appears much more complex than what I knew in the past. In fact, in a nearby town, there are 18 different departments at the srok, or district, office. Village governance, however, remains relatively simple. A village chief (*protien phum*), appointed by subdistrict officials with the approval of the district office, oversees village affairs, implements government directives, passes on government announcements, adjudicates disputes and divorce applications, and keeps track of vital statistics. The chief is assisted by two vice-chiefs (*anup protien*).

Sobay Looks to the Future

Sobay villagers in 1960 possessed limited knowledge of the world outside Cambodia and international politics. Now, however, their awareness of foreign and domestic politics seems to have been heightened by the political changes of the past few decades that direly affected their lives. Although newspapers are still rare in Sobay, people with radios listen daily to the Voice of America's

---

[7]Judy Ledgerwood (personal communication) participated in a survey of villagers in Prey Veng Province, many of whom lacked cooking pots, mosquito nets, and other basic items. She thinks that Sobay villagers are much better off than those she observed in Prey Veng.

Khmer language programs as well as to news broadcasts from Phnom Penh. In fact, the villagers were often more up-to-date on political developments than I.

In the summer of 1991, people were understandably anxious about the jockeying for power going on among the several political factions, especially the Heng Samrin/Hun Sen government, Sihanouk, and the Khmer Rouge. The latter were still active; they were not just in people's memories. One Sobay woman's son-in-law, a government soldier, was killed a few years ago fighting DK forces in the northwest-border region. A young man from West Sobay lost a leg when he stepped on a mine while working near the Thai border. Villagers hear (as I did one day) the thuds of distant explosions in mountains to the west where Khmer Rouge remain. On one afternoon, a loud blast frightened us; an unexploded mine in a nearby field had detonated, fortunately without harm to anyone. Everyone fears the Khmer Rouge could seize control again and reinstate a regime like that of the late 1970s. Hence, in mid-1991, Sobay villagers were following the political negotiations closely. They were cautiously optimistic that, after so many years of fighting, there could be peace in Cambodia.

The Legacy of Civil Strife

Democratic Kampuchea was an astonishing attempt to construct a radically new social formation at one stroke. Just as many DK irrigation projects were constructed without taking local topography and ecology into account, so the DK's doctrinaire and authoritarian policies largely ignored deep-rooted cultural forms. The DK seemed to believe that socio-political-economic organization, like the landscape, could be restructured by sheer force of will and effort—according to plan. In the same way ground was leveled; rice fields were reshaped into uniform plots; and canals, dikes, and dams were built to contain and direct water flow, the DK tried to reorganize society by leveling social classes, rationalizing methods of production via regimented labor teams, and imposing strict rules of organization and behavior that were meant to remold the populace into a new social order.

But under the more temperate and permissive policies of the PRK/SOC government, many fundamental aspects of prerevolutionary Khmer culture— including household production and consumption, family and kin networks, and religious beliefs and rituals—have reemerged as critical components of village life, although altered by events and a new context.

In an earlier article (Ebihara, 1987), I suggested that if pre-1975 Cambodia were taken as thesis, DK was in many ways an attempted antithesis of the old society, and present-day Cambodia can be seen as a kind of synthesis. The current political scene, for example, has several factions (including Sihanouk, the SOC, and the Khmer Rouge) jockeying for power in the face of forthcoming elections for a coalition government. In a similar vein, the economy and other realms of life incorporate elements deriving from pre- and post-1975 Cambodian society, but such features have been modified in various ways and appear in new syntheses. As Vandy Kaon, a Khmer sociologist, put it vividly in a May 1989 interview, "[Contemporary] Khmer society is like a kaleidoscope, a combination of the old and new but neither one nor the other. And changes are still happening."

Acknowledgments

I am deeply grateful to the PSC/CUNY Faculty Research Award Program of the City University of New York and to the Wenner-Gren Foundation for Anthropological Research for supporting my project. I express heartfelt appreciation to Dr. Judy Ledgerwood, who expedited and helped this research in numerous ways. I also thank Ms. Siwanny Roy, Ms. Mora Chan Tho, and Mr. Kheang Un for assistance in translations and transcriptions.

References

Ablin, David, and Marlowe Hood, eds. 1987. *The Cambodian Agony.* Armonk, N.Y.: M. E. Sharpe.

Boua, Chanthou. 1982. "Women in Today's Cambodia." *New Left Review.* 131:45–61.

———. 1983. "Observations of the Heng Samrin Government, 1980–1982." In *Revolution and its Aftermath in Kampuchea: Eight Essays,* eds., David Chandler and Ben Kiernan. New Haven: Yale University Southeast Asia Studies, monograph series no. 25.

Boua, Chanthou, and Ben Kiernan. 1987. *Oxfam America's Aid Program in Babong Village, Kampuchea.* Manuscript report for Oxfam.

———. 1989. *Oxfam in Takeo.* Manuscript report for Oxfam.

Carney, Tim. 1987. *Communist Party Power in Kampuchea (Cambodia): Documents and Discussion.* Data paper no. 106. Ithaca: Cornell Southeast Asia Program.

Chandler, David. 1991. *The Tragedy of Cambodian History.* New Haven: Yale University Press.

Chandler, David, and Ben Kiernan, eds. 1983. *Revolution and its Aftermath in Kampuchea: Eight Essays.* New Haven: Yale University Southeast Asia Studies, monograph series no. 25.

Curtis, Grant. 1990. *Cambodia: A Country Profile*. Report prepared for the Swedish International Development Authority, August 1989. Stockholm: SIDA.

Ebihara, May. 1968. *A Khmer Village in Cambodia*. Ph.D. diss., Columbia University. Ann Arbor, Mich: University Microfilms.

———. 1974. "Khmer Village Women in Cambodia." In *Many Sisters: Women in Cross-Cultural Perspective*, ed., C. Matthiasson. New York: Free Press.

———. 1987. "Revolution and Reformulation in Kampuchean Village Culture." In *The Cambodian Agony*, eds., D. Ablin and M. Hood. Armonk, N.Y.: M. E. Sharpe.

———. 1990. "Return to a Khmer Village." *Cultural Survival Quarterly* 14(3)67-70.

Frieson, Kate. 1990. "The Pol Pot Legacy in Village Life." *Cultural Survival Quarterly* 14(3)71-73.

Grunewald, François. 1990. "The Rebirth of Agricultural Peasants in Cambodia." *Cultural Survival Quarterly* 14(3)74-76.

Heder, Stephen. 1980a. *Kampuchean Occupation and Resistance*. Bangkok: Institute of Asian Studies, Chulalongkorn University, Asian Studies monograph no. 027.

———. 1980b. "From Pol Pot to Pen Sovan to the Villages." Paper presented at the International Conference on Indochina and Problems of Security and Stability in Southeast Asia, Chulalongkorn University, Bangkok.

Jackson, Karl, ed. 1989. *Cambodia 1975-1978: Rendezvous with Death*. Princeton: Princeton University Press.

Kiernan, Ben. 1980. "Conflict in the Kampuchean Communist Movement." *Journal of Contemporary Asia* 10:75-118.

———. 1983. "Wild Chickens, Farm Chickens, and Cormorants: Kampuchea's Eastern Zone Under Pol Pot." In *Revolution and its Aftermath in Kampuchea: Eight Essays*, eds., D. Chandler and B. Kiernan. New Haven: Yale University Southeast Asia Studies, monograph series no. 25.

———. 1985. *How Pol Pot Came to Power*. London: Verso.

Kiernan, Ben, and Chanthou Boua, eds. 1982. *Peasants and Politics in Kampuchea, 1942-1981*. Armonk, N.Y.: M. E. Sharpe.

Ponchaud, Francois. 1978. *Cambodia: Year Zero*. New York: Holt, Rinehart, Winston.

Twining, Charles. 1989. "The Economy." In *Cambodia 1975-1978, Rendezvous with Death*, ed., K. Jackson. Princeton: Princeton University Press.

Vickery, Michael. 1984. *Cambodia 1975-1982*. Boston: South End Press.

———. 1986. *Kampuchea, Politics, Economics, Society*. Boulder, CO.: Lynne Rienner Publishers.

6

Vietnam at the Starting Point: Just Another Successful Asian Economy?

David Dapice

Vietnam has clearly missed out on the two to three decades of rapid economic growth that have transformed South Korea, Taiwan, much of ASEAN, and parts of China. If the recently instituted economic reforms in Vietnam are pursued, and if Vietnam can overcome its diplomatic and economic isolation, some observers are tempted to think that the country may follow in the footsteps of other rapidly growing Asian economies. Is this bright future within reach?

This paper examines the initial conditions of four countries—South Korea, Taiwan, Thailand, and Indonesia—that have grown rapidly and, about a generation ago, showed some similarity to the Vietnam of today. I will contrast their early growth experiences with the current situation in Vietnam. My general conclusion is that Vietnam has some important differences from the economies of these countries at the start of their development. Vietnam probably will have to go through a period of reconstruction and slower growth for several years before it can accelerate to the growth rates of these other East Asian countries. Following policies similar to those of the successful nations may be desirable, but such a course is unlikely to immediately produce a high rate of growth.

My choice of the four nations discussed in this paper follows in part from a study tour I took with Vietnamese government officials. In December 1990, we visited Thailand and Taiwan; in January 1991, Indonesia and South Korea. We met with government officials, private sector executives, and academic experts. All four countries have grown enormously over the past 20 years; all have managed to increase exports rapidly; and all have done reasonably to very well in reducing poverty and improving health and education. South Korea and Taiwan initially emphasized labor-intensive manufactured exports, due to a lack of natural resources and relatively high-quality labor. Thailand, until 1985, grew mainly via agricultural exports and tourism. More recently, manufactured exports have been a leading sector in Thailand. Until the mid-1980s, Indonesia emphasized natural, resource-based exports, both oil and nonoil, after which it too began rapid growth in manufactured exports. All of the four had import-substituting industry, but had either limited protection or fostered competition so that much of it became more or less efficient. Foreign investment, outside of the minerals sector, was modest over most of the 20-year period in all four nations. This range of experience is relevant to Vietnam, which has modest but nontrivial natural-resource endowments and a relatively healthy and well-educated labor force.

The other obvious comparator, China, is not covered in this paper. One reason is the book's scope. Chapters 1 and 3 refer to socialist reform. The second reason is substantive. China is so large, so diverse, and so different that drawing lessons for Vietnam might be even more difficult than comparing the four nations that are discussed. While the success of Guangdong Province may well hold lessons for Vietnam, its unique ties to Hong Kong again push it beyond the bounds of this paper.

Basic Comparisons

Population, GNP, and Income Per Capita

There are many ways to evaluate the starting point of a nation. Three of the most basic are population, gross national product (GNP), and GNP per capita. Rather than take a common initial year, I choose to take 1960 for Korea, Taiwan, and Thailand; 1967 for Indonesia; and 1990 for Vietnam. These dates may be viewed as jumping-off points for burgeoning economic growth—in actuality for the first four, less certainly for Vietnam. Table 6-1 below shows population, GNP, and GNP per capita data for the initial years chosen for each country.

This table shows us that while Vietnam has a large population, it is very poor. Therefore, its total domestic-market size is also rather small. If subsistence food is deducted, its remaining economy is probably little larger than Thailand's at the time it started its rapid growth period, and certainly smaller

Table 6-1. Basic Data for Five Asian Nations

	Population (millions)	GNP* ($ billion)	GNP/Population
Taiwan (1960)	11	11	$1000
Korea (1960)	25	18	$ 700
Thailand (1960)	26	8	$ 300
Indonesia (1967)	111	17	$ 150
Vietnam (1990)	66	10–14	$ 150–200

*GNP in 1989–90 prices. It takes current US dollar estimates of GNP and real-growth rates in constant-price domestic currency to arrive at a calculated value of 1960 or 1967 GNP in billions of today's dollars. Vietnam's figure is, frankly, a rough guess.

than the other three countries'. This constraint limits the scope of efficient import substitution. Poverty is also a concern because it means that growth-oriented policies must be more cautious in their distributional impact. There are now more people very close to subsistence in Vietnam than there were in any of the other nations but Indonesia in the designated initial years. Vietnam appears to have less latitude to make mistakes and a smaller domestic market in which their firms can learn to compete behind a protectionist wall.

Labor, Land, and Capital

Vietnam's poverty extends to its capital stock as much as to its income. Infrastructure is very poor by any standard. Roads, telecommunications, and irrigation are sparse and poorly maintained. Much of the industrial capital stock is from the Eastern bloc and unlikely to produce goods of adequate quality or at competitive cost, even at the current, reasonable exchange rate. If the markdown of the estimated value of East Germany's industrial capital stock from $600 billion to $30 billion is any indication, Vietnam will have to rebuild almost from scratch.

In this respect, its initial capital stock is less favorable than Korea's or Taiwan's, which had been able to recover for a decade or more with U.S. aid. Likewise, Thailand's roads and ports were initially well maintained and were augmented significantly during the 1960s with U.S. assistance. Indonesia was perhaps most like Vietnam in this respect, but used foreign aid and oil revenues to repair and expand its infrastructure and other capital during its rapid growth. Poor in absolute terms, Vietnam's infrastructure and capital stock are also bad in relative terms. Progress made by other nations makes them much more attractive to foreign investors who want to export. The cost of being poor in 1990 may be higher in some ways than in 1960 or 1970.

Vietnam also suffers from a lack of land. It has only 0.1 hectare of arable land per capita, about the same as Taiwan in the 1950s and much less than the other nations. There are wastelands that could be planted to tree crops if capital were available. Improved and extended irrigation would also support some increase in food-crop areas. There is nothing to compare, however, with the potential in Thailand, where for more than 20 years most labor-force growth occurred in previously forested areas, even while the amount of land per farmer increased! Likewise, many of the Outer Islands in Indonesia have seen fairly substantial growth in areas cultivated. Vietnam, aside from tree crops, has no extensive agricultural growth path open to it.

One rather bright area is Vietnam's labor force. According to the 1989 census, its literacy is high (nearly 90 percent), its health is good, and labor has a reputation for learning quickly and working diligently. Wage rates are low, although government attempts to force the payment of unrealistically high minimum wages sometimes pushes the cost of labor up to Indonesian levels. About 42 percent of the population was identified as economically active in a recent census, a relatively low number due to the past relatively high birth rate and currently good school-enrollment rates. One reason for concern is the deterioration in public services with the onset of rapid inflation. This has diminished the quality and possibly the coverage of higher education and health services. Another concern, although it is also an opportunity, is the high rate of unemployment, as demobilized army veterans, returning guest workers from Europe, and more than one million new workers annually have swelled the labor force. On the other hand, population growth of just over 2 percent per year is low compared with the other nations when they began their rapid economic growth.

Debt and Debt-Service Ratios

A very striking difference between Vietnam and the other four nations is its severe debt burden. In 1988, debt owed (largely to the former U.S.S.R.) was nearly equal to GNP, and the ratio of debt service relative to exports was estimated by the International Monetary Fund (IMF) at about 40 percent. Even the dollar and other hard-currency debt is in arrears, including that owed to the IMF. Until the IMF debt is settled, no significant hard-currency loans will be available to Vietnam. With East-bloc aid virtually zero, Vietnam is in the unenviable position of owing a great deal and lacking any substantial, willing lender.

One positive point is that hard-currency debt is less than $4 billion and may possibly be renegotiated to a lower effective value. Debt owed to the former U.S.S.R. in transferable rubles could be paid down slowly with few real penalties, given the sharp falling off of trade with and aid from the former Soviet Union. If the hard-currency payments could be reduced to the $100–$200 million range and Soviet payments held under $100 million, the debt-service ratio relative to exports would fall as low as 10 to 20 percent—a still high but more realistic level.

The other four nations had debt-service ratios that ranged from 1 to 6 percent of exports, generally only a tenth of the 1988 Vietnamese level. They all had access to significant concessional and then commercial lending. Except perhaps for Taiwan, which has accumulated net assets, the other countries frequently tapped world capital markets. In Korea's case, the volume of borrowing was quite high over an extended period, and in Thailand and Indonesia, it was moderately high. Their ability to borrow prudently allowed these countries to adjust when economic shocks caused difficulty. This ability to borrow gave policy management significant flexibility and avoided the need for sharply contractionary policies.

Savings and Investment Levels

The measured Vietnamese savings rate is extremely low, probably in the range of 0 to 5 percent of gross output. Therefore, most or all past investment has been financed by foreign borrowing, at least according to the available statistics. It should be noted that official data are unreliable for several reasons. The most obvious one is hyperinflation, which makes evaluation of output difficult. In addition, private companies tend to evade official surveys for fear of drawing attention to themselves. The statistical network is not set up to catch private construction or other investment outside of the state-owned sector. For all these reasons, as well as the general deterioration of civil servants' pay and ability to work, it would be unwise to place very much weight on the available data.

Nevertheless, it is true that Vietnam's savings, defined as observed gross investment less net foreign borrowing, are quite low relative to income. This was also true for Indonesia and Korea when they began their rapid growth, but not for Thailand or Taiwan. For a number of years, Indonesia borrowed 5 percent of its GNP, and this amount equalled or exceeded its savings. Likewise, Korea's savings in the 1960s was far less than the 8 to 10 percent of GNP accounted for by foreign inflows. If successful nations have access to aid or commercial loans, apparently, they do not have to save at first. Savings ratios, in all cases, rose with growth to the point that savings now nearly equal or even exceed investment. It is easy to increase savings when incomes expand greatly.

There are reasons to hope that Vietnam's savings could rise quickly. Much ''consumption,'' such as purchases of gold and some stockpiling of durable goods or food, is really a form of household savings. These forms of savings cannot finance productive investment, so they are sterile economically. They are not now counted in domestic national savings. If a stable currency and safe bank accounts were available, much of this potential savings could be monetized and mobilized for productive investments. In addition, if small and medium companies grow fast, the Taiwanese experience suggests they will have a high propensity to save from income. This would raise the average savings rate rapidly. In other nations, even small farms can be an important source of savings. Some estimates from rural areas put the marginal rate of savings as high as 40 percent. Taken together, these three sources of savings could result in a much faster savings growth than is normally observed in economies not undergoing such rapid transformation.

The investment ratio in Vietnam has been estimated at around 8 to 10 percent of GNP, essentially the same ratio as Indonesia and Korea when they started out. Taiwan had a 20 percent and Thailand a 15 percent initial investment-to-GNP ratio. Given the condition of Vietnam's physical capital and depleted infrastructure, it is unlikely that investment of 10 percent a year will support much growth; there is too large a backlog of needed improvements. Vietnam's situation is different from that of Korea, which had a decade of repair and building, or Indonesia, where the sudden availability of foreign exchange allowed spare parts to restart idle factories. It is perhaps more like Korea in 1954. Time and money will be needed to build up productive capacity.

One way to think about investment levels is the incremental capital-output ratio or ICOR, the ratio of the investment rate to Gross Domestic Product (GDP) over the real GDP growth rate. It can be thought of as the dollars of investment needed to generate a dollar of continuing output. Fast-growing nations often have ICORs of 2.0 to 2.5 for considerable periods, but values of 3.0 to 4.0 are more usual. Nations such as India have had values of 5.0 or more. After some initial growth spurts, the ICOR of Vietnam may be between 3.0 to 3.5, implying investment ratios of about 25 to 28 percent to support 8 percent annual growth. This projection would require a long-term doubling to tripling of the current measured investment rate.

Macroeconomic Situation

Inflation is generally admitted to be bad for growth, especially as it reaches extreme levels. None of the four nations faced rapid inflation after they started growing. Thailand and Taiwan generally kept their annual inflation rates in the single digits. Korea averaged 10 to 20 percent a year during the early 1960s, but less over the entire decade. Indonesia fell into hyperinflation in the middle 1960s, but by 1969, its inflation rate had been reduced to 15 percent, and it was only 4 percent in 1971. None of the four nations faced sustained, rapid price increases once growth began, and they normally kept inflation below 2 percent a month except during the period of sharply rising oil prices. In general, by the 1980s, inflation for these countries was under 10 percent per year.

This record of low to moderate inflation stands in stark contrast to Vietnam, which, in several years, has seen prices at least double. While the pace of inflation slowed at times in 1989, the monthly inflation rate in 1990 and 1991 was over 4 percent. Such inflation threatens to undermine public confidence in the currency, the government, and the future. Certainly, rational calculation of future costs and prices is all but impossible in a high-inflation environment. The current inclination in Vietnam is to import, stockpile, and speculate rather than undertake fixed investment—recorded as only 3 to 4 percent of total income. This is not surprising given the interest-rate structure, which has reverted to a deposit rate below the inflation rate and a lending rate that is less than the deposit rate! There was a brief period with positive real interest rates, but these rates led to unemployment in state enterprises and financial scandals in private financial institutions. As a result, the policy was reversed. Meanwhile, tax collections have not risen as much as prices. This compounds the effect of the virtual elimination of aid from the former Soviet Union, since both tax revenues and aid have fallen in real terms. As the level of civil servants' salaries declines in real terms, officials either take on other jobs or collect extra income by taking advantage of their government jobs.

Clearly, inflation is doing immense harm. If it continues at its current pace, Vietnam's economy is likely to resemble Bolivia's, Peru's, or Indonesia's in the early to middle 1960s. Any possibility of sustained rapid growth will require a period of reconstruction and consolidation. Spending must be brought in line with revenues (or vice versa); the structure of spending must be focused on productive purposes rather than enterprise subsidies; and credit must be distributed more evenly and efficiently throughout the economy rather than extended mainly to failing state enterprises. While inflation might be reduced sharply if large infusions of aid were available and properly directed, reducing inflation to 1 percent a month for as long as a year is likely to be a somewhat longer process. (This is assuming modest aid levels of 5 to 8 percent of GNP on a net basis.)

Institutional Issues

Some of the most important differences between Vietnam and the four rapidly growing Asian nations do not show up easily in numbers. The absence of a legal market economy or private sector is a serious drawback. Laws, even well drafted, lack the infrastructure to enforce them. Banks are unfamiliar with market-based loans, having concentrated on administratively ordered loans to state enterprises—still 95 percent of state banks' lending. Letters of credit may not be honored. Getting local government approval can be very time consuming. Tax laws are often unclear. None of these problems is altogether unique to Vietnam, but it suffers from more of these problems more severely than did the other four nations.

In addition, the ideology of the Communist party still envisions bureaucratic guidance of the economy. At one level, this is unsurprising—all governments need to worry about macroeconomic stability, infrastructure, education, and environmental and health regulations. But at the operational level, this often means that the local government will demand ownership of joint ventures (with little or no actual investment), install their own workers at "official" wages, or otherwise intrude and cause uncertainty and delays. This problem will take time to overcome, although export processing zones may provide some immediate relief. Until changes occur in government practices, Vietnam will find it hard to attract foreign export-oriented, labor-intensive investment.

This last point is especially relevant because there is a perception, even in Vietnam, of a foreign investment boom. In fact, while approvals have indeed been high, there have been relatively few actual startups outside of oil and a few hotels. An export processing zone in Ho Chi Minh City may help accelerate the inflow of industrial investment, and this should begin operation in 1992. In addition, normalization would doubtless encourage more investment, and aid could help to ease infrastructure bottlenecks. However, the attitude of most investors, including the Japanese, is one of short-term caution combined with long-term optimism. Problems of land ownership, currency convertibility, and debt arrears will need to be resolved as well as regulatory, infrastructure, and legal hurdles before a true investment boom gets under way.

The regulatory issue is of special concern in that the provincial-level authorities often seem to be under only tenuous central control—a situation quite different from that in the other four countries, where local government is much more clearly subordinate. If the Vietnamese central government can collect taxes or effectively control foreign aid, it could extend its authority by using the power of the purse to reward or punish wayward provincial authorities. On the other hand, a great deal of investment may initially be channeled through Ho Chi Minh City, making it difficult to create uniform commercial policies throughout the country.

Another shortcoming is the inability of the bureaucracy to understand what is legitimately needed to provide a supportive environment for the private sector. The sharp reduction in aid from the former U.S.S.R. and concurrent drop in other government revenues has created tremendous temptation for government officials to use their positions for immediate gain. But beyond this, their lack of understanding that they need to play a positive role slows progress. Learning how to be honest and efficient banking regulators, tax officials, port managers, extension workers, or irrigation engineers takes time. There are some skills to build on, but much more needs to be done. Governments can help a market economy work smoothly. Vietnam has not had much experience with this.

Reconstruction

In the cases of Indonesia, Taiwan, and Korea, periods of reconstruction preceded the initiation of rapid development. This is easiest to understand in the case of Korea, where a war had just been fought. Taiwan also suffered in World War II. And Indonesia faced a violent, if brief, civil war and a longer period during which the government failed to maintain its infrastructure or establish an environment that attracted investment. In these countries, foreign aid was used—sometimes lavishly—to rebuild basic infrastructure, reestablish government organization, and get things back to normal. If Korea had tried to start rapid export-led growth in 1955 instead of the early 1960s, or if Indonesia had tried to undertake ambitious investments in 1967, each probably would have failed. During their reconstruction periods, investments that repaired or extended basic infrastructure, or got existing factories running, had a very high return. Investment was focused in these high-return areas rather than spread widely across lower priority projects.

Vietnam probably must undergo a period of at least a few years of repairing, finishing, or perhaps extending projects; training people; and establishing a less inflationary environment. During this time, Vietnam can not only build export processing zones but work out the process of managing the zones, the ports, customs, power, water, and so on. It will be a time not only to get interest rates in line with the rate of inflation but also to train bank staff, regulators, and accountants. During this period, the habit of encouraging rather than restricting private enterprise could be learned. Changing the psychology from one where private enterprise is suspiciously tolerated to one where it is welcomed would set the stage for much higher levels of longer term investment from both domestic and foreign sources.

This period will proceed faster if substantial aid resources are available: annual net flows of $500 to $800 million have been suggested as a reasonable figure, or annual gross flows of up to $1 billion. If a lesser amount is available, progress will be slower. It remains to be seen, even following normalization, how much aid would actually become available. Emerging capital demands in the Middle East, Eastern Europe, and possibly Latin America, combined with continuing problems in Bangladesh and Africa, suggest that there will be many demands on limited concessionary funds.

In addition, there may be some "enclave" investments such as oil and gas, coal, or hard minerals that could begin during the reconstruction period, as they often operate with much of their own infrastructure and outside normal government administration. These investments would not generate much employment, but would provide some foreign exchange and tax revenue. Progress on these investments is a function of Vietnam's physical deposits, its investment law, and the normalization of relations.

Oil prospects are moderately bright, as the estimated 70,000 barrels-per-day output in 1991 will rise by about 20,000 barrels per day for the next few years. On the other hand, this output is split with *Sovpetro*, the joint partner (which receives 40 to 50 percent of the gross value), and just about equals current consumption. Thus, gross 1991 sales of $500 million or so yield Vietnam only $250 million in net proceeds, all of which must be used to buy refined products. Coal exports will be an order of magnitude less, as they are now running under one million tons per year. Even by the end of the decade, by which time oil exports could equal a few hundred thousand barrels per day, the annual proceeds to Vietnam will not have offset the decline in aid from the former Soviet Union.

From Reconstruction to Development

Once a reasonably stable macroeconomic situation is established, and after some repair and basic extension of infrastructure is achieved, it should be possible to move beyond reconstruction. Presumably, at least a beginning will have been made in improving the regulatory environment. Banks will be able to make loans to sound customers, honor letters of credit, and make other transfers. Taxes will be collected in a more predictable and professional manner. Electricity and telephone connections should be easier to arrange, or at least have a defined waiting period. In this more settled environment, the government should have access to concessional loans, a renegotiated debt, and normal trade relations with all major trading nations. Foreign investment should also be a growing factor, as the underlying favorability of low-cost and skilled labor is no longer offset by other problems. (Direct foreign-investment approvals in Indonesia in 1990 exceeded $8 billion—nearly as much as Vietnam's entire GNP. An amount even one-tenth as much would become a major factor in Vietnam's economic growth.)

Peter Timmer and Vo-Tong Xuan have argued convincingly in their paper "A Food Policy for Vietnam" that agriculture will play a major role in any immediate progress. Rice, rubber, and coffee already provide export earnings. Possibilities in the export of fruits, vegetables, and fish and other seafood are promising. Over a longer period, tree crops could be planted on underutilized land. Substantial improvement in production and exports, however, will require large investments in improved irrigation, roads, storage, processing, and marketing facilities.

An increase in exports and production will also require changes in policy. Vietnam now receives $40 per ton less for exports of rice than does Thailand for similar quality rice because Vietnam is viewed as an unreliable exporter. Since Vietnam has little storage capacity, domestic consumers in the north get first call on southern production even if it had been intended for export.

Development of an information system, storage, and transport capacity is important to guarantee a certain level of exports. These steps alone could earn Vietnam more than $50 million per year.

With regard to rice, there have been growing problems associated with improper and excessive use of pesticides. The 1990–91 crop in the south may have declined 10 percent due to brown planthopper attacks. While the experience of Indonesia with integrated pest management over the last decade is relevant, it will take much more knowledge, training, research, and extension to get farmers to follow proper procedures and coordinate them with each other.

With the construction of export processing zones, it should be possible to attract foreign investment aimed at labor-intensive exports. These zones have proven initially useful to overcome problems such as sluggish or inadequate administration, port clearance, land titling, and infrastructure. All of these issues take time to solve in the larger society. Successful export processing zones also attract a critical mass of private-sector enterprise that can give rise to services like banking, freight forwarding, spare parts, and maintenance, which are also useful outside the immediate zone. In any case, to have a serious impact, the zones must serve as a first step only. Ultimately, many of their advantages can and should be transferred to any business anywhere in the country. Such a process is necessarily slow, but it can have a tremendous cumulative effect.

Nonetheless, it will be well into the 1990s before manufactured exports can have a major influence on the overall job picture. Even Thailand, with its manufactured exports tripling to $10 billion between 1985 and 1990 added only about 100,000 new jobs from them each year. The labor force in Vietnam amounts to 30 million and is growing annually at about one million a year. The increase in manufactured exports will not approach that of Thailand in absolute terms for some time, although Vietnam may be more labor intensive in its production methods.

It would be very helpful if manufactured exports grew at such a pace as to be of macroeconomic importance in the next few years. Yet the experience of the other countries does not suggest this outcome. In 1980, after 20 years of rapid growth, three-quarters of Thailand's exports came from natural-resource-based products, and manufactured exports amounted to less than 5 percent of GNP. In 1980, Indonesia was even further behind, with only $5 per capita of manufactured exports accounting for less than 1 percent of its GNP. Arguably, the import-substituting nature of their industrial growth had slowed the development of their export capacity, but even with a considerable base, it took five to ten years and changes in their domestic policies and in world exchange rates to spark really fast export-led growth.

The experiences of Korea and Taiwan similarly suggest that a period of consolidation, which both experienced in the 1950s, was useful in setting the stage for the rapid increase in exports observed in the 1960s. Even Korea, with its booming, export-led growth, increased its total exports by only $150 million ($600 million at today's prices) from 1960 to 1965. This slow growth suggests that, for Vietnam, large, immediate benefits will not come from this quarter, although rapid progress from the present small base (25 to 30 percent of total exports, or about $400 million) is quite possible.

Summary

Very few economies have attempted to do what Vietnam is now doing with so many disadvantages. Others have tried to shift from a socialist to a more market-oriented system, but typically with higher incomes and/or greater external support. Others have successfully emerged from hyperinflation and economic chaos. Indonesia did so but with a renegotiated debt, significant help from foreign aid and oil, and macroeconomic management that is widely regarded as among the best in the developing world. Korea overcame the destruction of a war, low initial savings, and a lack of industry, but only with a decade of generous U.S. aid and substantial capital inflows. In every previous successful case, a new government—in many cases a new regime—overturned many policies of the previous administration. In Vietnam, this has occurred to only a moderate extent during the reforms of the 1980s, although the changes, in fact, have been more than the change in official rhetoric.

Vietnam at present lacks access to international credit, to a full range of trading opportunities, and even to macroeconomic stability. It does not have many of the institutions necessary to start and sustain development. Its lack of an appropriate tax system causes reductions in real wages even to critical civil servants and undermines the ability of the central government to govern. As a result, the provincial governments play a large and more independent role. Clearly, without help, the nation will have difficulty creating stability, reforming its institutions, redirecting its economy, and changing to private-oriented ownership and market-driven investment. Yet, as important as outside loans and debt relief are, it is domestic policies that are most critical.

One way of viewing the different economic possibilities open to Vietnam is via a matrix in which internal policies (either "good" or "bad") are on one side, while the external environment (again, either good or bad) are on the other side. There are then four possible outcomes, as shown in the following matrix.

EXTERNAL ENVIRONMENT

		Good	Bad
INTERNAL	Good	1	2
POLICIES	Bad	3	4

What growth prospects for Vietnam would each outcome imply? What is meant by good or bad policies and external conditions? The implications of each scenario are discussed next.

1. *Good/Good:* In the best of all worlds, there would be a rapid move to normalization of trade and borrowing, renegotiated debt, and a rapid increase in foreign investment. The government would move to reconstruct infrastructure, limit loans to failing public enterprises, and get its macroeconomic house in order. Inflation would fall, the budget would move toward a balance as tax collections rise, and interest rates would move toward normal patterns, with lending rates higher than deposit rates and the deposit rates above inflation rates. Investment rates would rise rapidly, as both domestic savings and foreign inflows show strong growth. This would support GDP growth of 4 to 6 percent a year during the reconstruction phase, followed by faster annual growth of 7 to 9 percent by the middle to later 1990s.

2. *Good/Bad:* In this scenario, positive domestic policies are not immediately matched with support from the rest of the world. Trade with the United States is restricted, as is access to concessionary and commercial finance. Growth in this scenario would come to a greater extent from domestic savings, import substitution, and agriculture. Favorable terms of trade trends from some farm and mineral products would help. Tough bargaining to lower debt payments to the former Soviet Union and careful negotiation of hard-currency debt should reduce debt service even without a general agreement. Annual growth of 4 percent to 6 percent a year could be sustained under these conditions, as investment/GDP rises to 15 to 18 percent per year.

3. *Bad/Good:* In this unwelcome scenario, weak domestic policies are combined with debt relief and increased concessionary loans. These loans are used for political purposes, however—such as propping up inefficient public enterprises. Provincial governments continue to make foreign investment unattractive and even depress efficient, private domestic investment. Under these conditions, an initial spurt of growth is prematurely cut short as debt burdens again build up and poor infrastructure restricts the rapid growth of output. This path is tempting but amounts to a false start.

4. *Bad/Bad:* In this worst-case scenario, the hostility of the outside world is matched by poor internal economic management. Inflation remains high, public services deteriorate, and infrastructure remains inadequate. This case leads to stagnation, unemployment, and yet more inflation. The authority of the central government deteriorates further. With little security and bleak prospects, investment and output barely match population growth.

The basic lesson is clear. Because of its unfavorable starting point, Vietnam needs to exploit every possible opportunity to begin moderately rapid growth and then to accelerate. It badly needs debt relief, foreign aid, trade normalization, foreign private investment, development of oil and natural resources, improvements in agricultural infrastructure, and an early start on manufactured export-led growth. If it gets all of these and gets its policies pitched correctly, it can indeed crank up its engine of growth, at least in awhile. Even if the outside world is not so helpful, more moderate but sustainable growth is within reach. This accomplishment should be the immediate object of the Vietnamese government's economic management.

References

Central Census Steering Committee. 1990. "Vietnam Population Census 1989, Sample Results." Hanoi.

Council for Economic Planning and Development. 1990. *Taiwan Statistical Data Book 1990.* Republic of China.

de Vylder, Stefan, and Adam Fforde. 1988. *Vietnam—An Economy in Transition.* Stockholm: Swedish International Development Authority.

Drabek, Zdenek. 1990. "A Case Study of a Gradual Approach to Economic Reform: The Viet Nam Experience of 1985-88." Report No. IDP 74, Asia Regional Series, The World Bank, September.

General Statistical Office. 1991. *Statistical Data of the Socialist Republic of Vietnam, 1976-1990.* Hanoi: Statistical Publishing House.

International Monetary Fund. 1989. "Viet Nam: 1989 Article IV Consultation Report." Unpublished paper.

———. 1990. *International Financial Statistics, 1990 Yearbook.* Washington, D.C.: International Monetary Fund.

Ronnas, Per, and Orjan Sjoberg. 1990. "Doi Moi Economic Reforms and Development Policies in Vietnam." Papers and proceedings from an international symposium, Hanoi, December 12-15, 1989. Stockholm: Swedish International Development Authority.

Sachs, Jeffrey, and Susan Collins, eds. 1989. *Developing Country Debt and Economic Performance.* Volume 3. Chicago: National Bureau of Economic Research Project Report, University of Chicago Press.

United Nations Development Program. 1990. Chicago: "Report on the Economy of Vietnam." Hanoi, December.

Vo Nhan Tri. 1990. *Vietnam's Economic Policy Since 1975.* Singapore: Institute of Southeast Asian Studies.

World Bank. 1976. *World Tables 1976.* Baltimore: Johns Hopkins University Press.

———. 1991. "The Challenge of Development." In *World Development Report 1991.* Oxford: Oxford University Press.

Xuan, Vo-Tong, and C. Peter Timmer. 1990. "A Food Policy For Vietnam." Development Discussion Paper 351 (July), Agriculture and Food Policy Series. Harvard Institute for International Development, Harvard University, Cambridge, MA.

7

Food Policy and Economic Reform in Vietnam

C. Peter Timmer

Vietnam is still primarily an agricultural society.[1] If its physical production, shown in national income accounts, were valued at international market prices, more than 60 percent of gross domestic product (GDP) would originate in agriculture. Even the official statistics indicate that 55.5 percent of national income in 1990 came from agriculture and forestry, up from 46.6 percent in 1986. More than three-quarters of the labor force works in the agricultural sector. Furthermore, agro-processing is the single largest component of the industrial sector. In fact, nearly one-half of the industrial work force is employed in either agro-processing or the textile industry. Since the average Vietnamese household spends nearly two-thirds of its income on food, there is no doubt that the food and agricultural economy is the key to both economic growth and improved welfare for the rest of the 1990s.[2]

As the restructuring of Vietnam's economy gains momentum, policymakers are becoming aware of the important role to be played by the food and agricultural sector in generating employment, income, domestic savings, foreign exchange, and food security for the entire country.[3] Because of severe problems in restructuring the industrial sector, however, an expanding farm economy will have to focus on foreign demand for several key commodities, in addition to meeting domestic food needs.

Linking the fate of the rural economy to world markets requires Vietnam's farmers to compete with other suppliers in Asia and the rest of the world. Lower costs of production, greater efficiency of resource use, higher

---

[1]This chapter draws on my work on food policy in several Asian countries, especially Indonesia; on joint research on Vietnamese food policy with my collaborator, Professor Vo-Tong Xuan of Can Tho University; and on my participation in a technical assistance project to Vietnam, funded by FAO, that examined the relevance of Asian agricultural development policies to the Vietnamese environment.

[2]For general statistics on the agricultural economy of Vietnam, see Socialist Republic of Vietnam (1991).

[3]A particularly emphatic statement of the key role for agriculture is in Tien (1991).

quality, and higher yields will be essential for successful competition. These can be achieved only by an agricultural economy that integrates modern technology, knowledgeable farmers, and profitable markets for the output. Historically, only countries with efficient, market-oriented food and agricultural economies have integrated these components into dynamic forces for development.

From these lessons this premise follows: at least for the decade of the 1990s, Vietnam's agricultural sector must drive its economy. Traditional strategies for development have squeezed agriculture to foster growth in industry, at the inevitable cost of lower rural incomes. Food security often suffered in the process, and excessive reliance on food imports, sometimes from food aid, complicated the twin tasks of stabilizing domestic food markets while ensuring that the poor had access to them. If Vietnam is able to integrate its agricultural sector into the world economy in the context of an export-oriented macroeconomic policy, it can reverse this bias and follow a more rapid and more equitable path of economic growth.

Rapid Growth in Rural Income

The Vietnamese rural economy has long suffered from neglect—often from exploitation on behalf of centralized plans for industrialization. The agricultural sector is well diversified, with food crops making up about 50 percent of total output; industrial crops about 25 percent, and animal husbandry, including fisheries, the final 25 percent. Nonfood crops are important for rural incomes and export earnings, and significant investments are being made to stimulate their productivity. Coffee production has increased with assistance from Eastern European countries, Malaysian clonal materials are being used to raise yields of rubber, and tea acreage is expected to increase by 50 percent by 1995. On average, however, yields of export crops are quite low, partly as a result of poor management of state farms. Rubber yields, for example, are only one-fifth of those in Malaysia.

Livestock and fisheries also offer significant hope for expansion. Maize and sweet potato production is expanding to meet the need for feed, as production of pigs grows in response to higher rural incomes and increased demand for pork. Shrimp cultivation and ocean fisheries offer excellent export opportunities, although supplies of high-quality feed for aquaculture remain expensive and difficult to obtain on a reliable basis.

Within the food-crops sector, rice plays an overwhelming role. More than 80 percent of the value of food crops comes from rice, whereas maize, cassava, sweet potatoes, peanuts and other legumes, and Irish potatoes contribute less than 20 percent. Still, diversification of production is occurring as government controls are lifted. A study of the sweet potato economy in northern and central Vietnam, for example, found that ". . . substantial diversification is reflected in individual household income. This trend was already clearly indicated with regard to production itself. However, looking at the income, which has been expressed in money, it is clear that in percentage [terms], higher income elasticity goods such as meat, are the prime commodities to ensure high income" (Bottema et al., 1991, p. 81). Even with this diversification, however, the Vietnamese rural economy depends heavily on the success of rice.

But the rice sector has suffered great neglect historically, as the following observations by Prabhu Pingali and Vo-Tong Xuan (1990) attest:

> A comparison of per capita rice output from 1942 to 1986 reveals the depressed state of rice production in Vietnam. During this 45-year period rice output per capita in the Northern regions has remained stagnant at around 200 kilograms (unmilled rice). In the Southern provinces there has been a steady decline in per capita rice output during the same time period. Output per capita was around 420 kilograms of paddy in 1942 and is currently around 330 kilograms. During the period immediately following re-unification (1976–81) rice output per capita was around 270 to 290 kilograms. At the national level rice output per capita has been stagnant during this period at 260–280 kilograms, with the lowest levels being during the 1965–1980 period. A comparison with Philippines and Indonesia is illustrative. Rice is the staple food in both these countries also and the agroclimatic conditions are similar to Vietnam. Between 1950 and 1986 per capita rice output rose by 33 kilograms and 110 kilograms respectively, for Philippines and Indonesia. (p. 9)

An agriculture-led development strategy has the potential to reverse these trends. The starting point is to raise incomes in rural areas and to allow farmers, merchants, and rural industrialists to save and invest from their profits. These rural investments will form the catalyst for the rapid transformation of three key components of the rural economy: production of farm commodities, wage earnings by members of farm households, and a newly emergent nonfarm rural economy based on services and small-scale industrial activities. The short-run growth of urban incomes is likely to be feeble and highly uncertain as industrial restructuring takes place. Therefore, much of the demand for the goods and services produced by the nonfarm rural economy must come from exports and from rural households themselves.

Eventually, a healthy urban economy focused on labor-intensive industrial exports, as envisioned in Chapter 6 of this book, would also stimulate higher wages in rural areas. At this stage, Vietnam's real economic transformation will have begun. No attempt is made here to argue that agriculture should be the long-term basis of Vietnam's economy. On the contrary, rapid growth in agriculture in the 1990s will greatly enhance the capacity of the economy to industrialize at East Asian rates by the turn of the century.[4]

Food Supplies for National Food Security

Large Asian countries must produce domestically a large proportion of their basic food needs, especially to meet the domestic demand for rice. The world rice market is too thin and too unstable to permit any country to import regularly more than 2 or 3 million metric tons and still be able to stabilize its domestic rice economy. Somewhat unexpectedly in 1989, Vietnam found itself a sizable exporter of rice and thus dependent on the world rice market for export earnings. While this export status makes it easier to ensure the availability of rice supplies for domestic food security, dependence on world export prices to give rice farmers incentives to intensify production complicates two tasks: providing price stability for rice in both rural and urban markets; and giving farmers adequate price incentives to stimulate their production, incomes, savings, and investments. Without these investments, the rural economy is deprived of the catalyst it needs to stimulate the entire growth process.

In a country as large and geographically diverse as Vietnam, national food security requires movements of food from surplus to deficit areas. Significantly greater inter-provincial shipments of rice will be needed if farmers specialize in crops and livestock that fit their local comparative advantage. In principle, rice surpluses from the south could be shipped to the north, as they were in 1991 after cold weather damaged the early crop in the north. But the present transportation system makes this transfer expensive. Instead of high-cost rice, farmers in the north should be growing high-value fruits, vegetables, and livestock, as well as feedstuffs for the livestock sector. When appropriate crop varieties and markets are developed for northern farmers, importing rice from the cheapest source (probably south China) would save resources while permitting rice growers and millers in the south to build a higher-quality market for rice exports.

Vietnam's food security will depend on rice for many years. To guarantee continued adequacy of rice supplies for domestic consumers as well as for export, the government needs to make investments in new technology and rural infrastructure. These investments are crucial for maintaining competitive production costs and low marketing margins. The current export surplus

---

[4]There is no real disagreement between the perspective put forward by Dwight Perkins in Chapter 1, in which he argues the necessity of manufactured exports as the basis of long-term rapid growth, and my argument that agriculture must be used as the base in the 1990s to begin the growth process.

in rice is a welcome cushion, offering some flexibility in resource allocation for the early 1990s. But investments that will increase rice production must be made and maintained to ensure Vietnam's food security in the future.[5]

Rice, as noted, is not the only element in Vietnam's national food security. Rice supplies roughly 60 percent of the average daily caloric intake, but such staples as sweet potatoes, maize, cassava, and wheat also play a significant role, especially for low-income households and regions. Eventually, livestock and fishery products will become an important factor in food security. At the moment, however, both of these sectors are primarily income earners rather than significant contributors to food security at the national level.

The Strategic Context for Modernizing the Food Economy of Vietnam

No food policy can be designed in a vacuum. Policy design and implementation require sensitivity to what is feasible in the short run. Feasibility depends on context—that is, on the structure of institutions, markets, political power, and a host of other factors. For food policy, the crucial elements of context, in addition to technological capacity, are Vietnamese political realities, macroeconomic structure, institutional setting, and market environment.

Political Realities

The Communist party dominates Vietnam's political structure and, consequently, its machinery for determining economic policy. The public opposition that has thrown communist parties out of power in the Soviet Union and in Eastern European countries—the models for party structure in Vietnam— is nothing short of revolutionary. A vigorous debate has been waged in Vietnam for several years on how the party should respond to similar challenges at home. Partly because of this long period of political debate, an observer should not hastily draw parallels to the Eastern European experience. Vietnam is a far poorer country than any in Europe; it is, in fact, one of the poorest in Asia. No East or Southeast Asian country started its growth process from such low income levels with democratic political systems, although all the more successful countries are now grappling with the

---

[5]Discussions in Hanoi in August, 1991, revealed the concern of the senior leadership over the inability of Vietnam to maintain self-sufficiency in rice production, much less remain a major rice exporter.

introduction of more democratic institutions. In the short run—at least for the first half of the 1990s—Vietnam's political structure is likely to remain more centralized and subject to party control than any other in the region except China's.

Perhaps the main reasons for a continuing, powerful role for the Communist party are the leadership's overwhelming desire for stability and the public popularity that stability brings if it nourishes economic growth. This concern for stability, which can lead to fast economic payoff, has obvious implications for the design of both macroeconomic policy and price policy for rice.

But stability can also lead to stagnation. No market economy can grow for long without wide freedom of choice in investments, work location, or trading opportunities—all of which ultimately undermine political control by local, regional, and national party members. This tension between the efficiency of market allocations, and the individual decisions that support it, and the desire for political regimentation and control has plagued the democratic movements in Eastern Europe and the Soviet Union. The relationship between markets and government control is actively debated throughout Asia, including Vietnam. But experience in Asia shows that a gradual movement toward democracy, even within a single-party structure, seems to promote economic growth. This idea is gaining adherents within Vietnam.

Recognition by the Communist party of this relationship between markets and government control has translated into much greater authority for the National Assembly of Vietnam. In contrast to the mid-1980s, this body now has, with its increased powers, the potential to draft economic policy that reflects far more input from citizens and local organizations. An important test of this potential came in 1990 when a new agricultural tax law was debated. When the National Assembly challenged the bill, the government withdrew it. The government set up a new task force to formulate an alternative approach to agricultural taxation that will leave more income in rural areas.

A stumbling block in the design of a new national food policy, including the role of agricultural and land taxes, is the wide difference in agronomic and economic conditions between the northern and the southern provinces. Agriculture remains much more cooperatively based in the north, where higher population densities and lower crop yields contribute to a substantially lower standard of living. This difference between regions would worsen if the greater experience and willingness of individuals in the south to participate in market activities permitted them more rapid gains in income. As greater market orientation becomes the primary mechanism of growth, special measures must be taken in the north to find other sources of growth, provide greater resources for investment in infrastructure, improve access to credit, and teach farmers, after decades of communal farming, how to cope in a market environment. At some stage, equitable tax measures will be needed to transfer some of the rising surpluses in the south to the rebuilding effort in the north.

Macroeconomic Structure

The macroeconomic setting for a food policy determines whether the policy will succeed. Low inflation, fiscal integrity, positive real interest rates, and a competitive foreign exchange rate are necessary for the rural economy to create jobs, raise productivity, and generate resources for the development effort, including food, savings, and foreign exchange. The economic context in early 1990 in Vietnam was more promising than at any time in a decade, but each of the key factors in economic stability was poised on a knife edge. From mid-1989 to mid-1990, reforms of exchange rates and interest rates brought stability to the overall price level, but the restructuring of state-owned enterprises and reduction in price subsidies for their inputs meant that government revenues fell faster than expenditures. The budget deficit remained large and increased as a share of GDP, starting another round of inflation in late 1990. (See Chapter 8 for details.)

Unification of the official and free-market exchange rates in mid-1989 stabilized domestic prices and encouraged exports. But Vietnam's foreign debt service thereby assumed a much larger share of government expenditures, and trade profits were eliminated as a source of revenue. Financing this large external debt is also potentially inflationary, especially given Vietnam's limited opportunities to participate in world commerce. Arrears on convertible-currency debt in 1991 totaled more than three times the exports to the convertible-currency economies. Once the economic blockade is ended, most of these arrears must be settled before Vietnam can gain access to new credit, either from commercial institutions or from development agencies. For both domestic and foreign investors, great uncertainty hangs over the foreign-trade sector until mechanisms for resolving Vietnam's inability to pay its foreign debt are developed.

Credit Institutions

Domestic credit facilities are a major bottleneck in attempts to restart the economy down a market-driven path. The recent experience of Vietnam with pervasive fraud in private credit schemes demonstrates that the restructuring of state-controlled credit institutions might be the single most difficult task for the 1990s. The task is especially difficult in a communist country that considers it ideologically unacceptable to use interest rates as a mechanism for pricing and allocating capital. At stake is the "hard budget constraint" that Dwight Perkins, in Chapter 1, notes is required to make market pressures effective in enforcing efficient resource allocations. The "soft budget constraint" characteristic of socialist economies is the main reason their industrial structures are inefficient and produce so many items that consumers do not want; yet these industries provide their workers and managers with comfortable living standards. The rest of the economy, starved for the investment resources that offer high economic payoff in alternative uses, suffers the inevitable cost.

In market economies, investment resources are raised by paying savers a positive real rate of interest, and they are then allocated by financial intermediaries to investment opportunities that pay even higher returns. One reason for giving priority to Vietnam's rural economy in the 1990s is that individual or related households can do much of the savings and investment internally, thus removing the immediate need for modern institutions that are capable of efficient financial intermediation, which is usually essential for growth. The urban industrial sector cannot be restructured without these financial institutions, but they take considerable time to build. Indeed, apart from small-scale and local marketing activities, a modern marketing sector requires access to both liquidity and investment capital to carry out the functions of storage, transportation, and processing.

As noted repeatedly in the sections that follow, the rural economy has an important stake in the development of efficient financial intermediaries in urban as well as rural areas. Experience in the rest of Asia has demonstrated that farmers respond vigorously to price incentives and new technology, but only when the marketing system is reasonably competitive and efficient. Otherwise, household food security and local self-sufficiency become prime objectives. Raising productivity through specialization and trade is very costly without a functioning credit system that finances such trade. Government banks, especially when profit-oriented and unsubsidized, have been important actors in building these effective credit systems throughout Asia.

Institutional Setting
To a large extent, the institutional context dictates how quickly an appropriate set of prices and an effective marketing system can be established. Major questions exist about this context in Vietnam, however. Even the government's role in managing the economy is highly controversial. Traditionally, socialist economies have been managed directly through central plans, state ownership, and control of trade and finance. Market economies must be managed indirectly via control of interest rates, fiscal policy, and regulation of the "rules of the game" governing competition. The skills required for the

market approach, in the government and in industry and finance, are totally different from those appropriate for central planning. Economies that have developed along a market path have had time for both the public and private sectors to build these skills. How quickly this expertise can be acquired in the context of socialist restructuring is a matter of considerable concern and academic debate in both the East and West. Although technical assistance is readily available to help developing countries manage the process of structural adjustment when the starting point is a mixed capitalist-socialist system (like many in Africa), few Western experts understand the institutional rigidities and incentive problems inherent in communist-socialist economies.[6]

The most important institutional elements affecting the rural economy in the short run are property rights and the flexibility of labor and capital to seek their most productive uses. The nature of land tenure, the mechanisms to transfer property rights in land, and the freedom of labor to seek employment in various locations and occupations challenge traditional socialist control mechanisms. So too will the new organization of input distribution channels—especially for fertilizer and rural credit—which are needed to improve the efficiency of input use. The role of cooperatives and collectives in agricultural production and distribution must adapt to the emergence of private-sector institutions that will function in these areas. Finally, the agricultural extension service will lose its monopoly on access to farmers and farm groups, and information on technology and production assistance will be more openly available.

The privatization of agricultural holdings, especially in the south of Vietnam, seems to have been a leading factor in the recent growth of the sector. Private land holdings in the context of small-scale agriculture are important for two reasons. First, in the short run, private holdings encourage intensity of cultivation until the marginal product of effort matches the opportunity costs of the owner's time and management resources. All of this marginal product accrues to the farm household itself, thus maximizing incentives to use these resources efficiently. The experiences of both the Vietnamese and Chinese with reforming production systems, where responsibility for decisions about inputs and cultivation was returned to individual households, demonstrate that this incentive can have powerful production results in the short run.

---

[6]These institutional rigidities that challenge the restructuring of the industrial and financial sectors are additional reasons for focusing short-term attention on the rural economy. It is much less constrained by such rigidities because of the greater role of household decision making, once a suitable price environment and marketing system is in place.

Econometric evidence suggests that the contract system, initiated in 1981, raised the productivity of rice farmers in the north by about 12 percent and in the south by 16 percent (Pingali and Xuan, 1990). But a continuing need for large-scale imports of rice in the mid-1980s and famine conditions in several provinces in 1987–88 led to further policy changes to improve incentives for farmers. Resolution No. 10 by the National Assembly, in April 1988, moved agriculture to a full contract system of household responsibility. It also permitted long-term leases as the basis of land allocation, converted local cooperatives from decision-making bodies to service organizations handling inputs and technical assistance, and opened input and output marketing to private individuals and enterprises.

The second reason private holdings are important is that in the long run farmers have the incentive to save and invest in raising the productivity of farm resources. Many farm investments take years to show a payoff, and any uncertainty a farmer has about reaping the benefit severely slows the pace of investment itself. Such uncertainty can stem from unclear land titles or short lease horizons; it can also result from instability in commodity markets, inconsistent rules about marketing and access to foreign trade, and failure to establish and enforce basic property rights.

Other elements of food policy can deal with these additional sources of uncertainty, but they have only limited payoff unless both policy and practice establish in the household cultivator's mind the basic security of land holdings. Resolution No. 10 was an important first step in establishing this security, and farmers have responded impressively to it in the form of higher productivity. To reap the longer-run benefits of greater rural investment, the country must take further steps to enhance the confidence of farm operators and other rural investors, including legal guarantees of private property rights. In 1992, a high-level team was studying how to do this.

Input markets are in a state of flux. Although limited quantities of some agricultural inputs such as fertilizer and pesticides are available from private sources, district and provincial officials are still responsible for most input supplies and distribution. Shortages of foreign exchange, inadequate transportation, and poor marketing skills have created serious shortages of most inputs, thus sharply reducing the capacity of farmers to respond to new production incentives generated by privatizing economic activity and opening markets to foreign trade. Even when supplies are available, many poor farmers feel constrained by lack of cash and access to rural credit facilities. The ineffectiveness of rural credit institutions also blocks the emergence of private traders as the core of the agricultural marketing system. Without access to liquidity credits for the financing of crop purchases and access to investment credits for the purchase of trucks and for construction of mills and warehouses, the marketing system cannot function effectively. It cannot match the social costs of transportation, storage, and processing with the needs of consumers to have goods in different places, times, and forms.

Because of very high transactions costs in marketing, price margins vary widely across different regions and from season to season, even for standard commodities such as rice for export. Rural markets tend to be localized, lacking the benefits (and competition) of long-distance trade. Local and regional self-sufficiency persists as an important priority of provincial administrators, thus stifling a major source of higher productivity in the rural economy: the specialization of farmers in crop and livestock activities under local conditions that give them a comparative advantage in production.

Although farm households are generally the most efficient in making farm production decisions, rural cooperatives and collectives offer economies of scale in input and output marketing, in credit availability, and in transmitting new technology and knowledge to farmers. Now that the government no longer obliges farmers to belong to cooperatives, the managers of these organizations must serve their members more effectively to compete with private-sector suppliers. Some cooperatives are likely to survive the competition by offering their members more secure access to inputs, possibly at lower prices. Some cooperatives are likely to fail without government guarantees or forced farmer participation. Such failures will be a healthy reminder that cooperatives are meant to serve farmers, not the other way around.

Cooperatives and collectives have helped government extension programs spread high-yielding agricultural technology and new farming practices throughout the countryside. Through close links with agricultural universities and research stations, these extension services have been quite effective in reaching most farmers, although the input-delivery system has often failed to provide the crucial supplies—on time, in the right place, and in the desired quantity and quality—that are needed to make the new technology productive. The socialist allocation system for students and research workers has probably been instrumental in the success of the extension programs; however, the sharp reduction in central control over these resources threatens this effectiveness. Whether talented individuals making private choices about careers will choose agricultural research and extension is problematical; it has been difficult throughout Asia to recruit such talent for the agricultural ministry and related sectoral jobs, once freedom of opportunity and a dynamic private-sector economy beckon.

Market Environment

The market context in Vietnam is changing rapidly. While the legal status of merchants and traders has been established, their role remains in doubt until ancillary institutions and services are provided. Improved communications (especially telephones and telexes); long-distance transportation facilities; and normal commercial infrastructure that includes bonding arrangements, enforceable grades and standards, working capital, and long-term investment credits are all essential for developing a competitive commercial structure. Only such a structure can integrate the different rural economies with each other, with urban markets, and with foreign buyers.

It is easy to undervalue this commercial infrastructure and thus to underinvest in its development, both financially and in terms of institutional innovation. Marketing is the glue that holds an economy together and generates the signals indicating what farmers should grow and what consumers can buy. These signals to farmers and consumers challenge the established approach to managing the economy, especially in socialist economies with strong traditions of central planning. But to end allocation by central planning before the market economy has developed an effective alternative runs the risk of chaos in price formation and uncertain food supplies to cities and rural areas that are not self-sufficient in food production. No government can tolerate such turmoil for long, and yet, a hybrid arrangement in which plan and market coexist is harder to manage, even as a transitional step, than central planning alone.

In the reform of rural institutions, technical assistance based on comparative experience in other Asian countries can have a big payoff. The missions sponsored by the Food and Agriculture Organization of the United Nations in 1990 and 1991 started this technical assistance, and Vietnamese officials were very enthusiastic about the potential to learn from their successful neighbors. (In Chapter 6 David Dapice discusses the benefits of learning about comparative experience.)

Learning from the experiences of other countries is especially valuable in the management of price policy. No Asian country permits free markets to determine its rice prices, and Vietnam would be foolish to be the first. Yet markets are crucial for the signals they send out on resource scarcity and consumer demand. Managing a price policy to create the stability necessary for efficient producer and consumer decision making, while reaping the efficiency derived from market signals, is one of the key tasks of an integrated food policy. A well-managed price policy can serve as one of the few bridges available between the rigidity of a centrally planned system and the flexibility of a system of resource allocation that is less controlled but guided by market signals.

A Vietnamese Price Policy for the 1990s

In an era of tightly restricted budget resources, any significant policy initiatives must identify the fiscal revenues to be used. The alternative to finding new revenues is to rely primarily on changing the economic environment in which private-sector decisions are made and to do so without using direct subsidies as the vehicle. The price policy initiatives discussed here attempt to meet these stringent budgetary requirements, at least in the short run, but there are several longer-run dimensions of a rural-oriented food policy that will require investment of public resources. Although the rural economy can be expected to finance itself as it becomes the primary engine of growth, any public revenues generated, whether at the local, provincial, or national levels, will have multiple claimants. The investments discussed here should have high priority in budgetary allocations for two reasons: the rural sector will have generated the revenues in the first place; and the productivity of the investments in the rural economy will be at least as great as elsewhere, forming the foundation for further growth.

Two areas for policy initiative can be identified. The first is in maintaining the momentum of market reforms to promote the evolution of an efficient, competitive, private marketing sector. The second is in the complex set of pricing issues, which determine the economic environment in which marketing agents (as well as private businesses, farm households, and consumers) make decisions about production, consumption, and investment. The issues in pricing policy include undertaking efforts to control inflation, understanding how the exchange rate is set, setting prices for imports and exports, and defining an appropriate role for the government in stabilizing rice and fertilizer prices.

Market Reforms

Vietnam has already made great progress in opening its rural economy to private trade. The effects are quite visible: greater availability of fertilizer and other agricultural inputs, at least close to cities and major transportation routes, and more opportunity for farmers to market their produce. At least part of the remarkable surge in rice exports in 1989 can be attributed to the willingness and capacity of the private marketing sector to accumulate rice from farmers and store, transport, and process it before shipment to overseas customers.

Even so, the capacity of the private marketing sector is limited, its facilities are primitive, and many rural regions are barely touched by the opportunities that a dynamic market economy should offer. To reach the full potential of a market economy, further steps and market reforms are needed in three areas: improved communications facilities and rural infrastructure; an effective competition policy that regulates monopolistic practices among traders; and establishment of a rural credit system that would extend short-term liquidity credits to traders (and farmers) as well as investment credits to rice millers, truckers, and other market participants willing to invest in rural infrastructure.

Communications and Infrastructure. Low marketing costs are the secret to narrow margins between farmers and consumers, whether foreign or domestic. Marketing costs include transportation, storage, and processing as well as the costs of searching out information on available supplies and potential markets and the risks involved in buying commodities in one time and place and selling them in another. Therefore, when marketing costs are high and farmers are paid low prices for their output while consumers pay high prices, the blame can be laid partly on the high cost of gasoline, trucks, and highway travel; partly on high interest rates on liquidity credit; and partly on antiquated processing facilities with poor recovery rates. These real and visible costs of marketing can be reduced only through investment in rural infrastructure and processing facilities, along with commensurate investments in a rural credit system that will lower the real cost of capital to traders.

But part of the high marketing costs will remain invisible. The search for information about trading opportunities is central to the efficiency of price formation in market economies; but without reliable telephones, telexes, trade newspapers, and price information from central markets, this search is very haphazard, expensive, and subject to abuse. When information about market opportunities is not readily and cheaply available, established families or networks of traders have a material advantage over new entrants, thus limiting competition.

Furthermore, dealing in commodities is risky in a market economy because there is no guarantee that what is bought can ultimately be sold at a profit. In an economy like Vietnam's, which has long suffered commodity shortages, the idea that surpluses could appear that would bankrupt traders holding stocks may seem unlikely or even unimportant. In a market economy, however, prices must be free to go up *and down*, and traders, not the government, should face the risks of price movements. The risks are part of doing business and thus part of marketing costs. To eliminate these risks is to prevent the marketing sector from playing its crucial allocative role. But government should not increase the risks either. Arbitrary and capricious governmental price intervention is a danger of commodity trading in both developing and developed countries. Making the rules of price intervention clear is the most effective way of lowering market risk without displacing the market function of private traders.

Beyond establishing clear signals on its pricing policies, the government has a key role to play in making market information widely available and in improving the rural infrastructure to help lower marketing costs. In Vietnam, systematic improvement in rural roads, availability of electricity and telephones, and construction of docks and port facilities will have to await new budgetary resources and probably a renewal of foreign assistance from the

World Bank and other Western donors. But some improvements require coordination more than money, and some could draw on local revenues generated by increases in the tax base that arise from improved agricultural productivity. Without doubt, the most important step the government could take to lower the costs of marketing and improve the efficiency of the marketing system would be to articulate the policy itself and show its determination to spread market information as widely and fairly as possible.

A short-run investment strategy will then emerge automatically; where marketing bottlenecks exist, margins will be high. Low farm prices (relative to other areas) and high consumer prices can readily identify these locations. After investigation, the cause of a high marketing margin can be identified— then the road repaired, the ferry fixed, a bridge built, or additional competition brought into the market, possibly in the form of government offers to buy. The point is that the most pressing problems should be identified and fixed, rather than a comprehensive plan developed to rehabilitate the country's entire rural infrastructure. Such a plan will be needed when the budget can support the work. In the meantime, authorities must focus on lowering marketing costs in the most pressing locations.

Competition Policy. Little can be gained by turning over marketing activity from public bureaucracies to a private sector that uses monopolistic practices to restrict competition. In market economies, the government is responsible for regulating the competitive environment by fostering easy entry for new enterprises and preventing restrictive practices by established ones. In the transition from a socialist marketing system to a market-oriented system, preventing excess market power from falling into the hands of a few businesses or families is not easy. In Vietnam, the legal structure to support a regulatory approach does not exist. Encouragement of new enterprises may not work if access to credit is restricted and the infrastructure (especially communications and availability of information) is limited.

In this transition period, the Vietnamese government may need to set competitive standards by example—that is, by standing ready to buy and sell key commodities within a price range that reflects the competitive costs of marketing. Financial and administrative constraints on government marketing operations mean that activities must be restricted to essential commodities—perhaps only rice and fertilizer. Even for these commodities, the object is not for the government to establish its marketing agency as a monopolist but to serve as a competitive standard to prevent monopolistic abuses by the nascent private sector. Within a decade, competition policy should evolve to a regulatory approach, and direct marketing interventions would then shrink to a minor role.

Pricing Policy

"Getting prices right" is necessary for modernizing the agricultural sector, but price policy alone is not sufficient (Timmer, 1986). Institutional change as part of market reform and technology policy is also a crucial ingredient. Getting prices wrong, however, especially in the broader sense of distortions of the incentives presented to farmers, traders, and consumers, can easily short-circuit the entire growth process. Attention to price policy can pay high returns for modest fiscal costs, particularly in the early stages of market reform under severe budgetary constraints. Indeed, once productivity gains are won, pricing policy can be used to generate fiscal resources for reinvestment in rural infrastructure.

To play this energizing role, however, pricing policy must be set in a broad context that includes macroeconomic and international trade policies. For a country as poor as Vietnam, most agricultural prices must be determined by conditions in world markets. Thus the exchange rate for the *dong* will be the single most important price—influencing the decisions made by Vietnamese farmers, traders, and consumers. Rice prices are almost as important. Some mechanism for ensuring greater price stability for rice in domestic markets than has been the case in the world market would pay big dividends in raising productivity and generating political support. Without modern inputs, however, productivity gains will not be forthcoming. Consideration for the availability and prices of fertilizers, pesticides, and fuel for irrigation pumps, trucks, and river transport must also be factored into the design of price policy.

Fiscal Policy and Inflation. Controlling inflation is obviously essential for sustained growth. Steep inflation shortens the time horizon of investors and encourages unproductive speculation. It raises risks by confusing the allocative signals in market prices. Inflation makes the development of sound financial intermediaries in rural and urban areas nearly impossible. For many reasons, Vietnam has decided that inflation must be kept under control, although the economic blockade and inability of Vietnam to tap the resources of the International Monetary Fund, the Asian Development Bank, and the World Bank are making that control extremely difficult.

The fiscal austerity that must underlie the control of inflation brings high costs. The government has great budgetary needs. The most severe poverty seems to afflict government pensioners and civil servants, including teachers and rural health workers. Nearly all the country's infrastructure needs to be rebuilt or modernized. The large foreign debt must be serviced. Where will the money come from?

The countries considered to be the major success stories of East and Southeast Asia faced similar problems. (In Chapter 6, David Dapice furnishes details.) But South Korea and Taiwan enjoyed access to very large flows of foreign aid and military assistance in the early stages of their development, which greatly alleviated the pressures on domestic resource mobilization. Indonesia, Malaysia, and Thailand exported natural resources—especially oil in Indonesia, rubber in Malaysia, and rice in Thailand—that generated sizable tax revenues. While two of the fastest growing economies in the region, Singapore and Hong Kong, received no foreign aid and did not rely on exports of natural resources, they did not have to make large investments in rural infrastructure and an agricultural research and extension system capable of modernizing a backward agricultural economy.

Vietnam thus faces the prospect of controlling inflation and servicing its external debt without the resources that neighboring countries have mobilized to maintain growth. Agriculture must make a sizable contribution to closing this resource gap, but the government must take great care to have the growth process well under way in rural areas before it employs taxation and pricing policy to divert resources to public uses outside agriculture. Several years of stimulation now will pay far higher returns than premature efforts to tax agriculture heavily. The tax base is already established in the form of land taxes and taxes on agricultural exports, including rice. In mid-1990, the government was tempted to exploit this base more intensively as the easiest way to boost revenues, but the government would have sacrificed important growth opportunities by overtaxing agriculture at this crucial juncture. The debate in the National Assembly over agricultural taxes clarified these issues considerably and resulted in the formation of a high-level commission to study the question and make new recommendations.

Macro Prices and the Exchange Rate. In mid-1989, Vietnam established a very favorable macro price environment, which lasted until mid-1990. Real interest rates were positive, wages were low (indicating an abundance of labor), inflation was brought under control, and the exchange rate freely reflected the scarcity of foreign currency. The reforms since 1988 that led to this favorable environment were largely responsible for the dramatic turnaround in the Vietnamese economy. Especially in the rural sector, institutional changes and a return to household decision making have permitted a very rapid response to new incentives.

Maintaining this favorable price environment was increasingly difficult, however, as the budget deficit grew and inflationary pressures built up. Financing the deficit through monetary policy undermined interest rates. Efforts to reduce the burden of servicing the foreign debt by preventing depreciation of the *dong* at the rate of inflation immediately threatened agricultural exports and led to pressures for administrative controls on imports. In mid-1992, the macro price environment faced serious risks and required much determination on the part of the government to stabilize it. The rural economy continues to have an enormous stake in the macro price environment, however; the growth strategy based on rapidly rising productivity in agriculture and rural industry is threatened without this supportive economic environment.

Border Prices for Agricultural Commodities. Perhaps the dominant lesson from development experience since the 1960s has been the importance of an "outward orientation" for economic strategy. For agriculture as well as for industry, world markets provide the most appropriate signals about the relative scarcity and abundance of individual commodities, and thus of the desirability of producing and consuming them. Border prices—the prices a country pays to import or receives from exporting commodities—transmit these signals to domestic decision makers via the marketing system. As a starting point, countries restructuring their economies after decades of distortions induced by central planning and isolation from world markets should use border prices as a guide to what to produce.

Vietnam has gone a step farther. By actually opening up the economy to international trade in most commodities while keeping the exchange rate at a competitive level, the government has accelerated the restructuring. Market forces transmit border prices to Vietnamese decision makers, who are free to respond by importing or exporting. Unfortunately, the marketing system that transmits these signals is still very inefficient and costly. In addition, institutional rules are unclear for determining the participants in international trade, the licenses and permits required, and the role of government officials. The risks and costs of trading are thereby raised, but the more serious effect is to dampen the efficiency with which price signals from world markets are passed on to Vietnamese farmers, traders, and consumers. Because quick responses to opportunities in these markets will be an important source of growth for the entire economy, and especially the agricultural economy, the failure to transmit the correct signals will severely impede growth.

Price Policy for Rice. Rice prices are far too important to farmers, consumers, and the economy to be left to the whims of an unstable world market. Since the early 1970s, real prices for rice in world markets have varied by a factor of 10. Introducing such instability into the Vietnamese economy would place great burdens on consumers, who obtain roughly 60 percent of their food energy and protein from rice, as well as on producers, whose main source of income (low as it is) is the rice crop. The rice economy probably supports one-half of the employment in the country and contributes about one-sixth of national income. A high priority is to prevent sharp fluctuations in world market prices from destabilizing the domestic rice economy.

At the same time, the world rice market contains important information about the value of producing more rice. Vietnam is the world's third largest rice exporter and must take market conditions more or less as they are. Subsidies to rice farmers when world prices are extremely low, as in the mid-1980s, might be desirable on grounds of both equity and efficiency, but budget realities prevent their serious consideration. When world rice prices rise sharply, as they did in the mid-1970s, some protection for consumers is possible by taxing rice exports at a progressive rate, thus keeping domestic rice prices below world prices and generating budget revenues as well. Targeting some of the proceeds for reinvestment in the rural economy would help ease the burden on farmers and raise productivity in the future.

Apart from mechanisms to cope with these extremes in world rice prices, Vietnam's domestic rice prices must follow export prices, minus the necessary marketing margins between the farm gate and the f.o.b. price on board the export vessel. This export price is always below the equivalent import price, thus providing a significant bonus—perhaps 20 to 30 percent of the retail price—in the form of lower prices to consumers. The export price also forces farmers to compete with other efficient foreign producers (or with subsidies from rich countries), thus increasing the importance of access to cost-reducing technology and the modern inputs needed to raise yields. A low-cost, efficient marketing system also enhances the ability of farmers to grow rice for export, especially in a country as geographically diverse as Vietnam.

Price policy for rice then has two components: following the world export price in most years, while making investments that lower production and marketing costs; and preparing standby mechanisms to stabilize domestic prices if the world rice market suffers a serious shortage. Budget realities prevent a parallel effort to subsidize farmers in the face of a collapse in world rice prices, but investments to help farmers diversify cropping systems and to make the rural economy more flexible in response to changing market conditions can ease the burden of adjustment (Timmer, 1988). The announcement by the Vietnamese government in late 1990 that export taxes for rice would vary from 3 to 10 percent, depending on world market prices, indicates an appropriate balance between the concern for revenues and stability on one hand and farmer incentives on the other. If the world market price for rice in the 1990s stays at levels much higher than those in the 1980s, both Vietnamese farmers and the national budget will benefit.

Price Policy for Agricultural Inputs. Most modern inputs for agricultural production are imported. The availability and cost of nitrogen fertilizer (the "fuel" for the efficient plant engine of high-yielding varieties), pesticides for occasional outbreaks of insects and diseases that are not controlled genetically or by natural predators, and gasoline and diesel fuel for the irrigation pumps depend on world prices and the exchange rate for the *dong*. In a market economy, if these inputs have high productivity, farmers would be able to bid for the necessary foreign exchange to import supplies. But in a bureaucratic distribution system, constrained by limited access to foreign exchange, agricultural inputs frequently fail to arrive where and when they are needed and in appropriate formulations and qualities.

Pricing policy for inputs thus has two dimensions. Although most countries try to subsidize fertilizer in the early stages of adopting new plant varieties—to encourage farmers to experiment with new techniques—only a few countries have had the budget resources to ensure the success of such a policy. Given Vietnam's budget constraints, fertilizer (and other input) pricing will have to reflect the full costs of importing (or producing where appropriate) at a market exchange rate.

The second and more important dimension is formulating a distribution policy that overcomes the significant problems with availability of supplies and timely access by farmers to them. The policies and investments designed to stimulate development of the private marketing system for agricultural output will also serve to develop the input supply industry. No Asian country has been able to modernize its agricultural sector while monopolizing the distribution of fertilizer, seeds, pesticides, and fuel. But neither has any country turned all these tasks over to the private sector. The search for appropriate roles for both the public and private sectors in input distribution will require time and careful appraisal of results. An approach that encourages the two sectors to compete with each other, rather than dividing up tasks into various controlled products and regions, would better serve farmer interests.

Links among Prices of Inputs, Output, and Foreign Exchange. In a well-functioning market economy, farmers will continue to invest in productive inputs to produce additional output as long as the value of increased output is larger than the costs of the additional inputs needed to produce it (including the "costs" to the farmer of incurring the risk of the investment in the first place). If inputs, such as fertilizer, and output, such as rice, are tradable commodities with stable world prices, the foreign exchange rate becomes a crucial factor in determining the profitability of this investment, that is, of importing fertilizer to produce additional rice for export.

A simple calculation illustrates the point. The calculation is designed to illustrate the connection among prices for agricultural inputs, output such as rice, and the foreign exchange rate used to calculate the border prices in Vietnamese currency (*dong* or $VN) for both inputs and output. In the example, the border price for imported urea is U.S. $150 per ton (but shortages keep the market price above this level in domestic currency), the export price for Vietnamese rice (35 percent brokens) is $200 per ton, and the effective exchange rate is 6,000 *dong* per U.S. dollar. Assuming marketing costs to the farm level are 20 percent of value at the port, the relative price of paddy to urea at the farm level is about 0.48, as shown by the following calculations:

Border price for urea =

U.S. $150 per ton × $VN 6,000 =	
price at port per kilogram	$VN 900
+ marketing cost per kilogram	180
+ "scarcity premium" per kilogram	220
farm price of urea per kilogram	$VN 1,300

Border price for rice =

U.S. $200 per ton × $VN 6,000 =	
price at port per kilogram	$VN 1,200
− marketing cost per kilogram	240
farm price of rice per kilogram	960
× 0.65 = farm price of paddy per kilogram	$VN 624

The relative price of paddy to urea at the farm level = 624 ÷ 1,300 = 0.48.

If additional urea could be imported to eliminate the "scarcity premium," thus allowing urea to be priced at its import cost plus domestic marketing costs, the farm price could drop to 1,080 *dong* per kilogram, which raises the price ratio of paddy to urea from 0.48 to 0.58, an increase of 20.9 percent. If the price elasticity of demand for urea with respect to this ratio is −0.6 (a figure similar to Indonesia's at comparable levels of urea use), applications of urea would increase by 12.5 percent, from 200 to 225 kilograms per hectare. If farmers allocate the fertilizer to the rice fields with the greatest agronomic response, each kilogram of urea should produce about 5 kilograms of paddy. (Many fields will produce even larger amounts; so a response rate of 5 to 1 is conservative.) Paddy yields would increase by 125 kilograms per hectare, a figure calculated as follows: 225 − 200 = an increase of 25 kilograms per hectare, times 5 equals an increase of 125 kilograms per hectare in yield of paddy. The net foreign exchange earnings from this "investment" of six to eight months is the export value of the rice produced minus the import costs of urea, or a total of $12.50 per hectare. The rice is valued at $200 per ton, and 81.25 kilograms of rice are produced (125 kilograms of paddy times 0.65), for an export value of $16.25 per hectare. The additional 25 kilograms of urea per hectare cost $150 per ton, for an import cost of $3.75 per hectare.

Additional domestic resources, valued in *dong*, are used in these transactions. The assumptions used in the price calculations—20 percent marketing costs and 20 percent additional farm-level production costs—imply that

39,600 *dong* per hectare in domestic resources are required to produce the net foreign exchange earnings of $12.50 per hectare:

Marketing cost of
Fertilizer: 25 kilograms × 0.2 × 15¢ per kilogram × $VN 6,000 = $VN 4,500

Marketing cost of
Rice: 81 kilograms × 0.2 × 20¢ per kilogram × $VN 6,000 =   11,760

Production cost of
Paddy: 125 kilograms × 0.2 × $VN 624 per kilogram =   15,600
                                                                                                                    ─────────
                                                                                                                    $VN 39,600

Domestic resource cost per U.S. dollar earned = $VN 39,600 ÷ U.S. $12.50 = $VN 3,168.

Because the market rate for one U.S. dollar is 6,000 *dong* (when this example was calculated), the social profitability of importing additional urea for application on rice can be seen to be very high. Rice can "earn" dollars by using only 3,168 *dong* per dollar, while the market rate is 6,000 *dong*. Such highly profitable short-run investments typically occur only in economies that are badly out of equilibrium, those in which shortages and rationing of foreign exchange prevent prices from reflecting full social values and costs. Eventually, a well-functioning market economy brings the value to farmers of using more fertilizer much closer to its cost in world markets, delivered to the farm level. In the meantime, Vietnam has an important opportunity to increase its net earnings of foreign exchange quite rapidly by importing additional urea and distributing it as widely as possible in rural markets.

Concluding Observations

In a number of directions, the policy approach developed here appears radical in comparison with the Vietnamese reality. In other dimensions, however, the approach grows directly out of recent Vietnamese experience and draws on the most promising aspects of socialist concern for the welfare of the poor. The result is a hybrid: a cross between the rural-oriented growth strategies that have served several Asian countries so well and a socialist restructuring that directs opportunities and limited resources to the poor.

Implementing such a rural-oriented growth strategy, which has served several Asian countries so well, will be difficult, if only because no other country has faced the same set of circumstances and problems. Despite the difficulties, Vietnam now faces opportunities as well. The timing for a radically new approach to solving Vietnam's rural problems is propitious, partly because the challenge to the established way of doing business is so pressing and partly because the country is already well down the thorny path of policy reform.

The involvement of and support from a wide array of parties is required for the day-to-day implementation of the various components of the strategy proposed here. Agricultural research institutes must be incorporated in the strategy as well as district officers responsible for monitoring development of new rural credit offices. How are all of these components and agencies to be coordinated? A much greater reliance on market mechanisms is part of the answer, but coordination of government initiatives requires an agency with the capacity to grasp the overall agricultural policy framework and to carry out trouble-shooting investigations that identify emerging problems and propose solutions.

There is no particular institutional home for this capacity to monitor and evaluate. The planning agency, the ministry of agriculture, the finance ministry, or the food logistics agency are all plausible candidates, depending on the skills of the staff, the historical nature of their tasks, and the leadership at the top. Policy analysts often underestimate the power of, even necessity for, visionary leadership in the implementation of new strategic directions. Vietnam needs a clearly articulated vision of where a new agricultural policy is taking the country.

Regardless of the economic blockade, nearly all the resources, vision, and leadership essential to success in this endeavor must come from Vietnam itself. A country's food policy must satisfy its own unique needs in the context of an historical setting that no other country's experiences will duplicate. Not all mistakes must be learned from direct experience, however. Skills, resources, and comparative perspective can be borrowed from abroad if the policy framework is in place to use them effectively. Most Vietnamese leaders will assume that the most valuable resources the foreign community can bring to the country are financial, either as loans and grants from the donor community or as direct foreign investment by the private sector. Such financial resources will have high productivity, to be sure, especially because Vietnam has been cut off from them for so long and the budgetary situation is so desperate.

But equally valuable will be knowledge of how the outside world works. Vietnam has been cut off from this resource also, and, increasingly, knowledge is the engine of economic growth. This knowledge is not just scientific and technological, although that is important. A government needs to understand the organization and functioning of economies and the nature of competitive advantage in the world economy. Vietnam cannot hope to become rich without such knowledge, and it would take decades to learn on its own.

Speeding up the process will require technical and advisory assistance that serves the interests of Vietnam, but such assistance is useless until the country has settled on a strategic approach for its long march to modernization.

This chapter proposes one element of that approach, a rural-oriented food policy. The rural economy is selected as the focus for rapid growth because it is more responsive in the short run to new economic incentives, has great untapped potential to increase productivity, and is the home of most of the country's citizens, including its poorest. No country, however, gets rich by focusing all its resources on agriculture. Eventually, Vietnam must shift its attention to building a modern urban economy based on export-oriented industry and technology-based services. But by then, the rural strategy will have reduced poverty and stimulated the development of a much more effective array of linkages from farms to rural industry and to the urban economy. The rural economy will decline in importance, not out of neglect or heavy taxation but because its performance will have laid the foundation for the rest of the economy.

References

Bottema, Taco, Dang Thanh Ha, and Pham Thanh Binh. 1991. "Collective and Individual Production: Sweet Potato in North and Central Viet Nam." In J. W. Taco Bottema, Pham Thanh Binh, Dang Thanh Ha, Mai Thach Hoanh, and H. Kim, *Sweet Potato in Viet Nam: Production and Markets*, pp. 59–94. CGPRT Report No. 24. Bogor, Indonesia: Centre for Research and Development of Coarse Grains, Pulses, Roots and Tuber Crops in the Humid Tropics of Asia and the Pacific.

Dao Cong Tien. 1991. "The Renovation (*Doimoi*) of Agricultural Policy Mechanisms in Vietnam." Ho Chi Minh City: Ho Chi Minh City University of Economics.

Pingali, Prabhu L., and Vo-Tong Xuan. 1990. "Vietnam: De-Collectivization and Rice Productivity Growth." Los Baños, Philippines: International Rice Research Institute, Social Science Division.

Socialist Republic of Vietnam. 1991. *Economy and Trade of Vietnam, 1986–1990.* Hanoi: General Statistical Office, Trade Information Centre (Ministry of Trade).

Timmer, C. Peter. 1986. *Getting Prices Right: The Scope and Limits of Agricultural Price Policy.* Ithaca: Cornell University Press.

———. 1988. "Crop Diversification in Rice-Based Agricultural Economies: Conceptual and Policy Issues." In Ray A. Goldberg, ed., *Research in Domestic and International Agribusiness Management*, Vol. 8, pp. 95–163. Greenwich, CT: JAI Press.

Xuan, Vo-Tong, and C. Peter Timmer. 1990. "A Food Policy for Vietnam." HIID Development Discussion Paper No. 351. Prepared for presentation to the National Assembly of the Socialist Republic of Vietnam, June 1990. Cambridge, MA: Harvard Institute for International Development.

8

Vietnam: Successes and Failures of Macroeconomic Stabilization

David Dollar

Vietnam has made remarkable changes in an extraordinarily difficult environment. Soviet aid worth roughly $1 billion (in U.S. dollars) per year ceased abruptly, with no substantial replacement from the West. During the period of Soviet aid, Vietnam's economy grew only sporadically and was beset by hyperinflation. The withdrawal of assistance raised the prospect of an even poorer macroeconomic performance. However, the government responded to the external shock with an ambitious program of price liberalization and structural reforms. The reforms stimulated growth and reduced inflation well below the hyperinflation levels of the 1985–88 period. Within a short space of time, the country has completely reoriented its external trade, from the now-defunct Soviet Union to the dynamic market of East Asia. That this adjustment was accomplished without a recession is extraordinary and hints at the resilience and potential of the Vietnamese economy.

Unlike Eastern European economies trying to make a similar transition, Vietnam is a largely agricultural economy with a small state sector, an initial condition very favorable to swift transition. Furthermore, Vietnam is different from China in that its poor fiscal and financial condition provides compelling motivation to reform state enterprises quickly. On strictly economic grounds, Vietnam has arguably the best characteristics to support rapid development in a market environment.

One important lesson from recent years is that Vietnam in 1991, with virtually no foreign aid, was clearly far better off than Vietnam in the mid-1980s with massive aid from the Soviet Union. To be fair, some Soviet investment in infrastructure (i.e., hydropower) appears to yield a good return now; but much of the assistance served only to prop up an inefficient state-enterprise sector and an overblown bureaucracy. Vietnam provides evidence that good policies are more important than foreign aid. Having said that, it is still the case that foreign assistance can play a positive role in a poor country such as Vietnam, provided it is well targeted to public investments in economic and social infrastructure.

Although Vietnam's reform during 1989–91 was very impressive, the government did not succeed in fully stabilizing the economy. Inflation remained too high, and the economy faces a host of serious problems in the near term. It will be difficult for Vietnam to consolidate its stabilization program without renewed financing from the West. Stabilization requires that the country reduce the size and scope of the public sector. This adjustment will exacerbate, in the short run, an already serious unemployment problem and could interfere with the provision of important social services and the construction of economic infrastructure. Foreign assistance could ease these social problems and infrastructure bottlenecks. But in the absence of such assistance, it will be painful for Vietnam to stabilize and difficult for the economy to grow at more than 5 percent per year. Once the U.S. trade embargo is dropped and normal foreign assistance to Vietnam resumes, the economy should be able to reach a substantially higher growth rate.

The Starting Point

It is fashionable to lump Vietnam and China together as Asian socialist economies attempting to introduce market forces into their economies without fundamentally altering their political systems. While there are some obvious parallels between the two countries, there are also some important differences. In many ways, Vietnam is more similar to the East Asian Newly Industrialized Countries (NICs) in the early stages of their development than it is to China. The parallel is particularly strong between Vietnam and three of the NIC countries: before commencing their rapid development, high inflation and slow growth characterized Taiwan (late 1940s), South Korea (early 1950s), and Indonesia (early 1960s). In fact, each of these economies, in turn, was considered a "basket case" with little prospect for development. Vietnam has the same potential as these economies to stabilize and develop, and it would do well to implement many of the policies that they have adopted. Vietnam has better prospects of replicating the NIC experience than of following China's path of gradual socialist reform.

This assessment is based on six characteristics of Vietnam that have a crucial bearing on its current macroeconomic instability and that are likely to condition its socioeconomic development over the next two decades. The first is the country's strong natural-resource endowment, including its location. The nation is located in the heart of one of the most dynamic regions of the world economy. In addition, Vietnam is blessed with a long coastline, which means that most areas of the country potentially have good transport linkages to the rest of the region and the world. The long coastline is also an important resource for fishing and aquaculture, and the country has good land for rice production and a range of other tropical products. Finally, there are substantial and as yet untapped mineral resources, including oil and natural gas.

A second, and more important, characteristic of Vietnam is that the human-resource base is excellent. For an extremely poor country, Vietnam performs impressively in a range of social indicators, such as life expectancy, child and maternal mortality, literacy, and school enrollment rates. The wide diffusion of education and health services is a prerequisite for successful socioeconomic development, and Vietnam has established a good foundation of social services upon which it can build. In this regard, it is similar to NIC economies like Taiwan and Korea, as well as to China.

The state sector in Vietnam is smaller than in any other of the reforming socialist economies, a third important characteristic. In terms of the size of the state sector, Vietnam is more similar to developing market economies than to the reforming planned economies. This fact derives from the small share of industry in the economy and from the dominance of agriculture and services by the nonstate sector.[1] The difference between Eastern Europe and Vietnam in the weight of industry in the economy is particularly extreme, but even China is far more industrialized than Vietnam. China has many large state enterprises in heavy sectors like steel, fertilizer, machinery, and motor vehicles. In fact, each major city in China typically has a full range of these heavy industries.[2] In Vietnam, on the other hand, there is virtually no heavy industry. On the eve of the 1989 reforms, nearly half of manufacturing employment was concentrated in two labor-intensive sectors: textiles and food processing.[3] Much of this light industry was located in the southern half of the country and had been developed in a market environment. One of the implications of this absence of industry is that Vietnam was never a planned economy in the same sense as the Chinese, Soviet, or Eastern European economies.[4] To say that the only thing distributed through the Vietnamese planning apparatus has been Soviet commodity aid is an overstatement, but only a mild one. It is especially

[1]Revised national accounts for 1989 indicate that industry accounted for only about one-fifth of gross national product (GDP). Agriculture and services each accounted for about two-fifths. The small weight of industry and the large weight of services are very unusual for a socialist economy. These national accounts show that the nonstate sector produces almost two-thirds of GDP.

[2]On the prevalence of heavy industry in China and the lack of geographic specialization, see Gregory Chow (1985) or World Bank (1985).

[3]Out of 2.87 million manufacturing workers in 1988, 1.43 million were in food processing or textiles/garments/leather. (See Socialist Republic of Vietnam, 1991, pp. 33–35.)

[4]Fforde and de Vylder (1988) describe well how the Vietnamese economy was functioning in the 1980s.

true for the southern half of Vietnam, but it also captures the reality of the northern half fairly well too.

A fourth important characteristic of Vietnam is that the nation is in very poor fiscal condition. The government's savings rate remains negative, and the savings rate for the country as a whole is very low, less than 10 percent of GDP. In this fundamental respect, Vietnam is extremely different from China. Gross domestic saving was 36 percent of China's GDP in 1989. Government revenue collection as a share of GDP is nearly twice as high in China as in Vietnam, with the result that the Chinese public sector has significant savings. In addition, China's external debt in 1989 was around 10 percent of gross national product (GNP), even after a decade of openness and reform. Vietnam begins its era of reform with an external debt roughly equal to GNP. This large difference in the financial condition of the two countries limits the relevance of China's experience to Vietnam. In particular, China has been able to proceed slowly with price liberalization and state-enterprise reform because it has the fiscal resources to subsidize its firms. Similar policies in Vietnam's resource-constrained environment would inevitably produce inflation. This fiscal constraint makes Vietnam more similar to Indonesia, Korea, and Taiwan (in their periods of instability) than to China.

Vietnam's recent legacy of capitalism in its southern half is a fifth important characteristic. Many entrepreneurs have left the country during the past two decades, but still an important base of entrepreneurial talent remains. This capitalist legacy is one of the reasons that the nonstate sector has developed so dynamically in response to the reform program. Furthermore, the overseas Vietnamese are an additional resource, bringing managerial talent, capital, and technology to the economy. Economic links between overseas Vietnamese communities and the home country have sprung up rapidly in recent years.

A final important issue is that the south is richer than the north, by a factor of about two to one. The population is divided almost exactly between the two regions. Natural resources, however, are not distributed in the same way, with the north having considerably less arable land. Population density in the Red River Delta (658 persons per square kilometer in 1989) is nearly twice as high as in the Mekong Delta (355 persons per square kilometer). These differences in population density translate directly into inequality in amounts of arable land per capita. For rice production, sown area per capita is .09 hectare in the Red River Delta and .17 hectare in the Mekong provinces.[5] There are other important resources that are also distributed unevenly. The

---

[5]See Socialist Republic of Vietnam (1991), pp. 43 and 100.

capital stock for light manufacturing—the industrial sector with the most potential in the medium term—is concentrated in the south, particularly in Ho Chi Minh City. Furthermore, transport and other infrastructure is better in the south than in the north. The one exception in the infrastructure area is power: the north is amply supplied now that the Hoa Binh hydropower station is operating, whereas there are serious dry-season power shortages in the south. The regional inequalities are not simply a north-south issue either. The northern central coast, for instance, is far poorer than the Red River Delta provinces. And in the south, Ho Chi Minh City and its immediate environs has much higher per capita income than other areas in the south.

The 1989 Stabilization Program

Vietnam in 1988 presented a classic case of a developing country with macroeconomic instability. Price increases neared hyperinflation levels. Furthermore, the country had a massive balance-of-payments deficit that it could not finance. Vietnam, however, is not a typical developing country; in recent years, it has been a centrally planned economy in transition to a market-based system. Faced with a growing macroeconomic crisis, the leadership decided early in 1989 to adopt a bold combination of structural reforms and orthodox stabilization measures. The former involved liberalizing most domestic prices; the latter included raising interest rates, restraining the growth of credit, and devaluing the exchange rate. At the time, there were good reasons to be skeptical about the efficacy of these measures. First, these tools do not necessarily have the same effect in a socialist economy as in a market economy. Second, the measures lacked financial support from the International Monetary Fund (IMF) or the World Bank.

The stabilization program was amazingly successful for about one year. Inflation halted abruptly in the middle of 1989. Rice production increased substantially, and the balance-of-payments situation improved markedly. Some groups were certainly hurt by the stabilization measures, notably public-sector workers in the bureaucracy and in enterprises. Informal urban activity, however, expanded rapidly. The typical urban family earns some income from formal, public-sector employment and some from informal activities. Hence, even in urban areas, most families were better off in 1989 than in 1988. Certainly, in the main rice-growing areas, the Mekong and Red River deltas, family income rose materially.[6] Thus, in 1989, Vietnam presented

---

[6]The increase in per capita food-grain production provides an indication of the scale of the rise in household income. In Red River Delta provinces, the increase was from 287.7 kg. in 1988 to

almost a unique case of a rigorous stabilization program that made just about everyone better off—all at once.

By the end of 1989, however, the stabilization effort was coming undone. Monthly inflation rates returned to the 2 to 3 percent range by the fall of 1989 and continued to accelerate throughout 1990. The general price increase from December 1989 to December 1990 was 67.5 percent, and inflation continued at the same rate in 1991. The balance-of-payments situation deteriorated during 1990 and 1991. The collapse of the Soviet Union, one of Vietnam's main trading partners and aid donors, led to acute shortages of several key imported inputs, notably refined petroleum and fertilizer. The overall growth of real GDP, which had shown a healthy 8 percent increase in 1989, decelerated to 5 percent in 1990 and 3 percent in 1991.[7]

Vietnam's initial success with stabilization resulted from interest-rate and other price reforms. The economy returned to instability in 1990 and 1991 because these reforms were not backed up by sufficient retrenchment of the public sector. Some of the main features of the stabilization effort are captured in Figure 8-1, which plots the monthly inflation rate, beginning in January 1987, as well as the interest rate for household deposits in the formal banking system. Inflation reached nearly 30 percent per month in early 1988. During this period of hyperinflation, deposit interest rates were consistently below the inflation rate; not surprisingly, there were few deposits into the banks.

One component of the 1989 reforms was to raise interest rates, both for deposits and for lending. The deposit lending rate was lifted to 7 percent per month in the second half of 1988, and then to 9 percent per month in the spring of 1989. It can be seen in Figure 8-1 that inflation halted quite dramatically in the summer of 1989. Other price reforms complemented the interest rate adjustments. The government unified and devalued the exchange rate and legalized gold trading. As a consequence of these reforms, households shifted some portion of their liquid assets out of gold and dollars, which circulate quite freely in Vietnam, back into *dong*-denominated assets (i.e., domestic currency notes or bank deposits). In Vietnam, as in other

---

314.4 kg. in 1989. In Mekong Delta provinces, the increase was from 535.3 kg in 1988 to 631.9 kg in 1989. See Socialist Republic of Vietnam (1991), pp. 48–49.

[7]Official publications often cite the growth rate of net material product, which in recent years has been well below the growth rate of GDP. The reason for the difference is that net material product excludes most services, which have been a high growth area in Vietnam. In addition, the GDP growth rates cited here are calculated in 1989 prices, whereas net material product in Vietnam is calculated in 1982 prices. The latter discriminate against agriculture, another high-growth sector, particularly in 1989. Total food-grain production increased from 19.6 million tons in 1988 to 21.5 million in 1989. Production in 1990 and 1991 remained at the 1989 level. See the Socialist Republic of Vietnam statistical data (1991), p. 45.

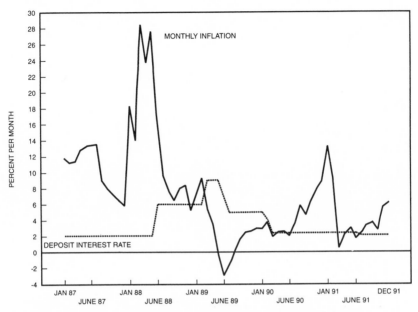

Figure 8-1. Monthly Inflation and Deposit Interest Rates (1987–91)

economies experiencing hyperinflation, people had largely stopped holding the domestic currency. The shift back into dong was only partial, but it had an important impact.

There is evidence to demonstrate this portfolio adjustment by households. First, the free-market prices of gold and U.S. dollars both fell precipitously in the spring of 1989—declines of roughly 20 to 25 percent. This drop can be seen in Figure 8-2, which plots the prices of three commodities—gold, dollars, and rice—deflated by the retail price index. This measure indicates the real purchasing power of these commodities over a typical retail basket of goods and services. The sudden drop in the real purchasing power of gold and dollars is consistent with the notion of a portfolio shift back into dong-denominated assets. In principle, a sudden change in the supplies of these commodities could also account for the price movements; it is unlikely, however, that any sudden, large increase in the supplies of gold and dollars occurred. More plausible is a sudden decline in demand for these items as a result of renewed confidence in, and hence demand for, the domestic currency.

Households in Vietnam have also maintained a significant share of their wealth in rice stocks, and in 1989, there was some shift out of rice into liquid dong assets—that is, households sold some of their rice stocks. This would tend to depress the price of rice in the same way that the prices of gold and dollars fell in the spring of 1989. It can be seen in Figure 8-2, however, that

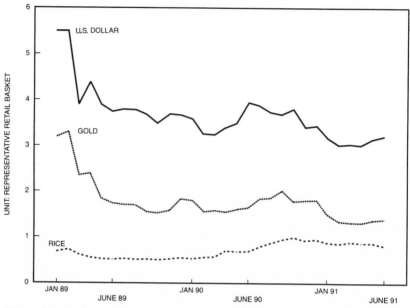

Figure 8-2. Real Purchasing Power of U.S. Dollars, Gold, and Rice (1989-91)

the decline in the relative price of rice at that time was very minor. The apparent reason for this is the liberalization of rice trading and rice exporting in the spring of 1989, with the much-publicized result that Vietnam immediately became a major rice exporter. That ability to export significant quantities of rice quickly prevented any sharp fall in the price of rice.

An additional piece of evidence concerning the portfolio shift into domestic currency is the dramatic growth in the dong deposits from households into the banking system. Figure 8-3 shows these household deposits (deflated into constant March 1989 prices) quarter by quarter from March 1989 to March 1991. (Above each data point is the real deposit interest rate, calculated as the deposit rate on nontime deposits minus the current monthly inflation rate.) Throughout 1989, real deposit rates were strongly positive, and household deposits increased tenfold between March 1989 and March 1990, albeit from a small base.

So there is strong evidence that the reforms of early 1989 succeeded in getting households to shift, at least partially, into dong-denominated assets. It was not simply the result of higher interest rates. In my view, it was the coordinated price reforms, plus trade liberalization, that restored confidence in the currency. Those price reforms included interest-rate increases, devaluation of the exchange rate, and liberalization of many other prices, including rice and gold.

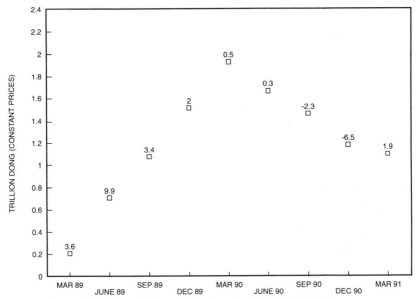

***Figure 8-3.** Real Household Deposits and Interest Rates (1989–91)*

There was also some increase in lending rates in 1989. Virtually all the lending from the banking system, however, goes to the government budget or to state enterprises, and it is not clear whether either client is very sensitive to interest rates. During the first half of 1989 the state bank evidently also restrained the expansion of credit to state enterprises. It is difficult to find data to prove this last assertion, but during my visits to enterprises in the summer of 1989, managers universally complained that credit was simply unavailable.

Monetary data for the end of each year tell a somewhat surprising story. As one can see in Table 8-1, domestic credit was growing very fast in 1987 and 1988.[8] In the latter year, for instance, credit rose 394.9 percent, and retail price inflation was an almost identical 393.8 percent. In 1989, the growth of credit slowed, but not by very much: the increase for the year was a startling 155.1 percent. It is remarkable that the accompanying inflation rate was only 34.7 percent. I interpret these data to mean that the reforms early in 1989

[8]There is quite a bit of uncertainty about the macroeconomic data for Vietnam. The figures in Tables 8-1 through 8-4 are estimates by World Bank staff based on primary data provided by the authorities. These figures are likely to be refined in the future. Revision of the data is unlikely to alter the basic macroeconomic story. I have chosen to present most of the data as a share of GDP, which facilitates the analysis. No doubt the estimate of nominal GDP will improve in the future. But even a significant adjustment in the estimate of the level of nominal GDP would not alter the analysis; it would merely change the denominators for all the figures expressed as a share of GDP more or less proportionally, so that the trends would remain as before.

Table 8-1. Monetary Data, 1987–90

	1987	1988	1989	1990
End of Period, as a Percent of GDP				
Total Liquidity (M2)	10.0	10.5	19.6	17.5
Dong liquidity	9.4	9.6	13.7	11.8
Currency	4.4	4.2	6.6	6.0
Dong deposits	5.0	5.3	7.1	5.8
Household	0.8	0.8	3.8	3.4
Foreign-currency deposits	0.6	1.0	5.9	5.7
Domestic Credit	11.3	10.8	19.0	15.7
Government	1.7	2.7	7.3	6.5
Enterprises	9.6	8.0	11.6	9.3
Percent Change from Year Before				
Total Liquidity (M2)		445.4	170.0	57.7
Dong liquidity		426.5	108.7	51.7
Currency		399.5	129.7	59.2
Dong deposits		449.8	92.2	44.7
Household		455.6	574.0	59.6
Foreign-currency deposits		734.5	759.5	71.6
Domestic Credit		394.9	155.1	46.0
Government		736.3	288.6	54.8
Enterprises		334.5	109.6	40.5
Retail Prices (December to December)		393.8	34.7	67.5

brought about a large increase in demand for real dong balances, as I have discussed. The monetary data provide additional support for this notion. For instance, household deposits as a share of GDP grew from 0.8 percent at the end of 1988 to 3.8 percent at the end of 1989. The ratio of the total money supply to GDP nearly doubled, from 10.5 percent to 19.6 percent.

As a result of the demand for real dong balances, the government was able to expand credit very substantially in the second half of 1989, generating only moderate inflation. Virtually all credit in Vietnam has gone to the public sector—either to the budget or to state enterprises. The pattern of credit creation has changed in recent years, however. At the end of 1988, most of the credit outstanding was to state enterprises (the equivalent of 8.0 percent of GDP) rather than to the budget (2.7 percent of GDP). In 1989 and 1990, however, new credit to the budget far outpaced new credit to enterprises—in 1989, for instance, by 288.6 percent to 109.6 percent.

It is ironic that the growth of the money supply and its main components slowed further in 1990, while at the same time inflation accelerated to nearly triple digits. The reason: in 1989 the government succeeded in getting economic agents to shift back into dong to a great extent, which provided some leeway to expand the money supply without generating excessive inflation. Such a large portfolio shift, however, is a one-time phenomenon, associated with the early stages of a stabilization effort. There was no further large change in the money supply as a share of GDP during 1990. Thus, during 1990, money-supply (M2) growth of 57.7 percent passed through directly into the price level, which increased 67.5 percent. Again in 1990, growth in credit to the budget exceeded growth in credit to enterprises.

In summary, the government has managed to gradually reduce the growth rate of the money supply. This has not, however, gradually reduced inflation. Because of the portfolio shift in the first half of 1989, inflation halted almost completely in response to price reforms and some restraint on the growth of credit. To consolidate this anti-inflation program, the government would have needed to exercise further restraint on the growth of credit in the second half of 1989 and in 1990. The financing of the budget through the banking system, however, continued at an excessive rate, and consequently inflation reemerged at a disturbing level.

Fiscal Developments

The fundamental source of inflation in Vietnam is a fiscal deficit that is large relative to the resources available to finance it, as Table 8-2, a summary of budgetary operations consolidated for all levels of government, shows. The most striking feature of Vietnam's fiscal situation is the low level of revenue collection. In 1988, only 11.3 percent of GDP was collected as government revenue. Transfers from state enterprises accounted for most of that revenue.

Revenue collection as a share of GDP declined significantly between 1986 and 1988. It is difficult to know for sure why this was so, but one plausible theory is that tax collection weakened as macroeconomic instability grew. The year 1988 was a low point for Vietnam in many ways, including the government's revenue performance. One would have expected the revenue situation to

Table 8-2. Summary of Budgetary Operations (as a Percent of GDP)

	1986	1987	1988	1989	1990
(1) Revenue	13.2	12.2	11.3	11.9	13.1
(2) Current expenditures	13.4	12.8	14.1	12.3	15.1
(3) Government saving [(1) − (2)]	−0.2	−0.6	−2.8	−0.4	−2.0
(4) Capital expenditure	5.6	3.9	4.4	6.4	4.5
(5) Overall deficit [(3) − (4)][a]	−5.8	−4.4	−7.1	−6.8	−6.5
Financing					
(6) Foreign loans and grants	2.2	1.4	2.4	1.5	4.0
(7) Credit from state bank (net)	3.6	2.9	2.9	6.0	2.5

[a]Figures do not add exactly due to rounding.

worsen further as the country embarked on price and institutional reforms during 1989 and 1990, because the reforms strengthened sectors that have not been well taxed (agriculture and the private sector) at the expense of state enterprises that form the core of the tax base. But revenue actually increased during the reform years, to 11.9 percent of GDP in 1989 and 13.1 percent in 1990. The sources of revenue, however, did change significantly in this period. In real terms, transfers from state enterprises declined by one-third between 1987 and 1990. At the same time, taxes collected from the nonstate sector increased slightly. The key to the overall revenue buoyancy in this period has been the rapid growth in oil revenues. A joint venture with the Soviet Union has begun to produce substantial quantities of oil in the past few years. The oil is sold for export, and a large fraction of the revenue accrues to the budget. Without this resource, the fiscal situation would be even more dire.

Throughout the past decade, revenues have been insufficient to cover current expenditures, as Table 8-2 indicates. Current expenditures (including interest) represented 14.1 percent of GDP in 1988. During 1989 and 1990, the government made a serious effort, with some success, to restrain these expenditures in its battle to halt inflation; as a result, current expenditures *excluding interest payments* decreased by about 1 percentage point of GDP. The retrenchment effort was sabotaged to some extent, however, by the fact that the government has had to increase its interest payments (included in current expenditures) from virtually zero to about 2 percent of GDP. Most of the government borrowing from the domestic banking system carries no interest, so that any interest payments recorded in the budget correspond to the servicing of external debt. The budget is compiled on a cash, not accrual, basis, so only interest actually paid is included. Total current expenditures (including interest payments) well exceed total revenue, making the government a significant dissaver. Government dissaving peaked in 1988 at 2.8 percent of GDP. Over the next two years, the government reduced its dissaving to 2.0 percent of GDP. Dissaving means that government revenue makes no contribution to financing the public investment program. Capital expenditure has been fairly modest in recent years, around 4 percent of GDP (except for 1989).

The government has had no noninflationary way of financing its overall fiscal deficit. Soviet assistance has helped somewhat. In 1988, for instance, some of the 4.4 percent of GDP in capital expenditure corresponded to Soviet projects (such as the Hoa Binh hydroelectric facility), with matching financing (under foreign loans). Even in 1988, however, these loans totaled only 2.4 percent of GDP and, hence, did not go very far in financing the fiscal deficit.

Some of the most important Soviet assistance came in a manner that did not contribute directly to financing the budget deficit. The Soviet Union has supplied important materials, including refined petroleum, steel, fertilizer, and cotton, on a grant or soft-loan basis. Until 1989, however, these materials were sold to enterprises at very low prices, so that the main benefit of the assistance went not to the government budget but to the enterprises. Thus, even in the heyday of Soviet assistance, the budget did not receive much direct support from that quarter. Nevertheless, the Soviet commodity aid did improve the financial performance of state enterprises, which indirectly supported the budget through enterprise transfers.

Even before Soviet assistance began to decline in 1989, the government had a large fiscal deficit that it could not finance. In 1988, the part of the deficit financed through state-bank credit amounted to 2.9 percent of GDP. In 1989, as Table 8-2 indicates, the overall deficit was 6.8 percent of GDP, while state bank financing of the deficit was 6.0 percent of GDP. Fiscal retrenchment in 1990, particularly in the area of capital expenditure, reduced the bank financing to 2.5 percent.

To maintain price stability, bank financing of the deficit will have to be reduced, probably to less than 1 percent of GDP. Hence, substantial fiscal adjustment is necessary to achieve economic stabilization. The difference between the bank financing in 1990 of 2.5 percent of GDP and a target of, for example, 0.5 percent of GDP does not appear at first glance to be too great. But a number of factors make this fiscal adjustment difficult. First, the government budget as presented in Table 8-2 fails to take account of the heavy external-debt servicing obligations that Vietnam has not been meeting. The government is attempting to reschedule its foreign debt. Even with very favorable rescheduling terms, however, Vietnam may have larger debt servicing obligations than the payments now indicated in its budget. In other words, normalizing its relations with the international financial community may impose additional interest obligations on the government, which will worsen the fiscal deficit. Such a result is not inevitable: it depends on the rescheduling terms that Vietnam can negotiate.

Furthermore, the level of the public investment program is woefully inadequate. To achieve a satisfactory growth rate, the government must increase its investment in infrastructure and the social sectors. The challenge it faces is to raise some essential areas of government spending, notably interest payments, infrastructure investment, and social expenditure, while reducing bank financing of the budget deficit.

Viewed from a purely macroeconomic standpoint, the fiscal adjustment required to stabilize inflation is not great. When viewed in the context of system reform, however, the problem becomes much more daunting. As a socialist government, the state in Vietnam has tried to produce a complete range of goods and services, and, frankly, has done a rather poor job of it. System reform requires the state to disengage from a wide range of activities, while at the same time stepping up efforts in other areas, notably investment in infrastructure, provision of social services, and the unfamiliar task of managing a market economy. Vietnam thus faces the difficult challenge of reducing its overall fiscal deficit and, at the same time, completely restructuring its public sector.

As the analysis of the monetary data in the previous section showed, the growth of credit to enterprises during 1989 and 1990 was restrained. On the surface, it appears that credit to the budget has been the underlying source of inflation. Furthermore, the budget no longer contains any major direct subsidies to enterprises. Nevertheless, the poor performance of state enterprises remains a problem that will have to be dealt with as part of the restructuring of the public sector. A large volume of credit to enterprises remains outstanding. Most of this is short term and was loaned at rates below the deposit rate. (By the first quarter of 1991, both deposit and lending rates were well below the rate of inflation.) Obviously, the banking system loses money if it lends at rates below those at which it takes deposits.[9] Losses of the state-owned banking system have to be covered out of the budget, so this indirect subsidy has fiscal implications.

In addition, the reduction in Soviet commodity aid has worsened the financial condition of enterprises. Many enterprises paid no taxes at all in 1989 and 1990, and real transfers from the state enterprise sector to the budget declined. The government is shifting to a system in which state enterprises, along with private companies, pay taxes according to fixed schedules. Improving the administration of this kind of nondiscriminatory tax system is an important component of fiscal reform in Vietnam. Such reform, in conjunction with an end to credit subsidies for state enterprises, will almost certainly deepen the financial crisis already experienced by many state enterprises.

To sum up, the fiscal adjustment in Vietnam during 1989 and 1990 was not large enough to consolidate the anti-inflation program. The government got a large windfall in the form of growing oil revenue. Oil revenue will continue to increase steadily, but it is unlikely that it alone will solve the fiscal crisis.[10] During 1989 and 1990, the increased oil revenue was more or less offset by declines in collections from state enterprises, which were partly the result of reduced Soviet commodity aid. The revenue-to-GDP ratio has been

---

[9]One branch manager described this to me as the "5-4-3" system of banking: "Take deposits at 5 percent per month, lend at 4 percent, and go bankrupt in 3 months!"

[10]The oil production target in 1991 was 3.5 million tons, compared with 2.6 million tons in 1990. Production from the White Tiger field is projected by the government to plateau at 7 million tons per year by the mid-1990s. Other producing fields are not likely to come on line before then. Hence, oil revenue should increase steadily, but not spectacularly, over the next few years.

fairly stable, and the experiences of other countries suggest that it is unlikely to increase very rapidly.[11]

In the absence of higher revenues, Vietnam will have to undertake substantial restructuring of the public sector to stabilize prices. The logical direction of adjustment is to reduce the size of the military and the bureaucracy and to close or divest nonessential state enterprises. Serious measures in this direction are already under way. For example, 600,000 soldiers reportedly have been demobilized, and employment in the rest of the state sector declined from 4.1 million in 1988 to 3.5 million in 1990. Most of the latter adjustment was in state-enterprise employment, not in the civil service. The government is now attempting to reduce the size of the civil service.

To halt inflationary financing of the budget, without external financial assistance, is a difficult task. As an illustration, assume that revenue in the short run can be raised to 15 percent of GDP, an ambitious but not impossible goal. If there is to be any public investment at all, current expenditure would have to be reduced as a share of GDP. Even with ambitious public-sector retrenchment, it would be difficult for the government to reduce current expenditure by 2 to 3 percentage points of GDP (from the current 15 to 12 percent). This would create the financing for a small investment program of perhaps 2 to 3 percent of GDP. With that level of investment for infrastructure, the power and transport sectors will be a constraint on overall growth, holding it to a moderate rate of 3 to 5 percent per annum. Thus, without foreign assistance, it will be difficult for the government to achieve macroeconomic stability and, at the same time, provide adequate financing for the social sectors and for necessary investments in infrastructure.

Balance-of-Payments Situation

Vietnam had serious balance-of-payments problems throughout the 1980s. Even with significant amounts of Soviet aid in the mid-1980s, the country had an unsustainable balance-of-payments deficit. With the announced phase-out of Soviet aid starting in 1989, the government was faced with an even greater crisis. This reduction in assistance was a major impetus behind the 1989 stabilization program. Soviet aid had financed some important investment projects in Vietnam. More important, soft loans supported the import of four key inputs: refined petroleum, fertilizer, steel, and cotton.

[11]Total government revenue of around 10 to 13 percent of GDP is typical for a developing country like Vietnam, with per capita income of around $200 in U.S. dollars. The revenue-to-GDP ratio generally rises as a country becomes more developed, but there are few historical examples of large increases over a period of one to two years (Tanzi, 1987).

The phase-out of Soviet aid meant that the economy would have to export more to finance imports of these essential inputs. The only alternative would be to find new sources of external financing. To deal with this mounting balance-of-payments crisis, the government unified and devalued the exchange rate with the convertible area early in 1989, and also liberalized external trade in rice and other commodities. The devaluation was quite extreme, as the authorities moved the official exchange rate to match the level of the parallel market rate. In the years following this reform, the official exchange rate has been devalued regularly in line with inflation, so that the real exchange rate has been fairly stable.

In principle, a sharp devaluation of the real exchange rate should improve the balance-of-payments situation through an increase in exports and/or a decrease in imports. There is considerable controversy, however, concerning how quickly the improvement will occur. Furthermore, in the environment of a planned economy, it is not at all clear what devaluation will accomplish. In practice, Vietnam got remarkable results from its real devaluation cum trade liberalization.

Table 8-3 lays out the main features of the balance of payments during 1988–90. Combining convertible-area transactions with those of the nonconvertible area presents a serious problem, as the latter trade has been carried out at artificial, fixed prices and denominated in a nonconvertible currency (that is,

Table 8-3. Balance of Payments (millions of U.S. dollars)

	1988	1989	1990
Current Account Balance	−764	−586	−339
Convertible area	−209	−218	−210
Nonconvertible area	−555	−368	−129
Trade Balance	−679	−350	10
Convertible area	−138	−9	97
Nonconvertible area	−541	−341	−87
Total Exports	733	1320	1782
Convertible area	465	977	1305
Nonconvertible area	268	343	477
Total Imports	1412	1670	1772
Convertible area	603	985	1209
Nonconvertible area	809	685	564
Services and Transfers	−85	−237	−349
Convertible area	−71	−210	−307
Nonconvertible area	−14	−27	−42
Capital Account Balance	418	300	249
Convertible area	−57	−34	176
Nonconvertible area	475	334	73
Errors and Omissions	26	67	−42
Overall Balance	−320	−220	−132

the "transferable ruble"). I have aggregated the two accounts employing the admittedly arbitrary cross-exchange rate of 2.4 transferable rubles per U.S. dollar. The result is my best guess about how to evaluate the nonconvertible trade in U.S. dollars.

In 1988, Vietnam had a large trade deficit, mostly within the nonconvertible area. Under my valuation method, somewhat more than half of Vietnam's imports were coming from the nonconvertible area, although a minority of its exports went in that direction. Concessional loans financed the large trade deficit within the nonconvertible area. Vietnam's merchandise trade with the convertible area was nearly balanced, but the country had large interest obligations (a negative item under "services and transfers") and principal repayment obligations (a negative item in the capital account) that it was not meeting. These accounts, compiled on an accrual basis, indicate what Vietnam should have paid in debt service each year. That it was not meeting these obligations is reflected in the large overall deficit for the balance of payments (U.S. $320 million in 1988). Vietnam had no financing for this deficit and as a result accumulated new external arrears each year roughly equal to the overall deficit.

As a result of devaluation and trade liberalization, Vietnam's exports rose dramatically during 1989. Hard-currency exports doubled, from U.S. $465 million to U.S. $977 million. Exports to the nonconvertible area also increased. Soviet assistance declined significantly in 1989; this can be seen in the reduced imports from the nonconvertible area and in the declining current-account deficit with the nonconvertible area. Overall, however, Vietnam was able to increase its imports in 1989 as a result of expanded earnings of foreign exchange from its exports. Still, Vietnam continued to accumulate external arrears, reflecting its inability to service its large debt or reach a rescheduling agreement with external creditors. Similar trends were evident in 1990: Soviet assistance continued to decline; exports to the convertible area continued to increase, although not as much as in 1989; and arrears continued to pile up.

Details of the changing pattern of trade can be seen in Table 8-4, which focuses on physical quantities of key imports and exports. It is amazing that Vietnam achieved such a rapid and large response to its trade reform. Part of the result was simple coincidence. As can be seen in the table, crude petroleum exports have expanded greatly. These increases, a result of earlier investments in the White Tiger field, cannot be attributed to the trade reform. Oil production and, hence, exports were projected to grow modestly to 3.5 million tons in 1991 and to 5 million tons by 1993–94.[12]

---

[12]Virtually all of Vietnam's oil production is exported, as the country has no major refinery. This situation is unlikely to change in the next three or four years, so oil exports and output will remain about equal.

Table 8-4. Major Imports and Exports (Thousands of Metric Tons)

	1988	1989	1990
Imports			
Fertilizer	2520	2956	2233
Convertible Area	400	506	1161
Nonconvertible Area	2120	2450	1072
Petroleum	2200	2305	2400
Convertible Area	0	0	1080
Nonconvertible Area	2200	2305	1320
Exports			
Rice	0	1425	1625
Convertible Area	0	1405	1455
Nonconvertible Area	0	20	170
Petroleum (Convertible Area)	680	1517	2600
Marine Products (Convertible Area)	13	15	29

The other major export success was rice. Vietnam was an importer through 1988, but as a result of trade and price reforms, it became an exporter of 1.4 million tons in 1989. Some of this volume probably arose from dishoarding, as the hyperinflation halted and households shifted out of rice, gold, and dollars. Much of the export, however, came from increased production. This is clear from the fact that the export success continued in 1990, when 1.6 million tons were exported. Exports besides rice and petroleum expanded as well in 1989, although no single product played an especially important role. In 1990, marine products (notably shrimp) emerged as another important export, with the quantity exported climbing nearly 100 percent.

Why did Vietnam get such a quick response to devaluation? Typically, such a devaluation spurs the incentive to export and, at the same time, creates financial hardships for firms that rely heavily on imports to produce for the domestic market. A sustained, real devaluation should generate a shift away from servicing the domestic market toward producing for export. The speed at which the shift occurs, however, depends on how rapidly productive factors can be moved from one activity to another. In the case of Vietnam, it turns out that resources could be moved very quickly because of several of the characteristics cited earlier. The country has good natural resources, and they were underutilized in the planned economy. Furthermore, Vietnam had the entrepreneurial talent to respond quickly to strengthened incentives, so output of a number of potential exportables—including rice and shrimp—increased very quickly.

At the same time, the devaluation had the predicted effect on manufacturers that use imported inputs to produce for the domestic market. During 1989, the effect was mitigated by the continued inflow of some supplies from the Soviet Union for which the Vietnamese government could control the prices to enterprises, thus minimizing the shock to firms. Table 8-4 shows that Soviet petroleum and fertilizer deliveries actually grew in 1989 (even though imports from the Soviet Union showed an overall decline). In 1990, however, nonconvertible deliveries of these two goods fell sharply, and Vietnam had to shift to hard-currency purchases for much of its supply. Since 1990, enterprises have had to pay world-market prices for these inputs.

While such price reform hurts firms that use imported materials to produce for the local market, Vietnam has an advantage in that its industry is mostly underdeveloped. Some enterprises in heavy industry are in serious trouble as a result of higher prices for energy and other inputs, but the number is small. In the heavy industrial area, Vietnam has a big advantage over socialist economies like those of Eastern Europe and China. In China, the kind of exchange rate and trade adjustment that Vietnam has undertaken would create financial problems for large numbers of heavy industrial firms, in such sectors as steel, fertilizer, and motor vehicles. In Vietnam, there are few such firms. Another one of Vietnam's important characteristics is that state-enterprise employment is concentrated in labor-intensive sectors like food processing and textiles. Manufacturing will probably not be at the forefront of export growth for some time. Nevertheless, many light-manufacturing enterprises are exporting to the convertible area and, as a result, are doing better now than several years ago.

The collapse of the Soviet Union in 1991 was a further big shock to Vietnam's economy. By the end of 1990, the economy had already largely adjusted to the end of Soviet aid, but a significant amount of barter trade was anticipated. The economic problems in the republics of the former Soviet Union resulted in their inability to follow through on commitments to supply fertilizer, cotton, and other inputs to Vietnam. Many state enterprises and household producers in the north of Vietnam had been exporting light manufactures such as carpets, footwear, and rattan furniture to the Soviet Union. The abrupt cessation of this trade in 1991 caused serious disruption to the northern economy.

To a large extent, the southern economy took up the slack, and total exports increased to about U.S. $2 billion for 1991. This performance is quite remarkable in light of the disruption of trade with the Soviet Union and natural calamities that held rice exports to 1 million tons. In 1991, marine products took over as Vietnam's number two export, after crude petroleum. The developments in 1991 unfortunately exacerbated regional inequalities. Southern firms that had been exporting products like pineapples, shrimp, and footwear to the Soviet Union have had to make a swift transition to producing for the East Asian market, whereas the northern producers of handicrafts, cited above, are now facing extreme difficulties. Overall, Vietnam's trade with former Council for Mutual Economic Assistance (CMEA) members has dropped to less than 5 percent of total trade; its main partners now are Japan, Hong Kong, Singapore, and Taiwan. Trade with mainland China is also on the rise.

Vietnam is already unusual among socialist economies in exporting 20 percent of GDP, and it has the potential to increase this figure quickly. There are a number of additional reforms that Vietnam needs to undertake to improve its trade performance. The government has done a good job managing the exchange-rate level, but the foreign exchange market functions poorly. That is a serious bottleneck for imports and exports. Furthermore, administrative barriers against importing materials and machinery remain. Finally, while the law on direct foreign investment is fairly liberal, in practice, foreign investors have to operate in a difficult environment, discouraging an activity that has the best prospect of increasing exports rapidly.

Even with further trade reform, however, Vietnam will remain in a difficult situation as long as the U.S. trade embargo remains in place and the country's relations with the international financial institutions (IFIs) are not normalized. The trade embargo limits Vietnam's access to the world's largest market and also discourages direct foreign investment from all countries. Normalizing relations with the IFIs similarly would provide the immediate benefit of new credits, as well as further indirect benefits. Financing from the IFIs could help Vietnam consolidate the stabilization program and improve the country's infrastructure, both of which should bolster direct foreign investment and growth.

Short-Term Prospects

Vietnam's macroeconomic performance during the 1980s was not at all unusual for a developing economy. Far too many countries have been faced with similar problems of high inflation and balance-of-payments crises. The usual sources of these problems have been excessive public-sector expenditure, financed by printing money, and weak incentives to export, particularly overvalued exchange rates and cumbersome import/export regulations. There is a generally accepted recipe for dealing with macroeconomic instability: the government needs to reduce the size and scope of the public sector and thus eliminate the source of excessive money creation. Furthermore, incentives to export need to be strengthened by devaluing the real exchange rate and liberalizing the trade regime.

The international financial community generally understands that a government undertaking such a rigorous structural adjustment program should be supported with new financing. The main reason is that the fiscal retrenchment at the heart of structural adjustment might limit the government's ability to provide necessary public services in the social sectors (health, education) as well as in infrastructure (roads, ports, electricity). International assistance targeted at these two areas can play an important role in generating satisfactory socioeconomic development in the new, stabilized environment.

While Vietnam's macroeconomic problems may be typical of developing countries, its recent experience with structural adjustment was anything but typical. The reforms it undertook in 1989 compare very favorably with other stabilization efforts. The exchange rate and trade reforms were very radical, and at the same time, the government made major improvements in monetary and fiscal policy. From 1988 to 1990, there was substantial retrenchment of the public sector, and the growth of credit to the government declined sharply. These reforms produced some immediate successes. Households resumed using the domestic currency to a great extent; that was the main reason why inflation halted dramatically in mid-1989.

Furthermore, the country was in a good position to respond to the improved incentive structure. The economy is largely agricultural, and there were significant amounts of unused resources in that sector. In response to the price reforms, rice output immediately increased and became a major export item. With a short lag, other primary outputs, such as marine products, expanded as well. What little industry there is in Vietnam is concentrated in labor-intensive sectors, so that some manufacturing firms were also able to respond quickly to the reform program. Overall, Vietnam got a remarkably fast and large supply response to its structural reforms.

External support, however, did not materialize throughout this period. Soviet assistance has ceased, and aid from the West is as yet minor. The typical developing country pursuing this kind of structural adjustment program would get assistance from the Group of Seven (G-7) industrial nations in rescheduling its external debt, clearing up arrears, and obtaining access to financing from the IMF and the World Bank. As of mid-1992, the G-7 continued to withhold this kind of assistance from Vietnam.

Vietnam will have difficulty stabilizing its economy in the absence of external assistance. The fiscal adjustment of the past two years has not been sufficient to consolidate price stability. Credit extended to the public sector generated a 68 percent inflation rate both in 1990 and in 1991. In an attempt to provide some subsidy to troubled state enterprises, the authorities allowed interest rates once again to become negative in real terms. The high inflation and negative real interest rates had not, as of this writing in early 1992, led to wholesale desertion of the domestic currency. But there is some danger that this will occur. In that case, we will see the reverse of what happened in mid-1989: households will shift their liquid assets out of domestic currency into dollars, gold, and stocks of rice, and inflation will likely accelerate back to hyperinflation levels.

To reverse the current instability, Vietnam will have to cut government expenditures and raise interest rates on loans to state enterprises. By further reducing the military and the bureaucracy, Vietnam could probably achieve macroeconomic stability and still continue to provide adequate resources for health and education. Little financing, however, would be available for new investments in infrastructure. Obviously, further large layoffs from the military and from the government would be controversial. In addition, eliminating the remaining indirect subsidies to state enterprises would almost certainly generate additional unemployment in that part of the public sector as well. What the government would get from this kind of adjustment is macroeconomic stability but probably only moderate growth in the 3 to 5 percent range. Poor economic infrastructure would continue to be a bottleneck, and the government would lack the financing to alleviate it. In the absence of external financing, the overall investment rate would also be modest at best and hold the economy back from rapid growth. So, the price of macroeconomic stability is likely to be serious public-sector unemployment that is not absorbed by rapid growth of the private sector.

This scenario is unappealing, but the alternative is likely to be worse. If inflation accelerates, it will be difficult to achieve any kind of growth at all in Vietnam. As long as the trade embargo and restricted financing continue, sound macroeconomic policies will probably generate only modest growth in per capita income. A return to the instability of the 1985–88 period, on the other hand, will almost certainly produce no growth in per capita income.

Obviously, an end to the trade embargo and normal access to international finance would greatly improve Vietnam's situation. The government must still undertake the fundamental restructuring of the public sector that I have described. Even under the most optimistic financing scenario, Vietnam's government will face a tight budget constraint and a need to use public resources wisely. Nevertheless, it can streamline the public sector more easily with some external assistance in hand. For example, it could persuade large numbers of soldiers and civil servants to give up their jobs in return for a modest, one-time payment. At the moment, the government lacks the resources to furnish substantial adjustment assistance.

More important, an end to the embargo and an increase in foreign assistance would enable the economy to grow much more rapidly. Foreign borrowing, used wisely, would enable the government to ease critical infrastructure bottlenecks. Improved infrastructure, plus an end to the embargo, would make Vietnam an attractive location for direct foreign investment, which could become an important source of growth. With more rapid growth, the economy could more readily absorb into new, productive activities the large amount of labor that must be shed from unproductive state enterprises and an overblown bureaucracy.

As of mid-1992, it remained uncertain when Vietnam would get access to foreign assistance. In the meantime, it remains in the government's interest to proceed with macroeconomic stabilization and the fiscal retrenchment required to achieve it. Without foreign capital, the results to be expected from structural adjustment are at best modest. The alternative, however, is a return to hyperinflation and macroeconomic chaos, which is likely to undo the good things that have happened in Vietnam's economy over the past two years.

Medium-Term Prospects

If Vietnam can stabilize its economy and obtain access to some foreign financing, the medium-term prospects for development are excellent. Foreign financing will be important for some time, as the savings rate is low and unlikely to rise very rapidly. As I have noted, the authorities will be doing well to make the government sector a saver to the extent of 2 to 3 percent of GDP. The need for public investment in infrastructure and the social sectors is much larger, so that resources from the international financial institutions and bilateral donors can contribute significantly to Vietnam's development, especially if they are well targeted to these priority areas.

In industry and agriculture, the country has to rely on the private sector to take the lead in development. No doubt, there will be some ongoing controversy within Vietnam about the role of the private sector. If the leadership is pragmatic, however, it will recognize that public resources to invest in commercial activities will be extremely limited. The Chinese strategy of providing ongoing support for state enterprises at the expense of the private sector is not likely to produce good results in Vietnam because of the public sector's relatively poor financial condition. Encouraging private-sector expansion is the best hope for financing new commercial investments. The domestic private sector is large compared with other socialist economies and has the potential to take over viable state enterprises quickly. Direct foreign investment can also be an important source of financing for growth, provided the authorities create a hospitable environment for the foreign private sector.

Vietnam clearly has the potential to grow rapidly once its economy is stabilized. Much of the financing for this growth will come from abroad initially; but if the economy grows successfully, the savings rate—both of the government sector and of the household sector—should rise gradually, allowing more and more of the investment in growth to be financed out of domestic resources.

The pattern of development is likely to be similar to that of the neighboring economies. The per capita natural-resource base is probably not as strong as in Thailand or Malaysia, although better than in Korea or Taiwan. The natural growth path would bear similarities with the paths followed by these other economies. Vietnam will grow most successfully if it exploits its comparative advantage in international trade. In the short run, much of that advantage will be in such primary goods as rice, marine products, and tree crops, as has been the case with Thailand and Malaysia. The weakness of the natural resource base in Vietnam, however, is likely to keep wages low, even with a strong export performance in the agricultural sector. Labor-intensive manufacturing, bolstered by policies encouraging the private sector and foreign investment, should soon develop export capacities. As with other East Asian economies, one would first expect to see exports of garments, shoes, and toys, followed shortly by simple electronics. As a consequence, exports (as a share of GDP) should rise sharply. Furthermore, surplus labor could be quickly absorbed into the labor-intensive sectors, reducing unemployment and poverty.

One important concern as the economy develops will be the imbalance between north and south. Not only is per capita income currently much higher in the south, but that region has better potential to respond quickly to the reform program. The shortage of electricity is holding the south back, but otherwise it has better infrastructure and natural resources than the north. Many countries have these regional disparities. In some cases, there are geographic factors that are nearly impossible to overcome. Northeast Thailand or western China, for example, are poor because they are isolated from the rest of the economy, and because it would be difficult and expensive to integrate them through improvements in infrastructure. The northern half of Vietnam does not have the same problem; its location is very good. The region's poor transport links with the rest of Vietnam and with the world are the result of history rather than geography. The same is true for the lack of capital stock in light industries.

Given the small amounts of arable land per capita in the north, Vietnam's best hope for reducing regional inequalities is to attract labor-intensive manufacturing to this area. The experience of other countries indicates that this should not be done through special tax incentives or regulations. The only way to attract the necessary investment is to make the area a low-cost location for production. Wages in the north are about one-half the level in the south, so the region potentially has a cost advantage. But roads, ports, and rail links are in poor condition, as are telecommunications facilities. In addition to these infrastructure problems, there are the policy issues itemized above: import restrictions, bureaucratic inefficiency, and regulations hindering direct foreign investment. The problems of streamlining the bureaucracy and improving infrastructure (except for power) are more acute in the north than in the south. If these problems are dealt with, then regional disparities should decline as the country grows.

Vietnam today is a very poor country, but its backwardness carries with it the potential for rapid growth. For a low-income country, Vietnam has impressive levels of health and education; the human-resource base is excellent. The fundamental lesson of East Asian development is that a strong educational base combined with an outward orientation of the economy will generate rapid growth. Vietnam can pursue this successful model of socioeconomic development if—and these are two big "ifs"—the government can succeed in reining in the overextended public sector, and the international community offers financial and technical support for this structural adjustment.

Acknowledgments

Opinions expressed are those of the author and do not necessarily reflect views of the World Bank or its member countries. The paper has benefited from the helpful comments of Börje Ljunggren, Peter Timmer, Thang-Long Ton, and Alexander Woodside.

References

Chow, Gregory. 1985. *The Chinese Economy*. New York: Harper and Row.

Fforde, Adam, and Stefan de Vylder. 1988. *Vietnam: An Economy in Transition*. Stockholm: Swedish International Development Authority (SIDA).

Socialist Republic of Vietnam, General Statistical Office. 1991. *Statistical Data of the Socialist Republic of Vietnam, 1976–1990*. Hanoi: Statistical Publishing House.

Tanzi, Vito. 1987. "Quantitative Characteristics of the Tax Systems of Developing Countries." In David Newbery and Nicholas Stern, eds., *The Theory of Taxation for Developing Countries*. New York: Oxford University Press.

World Bank. 1985. *China: Long-Term Development Issues and Options*. New York: Oxford University Press.

9

Population, Health, and Gender in Vietnam: Social Policies under the Economic Reforms

Joan Kaufman and Gita Sen

The Socialist Republic of Vietnam has made notable achievements in health and education. Despite a per capita income of less than $200 (U.S. dollars) a year, 84 percent of the female population is literate, the infant mortality rate is about 54 per thousand, and life expectancy exceeds 65 years. The economic reforms of the last several years appear to be revitalizing a stagnant rural economy and, if successful, will upgrade the standard of living. At the same time, some achievements in the social sectors are threatened. Furthermore, emerging challenges in health and population may not be adequately addressed.

Three major developments of recent years threaten Vietnam's health accomplishments. First, funds for development in all areas have become scarce, particularly in sectors like health, for which the productive payoff may not be immediate. This shortage of funds can be attributed to the sudden drop in Soviet aid, the continuing embargo, difficulties in tax collection, and reduced revenues from public enterprises during the transition from a centrally planned to a privatized economy. A second development is the shifting relationships between the central and the local governments. These include changes in responsibilities for financing investment (new and depreciated) and in the provision of supplies and salaries. The third change, linked to the transformation of the food production and distribution systems, may have both positive and negative effects on health. It may improve the supply and variety of foods but, at the same time, produce inequities in which poorer regions and households are worse off than they were under food-subsidy arrangements.

These three changes carry implications for health, population, and their gender dimensions through their effects on environmental sanitation and water supply, the infrastructure for health and family-planning services, and nutrition.

The near nonexistence of the infrastructure for water supply and waste disposal in rural Vietnam contributes to a variety of health problems. And, while water-supply and sanitation systems exist for many residents of the cities, they are in serious disrepair. These weaknesses, predating the current reform period, pose an impediment to further health improvement. On the other hand, a comprehensive health-services infrastructure (as distinct from the public-health infrastructure) was constructed during the prereform period, but chronic shortages of funds and supplies have threatened this infrastructure. And malnutrition remains a serious problem despite improvements in food production.

Each of these problems has gender dimensions that involve (1) the ways in which changes in the health system have affected or are likely to affect female access to health care and nutrition, (2) the impact of these changes on the work involved in health care provision (bearing in mind that in Vietnam, as in most societies, women have the main responsibility for maintaining the health of the household), and (3) the health issues that concern women and girls, such as reproductive health and maternal mortality.

Prereform: Achievements and Weaknesses in Women's Health Care, Literacy, and Employment

Achievements: Health Strategy, Programs, and Access

The Socialist Republic of Vietnam made access to health care a high priority in the North before and during the war and for reconstruction after the war. The achievements have been especially notable when compared with the usual economic correlates of improved health like per capita income, which remains quite low. Even prior to the Alma Ata Conference and Declaration of 1978 ("Health for All by the Year 2000"), Vietnam's health strategy emphasized prevention and construction of a basic health infrastructure. Soon after the French defeat in 1954, the government in the North began a massive training program for health-care workers. By 1965, nearly two-thirds of villages in the North had trained assistant doctors.

After Alma Ata, Vietnam adopted a 10-point plan that incorporated the primary health-care emphasis of "Health for All by the Year 2000" and added initiatives for setting up and reinforcing the health infrastructure and maintaining a record-keeping system for vulnerable groups (women, children, and the elderly). The primary health-care emphasis included six key programs: immunization for preventable childhood diseases, malaria control, provision of essential drugs, control of acute respiratory infections and diarrheal diseases, family planning, and maternal and child health services (including nutrition).

The health-services infrastructure was set up to work on a tiered system, similar to China's, paralleling government administration levels. Basic services were to be available at the grassroots level, and on the next tier, the commune health station was intended to serve a community of 5,000 to 10,000 inhabitants. Presently, 90 percent of the nearly 9,000 rural communes and most factories have health stations (Hoang Dinh Cau, 1990, p. 6). Some communes (mostly in the North) have extended services to hamlet health posts, where health education, prenatal checkups, and immunizations are carried out.

The commune health center is supposed to be staffed by four or five medical staff (depending on the population of the community), including a physician trained for five years. In reality, the staff usually consists of vocationally trained assistant doctors (vocationally trained for three years), nurses, and midwives—and sometimes a pharmacist. The center itself usually has little equipment and is often short of supplies and drugs. It serves mostly as an outpatient facility, except for child delivery, for which it is the main rural service facility. For supervision, training, and referral, the commune health center gets support from a district hospital with 50 to 200 beds, depending on the size of the district population (which ranges from about 100,000 to 300,000). The district hospital, in turn, gets backing from provincial and city hospitals with 100 to 200 beds each.

Access to these basic health services has helped the Vietnamese achieve generally good health, although the population is poor and mostly rural. The reported infant mortality of 53.8 per 1,000 live births compares favorably with countries like Bangladesh, where the rate remains a staggering 120 per 1,000 live births, or even more modernized countries like the Philippines, where infant mortality stands at 48 per 1,000 (Population Reference Bureau, 1990). Nearly 80 percent of children under five are reported by UNICEF to be immunized against the five main childhood diseases, and in many areas, trained midwives attend almost all births. In 1987, the World Bank estimated life expectancy in Vietnam to be 66 years (World Development Report, World Bank, 1991), an achievement that has eluded most other mainly rural countries besides China and Sri Lanka. Table 9-1 provides some basic statistics on Vietnam's health attainments compared with three other Asian countries.

Improvements in people's general health depend not only on the extent and quality of the public-health infrastructure and the health care delivery system but also on the people's knowledge and capacity to take advantage of the services available (including health-education messages) and to make their own contribution to improving public-health standards. Women's literacy plays a major role here, particularly because of their responsibilities for domestic labor, including health care, sanitation, and food preparation, and as care providers for children.

Table 9-1. Basic Social, Economic, and Health Data for Vietnam, China, Bangladesh, Philippines, 1986–1990

	Vietnam	China	Bangladesh	Philippines
Population[1] (in millions)	64.8	1120	114.8	66.1
Per Capita GNP[1] (in U.S. dollars)	< 200	330	170	630
Female Adult Literacy[2] (percentage)	84	55	22	85
Infant Mortality Rate[1]				
(per 1,000 births)	54	51[3]	120	48
Life Expectancy[1]	66	68	54	64

[1]Population Reference Bureau (1990). For Vietnam, Vietnam: Central Census Steering Committee (1990).
[2]The World Bank (1991). (Note: Data is for 1985 for all countries except Vietnam. For Vietnam, Central Census Steering Committee (1990).
[3]National sample survey by Chinese Ministry of Health (1986) as cited in Barister (1989).

Achievements: Female Literacy

Female literacy in Vietnam is high compared with other countries having similar per capita income levels.[1] Through strong emphasis on schooling and intensive adult-literacy programs, the adult literacy rates in 1979, among the population over 10 years of age, were 90 percent for men and 81 percent for women. By 1989, these rates were 93 percent and 84 percent respectively.[2] Disaggregated data, however, reveal substantial regional variation in literacy, especially between the northern and central regions of the country. A small-sample survey of women aged 15 to 49 years, conducted in northern, central, and southern communes in 1988, showed that while northern illiteracy rates were as low as 1 to 2 percent in the communes surveyed, rates in central Vietnam were closer to 14 percent, and southern rates were 4 to 5 percent (Ministry of University and Vocational Education, 1988, p. 10). This is probably related, at least in part, to population density and the remoteness of some regions. Ethnic differences in literacy also exist. Despite these regional differences, overall literacy might still be considered to be quite high.

Rural versus urban differences are also small compared to other heavily rural countries; the literacy rates in 1989 were estimated at 82 percent among rural women, compared with 92 percent among urban women (Central

[1]The weighted-average adult-female literacy rate for middle-income countries was 69 percent in 1985; for low-income countries the rate was 42 percent (World Bank, 1991, pp. 260–61). Vietnam, a low-income country, compares very favorably with these rates.

[2]In 1979, anyone who ever attended school was considered literate, which may well have overestimated the literacy rate. In 1989, the question about literacy was asked independently of the questions on schooling. The increase in literacy in 1989 occurred despite this change. Indeed, the low literacy of older women accounts for much of the difference between the two rates. In 1989, the literacy rates for men and women under age 45 were more than 90 percent. At higher ages, the female rate drops off sharply: 79 percent in the 45–54 age group; 61 percent in the 55–64 group; and only 31 percent in the group above 65, compared with 73 percent of men over 65 (Central Census Steering Committee, 1990).

Census Steering Committee, 1990, p. 45). The aggregate data also reveal no major differences between women and men in the extent of schooling.[3] Although there are signs that the economic pressures of the past decade are weakening this remarkable progress, it is clear that female literacy rates are more than adequate to enable most women to know about and to take advantage of whatever the health care system could provide.

Achievements: Women's Participation in the Labor Force

Classic socialist theory has always held that drawing women into productive work in the public economy is the path to their liberation from traditional oppression. In Vietnam, as in other socialist societies, this meant encouraging women's participation in the labor force while providing day care and facilities to make participation possible. According to the sample results of the 1989 census, 73.6 percent of the female population above the age of 15 was active in the labor force; and 67.5 percent of them were employed for more than six months in the reference period. The female economic activity rate is close to 90 percent of the male rate (Central Census Steering Committee, 1990, p. 62).

Women have a big share in all the major occupational classifications, the lowest being 33 percent of the "managerial/administrative" category.[4] Of course, a closer look at the gender distribution of employment reveals the usual distinctions: men occupy the well-paying jobs and positions of greater authority—that is, heavy-industry and administrative positions as well as political and bureaucratic slots.

The high rates of female economic activity are due in part to a tradition of high female participation in work and income earning. They are also partially the result of the long years of war, during which men were drawn into the armed services and were also killed in great numbers. (About 11 percent of Vietnamese women are widowed.) An additional contributing factor may be male migration in recent years. In 1975, the sex ratio was only 919 men per 1,000 women; by 1989, it had climbed to 947 men per 1,000 women.

The mass provision of child care to facilitate women's participation in economic activity outside the home dates back to the early years of the Socialist Republic of Vietnam. As one would expect, day-care centers were

[3]In 1989, sample results of the census showed that among the population over 10 years of age, 80 percent of the men and 74 percent of the women had only primary education, while 12 percent of the men had secondary or higher education compared to 9 percent of the women (Central Census Steering Committee, 1990).

[4]The other categories are professional/technical, 49 percent; sales workers, 68 percent; service, 45 percent; agriculture, forestry, animal husbandry, 55 percent; production-related work, transport, and equipment operators, 46 percent; others, 70 percent (Statistical Publishing House, 1990).

Table 9-2. Household Water Supply, Sanitation, and Electricity

% of housing units	1976		1987	
	urban	rural	urban	rural
without electricity	2	3	2	3
without running water	1	87	—	77
without toilets	4	91	4	93
without safe water	60	32	60	30
without sanitation facilities	2	41	2	40

Source: Statistical Publishing House (1990).

better distributed and facilities were more available in the northern part of the country. The quality of care also tended to be better in towns than in rural areas. Both the state and the cooperative sectors ran day-care centers; the latter accounted for as much as 72 percent of attendance in 1980. The number of children attending peaked at 1.2 million that year. Some 22.5 percent of children in the zero to three-year group attended day-care centers in 1986. This is a high figure for a predominantly rural population. Furthermore, cooperatives took much of the financial responsibility for the cost of child care (UNDP, 1990a, p. 206). Before 1971, no central agency was responsible for organizing child care. In that year, the Committee for Protection of Mothers and Children was formed, and its president was awarded the status of minister. The committee was given the task of developing a national child-care system.[5]

Weaknesses: Rural Health Problems Related to Water, Sanitation, Drug Shortages, and Poor Nutrition

While Vietnam has made impressive progress in setting up a primary health-care infrastructure and improving women's literacy and economic participation, both of which contribute to health care use, serious weaknesses remain in the public-health and health-services infrastructures. These weaknesses, which mainly concern the neglected sectors of water supply and sanitation, contribute to persistent rural health problems.

Table 9-2 reveals very little progress in improving household water provision or sanitation between 1976 and 1987. In urban areas, some early investment was made in water-supply and sewage-control systems (now badly in need of repair and renovation), and most urban residents have access to piped water. But little capacity exists in rural Vietnam, where 80 percent of the

[5]This included developing a training network; between 1976 and 1980, some 125,000 students received training at two central schools (as well as a number of smaller schools) through both full-time study programs, ranging from nine months to three years, and short-term courses (Eisen, 1984, p. 167).

population resides. About 40 percent of rural families have shallow wells, and the remainder obtain their water supply from rivers, lakes, streams, and rainfall, which serve multipurposes for washing clothes, bathing, and sometimes defecation (UNDP, 1990a, p. 196). In the Red and Mekong River deltas, the shallow-well groundwater is often too saline or full of minerals for regular use. People who depend on rainwater suffer regular shortages during the dry season and must buy their water supplies, which are often bottled river water from nearby areas. Only an estimated 30 to 40 percent of the rural population has a safe supply of water (UNDP, 1990a, p. 196).

Sanitation facilities are just as limited; virtually no hygienic disposal of human waste is available. Early efforts were made to construct communal village latrines, known as Ho Chi Minh models, but lack of maintenance has caused them to fall into total disrepair and disuse. A variety of traditional latrine types are currently used in rural Vietnam: in the North, excreta are often collected in pit or basket latrines and used untreated as fertilizer; in the South, traditional fish-pond latrines allow excreta to be deposited directly into ponds, where they provide fish with nutrients. These practices have contributed to a high incidence of intestinal parasitic diseases in the North—90 to 100 percent in many areas (Ministry of Health of the Socialist Republic of Vietnam, 1990)—and a variety of hygiene-related illnesses in both North and South, including high rates of gynecological infections in women; gastroenteritis and diarrheal diseases; and water-borne infections of typhoid, cholera, and viral hepatitis (Asian Development Bank, 1989, p. 82).

Shortages of supplies and drugs have plagued the health services since well before the economic changes began. A serious consequence of the U.S.-led trade embargo has been a shortage of medical supplies and drugs, which are manufactured in insufficient quantities domestically. A thriving black market in drugs and medical supplies operates in Ho Chi Minh City, supplied by overseas relatives of local residents who also sell these supplies to urban pharmacies. But little makes its way into the state-run medical system, especially in rural areas.

Moreover, nutritional status is low, and high rates of undernutrition and malnutrition increase the susceptibility to and progression of many diseases among the most vulnerable segments of the population. The average calorie intake is 15 percent below the Food and Agricultural Organization/World Health Organization (FAO/WHO) standards for Asian countries, and a disproportionately high share of calories comes from carbohydrates. Among vulnerable age groups, about 60 percent of children under six years of age suffer from a stunting form of malnutrition, and 14 percent are severely malnourished, while half of pregnant women suffer from iron deficiencies (UNDP, 1990a, p. 187; Tu Giay, Director of National Institute of Nutrition as reported in the *Far Eastern Economic Review*, Hiebert, 1991, pp. 16–17). The lack of vitamin A and D intake accounts for high rates of trachoma and rickets.

Table 9-3 presents data on the malnutrition of 571 children in Ho Chi Minh City in the mid-1980s. The data underlying the numbers reveal that early weaning with calorie-poor weaning foods; infectious and diarrheal diseases after weaning; and food shortages, especially of protein-rich foods, contribute to chronic malnutrition, wasting, and stunting in children under five years of age in Vietnam's largest city.

Vietnam's Current Health and Population Status and Challenges

Despite achievements in extending the availability of basic health services, preventable communicable diseases still dominate the morbidity profile. Table 9-4 lists the main causes of death and morbidity. National data of this type are sometimes highly unreliable. In the case of the mortality data in Table 9-4, two caveats must be made. First, we do not know what proportion of total deaths are due to noninfectious causes. Second, a rate of 3.2 deaths per 100,000 cannot make TB a leading cause of total deaths. Despite this, infectious diseases may still be a major cause of ill-health as the evidence in general appear to suggest. While health authorities have had considerable success in reducing morbidity from many of these communicable diseases, some illnesses like malaria and dengue fever (mosquito-borne diseases) persist, as do typhoid, cholera, and viral hepatitis.

Data cited in the UNDP report (1990a) show an increase in yearly incidence of malaria from 1,241 per 100,000 in 1978 to 1,359 per 100,000 in 1986—a high rate even within the region. The Asian Development Bank report (1989) cited a doubling in the rate over the same period. The

Table 9-3. Prevalence of Malnutrition Among 571 Selected Children by Age Group in Ho Chi Minh City (mid-1980s)

Age (months)*	Normal	Mild Wasting	Moderate Wasting	Severe Wasting	Stunted (Chronic)
0–6	76%	15%	2%	2%	5%
6–12	55%	29%	4%	3%	9%
12–24	29%	35%	7%	3%	26%
24–36	32%	28%	1%	3%	36%
36–48	23%	35%	6%	2%	34%
48–60	19%	44%	19%	9%	9%

*Age categories as given
Source: Duong Quynh Hoa (1988).

Table 9-4. Health Changes from 1978 to 1986

	1978		1986	
	Rank	Rate/100,000	Rank	Rate/100,000
Leading Causes of Mortality from Communicable Diseases				
Malaria	1	7	2	2.0
Tuberculosis	2	5	1	3.2
Salmonellosis	—	—	3	1.5
Dengue hemorrhagic fever	—	—	4	0.8
Viral encephalitis	4	1	5	0.8
Amoebiasis/bacillary dysentery	3	2	6	0.5
Tetanus	5	0.8	7	0.5
Shigellosis	—	—	8	0.4
Rabies	—	—	9	0.4
Measles	—	—	10	0.4
Leading Causes of Morbidity from Communicable Diseases				
Malaria	1	1,241	1	1,359
Diarrhea and salmonellosis	2	835	2	704
Influenza	3	410	3	494
Measles	4	218	5	112
Amoebiasis/bacillary dysentery	5	119	4	165
Whooping cough (pertussis)	6	153	10	72
Tuberculosis: pulmonary and other forms	7	138	7	78
Rabies	—	—	6	106
Dengue hemorrhagic fever	8	77	8	76
Shigellosis	—	—	9	73
Chicken pox	9	51	—	—

Source: UNDP (1990a, p. 193).

persistence of malaria may be due to the resistance of the parasite to chloroquine, reduction in spraying programs conducted with Soviet aid, and the return of infected soldiers from Cambodia in recent years.

These diseases have in common their links to the water supply. Mosquitoes breed in still water, as in ponds and improperly covered water tanks, and typhoid, cholera, and viral hepatitis are related to contamination of the water supply by improper treatment and disposal of human feces.

Women and children are particularly vulnerable to diseases linked to unclean water. A major contributor to infant and child mortality is diarrheal disease and subsequent dehydration post-weaning from unclean water supplies. Reproductive-age women reportedly suffer greatly from repeated gynecological infections, contributing to persistent morbidity in an already marginally nourished population. The high usage of intrauterine contraceptive devices (IUDs) may magnify the risk of more serious pelvic infections in rural women. While no hard data exist on the causes of these infections, most medical people suspect a culprit is bathing and working in ponds and rivers.

Table 9-5. Main Population and Demographic Data for Vietnam

Total population	64.4 million (1989)
Rural population	80%
Sex ratio (male/female)	94.7/100
Population growth rate	2.13%[1]
Total fertility rate	4.4
Population density	204 per square km.
Contraceptive prevalence rate	39%[1]

[1]National Committee for Population and Family Planning (1990).

For the treatment of diarrheal diseases in children and gynecologic infections in women, drugs are in short supply and are usually either unavailable (for example, oral rehydration tablets) or inappropriate.

The steady increase in population also challenges the health system. One consequence of health improvements has been consistent, prolonged population growth, especially since the end of the war. The postwar baby boom and continuous high fertility have pushed the total population to nearly 65 million (Central Census Steering Committee, 1990, p. 25). At its current growth rate of 2.13 percent (crude birth rate of around 31 per 1,000), the population will surpass the 80 million mark by the end of this century.

As about 80 percent of Vietnam's surface area consists of mountains, high plateaus, and jungle, population pressure on the limited agricultural land has grown to tangible levels in the Red River and Mekong River delta regions where most of the people reside. Table 9-5 lists the main population and demographic data. Given the challenge of providing adequate nutrition to children already born, the addition of several million new mouths a year strains already inadequate nutritional efforts.

In October 1988, after several decades of promotion of family planning, justified mainly in terms of the health of mothers and as a means to increase female labor-force participation during the war, the Council of Ministers adopted a more determined population policy.[6] It includes incentives and disincentives for promoting a national two-child policy. The age at which one can marry has been set at 22 years for women, and birth spacing of five years is promoted. All birth-control procedures, mainly IUD insertion and abortion, are not only free but also include small monetary incentives ($1 to $5 U.S.). Condoms and birth-control pills, where available, are free or heavily subsidized.

[6]As in other Marxist states, there has not always been unanimity among the top Vietnamese leadership about the link between population growth and economic development. This may have resulted in inadequate funding, compounded by bureaucratic fragmentation of central family-planning investment among the Ministry of Public Health, the Women's Federation, the Ho Chi Minh Youth League, the General Statistical Office, and others.

The disincentives include restrictions on living space for urban residents with more than two children and discontinuance of salary supplements or free delivery after the second child. Currently, hospital-based deliveries cost about $1.30 in U.S. dollars (World Bank, 1990, p. 90). Other disincentives, like the requirement to pay fees for schooling and health care for three or more children, have become meaningless as both these sectors now require fees for all persons. In fact, as in China, many of these disincentives are relevant only to urban couples, because the rural areas have no financial mechanisms to enforce salary deductions or deny benefits.

Use of modern contraception, mainly the IUD, by Vietnamese women reached 39 percent in 1989, but the fertility rate remains high at 4.0. Among recently married women, the average preferred family size is 2.5 children, and almost 60 percent of women questioned stated that they wanted no more children. This suggests a large unmet need for contraception (National Committee for Population and Family Planning, 1990, p. 49). The reasons behind this unmet need may be the high literacy rate among Vietnamese women, the motivational efforts of the national family-planning program, and the inability of the health infrastructure to offer either a choice or a reliable supply of contraceptives.

Indeed, the stream of births, occurring mostly at poorly equipped commune health stations or at home, contributes to a maternal mortality rate of 140 per 100,000 (UNDP, 1990b, p. 148). Despite the existence of safe-delivery facilities, usage rates are low in many areas, and prenatal screening is weak, especially in the central and southern regions. In a recently conducted small survey in three provinces, fewer than 20 percent of women surveyed in communes in Hue, Thua Thien and Long An had adequate prenatal visits (three or more), and only about 24 percent of women in communes in Hue, Thua Thien delivered at the commune health center or district hospital (The rates for medical-facility deliveries were 58 percent in Long An Province compared with 83 percent in Nghe Tinh Province in the North.) (Gunawan and Kaufman, 1991, p. 10). Where prenatal screening is haphazard, especially in the South, local facilities cannot handle complicated deliveries that have not been referred to higher levels in advance, and the maternal mortality rate from hemorrhage is reportedly high.

Constraints to Dealing with These Challenges under Reform

Other contributions to this volume have considered the acute shortage of development funds, and the factors behind it. The problem appears to have reached crisis proportions since the recent political and economic changes in

Eastern Europe and the related transformation of the economic links among member countries of the Council for Mutual Economic Assistance. The effects on the government budget can be seen from Table 9-6, which points to the existence of a problem prior to the changes in Eastern Europe.

The budget deficit leaped from 18 percent of government spending in 1984 to 45 percent the next year, and stood at 39 percent in 1989. Greater enterprise autonomy meant that the share of transfers from state enterprises in total revenue fell from 72 percent in 1984 to 41 percent in 1989. While higher tax revenues partially made up for this shortfall, the tax base is still quite narrow. So the government has had to cut back on capital expenditures. The share of capital in total expenditures fell from 23 percent in 1984 and 31 percent in 1985 to 20 percent in 1988, although it rose again in 1989 to 27 percent, partly as a result of reforms in current expenditures that year.

On the current expenditure side, the share of subsidies, which was 38 percent of current expenditures in 1984, fell to 21 percent in 1986 but rose again to 38 percent in 1988. The share of food subsidies fell from 34 percent in 1984 to 14 percent in 1986 as the government tried to reduce this support. But it had to reverse its position, and it restored food rationing in 1987. In 1988, however, attempting to reduce the budget deficit, the government cut the number of rationed commodities and raised their prices. The wage structure reform of January 1989 eliminated all consumer subsidies and boosted wages and salaries to 31 percent of current expenditures that year. After the exchange-rate reform, the government also dispensed with export subsidies. In May 1989, the government inaugurated fees for medical services, and, in September 1989, for education.

Table 9-6. Government Revenues and Expenditures (billion dong)

	1984	1985	1986	1987	1988	1989
Revenue	9.4	19.0	83.6	379.3	1617.0	3428.0
Transfers from state enterprises	6.8	14.7	60.4	284.8	971.0	1410.0
Expenditures	11.6	34.6	120.8	514.9	2710.0	5631.0
Capital expenditures	2.7	10.7	33.4	1116.1	549.0	1500.0
Current expenditures	8.9	23.9	87.4	398.8	2161.0	4131.0
Share of current expenditures (%)						
Wages and salaries	3.4	7.5	6.3	7.4	11.8	31.2
Subsidies (total)	38.2	25.5	20.8	37.8	37.6	—
Food subsidies	34.0	20.0	14.0	26.0	21.0	—
Deficit as % of total expenditure	18.0	45.0	26.0	27.0	40.0	39.0

Source: UNDP (1990a, Table 4.3).

What has been the impact of these changes on the financing of public-health infrastructure and of the health-care system? Traditionally, the various levels of government shared the financing of the health system, including infrastructure in water supply and sanitation, and construction, equipment, supplies, and salaries for health workers. The central government underwrote 75 percent of the investment for water supply and sanitation, while the provinces provided the rest plus operating costs. Since 1988, as part of the decentralization effort, the provinces have been expected to bear a larger share of the burden. That the provinces may have been unable to make up for the fall in central investment is indicated by the sharp fall in state investment (central plus provincial) in construction, from 860 million *dong* in 1980 to 140 million dong in 1988 at constant 1982 prices (UNDP, 1990a, p. 34). Although the allocations of this expenditure are not available, it is unlikely that investment in water supply and sanitation was protected in the face of such a steep decline.

This drop must also have affected community participation. For instance, the "three-hygiene work movement" (wells, bathrooms, and latrines)—a collaboration of people providing labor, government providing cement and iron, and health workers furnishing technical support—has probably suffered from the decline in government funding.

As far as the finances of the health-care system are concerned, they declined through 1988, but have shown some signs of a recovery since. Table 9-7 indicates that the share of health (and of social expenditures as a whole) in the government's current expenditures changed little through 1988. This stability masks a sharp decline in total *real* expenditures in the sector in the four years ending in 1988. Table 9-8 indicates a fall in total real expenditures, both current and capital, and a consequent decline in per capita health spending.

Since 1988, however, there appears to have been some turnaround. It is too early to judge whether this reflects the beginning of a trend since the government's finances are not yet on a sound footing. A significant part of the

Table 9-7. Functional Classification of Current Expenditure (% of total)

	1984	1985	1986	1987	1988	1989
Education	7.0	8.5	9.3	7.7	8.1	17.2
Health	3.1	3.1	3.8	3.3	3.1	5.5
Pensions and social relief	4.1	5.7	7.7	5.5	6.0	12.6
Other	3.7	2.3	1.4	1.3	1.0	1.2
Total Social Expenditure	17.9	19.7	22.2	17.8	18.2	36.5

Source: World Bank (1990, Table 5.3).

Table 9-8. Health Finances (at 1982 prices)

	1985	1988	1989	1990
Total government health expenditure (million *dong*)	228	110	241	282
Current	160	102	214	243
Capital	68	8	27	39
Expenditure per capita (1982 *dong*)	3.8	1.7	3.7	4.4

Note: The data in this table are provisional.

increase in capital expenditure after 1988 reflects equipment imports financed by external assistance. The rise in sectoral current expenditures after 1988 may simply reflect a change in expenditure categories; that is wages increased while consumption subsidies declined. It is unclear, therefore, how much of the rise in current expenditures is real and is percolating down to the primary health-care level. We also do not know whether the increased funds are being used to tackle the growing inequities that many long-time observers are noting in the health system—inequities that harm the poorer regions and households.

Indeed, some of the changes in primary health financing appear to have worsened the financial stringency after 1988 even as the health system's funding has improved overall. Traditionally, the district government underwrote the construction of primary health centers and paid for supplies, while the village or commune paid the salaries. The stepped-up devolution of fiscal responsibility to lower levels means that villages are now also responsible for the purchase of essential drugs. Some villages can do this easily through levies from improved harvests, but not all regions can, and those poorer regions are suffering a deterioration of health services.

In 1989, the government introduced market-oriented reforms into the health sector to stimulate cost recovery. A system of fees replaced the free services and drugs at district-, provincial-, and national-level hospitals. The indigent were exempted from fees with certificates from their local units. While primary care still remained free, local units were able to charge for drugs provided. The units had to buy these from retail pharmacies, which, after July 1989, were permitted to sell directly to the units as well as to individuals and hospitals (World Bank, 1990, p. 89–90).

Experiments in health insurance have begun as a means to generate funds to sustain and revitalize the floundering health system. Recent proposals include experiments using employee wage deductions in urban areas and user fees (not to exceed 1 percent of income) for the self-employed (farmers) to provide funds to neighborhood and commune health centers, which would then cover all higher-level hospital fees and drugs for the insured (Abel-Smith, 1990, pp. 8–15). Funds would be administered centrally to ensure cross-subsidization between poorer and richer areas. Salaries for all health-care workers, which, in any case, were previously so low that they failed to meet living expenses and are now reduced to only 30 percent of their former level in some areas, would be met out of taxes.

Most district and provincial hospitals are overstaffed for their current 50 to 60 percent occupancy levels (Abel-Smith, 1990, p. 3). The underutilization is due, in part, to the inability of people to pay the medical fees and, in part, to declining faith in deteriorating health facilities, where equipment often does not work and no drugs are available. The health reforms of 1989 also have allowed licensed private clinics to open in many urban areas and have permitted doctors to practice privately after office hours at public clinics. While still few in number, these private clinics often provide more convenient and higher quality services on a fee-for-service basis.

A similar substitution of private for public health care also occurred in China at the corresponding period in its reform. This trend could not compensate, however, for a serious attrition in the staff, supplies, and facilities of primary health centers in the poorer regions in the absence of concerted efforts to maintain financing. For example, after introduction of the contract system of agriculture in China in the late 1970s, many "barefoot doctors" (the main primary health-care workers in rural China) left health work to return to farming, when collective welfare funds were no longer able to guarantee them salaries.[7] Between 1978 and 1982, the number of barefoot doctors fell from 1.8 million to 1.2 million, a 33 percent reduction (Hsiao, 1984, p. 934). The number of rural midwives similarly declined, from 620,000 in 1975 to about 510,000 in 1986 (Young, 1989b, p. 52). (This was a particularly alarming trend given the dramatic increase in Chinese women entering childbearing during those years.)[8]

While no absolute attrition in staff is yet evident in Vietnam, there are some clear indications that the volume of health-service delivery is decreasing: medical examinations per capita have fallen from 1.7 in 1980 to 1.4 in 1989; beds per 10,000 population have dropped from 37 to 34.6 in the same

[7] The barefoot doctor was the backbone of China's rural primary health-care system—a model for the developing world promoted at the Alma Ata conference. These minimally trained, rural paramedics provided basic medicines and first aid, referral, health education, immunizations, family-planning supplies and education, and hygiene and sanitation work in much of rural China. While many of these barefoot doctors worked part-time, their salaries were mainly funded by cooperative health-insurance schemes in communes (now townships) and work brigades (now villages).

[8] Many of the remaining barefoot doctors and midwives, after passing county- or provincial-level exams, signed contracts with the former brigade governments to work out of village clinics on a fee-for-service basis.

period (General Statistical Office, 1990, Tables 122 p. 141 and 127 p. 149). Since the commune governments now pay only part of commune health workers' salaries, they must supplement their clinical work with sideline farming. This contributes to absenteeism. Staff absenteeism, along with fees for service and shortages of drugs and supplies, has reduced the use of health services at the primary level similarly to the reduction at the district and provincial levels. A survey conducted in 1989 by the Swedish International Development Agency (SIDA) in Ha Tuyen Province near the Chinese border found that 76 percent of farm women had not visited a health facility during their last illness episode (quoting SIDA in Heibert, 1991, p. 16). In rural areas, village-based traditional practitioners are taking much of the clientele away from the erratically staffed commune health centers.

Another area of concern is nutrition. In the largely rural, poor economy of Vietnam, nutrition depends on overall food availability per capita, on the regional dimensions of food-output growth (especially in the absence of adequate infrastructure for private markets), and on the public distribution system. Changes in the incentive system in agriculture have sparked significant increases in food output. Between the triennia 1980–82 and 1987–89, average food-crop production (in rice equivalent) climbed from 280 kilograms per capita to 307 kilograms—a decadal increase of 9.64 percent (General Statistical Office, 1990, pp. 33, 40, 41, Tables 27, 33, 34).

Distribution of the increased output, however, has been uneven. Table 9-9 shows that the decadal increase in food-crop production per capita was 20 percent or more in the Red and Mekong River deltas and in the central coastal area of the northland, but was negative in the central highland and the northeastern area of the southland.[9] Clearly, there is a growing disparity among regions in food-crop production. This would not matter if grain moved freely from surplus to deficit regions, but markets in the poorer regions have no such capacity at present.[10]

Reorienting the public food-distribution system could be critically important to achieving food security, especially in the poorer regions. As mentioned earlier, the rationing system provides fewer commodities at higher prices than before. Per capita food subsidies have not kept pace with the rise in the food-price index. Most of these subsidies, however, used to go to government employees and similar protected groups; an increase in wages, as part of the

---

[9]The decadal increase has been calculated between 1980 and the triennium 1987–89; provincial data for the earlier triennium were not available to us. Since 1980 was not a particularly good crop year, we believe that the stated increase is not an underestimate.

[10]See Xuan and Timmer (1990) for a discussion of regional differences in food availability and diet.

Table 9-9. Food-Crop Production

Production Per Capita Excluding State Sector (kg in rice equivalent)					
Region	1980	1986	1987	1988	1989
North mountains and midlands	226	244	237	248	268
Red River Delta	223	244	251	288	316
Central coast of North	185	250	221	219	226
Central coast of South	243	277	272	269	280
Central highland	298	270	246	238	236
Northeast of South	150	154	133	144	140
Mekong River Delta	453	517	462	535	631

Decadal Changes (1987–89 over 1980)					
	Total (million tons)			Per capita (kg)		

Region	1980	1987–89	% change	1980	1987–89	% change
North moutains and midlands	1.85	2.49	35	226	251	11
Red River Delta	2.69	3.90	45	223	285	28
Central coast of North	1.42	1.91	35	185	222	20
Central coast of South	1.43	1.84	28	243	274	13
Central highland	0.45	0.56	24	298	240	− 19
Northeast of South	0.97	1.07	10	150	139	−7
Mekong River Delta	5.50	7.76	41	453	543	20

Source: General Statistical Office (1990, Tables 27, 33, 34).

1989 reform, compensated for some of the reduction in subsidies. But neither the subsidies nor the wage reform have had much impact on rural people in poorer regions, few of whom are wage or salary earners. In the absence of further evidence, we can only speculate about the impact on nutritional status in these regions, especially on poor households and on vulnerable groups like children and pregnant women. To what degree these vulnerable groups have targeted food-security arrangements is unknown. A large project known as PAM (Project Antimalnutrition), run jointly by the World Food Programme, UNICEF, and SIDA in pilot areas in 11 provinces, extends food supplements to pregnant women having prenatal checkups and to all children under a certain weight.

Gender Dimensions of Health

An assessment of the health concerns affecting women in particular during a period of economic and social upheaval requires a focus along three dimensions: access to food and health care, the extent of women's work burdens, and health problems that particularly affect women. Unfortunately, almost no field studies exist for Vietnam that would supply the requisite data for analysis of some potentially important issues. So, in this section, we will point to some directions in which research may fruitfully be undertaken.

A brief look at the historical roots of women's current status provides a useful context for this discussion. Although the historical evidence is still rather thin, most accounts indicate the existence of two major periods in Vietnamese gender relations—the periods before and after Chinese rule. China ruled Vietnam for roughly a thousand years, from the first century B.C. to the tenth century A.D. Prior to this period, women appear to have enjoyed much greater personal autonomy and social status, at least in legend and oral tradition. We do not know, however, whether society was organized along matrilineal and/or matrilocal lines, both of which are known correlates of higher female status. Chinese rule consolidated patrilineality and patrilocality, so women could inherit very little from their parents, and daughters began to be viewed only as temporary family members whose labor and childbearing capacity would be transferred to another family on marriage. Confucian ideology reinforced women's secondary status and low social value, particularly among the wealthier classes.

These negative features persisted after the end of Chinese rule. Nevertheless, it is probably true that neither social practices nor ideological beliefs about gender were as demeaning to women in Vietnam as they were in China. The practice of foot-binding never caught on in Vietnam, and gender relations in peasant families evidently were based, at least to some extent, on ideas of partnership. Nonetheless, son preference and patrilineal inheritance made considerable inroads into rural social and economic life. Under such conditions, women's access to and control over productive resources and income is at stake, and also often their access to food and health care.[11] This is the first issue of concern, and therefore an area for greater research that could inform policymakers about how strengthening peasant, family-based production might affect women's well-being.

A second area of concern is the work burden of Vietnamese women. Traditionally, women performed a wide range of tasks in the country, even during the Chinese period and the colonial era. When men were drawn into the military forces during the struggle for national liberation, women had to

[11]For instance, gender differentials in access to food and health care are severe in many South Asian settings. However, Vietnamese women may not suffer as much from this because of the East Asian cultural context. On the other hand, son preference is strong and has been exacerbated by the number of male war deaths from which the sex ratio has not yet recovered. There may also be considerable differences in this respect between North and South, and between the hill regions and the deltas. The North was more affected by Chinese cultural hegemony, but it is also the area where the Communist party and the Women's Union have been working for the longest time to counter the ideology of female inferiority.

take on much of the burden of agricultural work. The "Three Responsibilities Movement," launched by the Women's Union in 1965, identified production, the family, and fighting as women's key responsibilities. Three conditions of the post-1975 period kept women's workload heavier than it would otherwise have been. These conditions were the continuing shortage of able-bodied men (a result of war deaths and disabilities), the labor demands of physical reconstruction in large parts of the country devastated by the war, and the renewed manpower demands of Vietnam's military action in Cambodia. At least part of the poverty of women-headed households in Vietnam is probably a result of their difficulties in recruiting labor to help them with productive tasks. About 20 percent of all households are headed by women, according to official data (Statistical Publishing House, 1990, pp. 19–20). These households are acknowledged to be disproportionately among the poorest in the country.

Vis-à-vis the work burden of women, two issues are of particular importance. One is the implications of some of the changes in the health-care systems on women's workload. The reduced availability of health care through the existing primary health system and the absence of alternatives, especially in poorer regions, may mean that people will have to travel longer distances for care. It is unclear how widespread is the practice of not getting treatment at health facilities as revealed in the SIDA survey cited earlier, and whether this failure to visit facilities when ill is a response to reduced supplies and health personnel or to increased workloads and time burdens on women (quoting SIDA in Hiebert, 1991). Although not clear, it is worth investigating. Also worth investigating is the extent to which women's unpaid family labor in health care is being substituted for health care hitherto provided outside the home.

The second issue of importance has to do with changes in the day-care system. Day-care facilities appear to be caring for fewer children and have become more expensive. The number of children in the zero to three age group who attended a day care rose from 564,000 in 1975 to 1.2 million in 1980, but declined to 700,000 in 1988. Much of this decline appears to have taken place in the cooperative sector, which accounted for almost three-fourths of day-care attendance in 1980. Cooperatives no longer allocate as much funding for day care, and parents are expected to bear the bulk of the cost burden (UNDP, 1990a, p. 206). As in health and education, this day-care cost may place a greater burden on poorer households and on poorer regions; in all cases, however, it constitutes a greater potential work burden for women who have primary responsibilities in these areas of child care. Of particular concern is the added work burden on female heads of households because of less day care. The resources and labor time of these women are already stretched thin.

Another area in which more research is needed is the area of health problems that particularly afflict women. As we have mentioned, the poor quality of water and sanitation systems means greater risk of gynecological infections. Exacerbating this problem is the use of the IUD as the main birth-control method. While the government promotes a better "method mix," shortages of supplies and information services deter program expansion. Despite strong government statements supporting population control, the service-delivery structure remains weak; there is little outreach for contraceptive promotion and education or for distribution of contraceptives to couples. Moreover, commune-level health workers responsible for family planning are overwhelmed with a multitude of other primary health-care tasks, and personnel retraining arrangements are weak. After assignment to commune health stations, local staff members are rarely updated with new medical knowledge and techniques.

The maternal mortality rate may also worsen as the public-health system declines, especially for poorer households and poorer regions. Some of our conjectures here may appear to be worst-case scenarios. But our knowledge of and experience with the recent changes in the Chinese health system justify erring on the side of abundant caution.

On a more positive note, changes in women's health habits and attitudes do seem to occur rapidly in Vietnam once supply and training problems are addressed, as can be seen from several donor experiments in providing services, supplies, or integrated primary health care that resulted in improved use of prenatal care, improved contraceptive use, and a shift away from IUDs (Gunawan and Kaufman, 1991, p. 12).

China and Vietnam: A Health-Care Comparison

Vietnam's economic reforms are similar in some respects to those undertaken by China more than a decade ago.[12] Both countries entered the reform period after achieving significant successes in primary health care and in improving the status of women. As China's reforms have evolved, however, there has been an unanticipated deterioration in the rural health-care system and in women's status in certain parts of the country. A review of the negative effects of these trends may be helpful for anticipating similar difficulties in Vietnam. Indeed some of these problems may be further magnified in Vietnam due to the poorer health status of its people and its weaker economy.

As in China, Vietnam has introduced users' fees for health services and drugs, which were formerly paid by collective funds. Many of the current

---

[12]Both countries have reinstituted family farming in rural areas. However, the reforms differ greatly in their approaches to trade and macroeconomic policy.

problems in China's rural health services can be traced to the curtailment of rural, collective health-insurance arrangements and the welfare funds (allocated from collective farming) that financed them. In 1975, before the rural economic reforms began, 85 percent of the Chinese population was covered by collective health insurance. By 1984, fewer than half of the rural health stations were still collectively financed (Hsiao, 1984, p. 934). Those that remained were mainly in prosperous areas. In poorer areas, the operation of many village-level health stations was contracted out and privately run on a fee-for-service basis. As noted earlier, the disappearance of collective funds out of which to pay salaries has led to a decrease in rural health personnel, including barefoot doctors, available to provide preventive and basic services.

In Vietnam, as in China, economic decentralization has shifted the responsibility for health financing to provincial and local governments. The effect of this decentralization in China has been to concentrate resources at the county level, the lowest unit financed by the state, at the expense of village and township services.[13] Township hospitals, the first referral units for the rural Chinese population, depend on local funds. All townships have suffered from a lack of reliable tax collection, and poorer townships have also suffered from the inability of local governments to provide subsidies. As a result, available beds in Chinese township hospitals declined from 775,413 in 1980 to 731,411 in 1984 (citing from China Health Statistics Yearbook, 1985, pp. 41–42 in Henderson, 1988, p. 36). We have noted a similar trend in Vietnam.

Although in China the shortage of rural funds stems from a nationwide redeployment of health resources to hospital-based curative care in the urban and county hospital systems, in Vietnam, the shortage of funds for rural health care is related more to the overall shortage of funds in the economy as a result of the war, the embargo, and the withdrawal of aid from Eastern Europe and the former Soviet Union. Unlike Vietnam, China was not aid-dependent in the 1970s before the initiation of reforms.

In China, what have been the health effects on the rural population from the changes and reforms just described, and how relevant are these effects to Vietnam? The main impact in China has been less access to good health care for poorer segments of the population. And about one-fourth of China's nearly 3,000 counties are classified as poor.[14] In these counties, and in others that have not experienced much economic growth under the reforms, the demise of collective health insurance has created a situation in which the

---

[13]Below the province level, China is administratively organized into prefectures, counties, townships, and villages. There are about 3,000 counties in China, and each county contains 15 to 20 townships, with up to 10,000 population.

[14]Poor counties are those with per capita incomes of less than $200 (U.S.) and infant mortality rates well above the national average of about 50 per 1,000 live births.

health infrastructure, especially for preventive services, cannot be maintained (UNICEF, 1989, p. 81). After more than a decade of reform in China, it is generally acknowledged that fee-for-service health care has undermined access for many segments of the population. Many richer areas have begun to reinstitute collective health-insurance arrangements, and a national health-insurance program is currently being formulated in Beijing. In Vietnam, where rural poverty is more prevalent, income-based inequity in access to health services is increasing with the change to fee-for-service care and can be expected to worsen unless cost-sharing arrangements are introduced.

In both countries, the disadvantaged poor—and especially women—suffer most from the semiprivatization of the health sector. In Vietnam, where poverty is more widespread and average income is lower, the impact of the reforms on the health of the poor may be even greater, despite nominal fees for service. In many areas of rural Vietnam, there is virtually no expendable income for fee-for-service medical care and medicines.

Little disaggregated information on health is available, but national data show an increase in morbidity from certain preventable infectious diseases in China in the postreform period, as illustrated in Table 9-10. Control of these diseases—dysentery, viral hepatitis, hemorrhagic fever, and typhoid—is related to hygiene education and basic sanitation efforts—tasks that were performed by barefoot doctors in the prereform period. But even though these preventable infectious diseases appear to be on the rise in China, China's health profile is characterized increasingly by chronic diseases that do not lend themselves as well to a primary-care approach.

Vietnam, on the other hand, remains a country characterized by infectious diseases that require a primary health-care approach. Here, too, there

Table 9-10. Incidence (per 100,000 population) of Infectious Diseases in China (1974–1984)

Disease	1974	1977	1980	*1984
Diphtheria	2.6	3.2	1.0	.33
Measles	110.9	107.9	299.9	60.14
Pertussis	73.3	70.3	32.3	20.96
Polio	1.2	.8	.8	.16
Dysentery	285.3	261.8	293.4	374.96
Viral hepatitis	26.5	27.9	48.4	67.55
Malaria	1090.8	442.8	336.9	87.70
Hemorrhagic fever	1.6	1.8	3.1	8.80
Typhoid, paratyphoid	.4	7.6	7.6	9.70

*According to Hsiao (1987) and others, the 1984 official Chinese estimates of childhood diseases may be seriously underestimated.
Sources: For the period 1974–1980, see Jamison (1984, p. 127). For 1984, see Henderson (1988), citing China Health Statistics Yearbook, 1985, p. 56.

has been a resurgence of infectious diseases, which had been largely controlled, and this regressive development bodes poorly for progress toward a health transition to a disease profile characterized by more chronic as opposed to infectious diseases.

The water supply and sanitation infrastructure are far more advanced in China than in Vietnam. China, however, had a longer period to consolidate its health-care system and improve its water supply and sanitation infrastructure prior to reform. Only about 10 percent of China's population must rely on untreated surface water for drinking, and almost all rural areas have centralized excreta-treatment arrangements. In Vietnam, basic health-education and sanitation efforts remain essential to begin to address the major health problems.

Finally, introduction of the family-based contract system of agriculture has done inadvertent harm to China's highly successful population-control efforts and gender equality initiatives. While preference for sons remains entrenched in many countries with patriarchal lineage and inheritance systems, China's socialist economic policies had, at least in part, eliminated the greater economic value of sons. Now, under the contract system, the economic value of sons has gained new life: daughters continue to marry out of the family; sons give elderly parents old-age support; and families view male labor as more valuable. The renewed son preference has undermined the "one child per couple" policy in rural areas of China in recent years; many rural couples now defy policy and continue to bear children until at least one male offspring is born.

China's similarities to Vietnam in the arena of son preference are striking. In Vietnam, son preference has been known to have had a pronatalist impact even before the recent economic changes (Nguyen Huyen Chau, 1988, p. 71). The renewed value of sons in the farm-based rural economy has deterred population-control efforts. The disproportionate sex ratio of men to women (94.7 males to every 100 females), which is a consequence not only of the war but also of the large outmigration of productive-age men in recent years, fuels son preference. This imbalance is particularly acute for the productive-age group of 25 to 44 years, for which the sex ratio is 87 males to every 100 females.

Yet, important differences must be noted between Vietnam and China. While both countries are experiencing a resurgence in son preference, Vietnam is unlikely to experience the extreme gender consequences from this preference that have occurred in China. While Vietnam *does* promote family planning and encourages a two-child limit, the policy is less coercive than China's, in part because Vietnam has learned from China's negative example. In China, the restrictiveness of the policy, which limits families to only one child, has resulted in such reported abuses as beatings of infertile or daughter-bearing wives, neglect or infanticide of girl babies, and abandonment of daughters. In

Vietnam, it is unlikely that such abuses will occur. On the one hand, son preference is less entrenched culturally, and on the other, there is no apparent mechanism in rural areas that prevents couples from continuing to bear children until they are ready to stop.

Conclusions and Recommendations

After a promising beginning, Vietnam's health system is now at a cross-roads. Over the last decade, a period of financial stringency as well as transformation in economic and social organization has placed considerable strain on the health sector. The quality of the public-health system has deteriorated. The water-supply and sanitation infrastructures, far from adequate before, still contribute to the spread of preventable infectious diseases, especially in rural areas. Preventive public-health efforts have not been maintained. Problems in the health-services system such as chronic shortages of drugs and supplies, lack of staff, and fees for service and drugs are forcing many people to forego medical care. Although a number of private alternatives have been implemented, they tend to be expensive, inadequate in coverage, and unable to offer preventive programs.

While the government maintains its commitment to protecting the health sector, financial stringency during most of the 1980s forced a decline in per capita health expenditure. The recent increase in external assistance to the health sector, as well as budgetary reforms, has produced a turnaround in the sector's finances at the aggregate level. But important concerns have to be addressed. What, if any, impact does this increase have on the accessibility of primary health care as opposed to secondary or tertiary care? Are the needs of poorer regions and households being met? How much of the increase is tied to individual (and perhaps isolated) projects that do not fully address the critical need for efficient and equitable resource planning? We believe that such donor assistance may be more effective if provided within the context of a strong government planning effort.

Strong government leadership is a continuing prerequisite for sustained health improvement during a period of economic reform. The government needs to play a particularly strong role in three areas. One area is investment in the water and sanitation infrastructure because of the persistence of infectious diseases. The erosion of collective organization at the local level has made it difficult to organize public-works programs, especially for projects deemed to have less immediate payoff to the productive sector. Alternatives, including better decentralized planning and new systems of local taxation and allocation, need to be explored.

A second area for government leadership is in the revitalization of preventive public-health efforts. Much of the earlier gain in health status can be attributed to preventive public-health campaigns, backed by a system of primary health-care centers. We believe this network should remain the backbone of the health system. Funding for this tier needs to be guaranteed to sustain its functioning.

A third area concerns mechanisms to protect equity in access to health services. Poorer areas, households, and vulnerable groups are at greater risk during the transition. Experience in other countries suggests that local-level health insurance rarely generates enough revenue to transfer health resources to these needier groups. A national health-insurance program may be a better mechanism for guaranteeing the health needs of all.

References

Abel-Smith, Brian. 1990. "Assignment Report: Vietnam." Unpublished consultant report for the Swedish International Development Agency, Stockholm.

Asian Development Bank. 1989. *Economic Report on the Socialist Republic of Vietnam*, Manila, October.

Banister, Judith. 1989. "A New Survey of Infant Mortality in China: A Research Note." Unpublished paper. Center for International Research of the U.S. Bureau of the Census, Washington, D.C.

Central Census Steering Committee. 1990. Vietnam Population Census, 1989: Sample Results. Hanoi: Socialist Republic of Vietnam.

China Health Statistics Yearbook. 1985. Beijing: People's Medical Publishing House.

Duong Quynh Hoa. "Assessment and Evaluation of Nutritional Status of Vietnamese Children in Community Health." In *Proceedings of the International Conference on Applied Nutrition, Hanoi, April 25–29, 1986*. Hanoi: National Institute of Nutrition and UNICEF.

Eisen, Arlene. 1984. *Women and Revolution in Vietnam*. London: Zed Books.

General Statistical Office. 1990. *Statistical Data of the Socialist Republic of Vietnam, 1976–1989*. Hanoi: Statistical Publishing House.

Gunawan, Nardho and Joan Kaufman. 1991. "Evaluation Report of the Integrated Project on Environmental Sanitation, Intestinal Parasite Control, and MCH/FP for Family Health in Vietnam." Tokyo: Japanese Organization for International Cooperation in Family Planning, July.

Hiebert, Murray. 1991. "The Cost of Care." *Far Eastern Economic Review*, January 10, pp. 16–17.

Henderson, Gail. 1988. "Increased Inequality in Health Care: Fact or Fiction?" Paper presented at the Conference on Social Consequences of the Chinese Economic Reforms, Fairbank Center for East Asian Research, Harvard University, May 13–15.

Hoang Dinh Cau. 1990. "Operation of Vietnam's Health Sector." Unpublished mimeo.

Hsiao, William C. 1984. "Special Report: Transformation of Health Care in China." *New England Journal of Medicine* 310:932–36.

———. 1988. "The Incomplete Revolution: China's Health Care System under Market Socialism." Unpublished paper from Conference on Social Consequences of the Chinese Economic Reforms, Fairbank Center for East Asian Research, Harvard University, May 13–15.

Hull, Terence H. 1991. "Government and Society in Southeast Asian Family Planning Programs: The Cases of Indonesia, Vietnam and the Philippines." Paper presented at the Annual Meeting of the Population Association of America, Chicago.

Jamison, Dean T., J.R. Evans, T. King, I. Porter, N. Prescott, and A. Prost. 1984. *China: The Health Sector.* Washington, D.C.: World Bank.

Marr, David, and Christine White, eds. 1988. *Postwar Vietnam: Dilemmas in Socialist Development.* Ithaca: Cornell University Press.

Ministry of Health of the Socialist Republic of Vietnam. 1990. "Results of a Prevalence Survey on Soil Transmitted Helminthiases." Hanoi: Socialist Republic of Vietnam.

Ministry of University and Vocational Education of the Socialist Republic of Vietnam. 1988. "Baseline Survey VIE/88/P07; Final Data." Unpublished report. Centre for Computational Design and Experiment, College of Construction, Socialist Republic of Vietnam, Hanoi, October.

National Committee for Population and Family Planning. 1990. *Vietnam: Demographic and Health Survey 1988.* Hanoi: Socialist Republic of Vietnam.

Nguyen Huyen Chau. 1988. "Women and Family Planning Policies in Postwar Vietnam." In David Marr and Christine White, eds., *Postwar Vietnam: Dilemmas in Socialist Development.* Ithaca: Cornell University Press.

Population Reference Bureau. 1990. *1990 World Population Data Sheet.* Washington, D.C.: Population Reference Bureau.

Statistical Publishing House. 1990. "Selected Indicators on Women's Status in Vietnam 1975–89." Hanoi: Socialist Republic of Vietnam.

UNDP. 1990a. *Report on the Economy of Vietnam.* State Planning Committee, Socialist Republic of Vietnam, Hanoi.

———. 1990b. *Human Development Report, 1990.* New York: Oxford University Press.

UNICEF. 1989. *Children and Women of China: A UNICEF Situational Analysis.* Beijing: UNICEF.

World Bank. 1990. *Vietnam: Stabilization and Structural Reforms.* Washington D.C.: World Bank, April 30.

———. 1991. *World Development Report 1991.* New York: Oxford University Press.

Xuan, Vo-Tong, and C. Peter Timmer. 1990. "A Food Policy for Vietnam." Development Discussion Paper No. 351. Harvard Institute for International Development, Cambridge, Mass.

Young, Mary E. 1989a. "Impact of the Rural Reform on the Financing of Rural Health Services in China." *Health Policy* 11:27–42.

———. 1989b. "Maternal Health in China." Unpublished mimeo. April.

10

Economic Reform and the Intensification of Rituals in Two North Vietnamese Villages, 1980–90

Hy V. Luong

Since the resumption of large-scale rice export in 1989 and 1990 after a four-decade hiatus, economic reform in Vietnam has been widely noted in the West for its success in improving agricultural productivity. Going beyond national statistics, I suggest that reform at the local level in the 1980s was closely connected with a fundamental transformation of the Vietnamese ideological and sociocultural landscape. The increasing prosperity, or at least reduced poverty, in rural Vietnam was inextricably linked to a major socio-cultural and ideological shift. My analysis of this interplay focuses on economic reform and the intensification of rituals in Hoai Thi and Son Duong, northern villages located 27 and 95 kilometers from Hanoi in the provinces of Ha Bac and Vinh Phu, and studied in the summers of 1987, 1990, and 1991.

I suggest that in both Son Duong and Hoai Thi, in the 1980s, economic reform had two major impacts on local ritual practices. First, the growing economic surplus and the movement away from collectivized agriculture toward household production in a multisector economy gave rituals both within and beyond the kinship domain a big push. Rituals and the reciprocal feasting system reinforced social relations in an agricultural community with constant natural threats to subsistence and with fewer subsistence guarantees and less assistance from the state. Economic surplus, especially in Hoai Thi, enabled villagers to organize increasingly elaborate ceremonies. Second, the Vietnamese state became more concerned with economic development and political stability than with socialist ideological transformation and, therefore, relaxed its control over local ritual practices.

Historical Backgrounds

Both Hoai Thi and Son Duong are agriculture-based communities with strong senses of identity, despite their nominal difference in administrative status. Like most northern Vietnamese villages (*lang*) in the 1980s, both underwent a fundamental economic and sociocultural transformation in connection with the restructuring of the nation's political economy.

Administratively, Son Duong is a commune (*xa*) that evolved from the merger of Son Duong with two smaller neighboring communities in 1946.[1] In contrast, for more than 100 years, despite its informal designation as a village (*lang*), Hoai Thi has been only a hamlet (*thon*) in the commune (*xa*) of Hoai Bao, a community situated 17 miles north of Hanoi.[2]

In 1990, with 761 inhabitants, 162 households, and 137 *mau* of land (49.3 hectares, including 44.25 hectares of cultivated land), Hoai Thi was the second smallest hamlet in Hoai Bao (population 6,513, with 1,377 households and 1,217 *mau* or 438 hectares). In 1991, Son Duong had 4,200 inhabitants, 876 households, and 1,024 *mau* of land (368.86 hectares, including 278.95 hectares or 779.86 *mau* of cultivated land).

The difference in administrative status between Hoai Thi and Son Duong has become nominal, however, since 1988. In that year, Hoai Thi was de facto restored to its nineteenth-century status as a separate administrative and economic unit, in parallel to the greater hamlet endogamy and its strong sense of sociocultural identity. This feeling was reflected in Hoai Thi residents' use of the vernacular term *lang* ("village") when referring to their community, as well as by their maintenance of a separate pagoda and communal house, in the same way that Son Duong villagers referred to Son Duong as a *lang* and maintained their own pagoda and shrine.[3] As an indication of the strengthening local identity in Hoai Thi, the rate of community endogamy increased to 75 percent (24 out of 32 marriages) for the 1986–90 period, while in general, only 50 percent of the 194 complete or incomplete couples in

---

[1]In the late 1920s, Son Duong and its two neighbors, Dung Hien and Thuy Son, possessed, in combination, 363.24 hectares of ricefields (1009 *mau*): Son Duong had approximately 216 hectares (600 *mau*) for a population of 1464; Dung Hien had 90 hectares (250 *mau*) for 240; and Thuy Son, a single-lineage village, had 54 hectares (150 *mau*) for 70 people. The land data comes from Son Duong (1987), and the 1927 demographic data from Ngo Vi Lien (1928).

[2]In the early nineteenth century, Hoai Thi was an independent village with its own mayor (*ly truong*) (Khong Duc Thiem, 1982, p. 116). By the late nineteenth century, it had been merged with two neighboring villages into the village of Hoai Bao (Ngo Vi Lien, 1928, p. 9; Vietnam, Historical Institute, 1971). In October 1946, two other neighboring villages were merged into Hoai Bao to create a new village with six hamlets.

[3]The communal houses of Son Duong, Dung Hien, and Thuy Son were destroyed during the Franco-Vietnamese war or in its aftermath, partly because of French bombing and partly with the encouragement of the local leadership (cf. Son Duong, 1987, p. 44).

residence in Hoai Thi represented intracommunity marriages. The 75 percent rate, while below the average of 81.8 percent in Son Duong for 1989, 1990, and 1991, was still remarkably high for a community of only 761 people, less than one-fifth the size of Son Duong.

The strong local identity partly accounts for the restoration of Hoai Thi as a separate administrative and economic unit. Following local implementation of Party Directive 10 (Luong, 1992, p. 212), issued in 1988 on a new contract system, the commune-wide cooperative, formed in 1979, became a nominal entity divided into six hamlet-level units with independent accounting systems. Also in 1988, the position of hamlet chief (*thon truong*) was created, equivalent to the village chief position (*ly truong*) in the precolonial period. The first *thon truong* was chosen among the three hamlet representatives to the Commune People's Council.[4]

In contrast to Hoai Thi, Son Duong and its two neighbors, Dung Hien and Thuy Son, gradually came to share the same identity as a *lang*, primarily for ritualistic and historical reasons. In the nineteenth century and throughout the French colonial period, Son Duong, Dung Hien, and Thuy Son were linked administratively, economically, sociopolitically, as well as ritually and historically. Before 1946, the original Son Duong had been the head commune (*xa*) in a same-name canton that, besides Dung Hien and Thuy Son, had included four other communes. It was administered by a canton chief and a deputy chief. The three communes used to share the same periodic rural market, which was located by the gate of Son Duong *xa* and in front of its pagoda. In the first half of the twentieth century, the elites of at least Son Duong and Dung Hien, if not of all three, had been linked through extensive school ties and class-based marital alliances. Son Duong, Dung Hien, and Thuy Son also worshipped the same tutelary deities, albeit in three different communal houses. At an important area festival on the third day of the third lunar month, the members of the three communes, male and female, young and old, joined in a ritual fight against the residents of Ngu Xa in the neighboring canton of Vinh Lai. Historically, according to a local Communist party historian, it was not until the early nineteenth century that the Kieu lineage seceded from Son Duong to form the tiny commune of Thuy Son and that Dung Hien followed suit. In this historical context, although Son Duong, Dung Hien, and Thuy Son kept the symbols of their common guardian deities in their own communal houses, the wooden figures and seats of the two deities were located only in the shrine in Son Duong. In the French colonial period, on the tenth day of the eighth lunar month, officials of the three

---

[4]All three representatives were party members. The other two were the village president and the head of the hamlet's women's association.

villages reportedly gathered at the shrine for a common worship ritual. Shared rituals and common historical roots made it easy in Son Duong to achieve complete integration of hamlet-level agricultural cooperatives in the late 1960s, as the following comments of a former Son Duong leader illustrate:

> When the [hamlet-level] cooperatives were merged, I headed the inspection team and joined the management committee of the new cooperative. In the context of war, the higher-level cooperative in Son Duong had fewer problems than cooperatives elsewhere. I told members of another village: "Your village [cooperative] has three fathers, while we have only one. Despite the earlier division of Son Duong into three villages [before 1945], we had the same customs and worshipped the same guardian deities. The earlier administrative division in Son Duong merely resulted from the conflicting interests of village notables in the past [that is, in the nineteenth century]. In your case, you had three different contests at the annual village festivals: rice cooking, wrestling, and group singing. You had three different traditions, hence the problems with a higher-level cooperative."

In the aftermath of the 1988 agricultural reform, the feeling of shared identity was the key factor in the decision not to restore Dung Hien and Thuy Son as separate administrative and economic units.

Economic Reform in Rural Vietnam: The Cases of Two Northern Villages

On the eve of the Sixth Party Congress in 1986, both Hoai Thi and Son Duong were predominantly agricultural communities that had benefited from the upsurge in agricultural productivity and the restructuring of Vietnam's political economy in the first half of the decade. In 1981, in response to a procurement crisis and declining productivity on cooperative land, the state had authorized the household contract system in agriculture. Under this arrangement, the household, through a two to five year contract with the cooperative, was responsible for transplanting, tending, and harvesting the rice crop. In other words, the household furnished 70 percent of the labor input in agricultural production, for which it received labor-point credit (Nguyen Huy, 1980, p. 11). In principle, the cooperative still did plowing, irrigation and drainage work, seeding, fertilizer spreading, and insecticide spraying, although in Son Duong, households also took care of plowing. Collectively owned land was allocated primarily on the basis of the household's adult work force. A contracting household's income was based not only on the value of each labor point in paddy and the number of labor points accumulated by the household but also on the crop yield above the cooperative's quota. In other words, the contracting household was allowed to retain the surplus.

In 1988, Party Directive 10 (Luong, 1992, p. 212) guaranteed cooperative members long-term leases on the contracted land and at least 40 percent of the production quota for fulfilling the transplanting, crop tending, and harvesting tasks. In Hoai Thi, under the new contract system, village households owned 10 percent of the cultivable land, the best land in the village, as "garden plots" (now called *ruong 10%*). The government levied no taxes on this land. Of the rest, 40 percent was allocated to *all* male villagers below the age of 60 and female villagers below 55; 40 percent was allocated to the adult work force; and 20 percent constituted reserve land temporarily allocated to the elderly or rented to successful village bidders but eventually allocated to demobilized soldiers or new cooperative members. Village households depended on the cooperative only for tractor plowing, irrigation and drainage, insecticide spraying, and crop protection, for which they were billed according to the size of their contracted land.

In the spring of 1988, the village leadership of Son Duong refined the household contract system. Agricultural households were divided into three categories: poor contractors (70 households), average contractors (412 households), and good contractors (350 households). Poor contractors were defined as households whose crop yields usually fell below the norm of 3.88 tonnes per hectare per crop (1.4 tonnes per *mau*) and who could not repay their paddy debts to the cooperative. Average contractors usually produced within the norm, while good contracting households clearly exceeded it. Village fields were also divided into three categories. The first category included 93.6 hectares of rice fields (260 *mau*), divided among all households on the basis of the number of consumers in the village (3,828). Each person—child or adult—was thereby entitled to 240 square meters (2/3 of a *sao,* or 0.06 acre). The cooperative divided agricultural taxes as well as the irrigation water, crop protection, and insecticide expenses for these 93.6 hectares among the village households on the basis of their holdings in this category.[5]

The second category included 132.8 hectares (369 *mau*), divided among the average and good contracting households on the basis of the active household work force (women from 16 to 55 years old, and men from 16 to

---

[5]The cooperative's leadership expected that with the annual crop-rotation index of 2.5, the 240 square meters would produce 210 kilograms of food (including both rice and secondary crops). With the allowance of 20 kilograms for taxes and the aforementioned expenses, each person would retain 190 kilograms a year, or 15.7 kilograms a month.

60). The cooperative supplied irrigation water, crop protection, insecticide spraying, and 13 kilograms of fertilizer per *sao* (360 square meters). The cooperative received half the production-quota figure of 90 kilograms (that is, 45 kilograms for a normal crop), of which 80 percent (36 kilograms) went toward taxes, water fees, insecticide, fertilizer, and crop protection. In the estimate of its leaders, the cooperative retained 20 percent of the production quota (250 kilograms per hectare, or 9 kilograms per *sao*, for a total of 33 tonnes of paddy per crop) for its obligations toward retired cultivators, to maintain an operating fund, and for management expenses.

The third category included 39.6 hectares (110 *mau*) of the most fertile rice fields, for which only the 350 good contracting households were allowed to bid. The cooperative provided an additional 12 kilograms of fertilizer for each *sao* of contracted land in this category. In return, the production quota was set at 170 kilograms per *sao* (4.72 tonnes per hectare) for each crop, of which the cultivator was entitled to one-half.

The cooperative's leadership adopted this contract system in 1988 to promote production efficiency in agriculture. They quickly altered it, however, to achieve greater equity. During my revisit to the village in 1991, I learned that of the 273.6 hectares (760 *mau*) of reallocated land, 31.25 hectares (86.8 *mau*, called 10–percent rice fields) had been equally divided among all residents of the village, regardless of age, gender, or occupational status (72 square meters per capita). The first two aforementioned categories of fields (for all villagers, and for average and good contractors) had been merged to create a pool of 180.76 hectares (502.1 *mau*), which the cooperative allocated on an egalitarian basis to all villagers, except for (retired) state employees. The third category (for good contractors) had grown in acreage to 61.9 hectares (171.9 *mau*), but it included only fields with less reliable yields. More important, the cooperative's role had been further reduced to crop protection, water control (irrigation and drainage), and tax collection for the state.

With the introduction of the contract system in 1981 and its liberalization in 1988, the average paddy yield per hectare per crop on cooperative land in Hoai Thi grew from 2.25 tonnes in 1980 to 2.43 tonnes for the 1981–87 period and to 2.81 tonnes in 1988–89.[6] In Son Duong, the yield rose from approximately 1.5 tonnes in 1980 to 3.45 tonnes in 1988–89. In Hoai Thi, per capita paddy production from cooperative fields increased from 187 kilograms in 1980 (a poor year) to 319.18 kilograms in 1989 and, in Son Duong, from 165 kilograms to 405.

---

[6]The crop yield in Hoai Thi approximated that in the Red River Delta in 1980 (2.29 tonnes per hectare), but lagged behind the latter in 1988–89 (3.41 tonnes per hectare) (Vietnam, General Statistical Office, 1991, p. 54).

Table 10-1 shows a breakdown of agricultural productivity in Hoai Thi and Son Duong in 1989—a year chosen to facilitate the comparison of incomes in the two villages with those in a nationwide study (Le Van Toan et al., 1991). Because of poorly kept village records and the decentralized production processes, precise figures on the production costs of some crops and animal

Table 10-1. Agricultural Income Sources in Hoai Thi and Son Duong (1989).

	Cultivated area (hectares)	Total yield in paddy or paddy equivalent (tonnes)	Production costs, miscellaneous levies, and tax	Net yield per capita (kilograms)
Hoai Thi				
Rice Crop on Contracted Land				
Chiem (5th month)	40.31	139.96	46.85%	169.7
Mua (10th month)	41.47	97.91		
Crops on "10%" Rice Fields				
(2 crops each year)*	5.508	32.130	31.85%	29.39
Secondary Crops +				
Soybeans	00.58	1.696	41.05%	1.98
Mung beans	00.576	0.81		
Peanuts				n/a
Maize				n/a
Sweet Potatoes				n/a
Animal Husbandry (herd sizes in 1990)				
Pigs	213 head	255.6	81%	
Cattle	14 head	10.5	54.7%	74.58
Buffalo	16 head	11.2	80%	
Total				275.19
Son Duong				
Rice Crop on Contracted Land				
Chiem (5th month)	203	834.56	49.5%	204.59
Mua (10th month)	216	792		
Crops on "10%" Rice Fields				
(2 crops each year)*	31.25	243.15	35.29%	39.19
Secondary Crops +				
Soybeans				n/a
Mung beans				n/a
Peanuts	54.4	242.25	43.18%	34.32
Maize	70.6	209.59	45.06%	28.68
Sweet Potatoes	30.8	151.38	20.98%	29.79
Animal Husbandry (herd sizes in 1990)				
Pigs	650 head	780	81%	
Cattle	342 head	256.5	54.7%	67.87
Buffalo	58 head	40.6	80%	
Total				404.44

*Yield and direct production costs assumed to be the same as for rice fields on contract with the cooperative.
+ Variation in total cost per hectare due mainly to the varying amounts and costs of chemical fertilizer (figures on fertilizer quantities from two households balanced against the aggregate data in the neighboring province of Ha Bac [see Phung van Thuc, pp. 203–10]). Other direct production costs (including water and crop protection) were roughly the same as for rice fields; tax was exempted for the winter crops of maize and sweet potatoes; and regular tax and local charges per hectare were levied on the bean and peanut crops.

husbandry are unavailable. I extrapolated production costs and net agricultural incomes per capita partly on the basis of the data from 1987, 1988, 1990, and 1991, and from other northern villages.

In Hoai Thi, according to the report of the hamlet chief, agricultural taxes amounted to 8 percent of the yield from contracted rice fields in the spring of 1990. The cooperative collected an additional 9 percent on average to defray water and plowing expenses. It levied 7 percent more to cover a variety of local expenses, including social welfare, cooperative management, crop protection, hamlet education, cemetery maintenance, village administration, and cooperative meetings and banquets. Of the 76 percent retained by the contracting household, seed and chemical fertilizer absorbed approximately 22.85 percent of the crop yield. Production costs, miscellaneous levies by the cooperative and the local administration, and agricultural taxes averaged 46.85 percent for the spring 1990 crop. Assuming no variation in this percentage from 1989 to 1990, the net paddy yield from contracted land amounted to 169.7 kilograms per Hoai Thi resident in both 1989 and 1990.

In 1989 in Son Duong, the cooperative collected 22 percent of the yield for agricultural taxes and for various cooperative and village charges.[7] Since Son Duong villagers had to apply more chemical fertilizer to obtain a higher yield, I estimated other costs to absorb 27.5 percent of the 1989 paddy production. Agricultural producers were able to retain 50.5 percent of the yield on contracted rice fields (cf. Le van Toan et al., 1991, pp. 30–33, 71–74). In Son Duong in 1989, the net paddy yield from contracted land amounted to an estimated 204.59 kilograms per person. Because the 10 percent household plots, under the permanent control of village households, were subject to little taxation and were at least as productive as the rest of cooperative land, I estimated for 1989 that they provided a net amount of at least 39.19 kilograms of paddy per capita in Son Duong and at least 29.39 kilograms in Hoai Thi.

In Son Duong, the secondary crops of maize, peanuts, and sweet potatoes yielded the gross equivalent of 545.33 tonnes of paddy, or the net

---

[7]The village accountant was unable to provide a breakdown of cooperative and village charges for 1989. In 1988, a mediocre crop year, agricultural taxes amounted to 11 percent of the crop yield on contracted land. An additional 11.8 percent was collected to defray collective water, insecticide, and crop protection expenses. And a total of 11.1 percent was levied to cover social welfare (.5 percent), cooperative management (2.3 percent), and general cooperative and village funds (8.3 percent). So the cooperative collected 33.9 percent of the crop yield in 1988. In 1989, with a higher crop yield, this percentage dropped to 22 percent. On the summer-fall crop in 1990, when the yield averaged 58 percent of that in 1989, the state granted a tax exemption, and the cooperative granted an exemption of various charges. For 1990, the village accountant reported that the cooperative collected only 7.1 percent of the crop yield (158 kilograms per hectare, in contrast to 875 kilograms per hectare in 1989).

Table 10-2. Paddy Yield per Hectare (tonnes)

	1986	1987	1988	1989	1990
Hoai Bao (commune of)					
Chiem (5th month)	2.50	1.93	3.48	3.47	n/a
Mua (10th month)	1.93	2.79	1.92	2.37	n/a
Son Duong					
Chiem (5th month)	4.17	2.78	3.17	4.11	3.89
Mua (10th month)	3.61	1.67	2.86	3.67	2.24

equivalent of 78.37 kilograms per person. In Hoai Thi, the small secondary crops of soybeans and mung beans (respectively .583 and .576 hectare) yielded the gross equivalent of 2.51 tonnes of paddy, or the net equivalent of 1.98 kilograms per person. I estimated that hog husbandry and buffalo and cattle raising added the net equivalents of 74.58 kilograms of paddy per capita in Hoai Thi, compared with 67.87 kilograms in Son Duong.[8]

Table 10-1 shows that, with the reforms of the 1980s, agriculture can sustain the livelihood of villagers in Hoai Thi and Son Duong in good harvest years, as 1989 was. Weather and occasional pest damage, however, render the rice yield erratic, as can be seen in the per hectare paddy yields in Hoai Bao and Son Duong for the 1986–90 period (see Table 10-2). It is not surprising that Hoai Thi villagers considered their village, up to 1987, to have been extremely poor, certainly the poorest village in the commune of Hoai Bao, because the local economy had relied almost exclusively on agriculture.

A turning point for many northern villages, including Hoai Thi, was the 1987 reform that removed private trade barriers throughout the country. Taking full advantage of their proximity to Hanoi, Hoai Thi residents earned sizable incomes from private retail trade. In contrast, the nonagricultural

[8]At the average monthly growth of 10 kilograms for each pig, the pig herd in Hoai Thi in 1990 produced 25.56 tonnes of live pigs, or 33.59 kilograms per capita. Each kilogram was equivalent to 10 kilograms of paddy at the market rate in the summers of 1989 and 1990. Because no precise figures were available for 1989, I assumed no change in the contribution of animal husbandry to household incomes from 1989 to 1990. In 1989, Son Duong had 650 pigs, 342 cattle, and 58 buffaloes. The pigs in Son Duong annually produced 78 tonnes of live animals (19.43 kilograms per capita). On the assumption that a cow can be sold within two years of purchase at an average weight gain of 150 kilograms, and a buffalo, within three years at a weight gain of 210 kilograms, the cattle and buffalo herds annually produced 297.1 tonnes of meat (in live weight) in Son Duong and 2.17 tonnes in Hoai Thi. In the summer of 1989 and 1990, in these parts of Vietnam, the prices of beef and buffalo meat were roughly the same as that of pork.

Lacking reliable information on the pork production costs in Son Duong and Hoai Thi, I assumed that they were approximately the same as in the northern province of Ha Nam Ninh (Le van Toan et al., 1991, pp. 33–35, 75). On the basis of the price of hay feed in Son Duong, I estimated that the production costs of cattle and buffaloes amounted respectively to 54.7 percent and 80 percent of the wholesale meat prices. On the basis of these rough production costs, I estimated that animal husbandry yielded the net equivalents of 74.58 and 67.87 kilograms of paddy per capita, respectively, in Hoai Thi and Son Duong.

income sources of Son Duong villagers remained modest, despite the close-ness of the village to two industrial towns: Cao Mai, 3.5 kilometers away, and Viet Tri, 17 kilometers distant. In the 24 Hoai Thi households (with a total of 147 persons) for which detailed participant-observation and interview data are available for the summer of 1990, 11 persons engaged in the hog trade, 10 in the delivery of alcohol in Hanoi, 3 in retailing tea and foods, 2 in food processing, and 1 in the construction industry. These figures are generally congruent with the rough estimate by a village leader in 1991 that of the 162 households in Hoai Thi, some 30 engaged in the hog trade, 50 in alcohol delivery, 20 in retailing other items, and 60 in the construction industry. (Although the state maintained an alcohol monopoly, moonshine could be found in every Vietnamese town and village.)

In Son Duong, in 1991, a local official estimated that only 200 villagers engaged in trade and did not earn much, about 70 worked at the two chemical factories in Cao Mai, 10 to 15 villagers worked in the construction and furniture-manufacturing trades in the village, and a small number of households produced bean curds. While precise data for 1989 on the size of the nonagricultural work force and its earnings were not available for either village, on the basis of circumstantial evidence, I estimate that in Son Duong total earnings from industrial sources remained stable from 1989 to 1990 at some 105 tonnes of paddy a year, or 26.15 kilograms per person. The commercial work force in Son Duong apparently grew significantly from 1989 to 1991, compensating for the decline of the mosquito-net-weaving handicraft and the local housing and furniture industries. According to my rough estimate, these income sources provided an additional 14.76 kilograms of paddy per person.

In Hoai Thi, in 1990, the nonagricultural work brought in an annual per capita income equivalent to 620 kilograms of paddy in the aforementioned 24 households.[9] Even if the 1989 nonagricultural income in Hoai Thi had stood at only 60 percent of the 1990 figure, it would have remained significant at 372 kilograms of paddy per person a year. No taxes were collected from these nonagricultural endeavors in either village.

In 1989, I estimated that the average annual net earnings per capita in Son Duong and Hoai Thi amounted respectively to 445.35 and 647.66 kilograms of paddy, or 37.11 and 53.97 kilograms of paddy a month, not

---

[9] In June 1990, an alcohol-trading trip to Hanoi (six hours round trip on a bicycle) brought a trader approximately 15,000 *dong* (equivalent to 35.7 kilograms of paddy on the local market). The trader regularly made 10 trips a month. My estimate is based on the assumption that the monthly alcohol profit averaged 150,000 *dong*, and that the profit from the hog trade remained in the same range as the alcohol-trade profit.

including local shares of agricultural taxes and pension and disability payments to retired cadres. (Paid in lieu of obligatory labor in public projects, the corvee taxes on men from 18 to 50, and on women from 18 to 25, partly offset these sources of income.) Although data on the income distribution in each village are unavailable, these monthly incomes, equivalent to 25.98 and 37.78 kilograms of rice, can be compared with the 1989 data from 17 villages in five provinces shown in a government study in Table 10-3.

In economic well-being, the typical Hoai Thi villager was probably in the upper half of Vietnamese rural dwellers, while the average villager in Son Duong was in the bottom quarter. Rising nonagricultural sources of income enabled Hoai Thi residents to adjust well to crop losses and higher paddy prices in the fall of 1990 and the spring of 1991 (losses respectively at 82 percent and 68 percent of the crops). In contrast, in Son Duong, villagers suffered great hardship with losses of 39 percent and 75 percent in these two crop harvests.

The temporary setback in late 1990 notwithstanding, Son Duong as well as Hoai Thi villagers benefited considerably from the economic reform of the 1980s. A sign of the growing disposable incomes in both villages was the construction or expansion of many houses in those years. In Hoai Thi, quite a few households owned televisions and motorcycles. Since 1988, many households with sizable incomes from trade have also hired laborers from other communities. The 1990 daily wages during the peak harvest season averaged 7.5 kilograms of paddy, plus meals. Accusations of labor exploitation were no longer heard because the practice had become widespread. By the summer of 1990, virtually all the houses were equipped with wells and brick outhouses. All but seven houses in Hoai Thi were constructed of bricks,

Table 10-3. Monthly Income per Capita in Rice in Rural Vietnam (1976–89)

	> 60 kg.	41–60 kg.	20–40 kg.	< 20 kg.
1976–80	12.5%	20.3%	34.3%	32.9%
1981–85	14.01%	26.99%	30.5%	28.5%
1989 (aggregate data)	18.4%	26.54%	45.62%	09.44%
1989 Provincial Breakdown				
Hoang Lien Son (northern highlands)	15.8%	22.27%	46.78%	15.15%
Ha Nam Ninh (northern delta)	10.09%	27.62%	54.86%	7.4%
Binh Dinh (central coast)	11.53%	25.18%	57.32%	5.97%
Dac Lac (central highlands)	21%	23.34%	35.25%	20.41%
Hau Giang (southern delta)	33.69%	31.55%	31.66%	3.1%

Source: Vietnam, Communist Party of (1991, pp. 45–46).

whereas before 1954 most reportedly were made of thatch. In those earlier days, the fields of Hoai Thi yielded only one crop, because they were inundated in the summer. Crop yields from the hamlet fields averaged only 1.1 to 1.4 tonnes a hectare (40–50 kilograms a *sao*). Annual paddy production amounted to only 130 kilograms per person. Villagers reported that their community had been so poor that, before 1954, the so-called upper-middle class peasants (up until the time of the 1955 land reform) had regularly worked as laborers in neighboring villages during the slack season. Even the two so-called rich peasants had worked as hired laborers during their more difficult days. The main secondary-income sources were petty trade, silk-worms, and weaving.

In Son Duong, at the time of primary field research in 1987–88, most houses had their own wells, and many had brick outhouses and outdoor bathing rooms. In 1985, according to the village administration, the percent-ages of houses with wells, brick outhouses, and outdoor bathing rooms reached 94 percent, 71 percent, and 49 percent respectively. In contrast, on the eve of the August 1945 uprising, there were only five brick houses, six private wells, and no outhouses or bathing rooms in the village. In the late 1980s, for transportation, village households possessed an average of two bicycles each, compared to one in the entire village before 1945.

Intensification of Rituals

Like numerous northern villages in the 1980s, Son Duong and Hoai Thi not only benefited from the nation's economic recovery but also underwent a sociocultural transformation. Most notable was the intensification of ritual practices in a selective revitalization of the pre-1945 tradition. The liberaliza-tion of the Vietnamese economy evolved out of the government's abandon-ment of an accelerated construction of socialism (from 1986 on), and from the state's increasing willingness to accommodate local concerns.

In Hoai Thi and Son Duong in the 1980s, ritual practices intensified, both between living individuals and between individuals and supernatural entities, and within the kinship domain and beyond, although there existed certain systematic differences between the two villages. More specifically, the gift-exchange and feasting reciprocity systems became much more elaborate, even among the households of numerous Communist party members in both villages, especially in Hoai Thi. Many rites of passage and rites of solidarity from the preindependence period (before 1945) were strength-ened. In Hoai Thi, around 1970, for the first time in two decades, the village had its own priest (*thay cung*), a native member who acquired his skills in his youth. The priest presided at the two monthly prayer sessions at the Buddhist pagoda, wrote house-protection amulets for villagers, gave consultations on the age compatibility of prospective spouses and on propitious wedding dates, and chanted Buddhist *santras* at funerals. Although no priest, monk, or nun lived in Son Duong, and villagers in need had to invite one from a neighboring community, ritual practices also dramatically intensified between 1987 and my brief 1991 revisit. In this four-year interval, the most visible physical changes were the restoration of the dilapidated pagoda and village shrine *(den)*, and the revival of the village market. The intensification of rituals was all the more remarkable because, as late as 1987, the village leadership had reported with pride the success of its wedding and funeral reform. (For elaboration on this point, see Luong, 1992, pp. 174–82.) The main differences between Son Duong and Hoai Thi in their ritual intensification processes lay in the greater intensification in Hoai Thi and the greater selectivity and innovation in Son Duong—differences that are probably rooted respectively in Hoai Thi's stronger economic base and in Son Duong's pre-1945 structure and its process of historical transformation.

In Hoai Thi, on a village-wide basis, the two monthly sessions at the pagoda and communal house were well attended. During my field-research period, about three-quarters of the 66 elderly women (above the age of 49) attended the two prayer sessions at the pagoda. Between 40 percent and 50 percent of the 53 elderly men were present at ceremonies on the same days at the communal house. In Son Duong, more than two hundred elderly women regularly took part in the prayer sessions at the pagoda on the first and fifteenth days of each lunar month, although at the recently restored *den*, the traditional home of communal deities' wooden figures, only the shrine guardian reportedly offered prayers and incense to the deities on those days. Even during the New Year, I was told, the shrine did not attract more than 40 elderly devotees, male and female. In a departure from the pre-1945 tradition and unlike the practice in Hoai Thi, the Son Duong elderly women's association *(hoi chu ba)* admitted into its ranks and to the pagoda a small number of "ritually clean" women in their forties—those who had ended sexual activities. In Son Duong, the attendance of women at the shrine and communal deity ceremonies also departed from the pre-1945 practice.

In Hoai Thi, the seating order among the elderly at the pagoda and communal houses was based strictly on age. In the pagoda, expanded in 1980, the outer part was reserved for junior members of the elderly group, women from 50 to 60 years old; the middle and inner parts were for older women above 60 *(cu em)* and 70 *(cu anh)*. The member recognized as the most senior was the honorary head *(cu thuong)*. In the reconstructed communal house, the elderly men were similarly divided and seated on their own mats.

Because the room was small, however, the three groups could not be seated according to distance from the altar. The importance of age in public rituals was reinforced by longevity-celebrating ceremonies, which the government-sanctioned elderly's association (*hoi bao tho*) organized on the fourth day of the first lunar month for villagers reaching the ages of 60, 65, 70, 75, and 80 or above.

In the Son Duong pagoda, the elderly women similarly divided themselves into three groups, new elderly women (*vai moi*), middle elderly women (*vai thu*), and senior elderly women (*vai thuong*). The most senior group was seated in the central wing closest to the altar, and the most junior, away from it in two side wings. Age and the date of entry into *hoi chu ba* determined seniority. A male party member in Son Duong remarked on this strict seating order in the pagoda and the impressive female organization:

> The elderly ladies form one of the strongest organizations to be found anywhere. Their discipline is impressive. On the first and fifteenth days [of the lunar month], the ladies automatically find their seats in the pagoda, with little dispute on the issue. If somebody is in the wrong seat, she will be asked to move and will automatically comply with the request. The voice of the most senior lady carries more weight with other members of the association than that of an agency head with his workers. Nobody takes any mat or bowls from the pagoda. On the ritual days, a few ladies voluntarily clean up the pagoda before the ceremonies. The ladies have a strong sense of their own obligations at the pagoda, perhaps because of the belief in religious virtues. At other forums, the attendance is not good, because people engage in disputes. Many villagers consider these meetings a waste of time. I have suggested to the local leadership that the bimonthly meetings of the elderly constitute a good forum for the dissemination of government policies and directives, such as on family planning. Those of us retired cadres who know a bit about Buddhism and can talk in a simple language relate easily to the elderly ladies. They listen quietly and attentively, unlike the audience elsewhere.

At the Son Duong shrine, seating was not strictly arranged except for the separation of men and women. The elderly worked out an informal gerontocratic order for themselves: those arriving early normally ceded the prestigious places to the more senior and late-arriving elderly.

In both Hoai Thi and Son Duong, the pagoda pantheons included not only the various Buddhas but also other deities. Most prominent among the latter was the child-guardian deity (*duc ong*) to whom, on behalf of their children, elderly women in both villages openly and regularly offered their grandchildren (*ban con*) for nominal adoption and protection against evil forces.[10] In Hoai Thi, *duc ong* was worshipped in the inner room as a part of

---

[10]Children also might be ritually adopted by other families that had raised a large number of children.

the folk Buddhist pantheon, in contrast to the practice in Son Duong, where the deity was recently moved from the inner room to an outer one, probably reflecting the villagers' recognition of the Buddhist deities as separate from the others.

In both villages, offerings to the pagoda deities at the two monthly sessions had become plentiful with incense, fruits, and occasionally rice cakes (*oan*).[11] In contrast, the semimonthly offerings in the communal house in Hoai Thi included merely incense, a bottle of wine, betel leaves, and areca nuts, while those at the Son Duong shrine were even simpler. In Hoai Thi, villagers also brought chicken, cooked gluant rice, and votive paper into the pagoda as offerings to *duc ong*, while in Son Duong the offerings did not include meat, in keeping with Buddhist doctrine. According to the retired head of the Hoai Thi Communist party branch, it was the elderly women from commercially enterprising families who regularly made the plentiful pagoda offerings. (In earlier decades, the offering was simply incense and prayers.) According to this former party head, however, none had dared suggest a link between the offerings and the offerees' trading successes. These elderly women, the senior party member's wife presumably included, simply said that their own children and grandchildren would ultimately consume the offerings.

In Hoai Thi, the ritual cycle was also marked by major ceremonies that indicated a certain degree of continuity with pre-1945 practices. Most important were the lunar New Year celebration and the festivity on the tenth day of the first lunar month, which had long been associated with *quan ho* folksong festival. On the latter occasion, the offerings at the communal house included cooked gluant rice and a large chicken, while those at the pagoda were sufficiently plentiful to permit each elderly woman to bring home a banana and a rice cake. As a part of the *quan ho* tradition, on this day, Hoai Thi invited singers from the village of Viem Xa in a neighboring district with whom they had been paired since time immemorial. The other important ceremonies included the village guardian-goddess worship on the fifteenth day of the tenth month at the communal house and, at the pagoda, the death anniversary of a former presiding monk on the twentieth day of the ninth month, the summer-beginning day on the fourth day of the fourth month, and the summer-ending day on the fourth day of the seventh month. These ceremonies were reportedly better attended and more elaborately organized than at any other point since 1954.

---

[11]In Hoai Thi, elderly men and women took turns providing for the offerings at prayer meetings.

In Son Duong, after the restoration of the pagoda and the shrine, villagers revitalized certain ceremonies. On the third day of the third month, although the ritual fight between Son Duong and Ngu Xa villagers had been banned for four-and-a-half decades, a simplified ceremony at the shrine had resumed. So had a ceremony on the tenth day of the eighth month (*ngay cau*). The offerings on these occasions regularly included meat and rice. At the pagoda, the elderly women's association also organized special ceremonies on Buddha's birthday (the eighth day of the fourth month, *le tam phat*); on the lost soul day (the fifteenth of the seventh month) with offerings of fruits, rice cakes, and fried mung beans and fruits; and on the anniversary of the last presiding nun's death almost two decades before—with the addition of pork to the offerings. On major holidays, the elderly ladies invited a priest or a nun from a neighboring village.

In Hoai Thi, the general expenses of the communal house and the pagoda were paid for with the revenue from a small piece of land (284 square meters) near the village cemetery under the care of elderly villagers—a practice not sanctioned by district authorities. In Son Duong, the revenue from a small piece of rather infertile land near the nuns' cemetery (less than 180 square meters) that had been continuously under the elderly's care since before 1945 helped to defray pagoda expenses. According to one report, the village also recently allocated 72 square meters of rice fields to the shrine in the care of its guardian.

In the 1980s, within the kinship domain in both villages, numerous rites of passage and solidarity intensified, and the structure supporting them was partly revitalized, although the process of intensification seems to have proceeded further in Hoai Thi than in Son Duong. In Hoai Thi, at least two of the three local patrilineages have been revived since 1982. Since lineage land is no longer available to defray the expenses of the founder's elaborate death anniversary and a feast gathering for the adult members of the patrilineage, contributions are required from member households on the birth of a son.[12] The contribution reportedly ranges from 5 to 30 kilograms of rice, or its cash equivalent. The contributions are put into a savings account, out of which the interest payments are used to organize the lineage founder's anniversary and to cover other expenses like the purchase of a funeral banner for lineage members. A lineage with large funds also makes house-renovation loans to its members at a low 20 percent annual interest rate. The visit to founding ancestors' graves by the representatives of all the

---

[12]If a family has no son and the son-in-law moves in with his wife's parents upon marriage, the matrilineal grandchildren are also allowed to join the patrilineage. No change in surname is necessary, because all the original inhabitants have the same surname of Nguyen.

households in the patrilineage is accompanied by either an informal gathering, or feast, to reaffirm kinship ties and to discuss the education of the younger generation.

In Son Duong, the patrilineal organization has been revitalized with the restoration of ancestral tombs and the one remaining ancestral hall, as well as with gatherings on ancestors' death anniversaries. (These are convened mainly on male ancestors' anniversaries. Female ancestors are usually commemorated with small offerings and participation by a few elderly lineage members.) Since funds are no longer available to defray meal expenses, households in the patrilineage are levied financial charges on these occasions. Attending are senior men of the households and a few of the senior elderly women. The ritual practice in both villages stands in contrast to the anniversaries in the more difficult time, from the mid 1950s to the late 1970s, when the chief of the lineage was solely responsible for offerings to the ancestor. In those days, the chief made small offerings without involving other elderly lineage members.

In Hoai Thi, parents' death anniversaries have also become considerably more elaborate in the last decade, despite the disappearance of altars and the absence of pictures of the deceased in some 70 percent of eldest sons' households—a result of the hardships during the French and American war periods. (Many village households had large pictures of Ho Chi Minh in central positions, in place of ancestral altars.) At the time of the field research, normally 60 to 120 people shared in a feast on a death anniversary—in a village of 761 residents. The guest list included not only close relatives but also the eldest son's friends and in-laws. The feast followed a prayer by adult relatives with joined hands and bowed heads, led by the eldest son, together with other guests' incense offerings. The eldest son's siblings made voluntary contributions to the feast, depending on their financial conditions. As the wealth of the village grew and the system of reciprocity became more elaborate, however, a parent's anniversary might be organized on consecutive days so that close friends and in-laws of younger sons could come. Invitations to them had to be made in reciprocation to their earlier invitations to younger sons on the occasions of their parents' anniversaries. Or the first and second sons in Hoai Thi might take turns organizing the parents' anniversary feasts: either the father's at the eldest son's house and the mother's at the second son's or, when only one parent was dead, alternating the anniversary feasts among the sons' households on an annual basis. (Grandparents' anniversaries were usually modest, consisting of a tray of food offerings at the house of the eldest grandson.) These patterns constitute a departure from the pre-1954 tradition since the village used to be a poor one with few large anniversary feasts.

In Son Duong, however, a death anniversary banquet with 30 guests was considered large; usually only family members and a few senior close relatives were present. A large celebration faced the pragmatic constraint of the eldest son's limited financial resources and often provoked criticism from fellow villagers. A resident explained the financial burden on himself as the eldest son:

> If, as the eldest son, I allow my siblings to contribute to a death anniversary on a voluntary basis as in the past, a woman making a voluntary contribution will bring her children, because a mother will not go to a feast by herself. [With numerous relatives,] a death anniversary becomes a financial burden. If in consultation with my siblings, I decide to extend the anniversary feast to the second and third generations and to specify the contribution from each guest, it will impose a hardship on some of my siblings who are not well off. A few families have tried this solution, but the practice has not spread because of the wealth disparity within the kin group. As a result, of the two main functions of a death anniversary, only the memorial function is regularly fulfilled.
>
> The gathering of relatives, as the second function, is only partly maintained nowadays. It is mainly a gathering of siblings, some of whom live far away. On the upcoming death anniversary of my father, my younger sibling in Hanoi will have to come back here for the ceremony. I will not grant any exemption. His presence is required in commemoration of our father. He may say that I am feudal, but I do not mind the criticism. Without this requirement, I may not see him for a long time, and our bond will be weakened. For this anniversary, I dare to invite only my siblings and a few elderly senior relatives, and to tell my children and their spouses to come.

Beyond the death anniversary rites of solidarity, within the kinship domain in both Hoai Thi and Son Duong, the major rites of passage such as month-old birth anniversaries, weddings, and funerals also have become more elaborate in the direction of pre-1945 practice. On the month-old birth anniversaries, especially of sons, offerings are made to the child's patrilineal ancestors. Close relatives and friends are also invited to a meal on the occasion, especially those who have tendered gifts to the child or the mother. Small gifts are normally offered on the occasion of the birth of the first child or a couple's first son. (Because of the close-knit kinship networks in the two villages, it is neither customary nor practical to present a gift on the birth of any close relative's child.)

In Hoai Thi, when a child marries, wedding feasts mark the occasion at both the bride's and groom's houses. Before the engagement and the marriage, however, the families consult with a priest about the compatibility of the couple's ages as well as about a propitious wedding date. As a part of the engagement ceremony, the groom's parents deliver tea, areca nuts, cakes, wine, and chickens to the bride's home as offerings and announcements to her paternal and maternal ancestors. Although the local-government ruling, restricting the size of the wedding feast by limiting the quantity of pork delivered by the groom's family to the bride's to 20 kilograms (for 120 guests), was still in effect at the time of my research, the customary delivery was twice that limit, depending on negotiations between the bride's and the groom's family representatives.[13] The bride's family contributions might also complement the outlay of pork. If a family was well connected, both in kinship ties and through the workplace, and if it was the wedding of the eldest child, the meat consumption might reach 80 kilograms (enough for 480 guests). The guest list included not only patrilineal relatives but also matrilateral first or second cousins. Beyond relatives, the feast for the first child's wedding was usually larger because the parents had to ask friends who had invited them on numerous occasions in the past. Explaining their flouting of the village-government ruling, residents would say: "It is a small village with the emphasis on sentiment." On the eve of the wedding, as a new practice, the two involved families also held receptions for the bride's and groom's acquaintances.

At the time of the field research, Hoai Thi villagers considered the size of death anniversary and wedding feasts an index of popularity and connections. The wife of the former head of the local party branch emphasized that most often small feasts reflected problematic personalities and social conflicts of the bride's or groom's parents. In the late 1980s, the average wedding feast for each side of a married couple involved 300 guests (50 trays). The food became more elaborate with the addition of highly valued Vietnamese salami (*gio*) to the main meal. In parallel to the larger feast was the bigger dowry, which used to be minimal—whatever parents could afford to give to their daughter or whatever the daughter had been able to save. By the late 1980s, although there was no set practice, a bride normally brought a blanket, a mosquito net, other household items, and often a bicycle to her husband's household for her own use. A son's wedding was estimated to cost 150 kilograms of meat (one or two pigs) and the cash equivalent of 1.5 to 2 tonnes of paddy.

The increasing wedding expenditures were linked to the elaborate network of gift exchange on the part of an increasingly prosperous peasantry. Among relatives, the customary gifts to the groom's side averaged 20 to 30 kilograms of paddy (26 percent to 39 percent of the village president's monthly salary), while the bride's family received few.[14] Gifts from the closest

---

[13]The bride's and groom's families negotiated on the quantity of meat, tea, areca nuts, cigarettes, wine, and occasionally food and cash coming from the groom's family. The family of the bride usually phrased the demand in terms of the large number of relatives who had to be invited.

[14]A former head of the local party branch estimated that the wedding gifts from relatives

senior relatives might amount to 100 kilograms. Given the close-knit kinship network and the high degree of village endogamy, there was reportedly no special favoritism to patrilineal relatives. These gifts had to be delivered before the wedding date. Each friend of the parents usually gave, on the wedding day, a household consumer product (usually a thermos, a pot, or a tray) and, since the late 1960s, a box of firecrackers. Nominal wedding gifts (less than 15 kilograms of paddy) were not recorded, but larger ones were noted for future reciprocity on the occasions of weddings, house construction, or a similarly important event. As a result, on the marriage of its son, a well-connected family with a lot of friends and relatives might have a wedding surplus equivalent to 1.2 to 1.6 tonnes of paddy (state salary for a full-time village cadre for 1.5 to 2 years).

As in Hoai Thi, wedding feasts in Son Duong were held at both the bride's and the groom's houses. As a part of the engagement ceremony, the groom's parents delivered tea, areca nuts, and cakes to the bride's home, principally for consumption by relatives and friends after ritual offerings to the ancestors.[15] The groom's parents were also expected to deliver chickens, rice, wine, betel leaves, and areca nuts to the bride's parents for engagement announcements and offerings to the bride's ancestors. (Offerings were made to her father's parents and paternal grandparents, to the head of his patri-lineage, to her mother's parents, and possibly also to paternal grandparents.) Despite village officials' ritual reform in 1986–87 and economic hardship in Son Duong from mid-1990 to mid-1991, the wedding became considerably more elaborate as certain rituals were revitalized and imported and as the size of the wedding banquet increased. Although the village administration in 1987 issued a ruling to limit the wedding banquet to 60 guests, by 1991 the bride's and groom's banquets had grown to at least 120 and 180 guests respectively. If the groom or one of his parents worked at a nearby state factory, the number might reach 600 guests, because coworkers had to be invited. It was standard for the groom's family to slaughter a pig of 70–80 kilograms, both for its own banquet and for the bride's family's banquet. (The groom's family contributed at least 10 kilograms of high-quality meat to the bride's family's banquet.) Wedding expenses had risen significantly not only for the groom's family but also for the bride's, because of greater dowry expected and the limited contribution from the groom's side to a larger

---

averaged 50 to 70 kilograms of paddy. His higher estimate might reflect the average larger size of wedding gifts to his family due to his power and connections in the community.

[15]The engagement gifts used to be distributed to senior relatives primarily within the patrilin-eage. Each household received an areca nut and betel leaves to mark the occasion. Each elderly relative also received a cake in recognition of his or her longevity and status.

banquet and reception. The dowry normally included clothes, pillows, blanket, and mosquito net. Wealthy families also added bicycles, cash, or gold (the equivalent of the rice field dowry given by the wealthy in the old days). The bride's family's expenses also rose because of the new practice of holding a reception for her on the eve of the wedding, with the necessary invitations to her numerous acquaintances. An elderly villager commented on these new practices:

> It is expensive to hold the bride's reception for her youth friends on the eve of the wedding. Parents complain about it everywhere, but to no avail. Even if parents take a strong stand against the reception, the daughters would say that they will buy the candies and cigarettes for the reception anyway. They can easily buy on credit. No parents have the courage of beating or heavily scolding their daughters [for doing that]. If the parents scold the daughter, she will just smile ear to ear, and the parents will have to pay quietly. Another innovation is the reservation of a part of the banquet for the bride's friends, up to 30 or 50 of them. Parents complain to no avail. [Did the bride's female friends not come to the wedding banquet in the old days?] Yes, but not as many. It was usually limited to two trays (eight people) and to the bride's closest friends. The only exception in the old days was when the bride was married to somebody against her will. She might ask for five to seven lavish trays for her friends as a way to incur unnecessary expenses on the groom's household, because the groom's household bore all the wedding expenses in those days.

In another recent revitalization of pre-1945 practices, the bride and groom bowed with joined hands before their ancestral altars. In a few cases, the ceremony also included the offerings of chicken and gluant rice to the ancestors—an element incorporated from a pre-1954 ceremony in the yard to the wedding god (called *cung to hong*).

Loans and gifts from close relatives before the ceremony as a part of reciprocal obligations helped to defray the wedding expense. These loans and gifts could amount to 100 kilograms of rice. Unlike people in Hanoi and many other communities, Son Duong villagers routinely refused cash gifts, except from the newlyweds' siblings and very close senior relatives (or unless delivered in private before the ceremony). (In many other communities, cash gifts were readily accepted, if not expected, from guests.) Small gifts in kind from the couple's closest friends could be delivered on the wedding day. An elderly villager elaborated:

> If somebody offers a cash gift at the wedding, the parents would automatically plead with the guest not to do it. A very close senior relative can give cash to a wedding, but only in private, and before or after the ceremony. More common are rice loans offered by close relatives. If the parents are not well off, they can also ask for loans (*di keu giup*) from other relatives and

close friends. A loan could be up to 100 kilograms of rice. All these loans have to be recorded and paid. Even if a close senior relative declares that the rice is a gift, it still has to be reciprocated on the occasion of his or her children's or grandchildren's weddings.

The elaboration of the wedding ceremony in Son Duong flouted the policy of the local administration, formulated in 1986 to simplify wedding rituals and to limit the banquet to 60 guests. These elaborate ceremonies departed not only from the style of ceremony dictated in 1986–87, but also from the simplified arrangements made during the American war, when a soldier might request marriage while on a brief home leave.

Although funerals were traditionally more simply organized in both villages, with a local priest's prayer session, they too had been undergoing an elaboration process. In both villages funerals were still simple in that there was no feast for local visitors. In Hoai Thi, a small meal was prepared only for overnight guests and family members. The quantity of meat consumed on the occasion usually fell within the limit of 20 kilograms set by the local government. The village elderly's association made a cash offering and loaned funeral dresses and flags, while the agricultural cooperative donated flowers, incense, and white funeral cloth.[16] In Son Duong, a larger family dinner had to be organized mainly for relatives who were still obligated to mourn for the deceased. As a new practice, gifts from junior relatives of the deceased have been accepted in cash (called *le den*) for at least a decade, and from the same-age association (those born in the same year) of a family member in the past two years. As an offering to the deceased, other guests bring incense and, to symbolize a close relation, a bottle of wine. The elderly association (*hoi bao tho*), formed with the encouragement of the local government, also offers a gift of incense, areca nuts, and cash, as well as a speech about the life of the deceased at the funeral.

In both villages, music has been recently added to the funeral and played from the death announcement until the burial ceremony. As an indicator of greater ritual intensification in Hoai Thi, the family of the deceased invites a four-member band to perform at the ceremony. In Son Duong, the village administration grants elders' request for music on the condition that the music is recorded on cassette tapes for reasons of economy. During the procession, music is played from a tape recorder, operated with electricity from a car battery, and carried with the deceased's picture on a table following

---

[16]In the era of state subsidies, the family of the deceased was able to purchase a coffin at state price with the cash donation from the elderly's association.

the coffin. (Since 1989, the agricultural cooperative no longer donates coffins but has loaned the battery and cassette recorder to its members at funerals.)

Many voluntary associations have been established in Son Duong since 1988, replacing similar pre-1945 associations for mutual assistance on the occasions of weddings, school examinations, elderly-honoring rituals, and funerals. (See also Luong, 1992, pp. 59–60.) Retired teachers formed the first contemporary voluntary association. Each member contributed 10 kilograms of paddy to establish a fund of 400 kilograms to be loaned to members at low interest, say 20 percent a year, for house construction or funeral expenses. By the summer of 1991, three same-age associations had also been formed among men approaching or above the age of 50. Membership dues varied but might amount to 200 kilograms of paddy, the interest from which was used for annual feasts, funerals, or weddings in members' households.

By 1990, in both villages, numerous other rituals had been intensified or introduced, harkening back to the pre-1945 era. During my field research in the summer of 1990, in every Hoai Thi household, offerings and a small feast were organized at the completion of the harvest. In the past decade and a half, in both Son Duong and Hoai Thi, house construction or reconstruction frequently has called for a consultation with a priest about a propitious date and offerings to deities, and in the case of Hoai Thi, the priest's issuance of a protective amulet. The amulet was either attached to a pillar near the ceiling or buried discretely in the floor. (According to the senior party member in Hoai Thi, amulets had not been used from 1954 to the end of the American war in the mid-1970s. Amulets were reportedly not yet widespread in Son Duong.) The recently reconstructed house of the young hamlet chief was not an exception in this aspect. Upon inquiry, villagers responded with the local dictum: *"Co than co thieng, co kieng co lanh"* ("Sacred power with deities, good luck with taboo observance"). In Son Duong in the past few years, shamans and fortune tellers have come from other villages on request and with greater frequency, although still surreptitiously. One villager specialized in manufacturing votive paper and objects (horses, clothes) for offerings to ancestors, gods, and ghosts on such occasions as bad-luck-chasing ceremonies, funerals, and death anniversaries.

The intensification of rituals in Hoai Thi and Son Duong in the 1980s does not indicate a total resurrection of local pre-1945 traditions. Ritual practices, both within and beyond the kinship domain, underwent a trans-formation, and the break with old practices in Son Duong is sharp compared with Hoai Thi. Of the life-cycle rituals in the kinship domain in Son Duong, weddings and funerals were radically simplified, and the supportive pre-1945 institutions were either eliminated or significantly altered. While the four basic wedding steps—preliminary inquiry (*le dam*), engagement, wedding-date request, and formal wedding—were retained, the burden on the groom's family was greatly reduced with the elimination of the cash bride price and financial sponsorship of the bride's family's wedding banquet. Abolished was the practice of delaying the marital union and consummation for up to three years after the wedding ceremony, during which time the bride remained at home with her parents.

The funeral feast and its attendant ceremonies were also abandoned. In the pre-1945 era, the funeral served as a marker of socioeconomic standing: a family of average means had to invite all male villagers with actual or honorary titles to a funeral feast; a wealthy household extended the ceremony to three days and invited all villagers; a poor family unable to afford a funeral feast felt an obligation to hold it later, when its financial conditions had improved (called *ma kho*, or a dry funeral). In return, the guests, including in-laws, close friends, and students, were obliged to offer cooked food (gluant rice and either a chicken or a pig head) to the deceased. Under the socialist government, for economy reasons, the elaborate offerings of the past were reduced to incense and flowers, and later, at the suggestion of the Son Duong administration, to incense and a funeral banner loaned by the village. Also certain ritual steps at the funeral symbolizing subordination and gender inequality were gradually eliminated: children no longer walked on canes during the procession and (since 1986) daughters and daughter-in-laws no longer lay in the courtyard in the path of the coffin in procession. With little class-based feast distinction in pre-1945 Hoai Thi, funerals there had always been more simply organized than in Son Duong. As a result, the ceremonies in Hoai Thi changed to a lesser extent, although as in Son Duong, the sons of the deceased no longer wore straw hats and walked on cane.

In Hoai Thi, the ritual process leading to a wedding was not fundamentally changed. As in Son Duong, the four basic steps—preliminary inquiry (le dam), engagement, wedding-date request, and formal wedding—were retained, although only the last two were marked by elaborate formal ceremonies. The main changes were the greater opportunity for the couple to know one another following the preliminary inquiry, the shorter interval between the engagement and wedding ceremonies, and the maintenance of elaborate ceremonies only for the last two steps.

In Son Duong as well as Hoai Thi, the ritual cycles beyond the kinship domain were transformed more than life-cycle ceremonies, although the changes were greater in Son Duong than in Hoai Thi. In both villages, state-sponsored ceremonies in the solar calendar on the foundation anniversary of the Communist party (March 2), the Veteran and War Memorial Day (July 27), and National Independence Day (September 2) were added to the ritual cycles. Popular activities such as sports were organized on National Independence Day, with some variation from one year to the next.

Many rituals in the pre-1945 ritual cycle were also eliminated or simplified, especially in Son Duong. Before 1945, for example, the ninth and tenth days of the eighth lunar month had marked the second biggest village-wide festival of the year (after the New Year), when villagers slaughtered pigs and buffalo for the worship of guardian deities at the communal house and the shrine, wore new clothes, and ate special festival foods. Although the ceremony and offerings to the deities were partly resurrected at the renovated shrine in the late 1980s, they paled in comparison to the old practice because of greatly diminished offerings, the abolition of feasts, and limited ceremony participation. Villagers had lost such ritual paraphernalia as cymbals, drums, palaquins, and ceremony banners. As mentioned earlier, the ritual fight with Ngu Xa villagers had been banned for more than four decades. The pig-slaughtering ceremony by each neighborhood (*giap*) on the third day of the first lunar month had disappeared since the Franco-Vietnamese war. In the pre-1945 period, at the pagoda on the lost-soul day, a four-square-meter paper model of the underworld was constructed, around which monks in formal yellow robes had prayed and performed rituals for an entire night. By 1991, these ritual artifacts and the monks' night-long prayer session were no longer maintained at the pagoda.

In contrast, in Hoai Thi, at least according to the village priest, the ritual cycle had been transformed to a lesser extent. Villagers no longer held the communal feasts on the eleventh day of the first month and the fourteenth day of the tenth month, or made offerings to deities on New Year's Eve or on the death anniversary of a Confucian doctorate holder (a member of one of the lineages in Hoai Thi) on the twenty-eighth day of the second month. On the guardian-deity worship day (the fifteenth day of the tenth month), chicken had replaced the ritually more important pork.

The symbolic structure of rituals also underwent less drastic changes in Hoai Thi than in Son Duong. The seating arrangement in the communal house of Hoai Thi in 1990 largely resembled the colonial-period order at communal house feasts, when younger male villagers could participate and when office occupants and honorary titleholders were placed further away from the altar than were the elderly. This seating arrangement contrasted with those in most other northern villages of the colonial period, which gave the greatest honors to mandarins, village literati, officials, and honorary titleholders (wealthy men awarded honorary titles on the basis of their contributions to state coffers). On the first-class mats in colonial Son Duong, for example, were all the current and former village-office occupants, holders of at least the honorary mayor title, and, as a reflection of the well-entrenched Confucian emphasis on scholarship, members of the association of literati, which included both Confucian scholars and holders of the Franco-Vietnamese *certificat d'études elementaires* (elementary-studies certificate). On the next level were former holders of lower-level village offices and honorary deputy mayors who obtained their titles for the equivalent of a landless laborer's annual income. On the lowest level were honorary occupants of general village positions, who purchased their titles from the colonial government for half of a laborer's annual income and who could provide a celebration feast for villagers in accordance with long-existing tradition. The poor without honorary titles were excluded from those feasts altogether in the colonial period. The informal gerontocratic order at the recently renovated Son Duong shrine therefore constituted a radical departure from pre-1945 practice in the direction of greater equality. Even at the village pagoda, where the pre-1945 order was largely maintained, it is not insignificant that the position of *vai hau*, a senior elderly woman who is also the wife of a powerful and respected male villager, was not restored.

The sharper break from pre-1945 practices in Son Duong than in Hoai Thi was rooted in differences in the pre-1945 socioeconomic structures and in the processes of historical transformation in the two villages. The emphasis on age in public-seating arrangements and the lesser class differentiation in the rituals of prerevolutionary Hoai Thi reflect the poverty of the village; it boasted no examination laureates and few wealthy members during the Nguyen dynasty and the colonial era. In the precolonial and colonial periods, however, Son Duong had been a prosperous agricultural community with considerable class differentiation and an elaborate class-based ritual system (Luong, 1992, pp. 61–79). As a result, the process of revolutionary transformation through class struggle in the land reform of 1954–55 was much smoother in Hoai Thi than in Son Duong. In Son Duong, the class-oriented ritual order at the communal house in the village-wide ceremonial cycle, and at funeral feasts in the kinship-centered system, was so strongly associated with a once-dominant class under attack by the state that its revitalization would have been highly problematic. But in Hoai Thi, the major public festival on the tenth day of the first lunar month was strongly associated with the *quan ho* folksong tradition, which the Marxist state promoted as an important part of the Vietnamese folk musical heritage (Dang van Lung et al., 1978, pp. 9–12). The maintenance of a gerontocratic ritual order at the pagoda and communal house was also facilitated by the absence of village officials and members of the powerful Communist party from those ceremonies, as secular power shifted from the communal house to the hamlet and cooperative offices, and as village officials were too young to attend the ceremonies of elders.[17]

---

[17]In Hoai Thi, as a result of the party-directed leadership rejuvenation in the late 1980s, the commune and hamlet officials residing in Hoai Thi were all in their thirties. The most senior party member in the community, the former head of the Hoai Thi party branch in 1968 and 1985–90,

Economic Reform and Historical Transformation of Rituals

The break from pre-1945 practices notwithstanding, in both Hoai Thi and Son Duong rituals have dramatically intensified since the mid-1980s. This intensification is all the more remarkable because ritual traditions came under critical attack from the Marxist state during the preceding four decades. In the 1946–84 period, citing the importance of a modern scientific world view and the necessity of collective economy measures during wartime and for socialist reconstruction, the state severely suppressed numerous "super-stitious" practices and directed the simplification of many other consumption-oriented rites of passage. In Hoai Thi, the attack was particularly sharp from 1954 to 1957, when worship of the village-guardian goddess came to a halt. The local government also prohibited the practice of offering children to deities for nominal adoption. Although it condoned ancestor worship and offerings, it divided the land of the *giap* (neighborhoods), partly to undermine the numerous religious ceremonies.[18] In 1955, the local leadership in Hoai Bao also discouraged lavish consumption by organizing weddings for five Hoai Thi couples at the communal house. The Youth Organization, who received tea and tobacco from the families involved, took charge of the event and organized the entertainment for the occasion. The older participants sang the traditional *quan ho* songs of that part of the country. Younger participants had to perform, regardless of musical talents, in a category specified in a lottery. There was neither a bride-receiving nor a bride-farewell ceremony. The bride-price institution came under attack. In general, the local government limited rituals to offerings to the couple's parents' ancestors and, in some cases, a small meal among the close relatives of the bride and the groom. (See also Tran Linh Quy, 1982, pp. 521–22.) The elderly reportedly understood the need for simplification and expense reduction because the country had just gone through eight years of the war with the French.

Although the Youth Organization still took charge of the wedding entertainment for a decade and a half after those five weddings in 1955, wedding feasts became larger in response to pressure in the community. Village officials, however, put pressure on parents through a local government ruling and through visits to families who were rumored to be preparing to slaughter pigs for wedding feasts. Citing the war and the country's economic problems,

had chosen not to attend the communal house gatherings. Son Duong leaders were also mostly in their forties, not yet entitled to attend shrine and pagoda ceremonies.

[18]During the land-reform period, many pagodas and communal houses elsewhere were also destroyed or partly converted into warehouses (Nguyen Khac Tung, 1990, p. 54).

the leaders demanded conformity with government guidelines. Although the pagoda prayer sessions were never discontinued despite low attendance, and although the communal house meetings resumed around 1958, village officials sanctioned the removal of a large number of incense burners and deity statues in the 1960s, taking them from their sacred location to the village pond—to the great displeasure of elderly women. By the order of the local party secretary, the outer wings of what remained of the communal house were also removed for the construction of an agricultural cooperative building in the 1960s. The pagoda and communal-house ceremonies then involved only prayers and incense. For two decades, the priest of Hoai Thi did not practice at all. He did not even have an altar at home during that time. Even as late as the mid-1970s, a priest from a neighboring community, who was often invited to funeral prayer sessions and house-construction ceremonies in Hoai Thi, was taken to the village and forced into confessing wrongdoing.

In Son Duong, an attack on class-oriented communal feasts and many ritual practices started as early as 1946. Well-educated young men in the community launched it in the name of national salvation and wartime economy. Communal-house rituals and feasts were attacked as hindrances to scientific progress and as a waste of resources needed for national reconstruction. The local leadership authorized the dismantling of the communal house, damaged by French bombs in 1951. In the 1960s, a local pagoda became a cooperative warehouse, and all statues were moved to the dilapidated remaining pagoda. Local officials considered lineage gatherings disruptive to communal unity and larger national causes and strongly discouraged them until the end of the American war. Under the pressure from the local government, ancestral halls were passed on as private properties to lineage heads. As an indication of the extent of suppression of ritual practices, the resurrection of funeral music in the mid-1970s by a deputy director of a provincial department at his mother's funeral led to his demotion.

Since 1975, however, rituals (especially kinship-centered rites of passage) have gradually intensified. The economy emphasis lost its appeal as war no longer posed an all-encompassing collective threat, and the promised prosperity seemed more remote than ever with the large-scale economic crisis in the late 1970s. In the early 1980s, the Communist party and the state issued numerous directives to their cadres to maintain pressure on local populations as part of socialist construction. (See Van Phac, 1985, and Tat Ung et al., 1983, p. 3.) The struggle was launched against "patterns of thought and behavior imposed by the feudal ruling class . . . against antiquated rituals, complicated and costly . . . funeral and wedding ceremonies, against superstitions . . . counter to modern science" (Chu Khac, 1987, p. 73). At the local level, in Hoai Thi, village and hamlet leadership attempted to revive the village-hall weddings and to eliminate wedding feasts by making a simplified village-hall ceremony a precondition for registration of the marriage.[19] In Son Duong, as late as 1986, in response to the resurgence of certain rituals, village party leaders instituted radical reform of life-cycle ceremonies. The village prohibited the serving of cigarettes at wedding and funeral receptions, restricted servings at funerals to tea and areca palm nuts, limited the number of wedding banquet guests to 60, and banned villagers' butchering of their own hogs for weddings. To reduce the cost of life-cycle events and to simplify the complex sequence of rituals, the village administration specified that (1) every wedding was to be held in the village office, (2) the engagement ceremony would require no more than five cigarette packs, half a kilogram of tea, and a few dozen areca palm fruits (instead of the virtually unlimited amount formally expected by the bride's family), and (3) in the case of a death, the corpse had to be buried within half a day. In return, the village cooperative provided, free of charge, a coffin, 10 packages of incense, and burial services for any deceased member. The village performing-arts group provided free entertainment at brief wedding ceremonies at the village office. The rationale for the reforms, according to the local party secretary, was to avoid the extraordinarily high costs of traditional ceremonies, which included status-oriented banquets and elaborate engagement-gift distribution:

> A well-off family probably managed a traditional ceremony all right. However, many others went heavily into debt on wedding and funeral occasions. If we take a [hypothetical] small family with two children, in the old days, six major costly banquets would have to be given: the wedding banquets for the two children, the funeral banquets for the parents, and two reburial banquets three years after each funeral. The costs were quite burdensome, especially if we take into account most parents' efforts to build houses for their junior sons. [Parents' houses were normally bequeathed to first sons.]

The state's efforts were unsuccessful. The authorities' argument on economizing reportedly evoked the response that it was people's own money, not government funds. Although officials in Hoai Bao imposed a heavy fine on hog slaughter for a wedding, many well-off villagers ignored the ban and willingly paid the fine. In the late 1980s, the national and local leadership finally gave in to the resistance to their tight control of ritual practices. In Hoai Thi, the prohibition on pig slaughter was lifted and even the offering of children to deities for nominal adoption no longer brought intervention. The local priest had carried on an increasingly thriving practice

---

[19]According to party and government directives, some villages instituted a drastically simplified marriage ceremony that lasted 25 minutes, with 15 minutes reserved for musical entertainment by the bride's and groom's friends (Tran Linh Quy, 1982, pp. 523–24).

since the late 1970s, and the local pagoda was expanded in 1980. Amulets were displayed in virtually every village house. In Son Duong, the village administration also gave up efforts to enforce the ruling on ritual simplification and allowed renovation of the pagoda and the shrine. By 1990, the rituals within and beyond the kinship domain in Son Duong and Hoai Thi had become more intensified than at any other time since 1954. The selective revitalization of traditional structures could be observed not only in Hoai Thi and Son Duong but also in numerous other northern villages during the past decade. (See Nguyen Khac Tung, 1990, p. 58; and Cao Nhu Nguyet, 1991, p. 243.) In 1990, on the national level, the Vietnamese government gave into the local resistance by allowing the manufacturing of votive paper and objects (Vietnam, Socialist Republic of, 1990, p. 7). In May 1991, it directed the provincial and district cultural offices to grant official requests for pagoda renovation.

In both Hoai Thi and Son Duong, opposition to state control was strongest regarding kinship-centered life-cycle ceremonies, which the state only wanted to simplify, and which retained the basic elements of the pre-1945 practices. These rituals were deeply embedded in the tight kinship networks of mostly endogamous communities, where the pervasive use of kinship terms for address and self-reference continually highlighted the rights and obligations of mutual assistance (Luong, 1990, ch. 2). The persistence of many ritual practices in the 1955–88 period was also aided by the high degree of community endogamy in North Vietnam, which rendered more intricate the local social network and made local cadres more susceptible to community pressure when implementing state policies. Mutual assistance among relatives became even more important when the diminished collective resources under the 1988 contract system prevented the Son Duong cooperative from drawing on its welfare funds to contribute a coffin to a funeral. In the context of the increasing importance of reciprocity among relatives and the maintenance of basic, traditional ritual steps in rites of passage, villagers considered the community-hall wedding ceremony to be a meaningless burden, as the comment of a retired Son Duong cadre indicates:

> In 1987, when you were here, the leadership tried to simplify ceremonies and to organize weddings at a village hall. But the change took place due to pressure from above. If the ceremony could simply take place at the public hall and end after the entertainment there, it might survive. But in reality, in the morning, the relatives still organized a delegation to the bride's house to ask for the bride. After asking for the bride, the bride's and groom's senior relative delegations went to the village hall for the ceremony, and then had to return to the groom's house. There were many complications. The public hall was simply too small, and many people had to stand chaotically outside. The bride's relatives could not simply see her off at the public hall, because

it was not the final destination. Everybody left after the public-hall ceremony for the groom's house where the ceremonial verbal exchange took place again. The basic steps still had to be taken. The public-hall ceremony was simply an addition, a complicating addition, especially when the weather was not cooperative. When there is no longer pressure from above, villagers invariably skip this additional step.

In Son Duong and Hoai Thi, since Buddhist *santras* are chanted as an essential component of any funeral, it is no coincidence that the elderly women's associations, based at the village pagodas, are the most resilient popular organizations; they have survived through the ebb and flow of religious rituals since 1954. Even in the heyday of socialist reconstruction, the elderly women could not be stopped from their monthly worship sessions at the pagoda. The pagoda remained an important local institution in both villages from 1954 to 1988. In contrast, since communal festivities and rituals were not directly related to life-cycle events, once the male-centered seat of power had shifted from the communal house to the party and village offices, these rituals suffered a precipitous decline.

In both Son Duong and Hoai Thi, in the 1980s, the economic reform and the concomitant ideological shift at the national level reinforced the intensification of local ceremonies. The growing economic surplus and the movement away from collectivized agriculture toward household production in a multisector economy gave rituals both within and beyond the kinship domain a big push. (cf. Potter and Potter, 1990.) As the household regained its role as the primary production unit and gained more resources vis-à-vis the cooperative (superseding the suprafamilial relations within the production team and the village) kinship ties became more important as a source of assistance in various domains, especially in such largely endogamous communities as Hoai Thi and Son Duong. The reciprocal feasting system reinforced kinship relations in an agricultural community with constant natural threats to subsistence and with fewer subsistence guarantees and less ritual assistance from the state. As the senior Communist party member in Hoai Thi observed, as villagers took more part in riskier trading activities, they also began to rely more on religious rituals, both in the household and at the pagoda, in an effort to gain psychological security. A large part of the economic surplus was channeled into consumption-oriented ritual activities, further stimulating agricultural production and consumer industries. The greater ritual intensification in Hoai Thi resulted from villagers' greater economic surplus and active engagement in risker trading activities.

Finally, in the 1980s, the Vietnamese state also became more concerned with economic development and political stability than with socialist ideological transformation. This was a time Marxist theoreticians increasingly viewed as a transitional period, lasting into the *foreseeable* future. The restructuring of the Vietnamese political economy was a part of that ideological shift. The state consequently relaxed its control of local ritual practices. The reform in Vietnamese agriculture and the changing sociocultural parameters were closely linked.

Acknowledgments

I would like to thank Diep Dinh Hoa, Börje Ljunggren, Shaun Malarney, Hue Tam Tai, James Watson, Alexander Woodside, as well as many participants in the Southeast Asia seminar at the Fairbank Center of Harvard University, for their comments on earlier versions of this paper. Professor Diep Dinh Hoa of the Vietnam Institute of Ethnology provided statistical data on rice-crop yields, expenses, and taxes in Hoai Thi, as well as on endogamy rates in both villages. Ms. Dang Thanh Phuong of the same institute, another member of our research team, also added some ethnographic details on Hoai Thi weddings and funerals. The research in Hoai Thi was a part of my collaborative project with researchers at the Vietnam Institutes of Linguistics and Ethnology. It was funded by a grant from the National Science Foundation of the United States and supplemented by a grant from the Social Sciences and Humanities Research Council of Canada. The research in Son Duong, on which this paper is based, was assisted by a grant from the Joint Committee on Southeast Asia of the Social Science Research Council and the American Council of Learned Societies, with funds provided by the Ford Foundation and the National Endowment for the Humanities.

References

Cao Nhu Nguyet. 1991. "Dien bien va thuc trang doi song nong dan" (The Transformation and Reality of Peasants' Lives). In Ban nong nghiep truong uong, ed., *Kinh te—xa hoi nong thon Viet Nam ngay nay* (Rural Vietnamese Economy and Society Nowadays), pp. 206–51. Hanoi: Nha xuat ban Tu tuong van hoa.

Chu Khac. 1987. "On the Formation of a New Socialist Way of Life in Our Country: Some Reflections." *Social Sciences (Vietnam)* 3–4:70–82.

Dang Van Lung, Hong Thao, and Tran Linh Quy. 1978. *Quan ho: Nguon goc va qua trinh phat trien* (Quan-ho Folksongs: Origin and Development). Hanoi: Nha xuat ban Khoa hoc xa hoi.

Khong Duc Thiem. 1982. "Su thay doi hanh chinh" (Administrative Changes [in the province of Ha Bac]). In Le Hong Duong, ed., *Dia chi Ha Bac*. (The Geography of Ha Bac), pp. 107–35. Bac Giang: Ty Van hoa Thong tin.

Le Van Toan et al. 1991. *Nhung van de kinh te va doi song qua ba cuoc dieu tra nong nghiep, cong nghiep, nha o* (Economic and Living Problems in Three Investigations on Agriculture, Industry, and Housing). Hanoi: Nha xuat ban Thong Ke.

Luong, Hy Van. 1990. *Discursive Practices and Linguistic Meanings: The Vietnamese System of Person Reference*. Amsterdam and Philadelphia: John Benjamins.

———. 1992. *Revolution in the Village: Tradition and Transformation in North Vietnam, 1925–1988*. Honolulu: University of Hawaii Press.

Ngo Vi Lien. 1928. *Nomenclature des communes du Tonkin*. Hanoi: Le van Tan.

Nguyen Huy. 1980. "Ve cac hinh thuc khoan trong hop tac xa trong lua" (On the Types of Contract Systems in Rice-growing Cooperatives). *Nghien cuu kinh te* (Economic Research) 118: 9–23.

Nguyen Khac Tung. 1990. "Buc tranh que—Mot chang duong" (The Rural Landscape—A Phase in the Trajectory). *Nghien cuu lich su* (Historical Research) 248:52–58.

Phung Van Thuc. 1982. "Nong nghiep" (Agriculture). In Le Hong Duong, ed., *Dia chi Ha Bac* (The Geography of Ha Bac), pp. 199–235. Bac Giang: Ty Van hoa Thong tin.

Potter, Sulamith Heins, and Jack Potter. 1990. *China's Peasants: The Anthropology of a Revolution*. Cambridge, England: Cambridge University Press.

Son Duong. 1987. *Lich su xa Son Duong: So thao* (A Preliminary History of Son Duong Village). Published under the editorship of the [Communist] Party Executive Committee in Son Duong Village. Viet Tri: So Van hoa Thong tin Vinh Phu.

Tat Ung et al. 1983. *Nhung chuyen thanh than* (Stories of Superstition). Viet Tri: So van hoa va thong tin Vinh Phu.

Tran Linh Quy. 1982. "Phong tuc tap quan cua nguoi Viet" (The Customs of [Ethnic] Vietnamese). In Le Hong Duong, ed., *Dia chi Ha Bac* (The Geography of Ha Bac), pp. 499–534. Bac Giang: Ty Van hoa Thong tin.

Tran Tu. 1984. *Co cau to chuc cua lang Viet co truyen o Bac Bo* (The Organizational Structure of Traditional Vietnamese Villages in North Vietnam). Hanoi: Nha xuat ban khoa hoc xa hoi.

Van Phac. 1985. "Mot so van de ve cong tac van dong nep song moi trong thoi gian toi" (Some Issues in the Upcoming New Lifestyle Campaign). *Xa hoi hoc* (Sociology) 10:44–48.

Vietnam, Communist Party of, Agriculture Section of Central Committee. 1991. "Danh gia thuc trang kinh te—xa hoi nong thon" (An Evaluation of Rural Socioeconomic Realities). In Ban nong nghiep trung uong, ed., *Kinh te xa hoi nong thon Viet Nam ngay nay* (Rural Vietnamese Economy and Society Nowadays), pp. 9–87. Hanoi: Nha xuat ban Tu tuong van hoa.

Vietnam, General Statistical Office. 1991. *So lieu thong ke CHXHCN Viet Nam—Statistical Data of the Socialist Republic of Vietnam, 1976–1990*. Hanoi: Nha xuat ban thong ke.

Vietnam, Historical Institute (Nguyen Dynasty). 1971. *Dai Nam Nhat Thong Chi*. Vol. 4. Hanoi: Nha xuat ban Khoa hoc xa hoi.

Vietnam, Socialist Republic of. 1990. *Luat thue tieu thu dac biet* (The Special Consumption Tax Law). Hanoi: Nha xuat ban Phap Ly.

11

The Political Economy of "Reform" in Vietnam— Some Reflections

Adam Fforde

The political economy of reform in the Socialist Republic of Vietnam is a unique topic: if, as one can argue without much difficulty, the Vietnamese economy has been essentially a market economy since 1989, then the leadership is the sole example in the world today of a ruling communist party that has abandoned the central-planning methods derived from Stalinist Russia.[1] Neither in China nor in the Soviet Union has the communist government been able to do this, and in Eastern Europe the question is now meaningless. Needless to say, this exercise in creative social change presents the Vietnamese Communist party with a sometimes bewildering mixture of opportunities and constraints. The process of reform, both deliberate and unconscious, dates from at least 1979.

People may argue against the notion that the Vietnamese economy today is a market economy. My main focus, however, will be on the changes that have taken place—and continue to take place—in the social relationships in Vietnam that may be referred to as political economy.[2] Apart from the now

---

[1]After the Fall of the South in 1975, the Democratic Republic of Vietnam (DRV or North Vietnam) and the Republic of Vietnam (South Vietnam) were replaced, in 1976, by the Socialist Republic of Vietnam.

[2]Loosely interpreted, political economy represents economic affairs that have to do with issues of power, distribution of rents and surpluses, the activities of the state, and other matters not usually considered under the conventional definition of economics as "the study of the allocation of scarce resources to competing ends." This paper takes a minimalist view of what constitutes a market economy, mainly for analytical convenience. It is difficult to think about the post-1989 Vietnamese economy in terms other than market economy. However, as should become clear, in the early 1990s, the economy lacked well-developed factor markets that could easily be described in conventional phraseology: most "modern" capital was still in the hands of state enterprises, which were yet to be reincorporated as state-equity companies, and rural-land access rights in the northern and central regions were influenced by traditional thinking and far more dominated by markets. In another study (de Vylder and Fforde, forthcoming), it is stressed that "for us, the key element is the nature of transactions in current goods and services, thus development of effective factor markets takes a secondary position."

burgeoning literature on Vietnam, this paper draws on a number of other works and works in progress, as well as personal observation.[3] These works tend to focus on the North because that is where the traditional system was imposed the longest and, therefore, where the shift away from the system has brought the most complicated developments. And as a professional economist, the author is biased toward economic rather than cultural-social matters.

The apparent success of the transition to a market system in Vietnam has raised a number of questions that evoke classic problems of the modern nation-state:

- What does the state represent, and to what extent is it subject to particular sectarian interests?
- If it is influenced by such interests, do they tend to make it stronger or weaker—more or less capable of mobilizing national energies?
- In practice, does the central government control the key levers of state power: the army, the currency, credit, foreign trade, the bureaucracy? Can the central authority enforce its will in areas it deems important, or does it have to give way to other powers within the national territory?

In a traditional Stalinist system, these issues are repressed by the ideology of Marxism-Leninism and the immense powers conferred on the central authorities by the system developed by Lenin and perfected by Stalin. In a society whose government openly approves of autonomous activities—a so-called civil society—the role of the state vis-à-vis the autonomous sectors has to be decided. The Vietnamese government, in accepting the right of all economic sectors to exist, has also accepted the importance of determining its own role.[4] Moreover, as a result of the reform process, these autonomous forces are now so powerful that they provoke the question of the acceptability of autonomous—unplanned—activities almost continually. The current debate over the Draft Socioeconomic Strategy, and the widespread hostility toward its emphasis on the "leading role of the state," has brought this question to the fore: What is, and what should be, the role of the state in the Vietnamese market-oriented system?[5] To shed light on this question, this

---

[3]Examples of some of the works on Vietnam are Melanie Beresford (1989), Zdenek Drabek (1990), Zamir Hasan et al. (1990), and Andrew Vickerman (1986).

[4]Since about 1988, the government and party have issued many decrees about this, hoping to convince a naturally skeptical population. See, for example, Vietnam, Socialist Republic of, (1988).

[5]See the forthcoming proceedings from the recent international symposium on the Draft Socioeconomic Strategy. Held in Hanoi in February 1990, it was organized by the Long-Term

paper will concentrate on the political economy of the state and in particular on the state sectors, such as state enterprises and trading companies.

Stages in the Transition to a Market Economy

Transition: An Overview

From the early 1980s, a revisionist strand has woven its way through Western analyses of Vietnam. Moving away from previous stereotypes, this line of thought emphasizes the important adaptations that were made to the traditional Stalinist model when it was adopted in North Vietnam (the Democratic Republic of Vietnam, DRV), then, subsequently, throughout the country after 1975-76.[6] One aspect of this argument is that these adjustments significantly "softened" (*mem boa*) the harsh, obligatory norms of the foreign model, perhaps in a way reflective of the national character and history.

Time will tell whether this interpretation is correct. It certainly makes the frequent failure of Vietnamese economic policy after 1975 easier to understand. And there is rather interesting evidence that shows that often the North Vietnamese economy responded to immediate local incentives rather than to the rigors of "socialist duty." Two examples are:

- the widespread erosion of the property-rights norms of the Stalinist model in the agrarian economy, in favor of local and household demands.
- the pressure from units in the state sector to expand various economic relations "outside" the plan while maintaining local interests.[7]

Planning Institute of the Vietnamese State Planning Committee in collaboration with the Stockholm School of Economics.

[6]Adam Fforde and Suzanne H. Paine (1987) argued that the DRV was a "weak state," lacking the power and resources to effectively impose the norms of the Stalinist model on North Vietnam. This was explored in greater detail in Fforde (1989a), which argued that North Vietnamese peasants, to a significant extent, managed to evade the pressure to adopt official norms. Melanie Beresford's work might be classified, along with these others, as revisionary, but I am not sure she would agree. Andrew Vickerman (1986) follows a similar line. And much of Alexander Woodside's work is in a similar vein. See, for example, Woodside (1989).

[7]The term "outside" draws upon Vietnamese vernacular and informal academic usage to capture the underlying dichotomy between "correct" activities within the formal socialist system and those activities beyond its reach. Frequent references in the established Western literature to "grey markets," and so on, miss many of the cultural and normative implications of activities carried out by such "outlaws." Also see Fforde and Paine (1987) for reference to evidence concerning these issues. That the North Vietnamese government did not like or wish to accept such deviations is abundantly clear from reading the Vietnamese literature, especially the preambles to economic decrees.

These developments were important because they imply that the nation-state was weak, incapable of attaining key goals that it had set for itself.

Although offering an explanation of what happened in the 1980s, the revisionist position conflicts with classic Western analyses from both the left and the right (to use unhappy and unfair but convenient labels).[8] Although in practice accepted by many Vietnamese economists, this view finds images of Vietnam as either an East Asian Prussia or some peasant-based social democracy perplexing. Classic analyses find it hard to explain the transition of the 1980s. How could hardline Stalinists have failed to construct socialism in a reunited Vietnam?

It could be argued that the transitional model of the 1980s simply developed and expanded trends visible prior to the beginning of reform. This is now an historical issue, however, and study of the mechanisms of the transition is now no longer of topical interest. Studies done in the late 1980s have been overshadowed by more recent events—key among them the abolition of central planning in 1989. Earlier analyses therefore belongs to history.[9]

But these conflicting views remain and are valuable in stimulating discussion of the transition, especially its origins. One important element of the revisionist view is its emphasais on the role played by spontaneous forces and the feebleness of the government in dealing with them.

The Transition from Central Planning to Markets—1978/79–1989

It is undeniable that the Vietnamese economy and polity changed radically through the 1980s. In the late 1970s, the economic system was essentially Stalinist, with orthodox Soviet institutions. After 1989, central planning was abandoned, cooperatives reduced to service organizations and residual property-rights holders, and most retail trade privatized. Until 1989, however, the core of the traditional model remained intact in the central and local authorities' direct residual control of resource allocation by administrative means. Central planning coexisted with market relations, or something very similar to market relations. This had important political effects, especially at the local and "line" ministerial levels.[10]

---

[8]Without going into a detailed literature survey, it is perhaps pertinent to ask where one can find studies of North Vietnam, prior to the early 1980s, that question prevalent assumptions about the nature of the DRV.

[9]Stefan de Vylder and Adam Fforde (1988) provide a description and analysis of the transition. A revision of this work is ongoing.

[10]"Line" ministry means those "owning" economic units (*cap chu quan*).

Origins of the Transition—North Vietnamese Socialist Economy Prior to 1979

The traditional Stalinist model relies on compulsion and a certain set of institutions to create forced economic development. The direct allocation of resources through the state distribution system permits these resources to be focused on priority sectors. The forced extraction—through state procurement—of required inputs to these same priority sectors allows very high mobilization rates, which usually lead to rapid industrialization and urbanization. However, a model such as this that relies on administrative methods that override direct material incentives forecloses alternatives without weighing their relative costs and benefits, and is therefore very inefficient. These two elements of the system—compulsion and replacement of markets by administrative allocation methods—create considerable social and economic tension. Thus, for this system, an apt slogan would be "prices do not matter much." In North Vietnam prior to 1975, however, prices in fact mattered rather more than they should have.

In the late 1950s and early 1960s, foreign aid fed the DRV industrialization drive. These resources came from donors who, without exception, also maintained central-planning systems. After some time, inflationary pressures built up, and free-market prices rose. Despite their collectivization in the late 1950s, farmers increasingly preferred free-market sales to deliveries to the state, and they began to sell produce on the free market. This extended to rice, the key staple.

During the early 1960s, the state's de facto response was to implicitly accept this preference, while explicitly condemning it. The state failed to eradicate the free market in rice through force—the traditional Stalinist solution.[11] Instead, the state struck a balance between its needs vis-à-vis the wartime struggle (on the one hand) and peasants' desire to get better prices for their goods (on the other hand). This development softened the norms of the Stalinist model, and one result was that resources moved away from the prescribed channels—the cooperatives and socialist trading network—toward the free market. Through the war years, foreign consumer-goods assistance was required to fuel the state trading-and-distribution system, which remained short of domestic inputs during this time. The war, the inefficiencies of the cooperative system, and the inability of agriculture to generate surpluses—all prodded the system toward the free market.

---

[11]Based on a secondary source referring to "diplomat's reports"; see Fforde (1989a).

This picture, of course, is a broad-brush characterization of actual events. The following developments reveal how the Stalinist model was adapted to Vietnamese conditions:

- The state failed to implement its own formal policy. Frequent decrees forbidding the free market in rice were widely ignored; local cadres were put under pressure to respect local interests. The old proverb "the writ of the Emperor bows to the customs of the village" (*Phep vua thua le lang*) still applied.
- Foreign aid was extremely important to preserving the institutions of the DRV state. Aid, supplied to the central government, went through the state distribution system.
- There was a self-defeating application of the traditional model, which, by failing to apply compulsion and permitting deviations, encouraged market-oriented behavior within the core institutions of the system. Cooperatives sought illegal expansion of household plots, workers sought additional cash income to buy food on the free market, and cadres sought ways of developing their prospects and those of their families.[12]
- There was a strong tendency toward equilibrium among various factors, rooted in a balance of incentives for respecting official norms and for conducting voluntary, own-account activities. This balance reflected traditional societal views and was easily captured in the language through dichotomies such as "inside-outside" (*noi-ngoai*).[13]

At any time the balance depended on such considerations as prices (especially the differential between the state and the free market), availability of goods, the political climate and the corresponding penalties for noncompliance with norms, and popular attitudes such as attitudes toward the war. These are very hard to analyze in any determinate manner, but it is not too difficult to view the adaptation of the traditional Stalinist institutions—their

[12]Interesting research remains to be done on the regional biases apparent in certain state appointments during the 1950s and early 1960s.

[13]"Unplanned" or self-serving activities were neatly described as "outside" activities. The apt phrase is *chan ngoai day hon chan trong*—"the outside foot is longer than the inside foot." For an early attempt to analyze the low-level equilibrium into which the Vietnamese economy appeared to sink (with capital equipment imports not used because of shortages of required current inputs), see Fforde (1984).

endogenization—in these terms.[14] A key factor contributing to this adaptation was the authorities' implicit recognition of a civil society—not to mention the participation of individual cadres in market activities to supplement low wages.[15]

But the continued attempts by the authorities to implement the DRV model, backed by foreign economic assistance, led to severe structural distortions in the North Vietnamese economy. Investment was scattered in a pattern that responded to political initiatives, bureaucratic logic, or whatever, leading to a capital stock that survived mainly via support from the state. This support came in the form of various subsidies, some of which were derived from the domestic economy (e.g., procured rice), but mainly from economic aid. One way of putting this is that the economy's "value relations" (*quan he gia tri*) were highly distorted. Most of the state's activities—the social sectors included—therefore depended upon two unreliable sources: (1) aid from China and the Soviet bloc, and (2) whatever resources the state could extract from the domestic economy.

The Weak State of North Vietnam: Failure in Economic Management

From a revisionist perspective, North Vietnam in the mid-1970s was a society with a weak state that had already softened the usually harsh norms of the Stalinist model in meeting local interests.[16] Compulsion through direct administrative means was muted in deference to market opportunities and the wishes of economic agents. The situation the state faced was this: either a drastic strengthening of repression was required to impose central authority and discipline, or spreading disobedience could force abandonment of the central-planning model altogether, allowing a more voluntary—market-based—mechanism to take its place.

A between-the-lines reading of North Vietnamese authors, published in officially approved sources at this time, clearly shows many of the underlying tensions in the DRV.[17] Thus, intellectual opposition to the operation of the traditional system apparently appeared early on but remained within the establishment (with certain important exceptions that remain to be properly

---

[14]See Fforde (1989a). Also, a study of these processes in state industry, by Fforde, is in progress.

[15]Civil society means areas of social and economic life that are autonomous relative to the control ambitions of the party and state. When civil society is *not* accepted, "anything that is not permitted is forbidden." That many state cadres and workers had significant informal income sources can be seen from Figure 11-5 (see page 323).

[16]The author would not claim that emphasis on the adaptation of foreign models is a novel theme either in East Asian history in general or in Vietnamese history in particular.

[17]See, for example, the writings of Dinh Thu Cuc, The Dat, Nguyen Manh Huan et al.

studied).[18] The natural intellectual pluralism of the society, therefore, like other expressions of local interests, could not be stifled.

It appears, however, that criticism often took two quite different positions. One, essentially static in its view of the world, upheld the possibility of creating a socialist system based on the traditional Stalinist model but without its many distorting effects, especially in the area of prices. This view insisted that the problem was not the model, but its implementation. The other position argued that because the Stalinist model avoided market-based exchange, the distortions arose; therefore, a market-oriented approach was necessary. Until the late 1970s, however, the Communist party tried to reinforce the traditional model and stiffen mechanisms for its implementation. Given the context, this was reactionary.

The Beginning of Change—The Crisis of the Late 1970s

The late 1970s saw the central authorities continue in their attempt to implement the Stalinist model—this time nationwide—despite earlier failures in the North under the DRV. In a reunited Vietnam with access to the Mekong Delta's abundant potential, conditions appeared more favorable than previously in the land-scarce North. Various decrees sought a recentralization of authority and compliance with party norms. However, the program failed. The government was unable to impose sufficient control on the economy, particularly in the Mekong Delta, with its large economic potential. Moreover, Western and Chinese aid was cut as a result of the Cambodian situation. These cuts mainly hit the state sector. At the same time, poor harvests and the failure of the Mekong collectivization drive pushed up free-market rice prices and therefore increased the pressures for decollectivization. The government's inability to force the needed rice out of the Mekong in 1978–79 showed once more that the Stalinist model inevitably would be softened in Vietnam.[19]

The political economy of the crisis in the late 1970s took the following form: escalating economic forces pushed the DRV system harder to accommodate local interests and to allow the expansion of autonomous, market-oriented opportunities. In the North (as well as the rest of the country), agricultural cooperatives started to break down, state enterprises started to

---

[18]For example, Bui Cong Trung, head of the Economics Institute in the early 1960s (Bui Cong Trung, 1959).

[19]The procurement strike was clearly of great historical importance. The relative roles of southern leaders and the Mekong Delta peasantry remain to be studied. Beresford (1989) discusses this incident.

"fence-break" and develop unplanned relations with suppliers and custom-ers, and direct links with foreign markets sprang up.[20] These latter links were particularly important in the South where industrial production relied heavily on hard-currency suppliers.[21] This economic upheaval was well described in the popular press and therefore was openly discussed—more or less.

The Transitional Model—1979 to 1989

As is well known, some 18 months after the important sixth plenum of the Vietnamese Communist party in mid-1979, official policy partially accepted the legality of these phenomena. The output contract system in agriculture, the Three Plan system in industry, and expanded rights for foreign trade were all sanctioned *subject to the condition that the core elements of the central-planning system would be preserved.* Here again, policy was essentially reactionary, seeking to defend the existing institutions and power structure while granting tactical concessions. To foreign observers, these reforms appeared, on the surface, to be liberalizing and were certainly presented as such by many Vietnamese spokesmen. In reality, conservatism drove this program in the early 1980s, with continued Stalinization of everyday life (restricting contacts with foreigners, limiting access to information, etc.) and thinly disguised hostility toward the free market and the private sector. On the other hand, the transitional model that was created set in motion powerful economic mechanisms. There followed a period of relatively rapid growth as compared to the stagnation of the late 1970s. Figure 11-1 shows percentage changes in produced national income from 1975–90.

It appears that the political consensus behind the transitional model lasted until around 1984 or 1985. The breakdown then was probably linked to the growing power of commercial interests, combined with rapid inflation and general confusion. The Sixth Party Congress of December 1986 marked the formal policy shift. It is worth recalling that Le Duan, the traditionalist secretary-general, died in the middle of 1986. The equally tradition-bound Truong Chinh acted as a six-month stopgap until the congress convened. Despite his past, Truong Chinh supported the new policy line in the period of preparation for the congress.

---

[20]The term "fence-break" is, like "inside-outside," taken from the Vietnamese. I first read it in an article by Dam Van Nhue and Li Si Thiep (1981).

[21]See, for example, reports on the Saigon Thanh Cong textile mill's activities with the Tourist and Marine Product Companies (1984).

The Sixth Congress appears to have targeted the end of the decade for abandonment of the residual elements of central planning, now condemned as the "bureaucratic subsidy system" (*quan lieu bao cap*).[22] The new attitude toward the nonsocialist sectors and free market was positive. After the congress, the de-Stalinization of everyday life proceeded.[23]

In fact, the transitional system lasted until 1988 or 1989, when the "re-reformed" output contract system drastically reduced the role of cooperatives; the two-price system was abolished, ending residual central planning; and foreign trade was greatly liberalized.[24] During the intervening period, the economy became increasingly "commercialized" and market oriented.[25] Perhaps most important of all, the attitude toward the private sector was reversed. Until 1986 and the Sixth Party Congress, party policy had been hostile to the private sector, but under the influence of such economists as Tran Phuong, appeared to seek implementation of the traditional model without creating conflicts between local interests and the priorities of the state. This chimera was what the party abandoned in 1986.

This departure from previous policy was particularly manifest in the arcane field of industrial-reform legislation. Prior to 1986, the modifying decrees to 25-CP (i.e., 146 and 156 of the Council of Ministers) mandated obligations to supply goods at low plan prices. From 1986 on, however, decrees (i.e., 306 of the Party Secretariat and 217 of the Council of Ministers) point toward removing such obligations and replacing them with the "commercialization" of exchange relations.

Thus the price-money-wage reforms of 1985, contrary to what many thought at the time, did not seek to liberalize the economy but rather to remove distortions by fixing state prices for planned distribution equal to

---

[22]This was revealed in various decrees, laying down the framework for reforms in the late 1980s. See Adam Fforde (1989b).

[23]I do not wish here to suggest that Vietnam became an open society. However, the political atmosphere lightened tremendously.

[24]The timing of events is muddied by the 1988 passage of the important Decree (No. 10) that liberalized agriculture, while administrative allocation of resources through central planning continued until 1989. Note also that foreign-trade liberalization occurred both formally and informally. With the effective opening of the borders, goods supplies on domestic markets soared, but the state effectively lost control of international economic relations. Most smuggling was either carried out or condoned by state organizations, with important implications for the political economy of the 1990s.

[25]The term *thuong mai hoa*, drawn from the Vietnamese (who are the experts), is often useful in describing complicated changes in micro and macro behavior that have to do with the development of markets. One element of this—crucial to the evolution of responsiveness of supply and demand to market price—is the creation of capital controlled by producers and consumers to back up their demands and ex ante supply decisions. Thus the growth of markets within the transitional model required the development of such capital, for which the Vietnamese term is "own-capital" (*von tu co*).

free-market prices. (This would appear to ignore the essential role played by compulsion in the Stalinist model and the necessary part played within it of economic distortions.) In any case, from the time of the Sixth Congress, supported by changes in the Central Committee that gave a greater role to local authorities, party policy sought to shift toward some sort of guided commodity/market economy.[26]

It is also worth recalling in this context that the early output contract system, dating from January 1981, had sought to preserve the cooperatives.[27] The work-point system had been maintained, and the base-unit still had been asserted to be the cooperative. Although a valuable increase in household autonomy was gained, permitting accumulation of capital and expertise, rural cadres still controlled an important part of the surplus. Moreover, with product markets still severely distorted against farmers and also very weakly developed, diversification remained risky and incentives poor.

At the macro level, rapid inflation was brought about by misconceptions driving macroeconomic policy and the state's unwillingness to cope with distortions created by past investment policy. As the economy became more commercialized, the traditional patterns of subsidy weakened. Parts of the state sector found it increasingly difficult to maintain access to resources, and workers and cadres saw their incomes threatened unless they had access to outside sources through the free market, either directly through second jobs or indirectly through their unit's commercial activities. The state's response was to print money in an effort to offset these processes, leading to inflation. By driving up free-market prices, the government, of course, added to the economic forces that were diverting resources away from the planned sectors and heading toward further commercialization. In this way, the system was continually jostled toward greater use of markets, while permitting accumulation of capital at the periphery.

The transitional economic system therefore settled into a dynamic state of crisis.[28] It ended when the 1989 anti-inflationary measures heralded the end of the two-price system and the introduction of a market economy. Two (among many) questions then arose: What had been happening to the political economy and the economic structure during the 1980s? What sort of market economy had emerged from the confusion? These remain the questions of the moment.

---

[26]See various papers by Carlyle Thayer (1983; 1985).

[27]This is shown, for example, by the title of Le Thanh Nghi's disseminating pamphlet (1981).

[28]This crisis of transition to a market economy is the main topic of de Vylder and Fforde (1988).

The Political Economy of the Transition

Any discussion of East Asian economic development involves the high-priority question of the state's role. The precise effects of state activities remain a matter of substantial debate, but it is important that countries with a long history as centralized nation-states take this issue very seriously (Hughes, 1988). Vietnam is no exception.

The traditional Stalinist-Soviet development model gave an extraordinarily important role to the state in economic development. It is the most extreme example of the "statist" developmental thinking common in the Third World after the Second World War. The shift to a market economy in Vietnam therefore required a movement of similar magnitude along a number of dimensions—economic, ideological, and political.

Economic Change—The Role of Distortion

It is perhaps trite to observe that the transition to a market economy is not at all the same thing as the transition to an effective and efficient market economy. Much of the work done by professional economists and others in the Third World and by other countries with market economies focuses on analysis of poorly operating markets. Problems are said to result from many factors, such as monopoly (natural and otherwise), lack of effective institutions (e.g., no clear and reasonably well-enforced law), and other, "structural" matters (e.g., largely subsistence-oriented agriculture).

A forthcoming work argues for the value of making a distinction between two different types of economic distortion created by central planning—plan distortion and market distortion (de Vylder and Fforde, forthcoming). Definitions of the two types of economic distortion are as follows:

- Plan distortion describes that aspect of the misallocation of resources by central planning that prevents a rapid shift to a market economy.
- Market distortion describes any part of the misallocation of resources by central planning that distorts the ensuing market economy.

The distinction is useful in thinking about the political economy of transition for at least two reasons. Plan distortion helps to assess the social-adjustment costs of getting to a market economy, while market distortion refers to the costs of then making that market economy operate efficiently. If the basic issue of political economy is *"kto kogo—ai thang ai"* (who wins, who loses?), thinking about the economy in this way may help to identify the obstacles to reform.

Reform Strategy and the Mechanisms of Transition

Consider the long-term strategy choices that may have confronted Vietnamese reformists in the early 1970s. The failure of the traditional economic model was clear. The economic costs were obvious, revealed in the lack of effective depreciation of industrial assets and the inability to finance reinvestment from the surplus generated. The underlying laws of motion of the economy were also easy to appreciate: the tension between plan and market, the endogenization of Soviet institutional models, the weakness of the state and its frightening reliance upon foreign assistance.

But the social costs of a rapid transition to a market economy were also undoubtedly high. Who would feed the cities if aid were cut off? What could the nonagricultural population produce to exchange voluntarily with farmers? Where would state revenues come from if the state sector—so obviously noncompetitive—closed down? At the micro level, a market economy requires producers to possess sufficient capital to participate freely in exchange. This is lacking in a centrally planned system: state enterprises, cooperatives, and farmers all lack the resources needed to develop market-oriented patterns of behavior.

More profoundly, how would the human capital adjust? Farmers, long constrained to work collectively in the brigades of cooperatives, would need time to accumulate experience and capital. Managers also, trained in central-planning methods, knew little about markets or cost accounting. The intellectual infrastructure built up in the 1950s and 1960s—intellectuals, lawyers, economists, planners—was based upon the Soviet model. What ideological and technical basis would the national government have, once the change had occurred?[29]

There are, of course, quite reasonable grounds for debate as to the speed with which these changes can occur. For more neo-classical economists (with optimistic assumptions about factor mobility under appropriate conditions), this speed is likely to be fast—perhaps two years. For those with a structuralist point of view (with pessimistic assumptions), the answer is likely to be that change would occur at a slower pace—perhaps a decade. In either case, there are significant political-economy considerations: "politics is the art of the possible." It was on such analyses that any effective, long-term reformist strategy would have to be built.

---

[29]Such questions are naturally more applicable to the northern and northern-central regions than to the South.

The Party and State—Changing Roles

Common sense suggests that a successful transition to a market economy without political upheaval demands a radical change in the nature of the state. That is, to effect a relatively smooth political transition, time is needed to allow the polity to evolve gradually rather than be subjected to radical and perhaps destructive change. The new basis of the party should therefore be permitted time to unfold—to make the transition from an orthodox implementer of the traditional central-planning model to the dominant political force in a market economy. However, it is far from unusual to find market economies run by single political parties. For example, neither South Korea nor Taiwan was a democracy during its own period of economic construction.

Thus, if the long-term goal in Vietnam was to create a market economy, it required eliminating the so-called plan distortions so that the social costs of shifting to a market economy would fall to acceptably low levels. These costs, furthermore, could be viewed in both political and political-economy terms. Politically, the dominant force (the party apparatus) had to shift its power base from the traditional pillars of the Soviet model—direct control through the plan over exchange relations, the state sector, the rural cooperatives, and foreign economic relations—to those appropriate to a market economy. In terms of political economy, the winners and losers of the transition had to be balanced off to retain the momentum behind the reform process without major upsets. In hindsight, this is what appears to have happened.

One hypothesis for explaining the 1980s transition is that forces with increasing political strength pushed for creation of an outward-looking economy within which the existing power structure could be transformed into a new one, made up of people who had started out working in the state sector. If such a transformation were effected, the establishment would change its power base without losing out personally. But by 1990, the party's dominant position had not changed, and positions at all levels were still held by people with strong interpersonal links based upon years of working together.

A Reexamination of the 1980s

A quick reexamination of the 1980s might be useful. In 1979–80 the Western and Chinese aid cuts, combined with the change in atmosphere at the eighth plenum in 1979, had introduced the period of "fence breaking" that culminated in 1981 with the passing of the two key decrees of the transitional model.[30] However, the reform package severely restricted the growth of the

---

[30]These were 25-CP in industry and CT-100 in agriculture.

free market and the private sector, which had mushroomed in the previous two years, growing at rates of 15 to 20 percent annually, as depicted in Figure 11-2.[31]

The transitional model created ample opportunities for the development of profit-seeking commercial activities by elements of the state and collective sectors, which were permitted—in practice if not absolutely in principle—to sell on the open market or exchange resources through such measures as voluntary swaps. The differential between state and free-market prices encouraged diversion into the free market of resources supplied by the plan. What it did not do, however, was open up the economy to independent, private-sector activities in crucial areas such as trade, industry, and foreign trade, which continued to be dominated by the state. The interesting point here is that the nature of state economic organization was changing fundamentally; it was becoming commercialized (*thuong mai hoa*).[32]

The residual element of central planning within the transitional model therefore helped create the basis for development of commercial resources that would then be available for profitable investment—although this was certainly not what most top policy-makers intended at the time.

Under this system, high profits accrued to any unit that could meet two conditions: first, get its hands on cheap resources supplied through the state system; and second, divert those resources onto the free market. This meant that good personal connections within the state system were an important ingredient of profit making. The ways in which these relationships were used had, however, changed. The associations involved individuals in the party in particular and the establishment in general. As the decade progressed, many people in the party and establishment came increasingly to support what was happening. It meant greater access to cheap resources through the state that they could then, in turn, use to local benefit. While local benefit often meant their own pockets, it did not mean that workers would not benefit. In fact, to obtain political support from ideologues, and to secure the labor effort required to produce for the market, adequate worker incentives had also to be considered.

Local benefit therefore involved a sharing of profits among various groups: workers, managers, superior levels, and others. Through this such mechanisms, commercial capital was created, leading to the preconditions for

---

[31]Note that policy toward the free market in staples did a u-turn in 1979, and that important members of the establishment *did* argue for a free-market approach at this time. See Fforde (1989a) and Nguyen Lam (1980). The latter author was, at the time, a senior member of one of the economics departments of the Party Central Committee.

[32]This term, once again, is drawn from the Vietnamese. I first heard it used (in 1988) to describe the way in which relations among state units were to change as part of the reforms.

a generalized market economy. But the political economy that it implied was not neatly fitted to clear definitions of ownership in terms of benefit and beneficiaries. Furthermore, a substantial part of these benefits derived from the high level of subsidy in the system, especially the availability of cheap inputs through the residual element of central planning. Thus, when and if the transitional system ended, much of this commercial activity would find itself exposed to sharply increased economic competition.

The emergence of capital had important regional differences. With an outdated capital stock derived from the socialist world, the northern state sector relied heavily on input supplies from the Soviet aid program. This was also true of the northern industrial cooperatives. In the South, however, the asset base was more competitive. In a common pattern, units within the state economy of the South sought out extra inputs through deals with hard-currency earners that enabled them to import needed inputs. This pattern, rather different from the North, led to the growth of highly profitable state-trading companies, often provincially or city based. But large areas of the southern economy remained integrated into the system of state subsidization through the supply of cheap goods, and these areas developed new political linkages in a way similar to the North. In all cases, however, the commercial-ization process radically changed the political economy of the country.

Thus, the transitional model created a powerful constituency in the party for further commercialization and reform. It created the potential for a successful transition to a market economy. It also, however, left partly unanswered key issues of economic efficiency and the role of the state in a market economy. But as plan distortions declined, the social costs of the shift fell away.

The weakness of central authority and planners in the face of de facto theft at lower levels was part of the transitional system.[33] At its root were profit-seeking individuals in the state and collective sectors. These people were probably close to the "local interests" who became important newcom-ers to influential positions in Communist party politics at the Sixth Party Congress in 1986.[34] As we have seen, this congress committed the party to the abolition of the old system. But what did this mean?

Here it is perhaps useful to pay attention to what can be called the "1985 thesis." Prior to the failed price reforms of 1985, which set off hyperinflation, the Vietnamese economy *could* have shifted to a stable system of voluntary exchange—that is, a generalized market economy or a fully commercialized

---

[33]Theft is the correct term. Government decrees repeatedly criticized and forbade state units from diverting plan resources to commercial use in so-called "Plan 2"and "Plan 3" activities.
[34]See various works by Carlyle Thayer for an examination of these trends.

system. In other words, it is argued, sufficient price response at the micro level already existed for a shift to a market economy. So why did it not happen? The answer is, in part, because of the opposition of old conservatives; apparently the interests of dominant forces would not then have accepted concessions to the private sector implied by the new model. Another factor was the conservatism of the (then) top leadership.[35] Sufficient time had not elapsed for arguments and evidence to accumulate to show that the more commercialized the unit, the more efficient and socially valuable it was.

To the classic intellectual reformers of Vietnam, trained in Eastern Europe, reform meant the market-oriented economic model, which (with variations) was and is familiar from market-socialist debates. These reformers, who appear to have played an important role in developing reformist legislation, can now be found, for example, in the Hanoi institutes. For the commercialized elements within the state and collective sectors, who had made money under the transitional system, reform more often meant more of the same; it did not necessarily mean a shift to a market economy, as the term would normally be understood. Why should it?

In the second half of the 1980s, it appears—with glorious contradiction—that the sharp increases in Soviet aid were an important factor in propelling forward, via the two-price system, the commercialization of the state economy (see Figure 11-3 following). The private sector shrank further (see Figure 11-4), and therefore, no independent, interest-based political force for development of a market economy emerged. In the agricultural sector, the party Agriculture Committee became alarmed by the deterioration in per capita staple production and by the famine crisis of early 1988.[36] As a response to this crisis, it published Decree No.10, which sacrificed about 50 percent of the cadre jobs in the cooperatives.[37] Freer domestic trade gave profitable state-trading companies better access to commodities. And through the closing years of the decade, a number of measures were introduced that helped to establish the basis for a market-oriented economy. These measures were promulgated in the context of hyperinflation as the state printed money in an attempt to balance the growing conflicts.

---

[35]Recall that Le Duan did not die until 1986.

[36]One of the main consequences of this famine appears to have been the creation of a far better national rice market through the removal of interprovincial trade barriers. Another is the theme of crisis in food production that runs through de Vylder and Fforde (1988), which still sits intriguingly besides Vietnam's emergence in 1989 as the world's third largest rice exporter.

[37]This figure comes from an official source. It has interesting implications for the real power hierarchy within the establishment: who is sacrificed when?

There was no real resolution of the issue of state property, and no real push to do so. The property issue remained, lurking behind many debates. In light of what has already been argued, however—that the transitional model created a commercialized state sector largely under the control of party cadres who were successfully managing their own transformation—the state property issue cannot be understood in purely technical "economic" terms; it is a matter of political economy. Furthermore, if this view of the transition is correct, and certain state enterprises had become competitive under market conditions, then it is the limits placed by state property on their expansion that are particularly arresting. In other words, what would the self-interest of this "state capital" seek, in terms of economic institutions?

Summary: The Development of a Business Interest

In summary, the transitional model was a catalyst for forces pushing for a shift to a market economy through the creation and development of a commercialized state sector. These forces combined with political support from within the party to bolster the market-oriented reformers. Underlying economic change reduced economic distortions and, therefore, the adjustment costs of the eventual shift to a market economy. But the process, involving as it did the commercialization of the state sector, greatly weakened an already ineffective central government. The state apparatus became confused in its objectives, as line ministries and local authorities became increasingly involved—through the state sector—in business activities. It is striking, to say the least, that the main source of equity funds for the Import-Export Bank was the "own capital" of the Ministry of Foreign Economic Relations.[38] It is also noteworthy that the main agents smuggling industrial goods into the South (thus creating great competition for Saigon manufacturers) were the Mekong Delta provincial authorities.

In hindsight, especially when the problems of the new economic system are considered, the absence of certain elements becomes analytically interesting. In other words, the transitional system could solve some problems, but not others. Underlying the transition was the weakness of the state in general, and the central government in particular. To manage effectively a market economy, certain basic functions of the central government in the economic sphere become of great importance—for example, contract enforcement between inter-regional joint ventures by business interests.

---

[38]Once again, this term "own capital" is drawn from the vernacular (*von tu co*) and literally means "the capital that the unit itself has." It was in common use by the end of the 1980s, and, of course, refers to and reveals the development and emergence of autonomous economic activities. Linguistic aspects of the reform process are discussed in Fforde (1990).

Vietnamese foreign trade expanded very rapidly in 1989. Official estimates put hard-currency export growth at more than 100 percent. Unofficial estimates as to the level of informal trade put it at around the same level as official values. One example of the continued weakness of central authority is the way in which the growth of foreign economic contacts was largely through smuggling or through weakly controlled but established channels— the state trading companies. There was actually little formal change in the foreign-trade regime. Thus, the rapid growth in Vietnam's participation in the world economy had no immediate, major systemic implications. A political economy had emerged that could cope with such shocks. Moreover, foreign investment was still rather unimportant in its effects on the political economy.[39]

This recourse to informal channels for rapid trade expansion meant that the state did *not* have to decide what it thought about the relative importance of alternative priorities. However, it also meant that the transitional system of the 1980s had failed to adequately address a key issue of national development based upon market economy: the role of the state in mediating between domestic and foreign economic interests.

Another striking aspect of the overall picture was the peculiar relationship between commercial and state interests. The private sector was relatively unimportant in state circles. At the end of the decade, it was still very small and had no formal political representation. It was the commercialized state sector that retained great political influence. This meant that commercial interests were still not extra-establishment. Accordingly, it was very difficult for the central authorities to resist calls for subsidies (via credit and tax breaks) to ease adjustment costs in the state sector. Furthermore, financial and fiscal discipline was hard to impose when the state structure was so deeply permeated with profit-seeking behavior. Thus, in 1990, when fears mounted concerning the potential for political unrest in the wake of Eastern Europe, policymakers were vulnerable to frequent appeals, appearing in the media, from the state sector for credit and fiscal assistance "to prevent unemployment mounting."

It appears that the resulting return of inflation did not prevent bankruptcies and unemployment in the state sector, and many of the resources, in fact, went into unproductive ventures. The lesson was driven home that effective management of a market economy requires a high degree of central authority. However, in the period of preparation for the Seventh Congress (July 1991) one implication of this—the need to curb the powers of local

---

[39]This is not, of course, likely to continue through the 1990s.

authorities—encountered the fact of their voting power in the party Central Committee. People would not easily vote against their own interests.

In Vietnam, empirical justification for any assertion is usually contentious; formal social and political structures, as reported, are often unreliable indicators of the whole picture.[40] In the end, the reader must make up his or her own mind. What is striking, however, is that, by the early 1990s, massive amounts of material were available to researchers, and there was easy potential for creating new data through surveys. The society was now far more open, thereby improving access to information.

Was the Post-1989 Vietnamese Economy a Market Economy?

The question of whether the Vietnamese economy was a market economy after 1989 is a contentious one. The answer depends on what one means by the term "market economy." It is reasonably certain that in the Vietnamese economy of 1990–91, the majority of inputs and outputs were bought and sold voluntarily by independent units who based their decisions primarily on considerations of profit, price, and personal welfare. There was no generalized consumer-goods rationing. With a few exceptions, there was no price control. Enterprises within the state sector had a single target (budgetary contributions), and farmers on the whole decided what to produce and how to dispose of it.

Some other aspects of the 1990–91 Vietnamese economy are as follows:

- Rice rationing continued, at a price that reflected quality differences, mainly to stabilize the market.
- Subsidized elements of the public-sector wage existed through cheap housing, health services, and so on.
- In parts of the state sector, legally binding contracts persisted, largely in the area of state-to-state trade. But these contracts had greatly declined in importance in 1990, since trade with the nonconvertible area had increasingly moved to a hard-currency basis.
- Farmers' access to land was often mediated through cooperatives and based on use rights, and these rights often constrained what farmers could do with the land. There was effectively a zoning system.

---

[40]This is not by chance. Some of the historical and systemic reasons for this should now be apparent to the reader.

Factor markets—for land-use rights, labor, and capital—also existed but were weak and primitive.

Land-Use Rights

According to the Vietnamese constitution, all land belonged to the state. The state allocated use rights to economic units. These are, in principle, transferable for benefit.[41] The holder of the use right was liable for the land tax upon it. If the economic unit was a cooperative, the farming family received the land on contract from the cooperative—that is, a lease system was applied. In practice, access to land through these contracts varied regionally. According to party policy, these leases should have been from 10 to 15 years in length for rice land, and longer for cash crops such as tea.

In the northern and central regions of Vietnam, land-use rights have traditionally been subject to collective restraints aimed at reducing risk and excessive social differentiation.[42] These constraints have long been seen as an important source of social stability in rural areas through their limitations on land concentration and the growth of landlordism. In many ways, the cooperatives, in 1989–91, appeared to have reverted to these traditional functions. Thus, the issues of how and when to allocate land to new families in a commune or village were handled by the cooperative, which maintained a right to revoke contracts. The cooperative, however, was, and is, evidently expected to pay compensation for any increase in the yield of the land resulting from the farming household's efforts.

According to dominant traditional thinking, land allocation in these overpopulated areas should have attempted to strike a balance between equity and efficiency. In fact, directives from the authorities usually required cooperatives to allocate land according to both household numbers and household resources and ability. In practice, however, there were abuses. Party cadres were often reluctant about giving away the cooperative's residual property rights (e.g., the length of contracts was often shorter than the party directives specified). But the evidence is that abuse has declined since the abolition of the work-point system in 1988.

In the south, where lower population density made such issues less important, farmers' access to land after 1989 appeared to have reverted to direct possession of use rights. The cooperatives had largely been abandoned, and farmers paid taxes directly to a tax station rather than (as in the north and

---

[41]In other words, while the authorities could not yet bring themselves to state that use rights could be bought and sold, they allowed them to be "ceded."

[42]The importance of these issues to an understanding of peasant attitudes is covered by James Scott (1976). See also Fforde (1983), which also surveyed some of the Vietnamese literature.

central region) through the cooperative. As a result, land for a new family was to be supplied by the family's relatives.

A recent survey, generally critical of conservative thinking, presented a picture of generally rising rural real incomes, which coincided with a variety of other observations (such as the buoyant supply of goods in rural markets) (Le Van Toan et al., 1991). Because of competition between state trading units, it was now rather difficult for local authorities to put too much pressure on farmers. Much still remained to be done, however, to develop rural markets and reduce the still-high margins between farm gate and f.o.b. or retail prices. These are typical problems of a market economy.

It will be interesting to see how the residual land-access rights of the northern peasantry influences the development of the national labor market in the 1990s. Despite a massive amount of rural underemployment now, relations between workers and employers will be less unequal than they otherwise would have been, because there is no landless class.

Enforcement of property rights in land use, however, remained weak. In upland areas, for example, it was very hard to prevent theft and forest destruction. Also, there was nothing to formally prevent large-scale private plantations, and southern commercial capital appeared to have already been invested in such crops as coffee in the Central Highlands.

Labor

Where foreign capital was not present, there appeared to be no limits on the hiring of labor by any economic component. Labor migration required population registration, but this appeared to constrain only those who could not find work. Temporary registration was reportedly easy for those with employment. But state workers who wished to relocate within the state sector found it very difficult to move. Migration from the overpopulated areas of the northern and north-central regions remained weak, because farmers would not resettle unless minimal infrastructure (schools, in particular) was available. This was true of farmers regardless of the apparent benefits to real incomes, for example from coffee small-holding.

The Capital Market

The Vietnamese capital market was also weakly developed. While foreign exchange could be obtained rather easily by anybody for a price and a large, informal credit market flourished, the lack of effective institutions made the capital market the Achilles' heel of the Vietnamese economy. Until foreign joint ventures grew significantly, almost all modern capital remained in the hands of state units, which, even if profitable, still found it difficult to mobilize capital easily in the absence of effective capital markets. Most of the equity for the nonstate commercial banks, however, came from the "own-capital" of state units, pointing to the direction of the system's natural evolution.

Most joint ventures within the country came from within the state sector, as state units sought to expand their profitable commercial operations. However, as these units remained formally owned by the state, it was hard to resolve such issues as shared risk and profit distribution. The policy position at the time of this writing appears to be that this concern can be addressed through the incorporation of such units as share companies. This process of incorporation would, however, involve cutting through the complicated web of interests that have grown up around state units in joint ventures and would therefore not be easy to implement. A program of experimentation is under way as of 1991.

Bank credit was still almost entirely concentrated in the state sector. The absence of clear rules about creditors' rights greatly increased the risk to banks lending to state units. And foreclosures on loans to the nonstate sector were now common, leading to asset seizure. The interest-rate structure was such that banks borrowed at a higher rate than that at which they loaned money, leading to a need for subsidies and state support. The usual lending pattern was that banks allowed state units a certain quota at a low level of interest, beyond which they paid a rate far closer to that on the free market. The extent to which this corresponded to the old two-price system was unclear. Banks, on the whole, were unwilling to borrow at real rates of interest because of the pressures such borrowing would put on their lending policies. Banks were unequipped with the normal powers of creditors in countries with more developed capital markets.

As it was, however, Vietnam appeared to be moving toward a credit-based capital market system, with the state banks playing the major role. This trend suggested that the state would have to bear a significant degree of the risk involved in commercial lending, which therefore comes back to the important issue of the relationship between the state and commercial interests which attracted much research interest in the late 1980s.[43]

Given the preceding discussion, it seems far easier to consider Vietnam in 1990–91 as a market economy—with important distortions and institutional peculiarities—than as anything else.

Reducing "Plan Distortions." Official statistics provide revealing indications of the process of reduction of plan distortions in the 1980s. However,

---

[43]See Wade (1988) for a discussion of this issue.

the business of measuring and tracking the process of commercialization is still in its infancy. We lack agreed-upon indicators.

In the first half of the 1980s, as we have seen, the private sector was strongly constrained and, after an initial, short recovery, the state's failure to deal properly with the pressure the cooperatives brought to bear upon farmers led to a growing agrarian crisis (de Vylder and Fforde, 1988). But the pressure of procurement on farmers, as measured by the gap between state and free-market prices, declined, as shown in Figure 11-6. Other important adjustments seem to have been in the state sector, where most factories, through of the Three Plan system, were able to develop their own capital supplies and acquire familiarity with the market.

At the same time, state workers diversified, moving away from the formal socialist sectors in both their earnings and expenditure patterns. This is illustrated by Figure 11-5, cited earlier in this chapter and shown here. Employment did not appear to change significantly, but, in fact, most urban state workers maintained at least two sources of income. Thus, the real allocation of labor time probably *did* change, with workers expending greater efforts in areas that give higher rewards. This, of course, was a continuation of a pattern going back to the early 1960s.

Winners and losers. The question remains, who has benefited from the changes during reform, apart from the commercialized state cadres, the market-oriented technocrats, and the top politicians who have supported reform? One aspect of the transition to a market economy that has been a manifest benefit to the majority is the rapid and substantial increase in mass living standards that has accompanied the abolition of central planning. For many farmers and workers, 1989 was a good year.

Trade

The discussion so far has focused on the state sector and the role of planning. The necessary corollary of a contraction in the role of central planning in resource allocation is an increase in direct relations between producers and consumers. The growth of the free market can be assessed through various statistics, as Figure 11-7 illustrates, and the state can be seen to have withdrawn from retail trade through the 1980s. While the private sector remained wary in 1990–91, growing from a low base, new job creation was limited and concentrated in services and trade.

The Work Force

Real incomes of state employees grew in the late 1980s as shown in Figure 11-8. Not only did the real money value of incomes increase, but the end of consumer-goods rationing also reduced the time required to wait in line, as well as the general degree of uncertainty in everyday life. There was a building boom as urban inhabitants expanded and improved the housing stock. Visible differences in personal consumption grew greatly. Food supplies in the northern cities, which used to be atrocious, improved beyond recognition. Development of the private sector allowed a return to the traditional pattern of out-of-doors eating.

Cuts in state-employment levels were substantial. Formally, some 500,000 (12 percent) jobs were eliminated between 1989 and 1990. These people were removed entirely from the state-employment system. There was a system of official severance pay, and, according to some official reports, about half the workers sacked under that system then obtained some sort of permanent employment. In practice, however, many more jobs were lost before the official system came into force, with state factories letting people go without wages. What is striking, however, is that by 1991 there did not yet appear to have been any reduction in real urban wages. This suggests that the nonstate sectors have recorded an appreciable employment expansion, but this is hard to gauge from the data.

On the whole, for those with employment, real incomes appear to have risen substantially. Indeed, the worst period for workers was probably the mid-1980s when they still depended upon rations. For those who were now unemployed, however, the old system represented a better time.

Farmers

By the end of the 1990s, farmers had better access to land and better markets. The domestic price of rice had risen fivefold in dollar terms since the mid-1980s, as depicted in Figure 11-9. However, the decline of the cooperatives had worsened the position of such groups as poorer families, and, some argue, women (Allen, 1990). Access to day care centers, primary health care, and other social services had declined. But the development of cash-crop production in food-deficit areas was striking as farmers learned that the rice market was now reliable and based on access to Mekong Delta rice. The rapid increase in per capita staples production in parts of the North was also notable. But state support for agriculture through rural credit, extension services, and further improvements in markets was still lacking.

Conclusions—The Emerging Post-1989 Political Economy

The transition to a market economy in Vietnam may, in historical hindsight, be seen as simply a variant of the conservative strategies implemented by other countries that replaced central planning with a market economy without first going through a political upheaval. These countries arguably include the Soviet Union prior to 1991 and China of the 1980s and early 1990s. They contrast with countries such as Poland, Hungary, and Czechoslovakia, where the events of 1989 saw the old leadership thrown from power. In any case, as the first country to abandon central planning *without* changing its government, Vietnam will reveal interesting lessons. The emergence in 1989 of a market economy from the transition of the 1980s resulted in a polity very different from that of the late 1970s and was certainly far from most people's expectations in the aftermath of the fall of Saigon in 1975.

One conclusion that is reasonably clear is that the flow of events after 1989 cannot be understood without looking at the political economy of change. The bitter debates of the early 1980s as policy remained reactionary, the shift toward abolition of central planning in the mid-1980s, the confusion of 1990–91, and the difficulties posed by the state sector all form elements of one historical process. In this process, traditional factors, such as the land question and regional issues, appear to coexist with newer issues bound up with the integration of Vietnam into the world economy of the 1990s.

With what political economy does Vietnam appear to have entered the 1990s? With the events that transpired after 1989, certain features of the new market-oriented system became clearer. Most capital was now controlled by economic units that primarily sought to use it for commercial ends: to profitably buy and sell in markets. This profit motive held true whether the unit concerned was a peasant family, a state enterprise, a private-sector trader, or a provincial import-export company. What differed among these units was their access to various inputs.

The state apparatus was increasingly uncomfortable with its distinctly schizophrenic role. On the one hand, commercialized interests within it acted with great autonomy. Characteristic elements within the powers of a normally functioning nation-state were strikingly lacking: control over international trade and foreign currency within its borders; ability to enforce government decrees in many areas (especially tax collection, contract enforcement, and use of state resources); and control over elements within it to whom decisions had been decentralized but who, in practice, acted as autonomous agents.

On the other hand, other interests within the state and party acted in obedience to commercial logic. That is, given access to resources, they used them in ways that were to their benefit. The result was that the state found it very difficult to separate its direct involvement in economic activities from its overall functions in "national economic management." This distinction has long been *theoretically* important in the Vietnamese reform process. What makes it less than practical in Vietnam is that a complete separation of the two functions is extremely unlikely in any polity, and (if comparative experiences are anything to go by) especially in East Asia. For Vietnam, the central question can be reduced to the following: what should and could the relationship be between the state and commercial interests?

It is easy to be pessimistic, for, with a GDP of perhaps $15 bn Vietnam's yearly output is comparable to a few months of Japan's trade surpluses.[43] The Vietnamese fiscal deficit of the early 1990s was around $200 mn; the list of key, central infrastructural projects on which the state placed such importance cost around $100 mn yearly. Furthermore, the chaos in the (former) Soviet Union not only removed Vietnam's main economic partner but denied Vietnam access to the military materiel needed to maintain its national security. Is such a situation one within which a country with a weak state can easily prosper? While development orthodoxy would suggest that the answer is no, consideration of the growth experiences of other countries "off the curve" (one example might be Italy) may suggest that judgment should be withheld.

References

Allen, Susan. 1990. *Women in Vietnam*. Stockholm: SIDA.

Beresford, Melanie. 1989. *National Unification and Economic Development in Vietnam*. London: Frances Pinter.

Bui Cong Trung. 1959. *Ban ve cai tao cong thuong nghiep tu ban chu nghia o mien Bac* (Discussion of the Reform of Capitalist Trade in North Vietnam). Hanoi: Su That Publishing House.

Dam Van Nhue and Le Si Thiep. 1991. "Ket hop loi ich cua tap the nguoi lao dong trong cong nghiep dia phuong." *Nghien cuu kinh te* (Economic Research), 5.

Drabek, Zdenek. 1990. "A Case Study of a Gradual Approach to Economic Reform: the Vietnam Experience of 1985–88." *World Bank Internal Asia Regional Series.*

de Vylder, Stefan, and Adam Fforde. 1988. *Vietnam—An Economy in Transition*. Stockholm: SIDA.

———. 1992. *The Economic Transition in Vietnam: Reflections on the Emergence of a Market Economy*. In progress.

Fforde, Adam. 1983. "The Historical Background to Agricultural Collectivization in North Vietnam—the Changing Role of "Corporate" Economic Power." Birkbeck College Discussion Paper no. 148. London: Birkbeck College, University of London.

———. 1984. "Macro-economic Adjustment and Structural Change in a Low-income Socialist Developing Country—An Analytical Model." Birkbeck College Discussion Paper no. 163. London: Birkbeck College, University of London.

[43]Estimates of per capita GDP of around $200 combine with a population of 65 to 70 million to give a total GDP near $15 bn.

————. 1986. "Unimplementability of Policy and the Notion of Law in Vietnamese Communist Thought." *Southeast Asian Journal of Social Science* no. 1.

————. 1989a. *The Agrarian Question in North Vietnam, 1974–79*. New York: M.E. Sharpe.

————. 1989b. "The Socialist Republic of Vietnam in the Twelve Months Since Mid-1988—Major Policy Changes and Socioeconomic Developments." Mimeo. Hanoi: SIDA, June.

————. 1990. "The Successful Commercialization of a Neo-Stalinist Economic System—Vietnam 1979–89," with a postscript. ANU Doi Moi Conference, Canberra, September.

————. In progress. *Curate's Egg or Dragon's Tooth?: Commercialization Processes in Vietnamese Industry 1979–89 and the Growth of a Business Interest.*

Fforde, Adam, and Suzanne H. Paine. 1987. *The Limits of National Liberation*. London: Croom-Helm.

Hasan, Zamir et al. 1990. "Viet Nam—Transforming a State-owned Financial System—A Financial Sector Study of Viet Nam." International Monetary Fund, Washington, D.C..

Hughes, Helen, ed. 1988. *Achieving Industrialization in East Asia*. Cambridge, England: Cambridge University Press.

Le Thanh Nghi. 1981. *Cai tien Cong tac khoan mo rong khoan san pham de thuc day san xuat cung co hop tac xa nong nghiep* (Reform Contract Work, Expand Product Contracts in order to Stimulate Production and Reinforce Agricultural Cooperatives). Hanoi: Su That Publishing House.

Le Van Toan et al. 1991. *Nhung van de kinh te va doi song qua ba cuoc dieu tra nong nghiep, cong nghiep, nha o* (Economic and Welfare Problems Through Three Surveys on Agriculture, Industry and Housing). Hanoi: Thong Ke Publishing House.

Nguyen Lam. 1980. "May van de ve tu tuong chinh sach kinh te hien nay" (Some Problems in Present Thinking about Economic Policy). *Tap chi cong san* (Communist Studies), 3.

Thayer, Carlyle. 1983. "Vietnam's Two Strategic Tasks—Building Socialism and Defending the Fatherland." *South East Asian Affairs*.

————. 1985. "National Leadership in Vietnam—Continuity and Change in the Party's Central Committee, 1960–1975," SSRC Brighton Conference, Brighton, England.

Vickerman, Andrew. 1986. *"The Fate of the Peasantry—Premature 'transition to socialism' in the Democratic Republic of Vietnam."* Monograph Series no. 28. Yale University Southeast Asian Studies Center for International and Area Studies. New Haven: Yale University.

Vietnam, Socialist Republic of. 1988. *Nhung quy dinh va chinh sach doi voi kinh te tap the, ca the, tu doanh va gia dinh* (Regulations and policies towards the collective, family, private and family economies). Hanoi: Phap Ly Publishing House.

Wade, Robert. 1988. "The Role of Government in Overcoming Market Failure." In Helen Hughes, ed., *Achieving Industrialisation in East Asia*. Cambridge, England: Cambridge University Press.

Woodside, Alexander. 1989. "Peasants and the State in the Aftermath of the Vietnamese Revolution," *Peasant Studies* Summer issue.

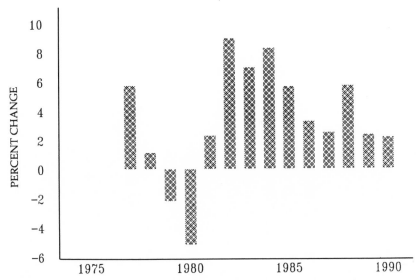

Figure 11-1. *Produced National Income (Year-on-Year % Changes). Three figures—11-1, 11-2, and 11-4—use the aggregate "Produced National Income" to assess the sectoral balance of the economy. This measure is net of incomes from overseas and, therefore, is conceptually nearer to the gross national product. Figure 11-1 shows how the growth record in the early 1980s was better than that of the period after the Sixth Party Congress in 1986.*

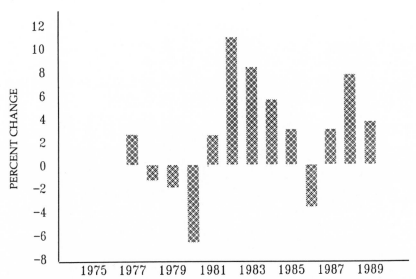

Figure 11-2. *Produced National Income—Nonstate (Year-on-Year % Changes)*

Source: Figures 11-1 through 11-8 were created by the author using data from a variety of official Vietnamese sources.

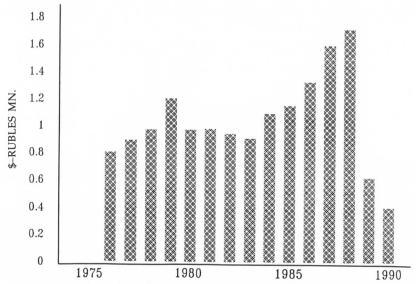

Figure 11-3. Trade Deficit ($-rubles mn.). Like many other people faced with the conundrum of comparing U.S. dollar values with rubles, the Vietnamese authorities simply add the two series together—"$-Rubles." This figure shows the sharp improvement in recorded trade from 1989.

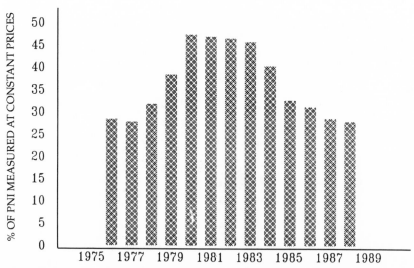

Figure 11-4. Private-Sector Contribution to Produced National Income (Constant Prices, %). Figure 11-4 confirms the data presented in Figure 11-2, which shows a reining in, after a growth spurt from 1980 to 1983, as the reactionary policies of the early 1980s attacked nonsocialist sectors. The private sector here shows a steady fall in its recorded share of total economic activity from 1980 to 1988.

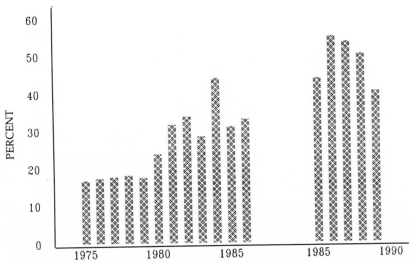

Figure 11-5. State-Employee Family Incomes from Informal (Other) Sources (% of Total). "Other" income sources refer to receipts not covered by such categories as wages, pensions, and allowances. It is therefore a useful proxy for earnings in the informal sector. Two series have been used, the later of which is in constant prices. The overall trend is, however, clear: there was a sharp rise in the proportion of state-employee incomes coming from "informal" sources in the decade between 1975 and 1985. Since then, the proportion has declined. This argues for the analytical importance of considering developments prior to 1989.

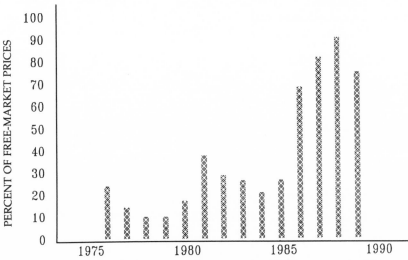

Figure 11-6. State Staples Prices as a % of Free-Market Prices (1978–90). This figure shows the steep reduction in the degree of distortion created by the state's policy of forced sales by farmers at low prices. The figure assumes a state-free market-price ratio of around 10 in 1979 (based upon personal observation); thus the figure's main point lies in the trend that it illustrates—the reduction in the gap between state and free-market prices—rather than the absolute gap, judgments about which rely upon the accuracy of the starting point. Note the deterioration between 1988 and 1989.

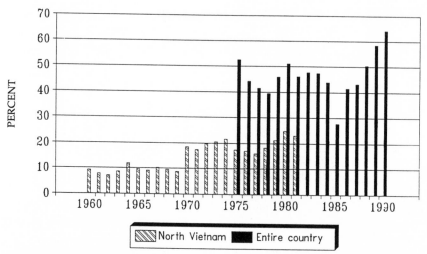

Figure 11-7. *Proportion of Total Retail Sales Controlled by the Free Market (%). In this figure, note the far higher extent of free-market retailing in the South during the late 1970s. Note also the decline in the free market's share during the early 1980s and the rather slow recovery, until 1989–90.*

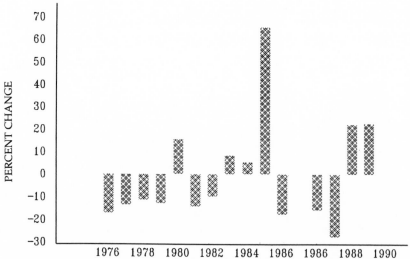

Figure 11-8. *Total State-Employee Family Incomes Deflated by RPI (Year-on-Year % Changes). This figure shows the instability of real income growth. The Retail Price Index (RPI) is, however, unlikely to be reliable.*

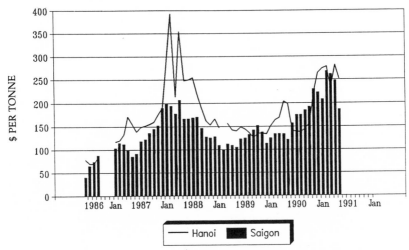

Figure 11-9. Retail Value of Rice in Local Dollars (Hanoi and Saigon, $ per Tonne). This figure is based on free-market information provided by the Institute of Prices and Markets in Hanoi. Note the widening of the Hanoi-Saigon differential during the food crisis of early 1988. Note also the secular shift—from around $75 a tonne in the mid-1980s to over $200 a tonne in 1990.

12

Political Renovation in Vietnam: Renewal and Adaptation

William S. Turley

"We should not allow the democratization movement to soar up and become uncontrollable nor allow deviations to go uncriticized and ungoverned, in order to avoid paying a high cost."

Tran Trong Tan, Director, Central
Committee Propaganda and Training
Department, June 1988

"[W]e do not tolerate pluralism. Democracy needs party leadership."

Nguyen Van Linh, Party General
Secretary, March 1989

"The vital lesson to learn in renovation is that in economic and political reforms, we should not be impatient and hasty. We must take harmonious, accurate steps. We cannot walk with one short leg and one long leg, nor can we walk lame with one leg."

Tran Xuan Bach, December 1989,
shortly before his expulsion
from the Political Bureau

"We cannot effect economic renovation without renovating politics at the same time. . . . Facts have shown that refusal or deliberate delay of political renovation will cost dearly even when the population's economic life is not so bad."

Nguyen Duc Binh, Director of Nguyen
Ai Quoc Institute, February 1990

In the West, among those who pay attention at all, the predominant perception of Vietnam's *doi moi*, or renovation, is that while the ruling Communist party remains committed to economic reform, it has followed the Chinese example in suspending political reform. The expulsion of Tran Xuan Bach from the Political Bureau in early 1990, partly for expressing views like the one above, may seem to confirm the validity of that perception. But this view reveals more about its proponents than about reality: Westerners, conditioned by events in Eastern Europe and the Soviet Union, do not perceive reform that falls short of transformation into liberal democracy as meaningful and therefore do not see the changes in Vietnam, even when they look.

Whatever the obstacles to political doi moi after 1989, advocacy of it did not die out, as the preceding quotation by Nguyen Duc Binh makes clear. Nor have the balance of power between party "liberals" and "conservatives" or events in other socialist countries been solely responsible for its fate. Although factional quarrels and international events have played a role, party ideocrats were wary of democratization before just such a movement got out of control in Eastern Europe. Reform-minded leaders ruled out pluralism for Vietnam before Tiananmen. And party journals have continued to publish articles arguing that political and economic reforms must coincide despite Bach's expulsion and a crackdown on dissent. It is not hard to see why foreign observers have misinterpreted the Vietnamese situation.

A review of the evolution of political doi moi requires a brief description of efforts to renovate seven institutions: (1) the bureaucracy, (2) the party organization, (3) the media, (4) elections, (5) representative assemblies, (6) mass associations, and (7) the legal order. The complex web of relationships among the party, state, and people is a separate but transcendent issue. Against this background, I will assess the prospects for survival, or transformation, of the Vietnamese political system. I argue that doi moi is continuous with, but not the end of, Vietnam's century-long struggle to formulate a response to the West, modernity, and the globalization of politics and economy.

Dimensions of Political Reform

In comparison with other reforming communist systems, Vietnam has enjoyed important political advantages. Coming to power through war and revolution rather than through imposition by outside force, the Vietnam Communist Party (VCP) in 1975 presided over an integrated political system with uncontested authority and legitimacy. After three decades of struggle, the party had eliminated all rivals and restored Vietnam as an independent and unified nation. The VCP leadership was among the most stable and genuinely consensual in the communist world, and the party's membership included a large share of Vietnam's most dedicated and patriotic people. It was a party, moreover, whose survival and eventual victory had depended on the mobilization of mass support, and it enjoyed broad, popular acceptance.

The postwar Vietnamese state, however, was as much a clone of other Marxist-Leninist systems as its leaders could make it. This began to change in about 1985. Beginning in 1979, the party introduced product contracts to stem declines in agricultural output, and sharp cuts in foreign aid disbursed through state channels drove many factories to obtain inputs through "unplanned" activities, which the party tolerated (Fforde and de Vylder, 1988, pp. 62, 68). The first reforms were thus piecemeal and essentially legitimized local responses to economic emergency. Few leaders showed any inclination to revamp political or administrative structures. It took a continuing economic crisis to convince the orthodox that "bureaucratic centralism," particularly of the military-logistic type that Vietnam had inherited from the war, was unworkable at Vietnam's level of development. Therefore, in June 1985, the Central Committee eighth plenum took tentative steps toward a market system and ordered the dismantling of the state's wage and price bureaucracies. These and other reforms were ratified at the Sixth Party Congress in December 1986 under the slogan, "Leadership by the party, mastery by the people, and management by the state." Administrative decentralization and consolidation reduced, in stages, the number of departments, offices, and personnel. By the end of 1989, the government had dissolved 12 ministries and ministerial-level state committees, closed 43.7 percent of offices at the department level, and laid off 50,000 workers (Vietnam News Agency, February 21, 1990). Two years later, the number of civil servants discharged and entitled to special compensation under Council of Ministers' Decision no. 176 had reached 550,000 (Radio Hanoi, September 18, 1991). Without more specific data as to the categories of civil servants involved and what alternative employment some may have found in the state sector, it is difficult to assess the overall impact of this downsizing, but the sheer numbers and references to the cost of pensioning them off suggest the cuts were significant.

Accompanying administrative decentralization was a drive to clarify the division of labor between party and state and reduce the duplication of effort. While the party was to retain a strategic role in policy planning, it was to cease interfering in day-to-day affairs of government. As stated in the June 1988 fifth plenum resolution, it was "impossible to effect renovation in the economic, social, security, and national defense fields without reforming the political system. The outstanding problem here is to clearly distinguish the party's function of leadership from the state's function of management . . ." (*Nhan Dan*, July 26, 1988).

But for the party to lead without commanding, it had to overcome an admitted crisis of confidence in its leadership, reverse the decline in its prestige, and recover popular support. The political crisis had resulted most directly from poor economic performance, administrative incompetence, and abuses of power by individual cadres; but expectations resulting from the party's own campaign to intensify popular participation in "socialist construction" following the war may have exacerbated the crisis in some regions.[1] Whatever the causes of declining confidence, the stimulus for the reforms that the party adopted to avert a crisis of legitimacy came from below.

However, the party retained tight control over the policy process and seized the initiative by reforming itself. In early 1987, the party opened a campaign to expel incompetent and corrupt members and step up recruitment of better-qualified ones. To make party members more attentive to public opinion, the campaign invited citizen complaints and denunciations. In the first six months of 1988, Party Control Committees in Binh Tri Thien Province received nearly 1,000 letters of criticism and complaint, which led to the discipline of 391 party members, including 115 who were expelled and 31 who were removed from their posts (Radio Hanoi, July 2, 1988). The Ho Chi Minh City party committee disciplined 424 members, expelling 172 and sending 16 to prison (*Nhan Dan*, July 31, 1988). By mid-1990, the campaign in Hai Hung Province alone had resulted in the punishment of nearly 10 percent of the province's 55,700 party members, including expulsion of 2,800 for violating party discipline, failing to have political awareness, or engendering distrust by the people (Radio Hanoi, October 10, 1990). The campaign continued into the spring of 1991, with some major effects on district-level party congresses that were being held to prepare for the Seventh National Congress scheduled for June. In Ho Chi Minh's native district of Nam Dan in Nghe Tinh Province, the campaign resulted in the disciplining of 795 party members, including the expulsion of 270 members and legal action against 19 cadres for corruption (Radio Hanoi, March 14, 1991).

Enlistment of the people in the campaign to reform the party and the reform of electoral and representative institutions (discussed following) implied reform of the media as well. In its own version of "glasnost," under the slogan "Let the people know, discuss, implement, and control," the party and government encouraged an unprecedented degree of critical reporting by journalists in the official press. Information began to circulate more freely through both official and unofficial channels. Books and periodicals began to appear without party or government sanction as censorship and other

---

[1] I am indebted to Ngo Vinh Long for pointing out the possible significance of this campaign for the "right to collective mastery," which General Secretary Le Duan spearheaded in the late 1970s.

controls were relaxed. In view of the burning or banning of many books in the South after 1975 and the subsequent postal interdiction of "counterrevolutionary propaganda" sent from overseas, this was a major change. The degree of openness did not approach Eastern European or Soviet standards, however, and several editors found themselves forced into early retirement for criticizing the government and party too vigorously. Still, the freedom was greater than anything the party had tolerated since the Nhan Van-Giai Pham affair in 1956.[2]

More meaningful popular involvement and greater openness in public affairs extended to the electoral system as well. In the past, elections for popular assemblies at all levels had eliminated all but docile, party-approved candidates from the ballot, and voters had made meaningless choices for powerless institutions with an understandable lack of enthusiasm. To overcome the popular cynicism, the elections for the National Assembly in April 1987 permitted a measure of competition. Whereas 614 candidates stood for election to the assembly's 496 seats in 1981 (1.24 candidates per seat), there were 829 candidates (1.67 candidates per seat) in 1987 (Kyodo News Service, April 7, 1987).

As before, the Vietnam Fatherland Front organized the nomination and screening of candidates, but people were permitted to nominate themselves and a few ran as independents. Electoral units also were made smaller to facilitate direct contact between candidates and their constituents. Although local officials, acting contrary to regulations, sometimes intervened against independents and on behalf of party members, reports in the official media indicated that people seized this opportunity' to ventilate their grievances with uncommon vigor.

The newly elected assembly then proceeded to operate under procedures designed to make it more than just a rubber stamp of the party Central Committee. To underscore the National Assembly's independence, the Central Committee shifted its plenum date to follow rather than precede the assembly session in December 1988, and deputies were allowed to choose among and amend alternate bills submitted by government ministers. Debate was free, and press coverage of the debates compared favorably with practice in more liberal systems. In a less publicized but potentially more important development, the assembly's staff and resources were augmented.

One of the most important items of National Assembly business in June 1989 was the reform of the People's Councils and People's Committees, the institutions that are supposed to institutionalize popular participation in state

---

[2]Named after two independently published journals of arts and opinion, the Nhan Van-Giai Pham affair paralleled the "Hundred Flowers" movement in China.

affairs down to the local level. After intense debate, the assembly adopted two laws—one on organization and one on election of the councils and committees. The chief aim of reorganization was to make the directly elected councils more independent and more powerful in relation to their standing executive bodies, the People's Committees. Empowering the councils, moreover, would have the effect of reducing what reformers decried as the "usurpation" of local government by party chapters whose members tended to dominate the committees. Although screening by the Vietnam Fatherland Front and a cap on the number of candidates continued, elections took place under a new electoral law in November 1989 that permitted more candidates than seats in all but 12 districts (Agence France Presse, November 18, 1989).

Mass associations, which the party had so expertly manipulated to mobilize society for war but allowed to wither afterward, also experienced a revival on the basis of more open procedures. For the first time ever, a National Congress of the Vietnam Collective Peasants' Assocation was held in late 1987. In October 1988, the Sixth National Trade Union Congress adopted a new statute for the Confederation of Vietnamese Laborers, the official union for 4 million workers. The Congress then proceeded to eject 70 percent of the old members from the confederation's executive committee and elect four out of the five independent candidates. In an atmosphere described as one of "openness and democracy" and "frank dialogue," Trade Union Congress delegates demanded, and won, a personal appearance by Premier Do Muoi to hear their excoriations of the government (Radio Hanoi, October 24, 1988). Similar efforts to reinvigorate the Vietnam Fatherland Front, the central umbrella organization of all mass associations, began with the front's Third Congress in November 1988.

Of course, it was never the party's intention to transform the associations into independent social forces; mobilizing popular support for party-defined goals remained the associations' key aim. Potentially contradicting that aim, however, the reforms sought to create something to which state and party cadres could be held accountable other than to their own superiors.

Renovation also spilled over into the legal system, although efforts to consolidate state regulations, decrees, decisions, resolutions, circulars, and directives into properly promulgated laws had begun earlier. The National Assembly adopted the country's first criminal code in July 1985 and followed this up with a criminal-procedure code in January 1989. These codes presumed the innocence of the accused, abolished detention without trial, and committed the state to the prevention of torture. Thousands of political prisoners were given amnesty in 1987 and 1988.

To support economic reforms, particularly those permitting a private sector and expanded interaction with the world economy, the assembly began introducing legislation on foreign investment, industrial ownership, taxation of private enterprise, civil contracts, labor, and so forth. As one Vietnamese social scientist observed, in such legislation were the beginnings of the socialist republic's first body of civil law, one purpose being to guarantee the right of people and organizations to do whatever the law did not expressly forbid (Dao Tri Uc, 1990). While shortages of resources and qualified personnel delayed full implementation of the new laws and codes and political interference in judicial proceedings and human-rights violations still occurred, renovation included the aim of creating a legal order (Amnesty International, 1990).

In sum, political doi moi, at least up to mid-1989, sought to address the problems of "bureaucratic centralism" and declining popular confidence with structural and procedural changes in every major institution. The pace and scope were moderate only by comparison with changes that overturned communist regimes in Eastern Europe, and the changes placed Vietnam in the vanguard of party-ruled states attempting an orderly renewal. While economic renovation had certain spontaneous features, on the political side it was initiated entirely within the party, on approval from the top.

1989

Of course, political reform is almost never decreed in a vacuum. Where social pressures for change are absent, the elite has little incentive to revamp the political system that sustains it in power. As the experience of communist regimes everywhere has vividly demonstrated, even presumably "totalitarian" systems are susceptible to pressures from below. It may be useful to generalize from the experience of the Soviet Union and China and from the qualitatively different experience of Eastern Europe. The more firmly entrenched and legitimate the regime, the more likely pressure for change and proposals for reform will arise from within the apparatus of power itself, as in China and the former Soviet Union. Where the regime is less firmly grounded on popular acquiescence, habit, or consent, the more likely pressures and programs of reform will originate outside that apparatus, as in Eastern Europe. In this comparison, Vietnam has more in common with the Soviet Union and China than with the Eastern European countries. It is somewhat more like the latter, however, in the way that events elsewhere in the socialist community have resonated in its own domestic debate.

Up until the Chinese and Eastern European upheavals in 1989, pressure to increase the pace and scope of political doi moi appeared to grow. Citing Gorbachev's pathbreaking speech to the Nineteenth CPSU All-Union Conference, articles in Vietnam's official press condemned the deformation of socialism through "usurpation" by an all powerful party-state (*Quan Doi Nhan Dan*, January 19, 1989). Nguyen Huu Tho, the chair of the National Assembly, called for making state officials elected to the assembly nonvoting members and uncapping the number of candidates permitted to run in elections (Nguyen Huu Tho, 1989).

An influential academic described to me in late June 1989 his institute's officially sanctioned research, which he described as "strange for us and for the organs that have ordered us to do this work," on how to organize electoral procedures and representative institutions to better aggregate the interests of a multiclass society. Obviously aware of currents in Eastern Europe, his institute was also conducting research on the socioeconomic impact of the party's power monopoly with a view to recommending whether it should accept pluralism within the party or share its leading role with other parties. The party's opposition to pluralism, he said, was temporary, as reform logically would lead—eventually—to the appearance of other parties.

But most senior leaders, including radical economic reformers, were, by instinct and training, opposed to any dilution of the party's power and centrality in public affairs. While embracing administrative reform as necessary to unleash productive forces in the economy, these leaders predicted that unchecked demands for "absolute democracy and openness" would lead to a "chaotic and anarchic situation" (Tran Trong Tan, 1989). As pressures mounted in Poland and Hungary for multiparty democracy, but weeks before the Tiananmen incident of June 4, 1989, Party General Secretary Nguyen Van Linh declared to the Central Committee's sixth plenum that "we do not tolerate pluralism" (Nguyen Van Linh, 1989a).

Given this orientation, it is not surprising that Vietnamese leaders reacted as they did to the assaults on communist regimes in Eastern Europe and China. At the Central Committee's seventh plenum in August, 1989, Nguyen Van Linh sternly denounced "bourgeois liberalization, pluralism, political plurality, and multiopposition parties aimed at denying Marxism-Leninism, socialism, and the party's leadership." He also reaffirmed the principles of proletarian dictatorship, democratic centralism, and "the purity of Marxism-Leninism" (Nguyen Van Linh, 1989b). Subsequent statements and resolutions reaffirmed these positions and made stability the highest political priority. Tighter party and state controls over the media were announced at congresses of the journalists' and writers' associations in the fall of 1989. In December, an anticrime campaign that resulted in the arrest of 9,800 people in its first week had a chilling effect on political discussion, whether or not that was its aim (Radio Hanoi, December 10, 1989). The Central Committee's eighth plenum in March 1990 unveiled measures to renew "the party's leadership over the masses" and removed Tran Xuan Bach from the Political

Bureau for violating "party organizational principles and discipline." When foreign participants arrived in Hanoi for a workshop on reform in June, they were told not to criticize the party's positions on pluralism, the socialist line of development, and the party's leadership monopoly.[3]

The themes and terminology of public discourse in Hanoi, not to mention the sensitivity regarding politics of any but the party-approved ritual kind, seemed to echo the hard line in Beijing. Were the Vietnamese pushed by geopolitical realities and their own ideological proclivities, not to mention a sudden appreciation of shared "Asianness," into harmony with China? Into a defensive, xenophobic, security-obsessed suspension of political reform?

The Vietnamese Model

Before jumping to that conclusion, it is well to consider the Vietnamese interpretation of events in other socialist countries. Far from concluding that the Eastern European regimes should have suppressed popular protest with a whiff of grapeshot, the dominant view in Hanoi was that the ousted parties had reformed their politics too little and too late. With respect to Tiananmen Square, some Vietnamese expressed confidence that the same could not happen in Hanoi. They argued that Vietnamese students have a less dissident tradition (though they do not), and that the party was prepared to respond quickly, flexibly, and preemptively to popular pressures.[4]

An official summation came from Vo Chi Cong in a speech before the National Assembly in December 1989. In Eastern Europe, said Cong, regimes collapsed because they had adapted too slowly to the information explosion, growing popular political consciousness, and the scientific-technical revolution since the 1970s; they had violated the principles of "socialist democracy," alienated the masses, and lost popular support; and they had clung too long to an outmoded economic model (Vietnam News Agency, Dec. 19, 1989). In other words, by clinging rigidly to Stalinism, they had made themselves brittle and therefore easily broken. Vietnam, he said, would not commit this error.

[3]The author was an organizer of this workshop, which brought nine western academics together with a dozen Vietnamese for three days of discussion under the auspices of the Social Sciences Research Council and Vietnam's National Center for the Social Sciences. A selection of papers presented there may be found in Turley and Selden, 1992.

[4]The youthful radicalism of the party's gerontocratic leaders and the student protests in South Vietnam during the 1960s evidently were forgotten, perhaps because student dissidence has been relatively absent from the North since 1954. But, when several hundred students protested poor living conditions and low scholarship pay at several Hanoi colleges and universities during May and June 1989, the government did respond preemptively (Agence France Presse, June 17, 1989; Radio Hanoi, June 23, 1989).

There could be disagreement over the pace and scope of reform, but regarding the basic question of need, the choice was to "renew or die."

So the Vietnamese did not turn their backs on political doi moi. On the contrary, they resolved to press on, though in a form inspired by their own mobilizing past rather than by liberal principles. This form was "conservative" in the limited sense that it emphasized the maintenance of stability and the shoring up of the party's power monopoly in a framework of "democratic centralism." But it was renovative in the sense of preserving reforms already made, while expanding mass participation in public affairs with the intention of restoring popular acceptance of party leadership.

Whereas previous reforms had strengthened state-mass linkages through popularly elected representative assemblies, post-1989 reforms attempted to restore the party as the primary channel of communication between leaders and "the led." The Central Committee circulated drafts of important resolutions for public debate prior to its plena, beginning with the eighth plenum resolution in March 1990. That resolution, on the theme of "the renewal of the party's leadership over the masses," came under attack from youth groups as "old and unattractive" and from the southern leader Tran Bach Dang for repeating themes heard "hundreds of times before" (Radio Hanoi, February 17, 1990; Radio Hanoi, March 5, 1990). Still, debate was held and was well reported.

In August 1990, the ninth plenum initiated a similar debate on five draft resolutions to be submitted to the Seventh Party Congress in June 1991. This debate was conducted within the confines of local party committees and congresses, but apparently little attempt was made to stifle dissent or hide internal divisions. It was reported, for example, that some delegates to the congress of central mass-mobilization party organizations in April 1991 suggested changing the names of both the party and country (Hanoi Vietnam Television Network, April 28, 1991). At the Ha Nam Ninh Province congress, the issue of land use, ownership, and inheritance was hotly debated, with 370 out of 499 delegates supporting long-term leases and right of transfer (Radio Hanoi, April 28, 1991). A report on the Thua Thien-Hue congress gave voting figures on five discrete issues, including whether the VCP's status as the political vanguard of the working class should be written into regulation (290 out of 301 in favor) (Radio Hanoi, May 6, 1991). In this somewhat crude way, the party sought not only to rally the support of its members for what the center already had decided, but also to present itself as an instrument of interest aggregation.

A major topic of these resolutions was the revitalization of mass associations. This, of course, had been a theme of reform from the beginning, but emphasis shifted from making the associations more independent and responsive to their members' interests to restoring their traditional role as instruments for mobilizing mass support for the party and its policies. A vivid example in practice was afforded by the new national Veterans' Association. Formed in February 1990 partly to preempt potentially dissident unofficial organizations such as the Club of Former Resistance Fighters in Ho Chi Minh City, the association organized politically reliable veterans to help local party chapters cope with situations ranging from the suppression of "outside reactionary elements" and settling land disputes in the South to the maintenance of public order (Radio Hanoi, Sept. 17, 1990).

The other major thrust of post-1989 reform was the intensification of the party's purification and reorganization. This action continued the effort to make party members exemplary in their moral behavior and political commitment. Since party surveys had shown that only 30 percent of members had "truly maintained revolutionary quality and ethics," while 60 percent had failed to do so, and 10 percent were "degenerate" (*Tap Chi Cong San*, Feb. 1990), this campaign had the potential to result in a major purge. And as indicated earlier, one method of identifying members who lacked "revolutionary quality and ethics" was through citizen complaints and denunciation, thus providing a measure of popular participation in determining membership and mobility within the power structure.

As for representative assemblies, these continued to be elected under the somewhat more open procedures. In November 1989, 480,000 candidates contested 383,000 People's Council seats, and at the province level, an unprecedented 53 percent of the deputies elected were university graduates. At a National Conference on People's Councils in April 1990, the theme was finding ways for the councils, at all levels, "to operate with real power . . . and overcome the perfunctory manner of operations recently observed" (Radio Hanoi, May 21, 1990). The National Assembly continued to hold lively debates and cast divided votes; however, when legislation was vital to state-party interests, the number of independent voices was small.[5]

Political doi moi since 1989, then, has preserved the institutional changes introduced since 1985 while attempting to strengthen "socialist democracy." This concept of democracy is the orthodox Marxist-Leninist one of voluntary popular involvement in the implementation of decisions made by the party, but it has a special meaning in the Vietnamese context. Perhaps more than any other communist leadership, senior Vietnamese have kept faith that

---

[5]During the December 1989 session, rancorous debate on a new press law caused the Assembly to meet 21 times, including once at night. After repeated amendment, the law passed by a margin of 422 to 37 as reported in *Saigon Giai Phong*, January 5, 1990. In the June 1990 session, only 16 delegates out of 416 present cast votes against amendments to the criminal code and other bills concerning the courts and judicial procedures as reported on Radio Hanoi, June 27, 1990.

popular participation under party tutelage can combat bureaucratism, maintain an organic relationship between local party organs and the people, and preserve or restore mass support for the regime. Therefore, the party gave considerable attention to mass associations, public discussion of the party's draft resolutions, and citizen complaints about party members.

In responding this way, the party was simply revitalizing mass-regarding practices it had used previously to cope with threatening situations. As in China, the party's rise to power in an extremely competitive political and military environment had forced it to perfect such practices despite its authoritarian internal structure (Womack, 1987, 480). Leaders who themselves had risen to power during those struggles, winning national independence and unity against great odds in the process, naturally fell back on solutions that had worked well for them in the past. As in wartime, political doi moi attempted to recreate social harmony based on cadres' virtuous behavior, popular involvement in public affairs, and the masses' willing sacrifices under the party's benign guidance. . . Socialist democracy in the Vietnamese context was democratization in the mass-mobilizing sense.

All this is not to say that political reform based on the wartime model has had no critics. On the contrary, Vietnamese intellectuals educated in Eastern Europe and the Soviet Union had been influenced by heterodox currents in European socialism, and various concepts of liberalism and pluralism were the subjects of intense discussion up to mid-1989. Following the party's firm rejection of liberalism and pluralism in any form, the Seventh Congress draft texts provoked criticism in the party itself. The most widely publicized criticism came from Colonel Bui Tin, deputy editor-in-chief of the party newspaper *Nhan Dan* (The People). From the safe location of France in November 1990, Colonel Bui Tin delivered a "citizen's petition" to the Vietnamese ambassador in Paris and gave a long interview to the British Broadcasting Corporation in which he defended socialism as a socioeconomic system but called for a "democratic system really based on the people" that implied pluralist elements.[6] Perhaps more influential internally was a letter addressed to the party by Nguyen Khac Vien, a former intimate of Ho Chi Minh and a prestigious party intellectual. While not questioning essential socialist values, Nguyen Khac Vien blamed the country's ills on the party's

---

[6]Fragments of the BBC interview are translated in FBIS-EAS, February 8, 1991. I am indebted to Georges Boudarel for providing me with an apparently complete handwritten transcript in Vietnamese.

overweening interference in state affairs; castigated the party apparatus for trying to resurrect the past; and condemned the party's refusal to grant greater freedom of the press, thought, and assembly.[7]

Colonel Bui Tin and Nguyen Khac Vien no doubt spoke for others, but theirs were the voices of a tiny, isolated intelligentsia speaking from within the party. Neither of them threatened to leave the party, taking a faction with them as Boris Yeltsin had done in the Soviet Union. And they called not for the overthrow of socialism or for multiparty democracy in the Western sense, but for evolution toward a more open political process based on socialist values adapted to the needs of an industrializing society in an interdependent world.[8]

The debate was not between "conservatives" and "liberals"—meaningless terms in the Vietnamese context—but hinged on a difference of emphasis implied in the terms adaptation and renewal, with supporters of each claiming to embrace renovation. Adaptationists argued for the adjustment of both form and ethos to changing domestic circumstances and international standards, breaking if necessary with certain elements of the revolutionary past. Underscoring the failure of highly centralized political systems to meet the challenges of high-technological industrialization and global economic interdependence, they maintained that over the long term the most successful social systems were those based on political equality, direct participation, and personal freedom. The implication, of course, was that Vietnam's political system should permit a greater measure of these things.[9]

Renewalists replied that adaptation disguised a crude and unprincipled urge to imitate "'the world outside,'" ignoring the fact that no matter how much the world has changed, "politically and socially it still cannot overcome the bitter antagonism between capitalism and socialism" (Tran Xuan Truong, 1990). The solution, according to this line, was to revitalize institutional forms and ethos from the Vietnamese revolution's own past. Renewalists thus stressed continuity over change, while accepting the latter as necessary to develop the economy and attain socialism—goals that they shared with adaptationists.

Forward to the Past

The current trend in Vietnam's political reform does not satisfy the element that yearns for faster movement toward something more open and

---

[7]For a description of the Nguyen Khac Vien letter, see the article by Jacques Bekaert in the *Bangkok Post*, March 15, 1991 (FBIS-EAS, March 18, 1991).

[8]Bui Tin in his early 1991 BBC interview observed that the people "still want the party to revamp itself," though in the long run "real democracy is possible only if there is a multiparty system."

[9]For a statement of the adaptationist position, see Phan Dinh Dieu, 1990.

in step with perceived international norms. But it is still reform of a kind. In the past, the Vietnamese chanted the mantra of adapting Marxism-Leninism to their special circumstances, but in fact they always looked for ideas and support in foreign models and a united bloc of like-minded states. Now, for the first time in the party's existence (assuming it does not wish to accept direction from Beijing), it is truly on its own and must devise its own solutions. Alone and adrift since the collapse of the Soviet-centered socialist world order, the party must come to terms with its domestic environment without help or inspiration from abroad. The dynamic is no different from that which throughout history has caused the pieces of decaying empires to indigenize imperial institutions, gradually replacing imperial uniformity with national diversity. What kind of political system, then, should we expect to evolve from Vietnam's continuing attempt to indigenize Marxism-Leninism in a post-communist era?

The answer to that question first requires some discussion of prospects for the system's survival in its present form. From one perspective, they are not brilliant, for the party faces several crises that will be very difficult to overcome without unleashing forces of change that have swept other parties from power. One crisis already mentioned is low public confidence in the party's leadership. Although caused initially by such failures as poor economic performance, administrative incompetence, cadre corruption, and elite privilege, reform may actually worsen the problems by focusing attention on the contradiction between supposedly voluntary mass participation and the party's leadership monopoly. This contradiction is most apparent in the case of mass associations, which have been given a new freedom of operation yet must continue to accept the party's vanguard role in their internal affairs. Tolerated in wartime, the contradiction is felt more acutely in peace. The result is not the hoped-for gain in legitimacy but popular cynicism or indifference toward the public sphere. The more the party relies on mobilization to recover popular support, the more it risks driving people into private lives. The obvious way out of this crisis—allowing independent political organizations—is also a slippery slope terminating in the end of the party's power monopoly.

A second crisis involves leadership change, specifically the replacement of leaders who fully internalized the party's ideology and unique ethos on the road to power.[10] Over 70 percent of members who held leadership posts from district to central level in the late 1980s had joined the party between its

---

[10]This and the next two paragraphs owe much to conversations I had with Huynh Kim Khanh periodically for a year before his death. His thinking on these issues can be found in his last paper (Huynh Kim Khanh, 1990).

founding in 1930 and the August Revolution in 1945. This generation provided Vietnam decades of leadership unique in the communist world—indeed, unique almost anywhere—for its stability, unity, and experience in leading the nation through revolution and war. During preparations for the Seventh Congress, a large portion of these members, most of whom exceed 60 years of age, were "screened and retired" (Nguyen Dinh Huong, 1988). The screening was in fact a search for successors who would be "steadfast and fully qualified" to carry out doi moi as presently framed. Of the 1,176 delegates to the congress in June 1991, 61 percent attended for the first time and fewer than 20 percent were over 60 years of age (Radio Hanoi, June 21, 1991). While these figures suggest a major turnover, it is highly unlikely that succeeding generations will be as uniform in experience and outlook, or as consensual in leadership style, as the outgoing one.

The third major crisis can be described only as a loss of faith—in Marxism-Leninism, the ideal of proletarian internationalism, the party's version of history. This ideological crisis was inevitable for a movement that drew sustenance for so long from the super-heated idealism of war and revolution, only to face frustration, fatigue, and failure afterward. But it has been much exacerbated by the repudiation of Stalinism, even socialism in any form, in the countries to which the Vietnamese once looked for guidance to modernity. Every new liberalizing measure in the Soviet Union set off reverberations in Vietnam.[11] The party still has many true believers, of course, but widespread skepticism is openly admitted. The questioning of received verities challenges even the historical necessity of Vietnam's two wars for independence and unity (Dao Loc Binh, 1990). The proportion of party members under 30 years of age actually declined at the very time its ranks have most needed to grow, and the party's youth wing, the Ho Chi Minh Youth Group, lost half a million of its 4 million members in the first nine months of 1990.[12] For good reason, party leaders cannot be sure that generations to come will preserve or build on their work.

In historical perspective, these crises are not problems of and for the Vietnamese communist party alone. For they are symptoms of Vietnam's inability thus far as a nation to recover its socio-cultural equilibrium, or what

[11]An excellent example was a call for the depoliticization of the People's Army, which "has laid the ambition of some individuals or groups of people to seize control of the Army . . . [and] gradually cause the revolutionary Army to . . . become a bourgeois-style professional army," according to Maj. Gen. Le Quang, 1990. This call followed Gorbachev's decree abolishing the political departments of the Soviet Army and the KGB.

[12]The decline in members was from 23.5 percent to 21.3 percent between late 1986 and the end of 1988, according to *Tap chi Cong san*, February 1990. For a discussion of the decline of Youth Group membership see Agence France Presse (Hong Kong), September 28, 1990.

the French Vietnamologist Paul Mus referred to as "balance," and of the country's continuing inability to formulate an effective response to a rapidly changing world. It can be recalled that colonial destruction of traditionalist resistance toward the end of the nineteenth century splintered the Confucian consensus and caused Vietnamese intellectuals to search for an alternative doctrine of state. The influx of highly diverse ideas, however, led to greater ideological fragmentation of the Vietnamese elite than the nation had ever known. That fragmentation began to resolve itself in the gravitation of the intelligentsia to Marxism-Leninism during the 1920s and 1930s, and from then onward, it was the Vietnam Communist Party that defined the terms of Vietnam's entry into the modern world. Now, the party faces the future without a legitimating model abroad, without a blueprint, and without unity in its own ranks.

Prospects

One must not overlook, however, the very significant sources of resilience in the Vietnamese political system. Perhaps most important, the VCP achieved power through war and revolution rather than imposition by the Soviet Red Army. So the VCP is fundamentally more legitimate than its fallen Eastern European allies ever were. In the course of that struggle, it built a political structure in the hamlets and villages and rooted itself in popular patriotism without serious competition at the local level from its elite nationalist rivals. As a result, the VCP not only monopolizes power but is also identified with Vietnamese nationalism and sovereignty. In these respects, it is more firmly entrenched and more broadly accepted than the party of the former Soviet Union was, and than the party in China is (though only time will tell whether this is saying much). The admonition by senior leaders that Vietnam faces a choice between the party and chaos is self-serving, but it is not without a grain of truth.

Moreover, it must be remembered that Vietnam remains a predominantly agrarian society at a low level of economic development—more agrarian and poorer than China.[13] There is no middle stratum of merchants, managers,

---

[13]With about one-third the Gross National Product per capita, Vietnam has nothing yet to compare with China's long-established heavy-industrial centers; booming export processing zones; large numbers of students abroad; massive foreign investment; double-digit growth and resulting burgeoning, self-confident, and knowledgeable class of managers, entrepreneurs, skilled workers, and technicians. One similarity that provides each country a kind of shadow civil society—the white-collar intelligentsia abroad in Hong Kong and Taiwan for China, the emigré diaspora for Vietnam—is, in fact, an important difference in that the Vietnamese state is not threatened by the potential to interact with this intelligentsia through territorial incorporation.

entrepreneurs, and professionals to articulate alternative policies or to organize opposition. There is no national church and no movement like Solidarity to provide leadership and organization or a focus of loyalty outside the party, state, and affiliated mass associations. A civil society of relatively autonomous, nonpolitical social and cultural space, located outside but interacting with the institutional framework of the state, whose emergence and gradual expansion played such an important role in the political upheavals in Eastern Europe and the Soviet Union, can hardly be said to exist in Vietnam. Although Leninist theory and practice—as exemplified in the arrest, trial, and conviction in 1991 of the Amnesty International activist Dr. Nguyen Dan Que for "activities aimed at overthrowing the people's government"—has done its part to prevent the emergence of a civil society in Vietnam, economic, social, and historical conditions would have made it weak even in a more permissive political environment. By comparison with other "real" socialist countries, Vietnam has yet to develop a politically meaningful, self-organizing society outside the nexus of party, state, and people.

One must give credit too to a lesson from the party's revolutionary past, namely, the senior leaders' firm belief that the revolution will survive only so long as it enjoys a sympathetic environment. Steeped in this myth of "people's war," party leaders have a long history of striving for popular support through organizational preemption. While believing that "unprincipled" and "overhasty" concessions to opposition forces were partly to blame for the unraveling of other regimes, Vietnamese leaders at least understand the need to change rather than wait for change to be forced on them. Moreover, though gerontocratic, none of them has personal stature or charisma that is crucial to regime stability. Unlike Honecker, Ceaucescu, Zhivkov, Kim, Castro, Deng Xiaoping, or Ne Win, Vietnam's leaders can retire or die without taking the system down with them.

The greatest challenge to the regime lies not in any imminent danger of collapse but in the long-term task of institutionalization in the absence of a proven model. In this situation, the only way ahead is to proceed empirically, and this is just what General Secretary Nguyen Van Linh advocated in September 1989: "Principles are merely major guidelines. How common principles are manifested specifically in space and time in life must be answered through life itself. General abstract principles do not exist. Truth is always concrete and revolution creative" (Nguyen Van Linh, 1989c). Like Deng Xiaoping's summons to pragmatism *before* Tiananmen, this statement opens the door to experimentation.

Given Vietnam's experience and existing institutions, where does experiment lead? Most likely it leads toward a political system resembling the familiar East Asian model, whose main components are Confucian political culture, colonial heritage, agricultural reform, export-led development, continuous industrial upgrading, emphasis on education, continuity in a ruling elite or party, and a strong authoritarian state. Significantly, following the Sixth Party Congress, the Council of Ministers approved research into the relevance of tradition to development, which supported the integration of traditional values into Vietnamese socialism.[14] Moreover, a good deal of officially sanctioned social science research in Vietnam has focused on the political economies of the four Asian "tigers," particularly South Korea. Bereft of stable, successfully developing, and authentically socialist allies, the Vietnamese already have looked for comfort in the traditions they share with prospering neighbors.

But there is an important difference between Asia's capitalist authoritarians and the Vietnamese: the legacy of a mobilizing past, with its norms of mass participation and communal autonomy. Under political doi moi, citizens are not supposed to be mere subjects, as authoritarians elsewhere have treated them. They are regarded, rather, as active participants, albeit under the party's guidance, in the management of local affairs and the monitoring of state behavior. Although the VCP has long advocated such participation under the rubric of "popular mastery," doi moi has committed the VCP to the "perfection" of this fundamental element of "socialist democracy." Whatever the formalism of participation under one-party rule, doi moi expands popular involvement in public affairs. Under such a regime of mobilizational authoritarianism, popular involvement in public affairs is both legitimate and encouraged, while in the conventional, nonparticipatory form it is suppressed.

This notion of an East Asian model with socialist characteristics deserves more attention than I can give it here. But the interaction of politics and economics in a Vietnamese variant of this model deserves brief comment. A question the Vietnamese themselves have posed is how far economic development can proceed under existing institutions without causing significant change in the political system. As discussed elsewhere in this volume, a keystone of economic doi moi is the "multisectoral economy," and already the private and cooperative sectors generate more than two-thirds of gross national income. At what point will the plural economy produce significant pressures for the pluralization of politics? Both Marxist and liberal social science predict that market-based economic development will lead inevitably to such pressures through the creation of an autonomous middle stratum of entrepreneurs, professionals, and managers.

[14]A reflection of what was apparently a major undertaking can be found in Tuong Lai et al., 1989.

Such pressures do not, however, require accommodation in Western-style parliamentary institutions and practices. As Asian examples suggest, economic development can take place under single-party rule for a long time, and single-party dominance is the Asian norm even in systems whose constitutions permit competition.

In Vietnam, it is difficult to imagine the social base on which a party capable of rivaling the VCP could be built in the foreseeable future. A welter of fractious patronage groups, yes; a party with symbolic power, patriotic appeal, and a national following, no. No party besides the VCP has ever had a mass membership in the countryside as well as towns and cities of all regions. The party, moreover, must uphold the single-party system not only for ideological reasons but also because, as the leadership and probably most members believe, competitive politics would exacerbate regional divisions and invite disruption by overseas Vietnamese.[15] Economic development is more likely to restructure politics within the VCP itself than to create credible alternative parties.

Even so, economic development under doi moi does have the potential to be politically destabilizing. Although a high level of development is associated with stability, a high rate of growth in poor countries redistributes income, social prestige, and political power, mobilizing the "losers" into dissidence. The shift from central planning to markets merely aggravates the situation by exacerbating inflation and unemployment at the same time that it raises expectations of immediate improvement. To maintain stability during rapid growth and reform, governments must either suppress opposition or preempt it by coordinating political reforms with economic ones. Up to the present, the Vietnamese have used coercion in moderation and emphasized preemption, avoiding what they believe to have been the Soviet mistake of liberalizing politics without concomitant economic reform and the Chinese error of marketizing the economy while resisting political change. The fact that Vietnam has been spared violent upheaval while other communist parties have been overthrown or shaken may suggest that this middle way is working.

But Vietnam has not yet experienced sustained rapid growth, the kind that destabilizes. A long growth spurt resulting from foreign trade and investment after the United States lifts its embargo could be the most serious challenge on the horizon to Vietnam's political stability.

---

[15]See General Secretary Linh's comment that multiparty politics would "create conditions for the reactionary forces of revenge within the country and from abroad to rear their heads . . ." in his political report to the Seventh Congress. Radio Hanoi, June 24, 1991.

References

Agence France Presse (Hong Kong), June 17, 1989. In Foreign Broadcast Information Service, *Daily Report: East Asia* (hereafter FBIS-EAS), June 19, 1989.

Agence France Presse, November 18, 1989. In FBIS-EAS, November 20, 1989.

Agence France Presse, September 28, 1990, citing *Tien Phong* (Vanguard monthly) magazine. In FBIS-EAS, October 1, 1990.

Amnesty International, U.S.A., 1990. *Vietnam: "Renovation (Doi Moi), the Law and Human Rights in the 1980s.* New York: Amnesty International, U.S.A., February.

Bangkok Post, March 15, 1991. In FBIS-EAS, March 18, 1991.

Dao Loc Binh. 1990. "Some Views on the World Situation and the Revolution," *Quan Doi Nhan Dan* (People's Army daily), October 28. In FBIS-EAS, July 2, 1990.

Dao Tri Uc. 1990. "Phap luat Viet Nam trong qua trinh doi moi kinh te xa hoi" (Vietnamese Law in the Process of Economic Renovation), paper presented at the workshop on Renovation in Vietnam, Hanoi, June 27-30, p. 3.

Fforde, Adam, and de Vylder, Stefan. 1988. *Vietnam—An Economy in Transition.* Stockholm: Swedish International Development Authority.

Hanoi Vietnam Television Network, April 28, 1991. In FBIS-EAS, May 17, 1991.

Huynh Kim Khanh. 1990. "The Rescuing of a Revolution: Political Renovation in Vietnam and the Road Ahead," presented at a conference on "East Asia: The Road Ahead," at the Institute of East Asian Studies, University of California, Berkeley, March 29-31.

Kyodo News Service, April 7, 1987. In FBIS, *Daily Report: Asia & Pacific* (FBIS-APA), April 7, 1987.

Le Quang (Lt. Col.). 1990. "Thuc chat quan diem 'phi chinh chi hoa quan doi' " (The True Nature of the Call for "Depoliticization of the Army"), *Tap Chi Quoc Phong Toan Dan* (All People's National Defense monthly), November, p. 87.

Nhan Dan (The People daily), July 26, 1988. In FBIS-EAS, September 29, 1988.

————. July 31, 1988. In FBIS-EAS, August 16, 1988.

Nguyen Dinh Huong. 1988. "Formulate Plans for Leading Cadres," *Tap Chi Cong San* (The Communist monthly), July, pp. 22-26. In FBIS-EAS, September 13, 1988.

Nguyen Huu Tho. 1989. "Renovation of Mechanism—Pressing Need of the Renovation Process," *Tap Chi Cong San*, March, pp. 1-4. In FBIS-EAS, May 5, 1989.

Nguyen Van Linh. 1989a. Speech at closing session of sixth plenum of the central committee. Broadcast over Radio Hanoi, March 31. In FBIS-EAS, March 31, 1989.

————. 1989b. Speech at seventh plenum of the central committee. Broadcast over Radio Hanoi, August 28. In FBIS-EAS, August 29, 1989.

————. 1989c. Speech at the Nguyen Ai Quoc Institute, broadcast over Radio Hanoi, October 2. In FBIS-EAS, October 3, 1989.

————. 1991. Political report to the Seventh Congress, broadcast over Radio Hanoi, June 24. In FBIS-EAS, June 16, 1991.

Phan Dinh Dieu. 1990. "Stabilization and Development in the Current Situation," *Tap Chi Cong San*, September, pp. 25-29. In FBIS-EAS, November 30, 1990.

Quan Doi Nhan Dan (People's Army daily).

Radio Hanoi, July 2, 1988. In FBIS-EAS, July 8, 1988.

Radio Hanoi, October 24, 1988. In FBIS-EAS, October 27, 1988.

Radio Hanoi, March 31, 1989. In FBIS-EAS, March 31, 1989.

Radio Hanoi, June 23, 1989. In FBIS-EAS, June 26, 1989.

Radio Hanoi, August 28, 1989. In FBIS-EAS, August 29, 1989.

Radio Hanoi, December 10, 1989. In FBIS-EAS, December 12, 1989.

Radio Hanoi, February 17, 1990. In FBIS-EAS, February 20, 1990.

Radio Hanoi, March 5, 1990. In FBIS-EAS, March 15, 1990.

Radio Hanoi, May 21, 1990. In FBIS-EAS, May 25, 1990.

Radio Hanoi, June 27, 1990. In FBIS-EAS, June 27, 1990.

Radio Hanoi, September 17, 1990. In FBIS-EAS, September 21, 1990.

Radio Hanoi, October 10, 1990. In FBIS-EAS, October 10, 1990.

Radio Hanoi, March 14, 1991. In FBIS-EAS, March 20, 1991.

Radio Hanoi, April 28, 1991. In FBIS-EAS, May 22, 1990.

Radio Hanoi, May 6, 1991. In FBIS-EAS, May 30, 1991.

Radio Hanoi, June 21, 1991. In FBIS-EAS, June 26, 1991.

Radio Hanoi, September 18, 1991. In FBIS-EAS, September 24, 1991.

Saigon Giai Phong (Liberated Saigon daily), January 5, 1990. In FBIS-EAS, January 25, 1990.

Tap Chi Cong San. February 1990. In FBIS-EAS, March 27, 1990.

Tran Trong Tan. 1989. "How to Clearly Understand the CPV Central Committee Political Bureau's Conclusion on Ideological Work," *Nhan Dan*, January 23, 24. In FBIS-EAS, March 1, 2, 1989.

Tran Xuan Truong (Maj. Gen.). 1990. "Renovation or Adaptation," *Quan Doi Nhan Dan*, October 15. In FBIS-EAS, November 30, 1990.

Tuong Lai, et al. 1989. "Truyen thong va hien dai trong su nghiep moi cua chung ta" (Tradition and Modernity in our new Task), *Xa Hoi Hoc* (Sociological Review monthly), January, pp. 45–64.

Turley, William S., and Selden, Mark (eds.). 1992. *Reinventing Vietnamese Socialism: Doi Moi in Comparative Perspective*. Boulder, Co.: Westview Press.

Vietnam News Agency (VNA), February 21, 1990. In FBIS-EAS, February 23, 1990.

———. December 19, 1989. In FBIS-EAS, December 20, 1989.

Womack, Brantly. 1987. "The Party and the People: Revolutionary and Postrevolutionary Politics in China and Vietnam," *World Politics*, XXXIX, July 4, pp. 479–507.

13

Concluding Remarks: Key Issues in the Reform Process

Börje Ljunggren

In this volume, reform in Indochina, Vietnam, Laos, and Cambodia has been addressed from a number of perspectives by scholars and practitioners with wide-ranging experiences and backgrounds in the region. Economists, political scientists, anthropologists, a journalist, an aid administrator, and others who have contributed to this book bring their specialized knowledge and expertise to bear on the issues of reform. Some have looked at the region of a specific country from a macro perspective; others have documented conditions in a specific village. In all the chapters, there is a unifying theme: ongoing economic reforms go far beyond the mending of an ailing socialist system. None of the countries today is a centrally planned economy. Markets, although imperfect, now govern prices, agriculture is no longer collectivized, and the private sector is already of considerable importance in all three countries.

However, while they share some common conditions, these countries also differ in important respects. Laos is carrying out its reform under conditions that are, in many respects, normal for a deeply underdeveloped socialist country undertaking adjustment and reform. It enjoys substantial support from international financial institutions (and is actually risking to become addicted to aid, mobilizing very limited financial resources of its own). Vietnam, on the other hand, is undertaking its reform almost totally without international support (U.S. $2 per capita) while facing a continued U.S. embargo. Nevertheless, its economy has undergone profound systemic changes, especially since 1989. Cambodia's situation is extremely difficult and remains so even after the international agreement reached in Paris in October of 1991. The country will continue to suffer for a very long time from the losses of the Pol Pot years—the vast majority of its trained manpower did not survive. In her paper in this volume, May Ebihara tells the story of the Pol Pot years from the point of view of the village where she did field research almost 30 years ago. Still, for Cambodia, the past decade has been a decade of recovery as well as reform. The achievements of the Hun Sen regime are greater than generally recognized. But so are its current problems. The public sector is in a state of limbo, threatening the legitimacy of the state, and further weakening the institutions on which future developments (beyond the elections scheduled for 1993) depend.

Despite major differences with regard to endowments as well as current conditions, all three countries now face a number of critical issues in their reform efforts. Discussed here are the four key issues that we have considered to be of particular long-term importance:

- state capacity to manage reform
- domestic resource mobilization and international aid
- reform and the social sectors
- the political dimension of reform

State Capacity to Manage Reform

What is "the developmental strength of a state"? (White, 1984, pp. 98–100). This question is occupying an increasingly large number of political scientists. In his monograph, *Democracy and the Developmental State,* Georg Sorensen has tried to identify the key elements of the "developmental state" (Sorensen, 1992).

Sorensen suggests that three elements are of particular importance. Two of these core elements—autonomy and capacity—are structural features, while the third one—statecraft—is what Sorensen calls a "policy element." The elements are set in a larger context that includes the sociohistorical framework of the state on the one hand, and the outcomes the state is able to "produce" on the other (Sorensen, 1992, p. 24). To do justice to the model, each one of the elements would have to be presented at some length. However, a brief summary of the concepts does shed light on the questions that one has to address when trying to assess the developmental strength of Vietnam, Laos, and Cambodia. The concept of autonomy, which Sorensen uses with reference to a work by Theda Skocpol, means at a minimum that a state "may formulate and pursue goals that are not simply reflective of the demands or interests of social groups, classes, or society" (quoting Skocpol, 1985, p. 9, in Sorensen, 1992, p. 15). The second element—capacity— "basically means that there is an efficient bureaucratic apparatus, guided and shielded by a political elite that gives priority to economic development" (Sorensen, 1992, p. 22). The essence of the third element, statecraft, pertains to the ability of a state "to shape the environment to one's own advantage" (quoting Chan, 1988, p. 219, in Sorensen, 1992, p. 13).

Democracy is, as Sorensen sees it, no prerequisite, as shown by East Asian examples such as Taiwan and South Korea, but Sorensen argues that one important factor behind the trend toward democracy in these countries " is the tendency for the developmental state to undermine authoritarianism through its very success: rapid economic development produces stronger social forces outside the state apparatus: private business, an industrial labor force, etc." (Sorensen, 1992, p. 49).

Sorensen's analysis does not focus specifically on the question of the role of the state and party apparatus, on the one hand, and the market on the other. However, in his analysis of China, he discusses how the monopolization of power by an elite may lead to petrification, retarding economic development and reducing the ability of the system "to deliver." In the case of Vietnam, Laos, and Cambodia this question of monopolization of power by an elite is closely related to Sorensen's core elements. In the tradition of marxist-leninist one-party states, they would have a political elite that would not see any limits to its own right to interfere, would not leave any defined area for an efficient bureaucracy with integrity of its own, and would not provide the space required for statecraft to develop institutionally. We will return to the broader question of political change in the sections below about the dynamics of revolution and reform.

In his oft-quoted essay entitled "On the Sequencing of Reform in Eastern Europe," Hans Genberg concludes that "macroeconomic stabilization should be placed at the beginning of the reform sequence with the proviso that the policies introduced include the elimination of the principal causes of fiscal imbalances, namely the easy credits to and subsidies given by the government to state enterprises" (Genberg, 1991, p. 27).

Genberg addresses a critical aspect of the reform processes in Vietnam, Laos, and Cambodia. None of the countries confronted this macroeconomic stabilization issue until later stages in the process, and inflation has been a major threat to their reforms. (In the case of Vietnam, inflation hovered for years at an annual rate of several hundred percent.) Genberg's conclusion, however, has two dimensions. One concerns which policy measures to choose when launching a reform; the other underlying one, concerns the capacity of a country to make the analysis, formulate policy, implement policy, and monitor its implementation, that is the institutional capacity required to formulate policies and pursue reform. The ability of a country to create efficient—and legitimate—institutions is the ultimate test that determines whether it can forge ahead as a reforming economy.

Present state structures in Vietnam, Laos, and Cambodia are the product of a Marxist-Leninist tradition, hence different from the structures needed today. While trimming their huge bureaucracies, which are generally oversized and underpaid, all three countries must build institutional capacity to manage change. This demands a radical change in the way the state is perceived as well as in the relationship between state and party. In the longer run, the whole "polity" of the society must develop a new openness, that is, transparency, free debate, and accountability on which a continuous reform process can be built.

What is required is clearly not an abdication by the state through, what Lance Taylor calls, "wholesale liberalization moves," but prudent "hands-on management of a mixed economic system" (Taylor, 1988, p. 168). Market and state will remain imperfect, the commanding task being to develop both. Dismissing the state would be as detrimental as the traditional socialist "sin" of not recognizing the market. Virtually all cases of successful economic development have involved a measure of state intervention. Interventionist strategies demand, however, considerable prudence, skills, and flexibility, and a readiness to accept mistakes and correct them, in other words, the qualities that constitute the "developmental state." Special interests must not be allowed to control interventionist policies and corruption must be curtailed. Communist *nomenklatura*, as Kornai, Ferdinand, and others have noted, obviously constitutes a major obstacle to the developmental state (Kornai, 1992, Ferdinand, 1989).

To what extent then has the role of the state and the party in the emerging market economies of Laos, Vietnam, and Cambodia been redefined? We have seen how central planning has been dismantled, and how the state and collective sectors have been reduced while the nonstate sphere has expanded through decollectivization of agriculture and a growing role for the private sector in manufacturing, construction, and services. The new, emerging role of the state is also illustrated by recent efforts to separate state and party, rule by law rather than decree, reduce the bloated bureaucracies, and reform public administration.

Laos. Among the three countries, Laos has been the most consistent when it comes to addressing the question of the role of the state in a developing market economy. The state has disengaged itself from involvement in productive activities having passed through the stage of ambivalence. The ongoing reform of the banking sector and the introduction of a new tax system are current examples of its effort to build institutions geared to the needs of a market economy. Like Vietnam, Laos is making serious efforts to create the legal framework for a mixed economy. The comparative advantage Laos has over Vietnam is that it did not build up the heavy bureaucracy that Vietnam did and, hence, has less vested interest in the old structures, such as a relatively large state-owned enterprise sector and an entrenched party machinery. Successful reform of the state assumes that the tasks of building new institutions and dismantling and revamping old ones are addressed simultaneously and with equal fervor.

The Lao draft "Policy Framework for the Public Investment Program, 1991–1995" contains the clearest statement about the role of the state in a reforming economy made so far by any of the three countries:

> The Third Five Year Plan calls for the private sector to be the main engine of growth in the manufacturing sector. The Government role increasingly will be restricted to maintaining an economic environment to promote private sector growth, ensuring that appropriate infrastructure is constructed, and ensuring that skilled labor is available. However, as the public sector still dominates manufacturing, policies to improve the efficiency of state-owned enterprises until they can be privatized will be important. (Lao P.D.R. 1990b, p. 42)

Both this document (prepared for the government by a consultant team) and the outcomes of the Fifth Party Congress held in March 1991 indicate that there is reason to believe that the Lao notion of the role of the state has indeed changed. In the "Political Report of the Executive Committee of the Central Committee of the Lao People's Revolutionary Party (LPRP)" presented by the Fifth Party Congress, a strong emphasis is put on "eradicating the leftovers of the centralized bureaucratic management system, utilizing the market-oriented economy adjusted by the state, promoting the strong development of market economy" (Lao P.R.P., 1991, p. 17). The state "will not directly manage the business production but it will concentrate mainly on playing its role of macro-adjustment with clear and firm economic instruments and on a legal basis" (Lao P.R.P., 1991, p. 18).

The idea of development through all-encompassing mobilization by party and state has, over a decade, given way to the idea that the main function of the state is to create the physical and social infrastructure and the stable policy environment that is required for equitable market-based development. The prevailing neoclassical notion of the role of the government in planning and finance in a market-oriented economy is "to 'plan' the physical, social, and physiological *environment* of private agents rather than to plan what these agents are supposed to do" (quoting Lindbeck, 1986, p. 8, in Wade, 1990, p. 13). Less than 10 years ago, the Lao government would have regarded such a notion as a negation of its deepest convictions. Today, that is no longer the case; the government obviously does not exclude public interventions in the economy. In some respects, the Lao government may actually underestimate what will be required of government, beyond adjustment and reform, for large parts of the country to develop.

The shortage of trained manpower, reflected in all institutions in Laos, will delay the buildup of the institutions required for a functioning Lao economy. Government offices are overstaffed by extremely poorly paid officers. There are very few Western-trained economists. As the reform has evolved, Laos has been receiving rather substantial technical assistance that has generated a noticeable degree of mutual confidence. The country must, however, attach the highest priority to building up its own institutional capacity to undertake policy analysis. For this to be possible, Laos must develop the institutional capacity to collect data and do analytical work, including allowing research activities that are not controlled by party and state. Today, hardly any social science research that can be regarded as academically free is undertaken in Laos. (Neither Laos nor Cambodia has any indigenous research capacity, while Vietnam has a large number of research institutes whose freedom to pursue research has increased significantly during the last few years. Lack of adequate training, lack of access to professional literature, and inadequate salaries are often perceived by economists to be problems at least as serious as the control exerted by the party and the state apparatus.)

Vietnam. Vietnam represents, in some respects, the opposite of Laos and Cambodia. Its literacy rate is one of the highest in the world for a least developed country, and it has a wide range of institutions of higher learning and research. Few observers doubt that a nonisolated Vietnam has the capacity to bring about rapid economic change in the medium term. Provided continuous reform, its capabilities to generate development are qualitatively different from those of Laos and Cambodia. But Joel Migdal's assessment of Vietnam's capabilities obviously is not based on its ability to manage systems change, as he says, ". . . it is true that only a handful of Asian, African and Latin American states fall high on the continuum of 'stateness,' or state capabilities. Israel, Cuba, China, Japan, Vietnam, Taiwan, North Korea, and South Korea have been the highest in state capabilities from those continents" (Migdal, 1988, p. 267).

Vietnam's reform process has become increasingly far reaching. There has, however, been considerable ambivalence within the Communist Party of Vietnam regarding the fundamental question of how to redefine the role of the state and the collective. The nomenklatura sees its interests threatened. The documents prepared for the Seventh Party Congress and the outcome of the congress show that influential interests within the party would like the state and the provinces to maintain a significant role in manufacturing as well as in "whole-sale trade, combined with retail trade of essential goods" (Vietnam, Communist Party of, 1991). Also, while granting peasant families long-term tenure on land, they still would like to "enhance the role of [cooperative] managers' boards in managing and regulating production. . . ." The new constitution, adopted on April 15, 1992, may be seen as reflecting the same ambivalence. The economic system is described in the following way in a new paragraph of Article 15 of the *1992 Constitution*:

> The state develops a socialist-oriented multi-sectoral commodity economy driven by the state-regulated market mechanism. The multi-sectoral structure of the economy with diversified types of production and business organisation is based on ownership by the entire people along with collective and private ownership, of which the first two are the cornerstone (Vietnam, Socialist Republic of, 1992, p. 7).

The article is a fascinating example of Vietnamese consensus building. It does, however, constitute a radical departure when compared to the same paragraph in the old constitution (1980), according to which the economy should be transformed directly into a socialist economy "without going through the stage of capitalist development" (Vietnam, Socialist Republic of, 1981, p. 17). When looking at what actually happens in Vietnam—and has happened during the last decade in Vietnamese society—and considering the precarious economic realities of the Vietnamese state, it becomes evident that a gradual adjustment to a more limited notion of the role of the state and the cooperative is gaining increased acceptance also within the party. Reforming a party with the ideological traditions of the Communist Party of Vietnam is a process that is bound to take time, as it involves fundamental principles as well as narrow self-interests.

Another important, interrelated reason that the reform process is cumbersome is the state of Vietnam's civil service, and the relationship between the civil service and the party apparatus. The country's large civil service is in need of thorough reforms. So far, it retains much of its old bureaucratic form and distributive roles. However, the government has begun to restructure the public sector, and employment within the sector as a whole, including the civil service, the army, and state enterprises, declined by more than 20 percent between 1988 and 1991, shedding more than one million in all. The dismissal of another 400,000 is supposed to be completed by the end of 1992.

The bureaucracy, however, needs more than a reduction in size. It also needs reform. A basic requirement is profound salary-reform, which would allow government employees to survive on a public salary. The present situation inevitably leads to increasing absenteeism, corruption, and public cynicism. Certain changes are in the offing. Hence, in the "Strategy for the Socioeconomic Stabilization and Development of our Country up to the Year 2000," adopted by the Seventh Party Congress, the two major objectives are (1) "To revamp the State apparatus in order to enhance managerial effectiveness and strengthen judicial processes," and (2) "To fundamentally renovate State employee work in line with the new system."

Regarding personnel, the strategy further states that it will be necessary to "make a clear-cut distinction between *elected personnel* operating on a fixed-term basis and *professional administrators and public employees*" (Vietnam, Communist Party of, 1991, pp. 193-95). In fact, a minister of personnel, with the task of developing a more professional civil service, has been appointed. How far this will lead is not clear. The party has shown concrete interest in changes, such as career planning, that would lead to a more independent civil service. A crucial question is how much change the party will ultimately consider compatible with its leading role.

Training is another critical need, especially in areas at the core of the reform, such as economics and management. Few persons in government have training in macroeconomic management, and government policy is formulated on the basis of insufficient documentation. Only recently have possibilities to study abroad at Western institutions been available, and it will take many years before Vietnam has a reasonable number of adequately trained economists. A number of senior Vietnamese officials have, over the years, developed a good grasp of the nature of a market economy. Their understanding is, however, insufficient for Vietnam to be able to assess advice critically and draw on expertise. Institutional capacity is lacking, and it will develop only after Vietnamese have received adequate training abroad and after reform has penetrated universities and other institutions of higher learning.

Cambodia. Virtually no other country has faced such a daunting task of rebuilding a society as Cambodia. Still, a fragile foundation was laid during the last decade through reconstruction and reform. Whatever has been created is, however, very rudimentary, and in the absence of a political solution, the state is becoming increasingly weak and inefficient. It is unable to raise the bare minimum of revenue that would allow it to pay a civil servant or a teacher a salary worth the name—even though trade and commerce have produced ostentatious wealth in some sectors. The state is facing a crisis of legitimacy, aggravated by growing corruption. The public sector may be said to be in a state of limbo, revenues in 1992 amounting to as little as 4 percent of GDP.

The country is in extraordinary need of carefully designed training and advisory programs in almost every field—the economic field being a critical one. Until now, Cambodia has managed its economy and pursued reform with practically no external advice, with virtually no one trained in the macromanagement of a market economy within the present administration in Phnom Penh. Cambodians in exile could play a role in the development of their country's economy, if brought back by the United Nations. Technical assistance is urgently needed.

Since August 1987 when the Phnom Penh government announced its "policy of national reconciliation," and since the subsequent dialogue between Prime Minister Hun Sen and Prince Sihanouk, the Hun Sen government has de facto been involved in a major reform of the state. In part, the process has been outright crisis management. However, it has also taken shape as Prime Minister Hun Sen and the reformists around him try to find more viable paths to "nation building." "The question is nation building. We are not looking to build up Marxism or Communism. We are looking to improve the welfare of the people" (quoting *The New York Times*, April 11, 1989, in Hess, 1990, p. 157). In a speech on planning delivered in January of 1991, Hun Sen addressed the question of how to reform the state: "We must direct our economic management in accordance with the requirements of the merchandise economy [the market] and the increasing role of the state of Cambodia in international trade, instead of sticking to an economic system with heavy red tape" (information provided by Grant Curtis). In October 1991, only days before the convening of the final Paris Conference on Cambodia, the ruling Kampuchean People's Revolutionary Party adjusted to the new realities by explicitly endorsing a free-market economy and multi-party democracy. The party also declared, as reported by the *Far Eastern Economic Review* in an article entitled "Exit Heng Samrin," that Prince Sihanouk, not president Heng Samrin, would be its presidential candidate (Hiebert, 1991). The ambition to remain a political force rather than ideology has obviously been of decisive importance in shaping the strategy.

What is clear is that the conceptual role of the state and the party is undergoing fundamental change. Equally clear is that it undoubtedly will take decades—without civil war and isolation—before Cambodia will have an administration with salaries and institutional practices at levels that may give it a measure of integrity. The strategies and tactics of the Khmer Rouge are a foreboding and continuous threat.

Domestic Resource Mobilization and International Aid

The experiences of other developing countries indicate that a necessary—but in no way sufficient—prerequisite for the longer term development of Vietnam, Laos, and Cambodia is that they gradually manage to achieve public and private investments, including foreign investments, that total at least 20 percent of their GDP. Equally important is that these investments are used efficiently to ensure a good balance between public investments in fields like human resource development and physical infrastructure and private investments within the main sectors of the economies of these countries.

The current investment levels are either low (probably around 15 percent in Laos), very low (8.5 percent in Vietnam), or exceptionally low (Cambodia);

actual investments most probably are higher than the statistics show because the national accounts do not reflect the expansion of private investment in construction and the informal sector, nor do they adequately capture private agricultural investments. Vietnam's public investments have fallen to less than 4 percent of GDP (1990), a level that would be extremely low for any country and that seems almost unimaginable for a country that, until recently, has regarded the state as the "engine of development."

Both Vietnam and Laos suffer from very low levels of revenue, estimated at 11 to 12 percent of GDP. Cambodia's figure is unknown but is estimated at 4 percent of GDP (1992). All three countries have seen their traditional sources of revenue dwindle. In the past, central planning and the system of controlled and distorted prices of inputs and outputs determined the volumes of turnover and enterprise taxes that state-owned enterprises would transfer to the budget. During the last few years, however, this dominant source of revenue has fallen drastically (by 50 percent in Vietnam), at the same time that aid from the former Soviet Union has ceased to be a source of revenue.

Expenditures are also very low. Recurrent expenditures in Vietnam equaled 15 percent of GDP in 1990. The level in Laos is even lower (11.3 percent in 1990), while Cambodia's total government expenditures, according to one of the few existing sources, stand at around 8 percent of GDP. Still, current expenditures exceed revenue. Public savings are therefore negative; external assistance finances not only the public investment programs but also parts of public consumption. Cambodia is facing a large, unfunded deficit.

Nothing is known about private savings. While they certainly exist and— judging from the considerable import of gold and the volumes of dollars in private hands—may be rather significant, savings in the form of bank deposits are small to negligible. A significant beginning was made in Vietnam in 1989, but the resurgence of inflation and negative real interest rates have reversed the trend, causing a preference for other forms of savings. The real interest rates in Laos have been highly positive for more than a year, but confidence in the banking system has been lacking—one reason being the difficulty of withdrawing savings at will. According to one recent study, significant increases in financial savings through the banking system have been occurring during the last two years (Pham, 1991, p. 50).

A crucial task lying ahead for all three countries is to build the volumes and structures of revenues and savings necessary for the state to be able to shoulder its role in the development process. Long-term development cannot be based on aid flows that are not combined with growing domestic savings. Such imbalances inevitably lead to aid dependence and distortions that hamper the development of viable institutions and programs.

Laos is, as we have seen, at great risk of falling into a position of such dependency. Enjoying easy access to aid, it annually receives development assistance in the order of $30 to $40 per capita, on generally soft terms. It is crucial that the aid Laos receives during the rest of this decade is provided in such a way as to strengthen the general viability of the economy by contributing to the development of sound public finance and significantly reduced external deficits. If donors, in their eagerness to provide assistance (and disburse funds), do not assure that their cooperation really contributes to, rather than substitutes for, domestic savings, they will be doing Laos a disservice. Recent developments in private savings and foreign investments indicate than Laos *may* be in the process of becoming less heavily dependent on aid. The trade deficit, however, continues to be exceptionally large, corresponding to 14 to 15 percent of GDP.

Vietnam is undertaking its adjustments while receiving barely any aid from the former Soviet Union or the West. While aid never will play the same role in Vietnam as it does in a small country like Laos, it should reach a level corresponding to approximately 5 percent of GDP three to four years after the normalization of relations with the IFIs, or three times the present level. Foreign investments could reach that level too, given the necessary institutional development and steadily improved confidence among investors. To realize its growth targets, Vietnam would have to mobilize domestically at least the equivalent of these flows. While aid may negatively affect the propensity of a country to save domestically, properly managed aid flows to Vietnam at this stage should have the opposite effect, giving the reform the momentum it needs to stabilize the economy and harden the budget constraint.

Vietnam's search for what William Turley has called "a new balance" is clearly influenced by the circumstances under which it is being pursued (Turley, 1991, p. 22). A scenario in which Vietnam seeks adjustment and stabilization with the support of the international community would be different from one of continued isolation. Trying to build an open economy while facing an embargo is indisputably an exceptional task. It is no small accomplishment to have pursued the reform process against such odds, making decisions like the 1989 price-reform decision without "anesthesia."

In Cambodia, vital functions of the country's economy have for a long time suffered from a critical shortage of foreign currency as well as technical support. Nine months after the Paris agreements, this is still the case. The opposite might, however, soon be the case, provided that the peace process does not face insurmountable obstacles. Huge quantities of aid are likely to be made available, which will put the country—and the international community—to severe tests. How does one provide aid efficiently to a country as institutionally weak as Cambodia after Pol Pot? How does one furnish it in forms that contribute to steady and sustainable growth rather than chronic aid dependence, an oversized public sector, or the kind of corruption that easily follows in the wake of large aid flows?

Almost nothing has been done to help the country develop capacity to receive aid. Traditional donor behavior could therefore have detrimental consequences, that is, if vast numbers of donors and their consultants invade the country in "flocks," without a proper coordination mechanism among themselves and between them and the government. The subject of coordination was on the agenda of the 1989 Paris Conference on Cambodia, but very few concrete measures were taken afterward. Valuable time was lost, causing a destabilizing vacuum after the signing of the Paris agreement.

While seeking a political solution, the international community should have widened its role and gone beyond its narrow definition of what may be allowed under prevailing circumstances. The main principle, according to which only nondevelopmental assistance could be provided, should have been replaced by a principle allowing broad-based humanitarian work and—first and foremost—basic preparatory work. A task force should have been set up with the mandate to undertake necessary studies, find training opportunities abroad, and so on. The winding down of support from the former Soviet Union gave the issue of redefinition a new urgency, as fuel and fertilizer ceased to arrive and the fiscal situation grew worse.

What Cambodia has managed to build since 1978 would have stood a much better chance of surviving the current critical period if efforts to reach a political solution had been combined with a systematic effort to develop machinery and programs for a comprehensive rehabilitation and reconstruction program—including efforts to keep the public sector (key government functions, primary schools, health centers, etc.) from disintegrating. The fact that the United Nations Transitional Authority in Cambodia (UNTAC) appeal issued in May 1992 included budgetary support was an important indication of a more comprehensive United Nations' approach toward Cambodia during its critical years of transition (UNTAC, 1992, p. 2). No measures have, however, been taken, and the economy is drifting toward hyper-inflation.

Reform and the Social Sectors

It has been generally assumed that a socialist system caters to basic social needs such as health care and education better than a market economy at an equally low level of development. It is also frequently assumed that structural adjustments as such, rather than the underlying economic crisis, constitute a threat to what has been built up under socialism. In this section, some observations will be made about this relationship between reform and social services, primarily on the basis of Vietnam's experiences.

Vietnam has been an important case in point. Although its income per capita is among the lowest in the world (around $200), both life expectancy at birth and literacy have been higher than for many middle-income countries. Life expectancy at birth is 63 years, according to the United Nations Development Program (1990), and 66 years, according to the World Bank (1989), and the adult literacy rate is 88 percent (1990) (UNDP, 1992; World Bank, 1991). The infant mortality rate was roughly halved between 1960 and 1979, from 156 per 1,000 live births to 83, and it was reduced by nearly another 50 percent during the next 10 years to a level of 45 per 1,000 live births in 1989. (Mortality ranged from 26 in Hai Phong to 78 in certain parts of the Central Highlands.) Like Kerala, Sri Lanka, and China, Vietnam has clearly been a "positive deviant" in health and education. In addition, not only public-sector employees but also members of cooperatives (the bulk of the labor force) have enjoyed social safety nets, including a childcare system that enrolled millions of children. The overall shortage of food and common childhood infectious diseases have caused widespread malnutrition and stunting, but rudimentary entitlements under an elaborate food-distribution system have prevented mass starvation. Continued, high population growth rates (2.1 percent per year) have put heavy pressure on the system. An increasingly critical fiscal situation has threatened to undermine the quality of services as shortages of essential supplies have worsened and the real value of the salaries of health workers and teachers has declined. A serious effect of the prevailing financial crisis of the state was that impressive social gains were threatened. If this tendency were allowed to continue, it would not only undermine an element of the legitimacy of the state, it would also mean the loss of a comparative advantage in the competitive world in which Vietnam seeks investors and markets.

In 1975, when the revolutionary government came into power in Laos, the social indicators were poor. Life expectancy at birth was estimated to be 40 years, and the rate of literacy to be around 50 percent. (However, available data at that time did not have nationwide coverage, and the quality of the data was poor.)

The new government had high social ambitions, and preventive health care and literacy campaigns were salient features of its programs during the early years after the revolution. Improvements took place in both life expectancy and adult literacy. But, the lasting impact of the highly politically charged mobilization programs was much more limited than assumed at the time; both primary health care and basic education systems remained very weak due to a severe shortage of trained manpower, deficient management, low budget priority, and extremely limited donor support.

Laos has recently begun to undertake its first systematic surveys ever. When they are completed, the country will have baseline data for social-policy planning. The current official statistics show life expectancy at 50 years, while adult literacy has been assumed to be as high as 84 percent. However, it has become increasingly clear that existing official figures, especially the literacy figures, are of dubious quality. Actual literacy figures may be as low as 50 percent. Today, such figures may be found not only in international estimates but also in official Lao documents.[1] Certain parts of rural Laos still have among the highest infant mortality rates in the world—above 200/1000.

In its new public-investment program, the Lao government gives priority to health and education, although not yet reflected in actual budget allocations. New possibilities for developing the health and education sectors are emerging as the fiscal situation continues to improve, especially as donor involvement in the social sectors increases. It may, however, take another decade before really significant results are achieved beyond the Vientiane plains because of the present low level of organization and training. The low educational level in Laos will continue to be a major barrier to development for a long time to come.

UNICEF presents the following picture of the health conditions prevailing in Cambodia after the Pol Pot years: "With an estimated 263 out of every 1000 children dying before their first birthday (the highest infant mortality rate in the world), the majority of the population severely undernourished, the health infrastructure almost completely destroyed, and only 50 doctors surviving in the entire country, the task of rehabilitation and reconstruction was almost unsurmountable" (UNICEF, 1989, p. 2).

The new Cambodian administration, largely organized by the Vietnamese authorities, had to undertake the training of teachers and health personnel and the rebuilding of schools and other essential social services under conditions of extreme scarcity, and with very limited international support. Much more was accomplished than the world community has recognized. In November 1979, 5,300 primary schools were opened with almost a million pupils enrolled, and during the years 1979–84, more than 40,000 teachers

---

[1]In 1991, both the World Bank and UNDP chose to adjust the figures they quote. The World Bank (1991) in its *World Development Report* estimated adult literacy to be 55 percent, while UNDP (1991) in its second *Human Development Report* presented the figure of 50 percent. A similar figure is quoted in the Lao document prepared for the UNDP Round Table meeting on Laos held in Geneva in March of 1992 (Lao P.D.R., 1992). The low level of educational development is confirmed by recent data on the mean number of years of schooling. According to the UNDP (1992) *Human Development Report,* the figure is as low as 2.9 years.

were trained or retrained. The teacher-training courses, however, lasted from only a week to four months. Today, 20 provincial-level teacher-training colleges give students one year's initial training after completion of secondary school. The university was, however, reopened as recently as in 1988. So far, it offers only elementary training in a limited number of fields.

By 1989, no fewer than 55,000 teachers who had received some (albeit rudimentary) training were teaching. Around 90 percent of school-age children were enrolled (UNICEF, 1989, p. 9). However, the dropout rate was—and is—high. A few years ago, around 66 percent of children enrolled continued to the second grade (UNDP, 1989, p. 147). Recent assessments indicate that the rate may be even higher today. According to information provided in October 1991 by the UNESCO representative in Cambodia, there were 460,000 pupils in grade one, but only 125,000 in grade five. Since then, the overall quality of social services has declined. Growing fiscal difficulties have aggravated the situation within the public sector, and teachers often receive their extremely meager pay several months behind schedule.

The health and education conditions prevailing in Vietnam, Laos, and Cambodia are different in several fundamental respects. Vietnam is the only country that had built up comprehensive systems that have provided services of any quality. Still, all three countries face questions of how to organize and finance their social services. Current budget allocations are exceptionally low.

In 1989, Vietnam's combined current expenditure on education and health accounted for approximately 2.5 percent of GDP, compared to an average of 4.2 percent for all Asian countries. Public expenditure for health actually amounted to less than 1 percent (a recent World Bank study puts the figure at 0.8 percent). Even so, in 1991, these two sectors—education and health—absorbed around 20 percent of total current expenditures, and according to recent estimates by the World Bank, Vietnam has now actually increased real allocations in favor of health and education.

Still, Vietnam's fiscal situation remains very serious and this has many adverse effects. The health sector is suffering from a severe shortage of drugs, medicines, and contraceptives, and a general deterioration in the quality of health care. Low morale among health workers, at least partly induced by declining real wages, constitutes an important underlying cause of this deterioration. The devoted health worker of the past, whose low salary was supplemented by rice and other basic food items through the rationing system, has now become a person trying to survive by adding on a second job, a private practice, farming, or a combination of such activities.

A new fiscal foundation must be laid before it will be possible to pay teachers, nurses, and other social service personnel, so that they can afford to devote themselves fully to their professions. While the average pay for a primary school teacher in other Asian countries in the mid-1980s amounted to 2.6 times the per capita GDP, the average pay in Vietnam was estimated to be in the range of 0.8 to 1.2 times the per capita GDP. Such salary levels inevitably cause severe incentive problems. The positive side of the picture is that the country's trained manpower represents an important potential—an asset on which to build better-functioning systems.

Vietnam is trying several approaches to deal with the fiscal limitations on the social sectors, including decentralizing to lower administrative levels, introducing school and medical fees, allowing private schools and health care alternatives. Vietnam is also moving away from its strongly curative bias and has begun investigating the possibility of introducing a health insurance system. No comprehensive picture of the emerging system exists at this stage. But it is clear that private forms of education and health service are becoming common. In fact, private expenditure on health is becoming substantial as the bulk of drugs and medicines is bought in the market rather than provided through the primary health-care system. In a 1992 health-sector study, the World Bank notes, on the basis of two household surveys, that private expenditure may be as high as 59 to 69 percent of total health care, reflecting the paucity or nonavailability of medicine in the primary health-care system. Access to services varies greatly among provinces and income groups.

While no definitive conclusions can be drawn from recent experiments, three general observations can be made based on developments in Vietnam. First, the Vietnamese efforts to decentralize, which have been driven by budgetary concerns, have led to a rapid deterioration of services in poor areas that are unable to raise required revenue to pay health workers or provide medicines. It is clearly urgent to give more support in the central budget to particularly poor districts. Second, user fees, at the modest levels now being charged, appear justifiable as longer term elements of the public-service system, provided that particularly vulnerable groups are protected. User fees may not only cover costs but also stimulate public involvement and concern for the quality of services. The equity impact of such fees should be carefully monitored to make sure there are no barriers to access. Third, while there should be some latitude for privately provided forms of social services such as private medical practitioners and private schools, the provision of education and health services must remain a fundamental task of the state.

As the fiscal situation improves all three governments must give high priority to allocations for education and health. The objective must be to bring the allocations to levels of GDP comparable with other Asian countries. The last observation may appear superfluous, especially as regards Vietnam. But reported increases in the primary school dropout rate show that even Vietnam may need to renew its traditional social commitments. Significant improvements in education and health, both quantitative and qualitative, should be seen as a primary purpose of present economic reforms. Improved education and health are litmus tests of whether growth is translated into welfare.

A crucial question, of course, is whether Vietnam, Laos, and Cambodia would have been better off socially without market-oriented reforms. In the short term, certain groups might have been better off. Without reform, however, all three countries would have had large and growing food deficits and decreasing amounts of foreign currency available for food imports. The budget situation still would have been critical, and the countries would have been even less prepared to absorb the shock from the Soviet pullout. Long-term economic-growth prospects would have been considerably diminished and so would the prospects for establishing a viable fiscal base for social services. It does not follow as an automatic result of the reforms that education and health services will improve in all three countries, or even in any single one of them. The reforms only put improvements within economic reach, provided there is the political will to transform economic gains into social progress.

The Political Dimension: The Dynamics of Revolution and Reform

Colonization and war produced a strong anticolonial tradition in Indochina, primarily articulated by the Marxist-Leninist movements. Once in power, these movements tried to realize their dreams of planned societies free of exploitation. Their ambition was to strike the kind of balance between equity and economic efficiency that has been a main objective of the Soviet Union and other socialist countries. The Soviet, the Chinese, and other examples had shown that such societies could be built, and that they had, as Kornai put it, an "elementary viability" enabling them to generate considerable economic growth (Kornai, 1992).

In their revolutionary fervor, the leaders—to use their own terminology—transgressed fundamental rules regarding the relationship between the development of the forces of production and the relations of production. They committed what Nguyen Van Linh, former Secretary-General of the Communist Party of Vietnam, declared to be grave "leftist errors" and "subjectivism, voluntarism in defiance of objective (economic) laws" (quoting in Vo Nhan Tri, 1990, p. 75).

Collectivization of agriculture in the Democratic Republic of Vietnam (the DRV or North Vietnam) in the 1950s, in the southern part of united Vietnam in 1977–78, and in Laos in 1977–79 are more traditional examples of the "transformative ambitions" of socialism; that is, the ambition to move forward through drastic changes in the relations of production (Woodside, 1989, p. 292). The latter two were not brought to the extreme of large numbers of people, such as landowners and rich peasants, being killed, but the agrarian reform in North Vietnam in 1953–57 did have that result. According to some accounts, as many as 50,000 people were killed, while others regard 5,000–15,000 killed as a more likely figure.[2] According to some observers, who so far have not published their material, party cadres were also executed.

None of these three drastic moves to change the relations of production produced the envisaged results. Particularly significant for this analysis, all three efforts led to severe self-criticism, and the agrarian reform in Vietnam in 1977–78 and in Laos in 1977–79 led to profound changes in the party line. The emphasis is no longer on socialist transformation of the forces of production through colle ivization, nationalization, or other traditional measures. Today, the motto of the Indochinese regimes is rather "to liberate and exploit all potentialities for the development of productive forces," not only in the state sector and the collective sector, but also in the household economy, the small-commodity production sector, the private capitalist sector, the "state-capitalist" sector, and the "subsistence economy," through the "correct use of the commodity-money relationship" (Vietnam, Communist Party of, 1987). Developing market forces came to be viewed as an "objective necessity" (Vo Nhan Tri, 1990, p. 247).

From a distance, it may seem as if Vietnam has been trying to implement a blueprint ever since "socialist transformation" began in 1958. In reality, the Vietnamese path has been considerably more complex and dialectic, characterized by often intense debate about strategy as well as tactics. Originally, this debate was primarily over the choice of methods for reaching the socialist goal and the speed at which one should travel. The approaches selected were similar to those tried in the Soviet Union, the goal, for example, being to increase the efficiency of how state-owned enterprises were managed by the center (Hewitt, 1988, pp. 221–56).

Beginning in 1979, a process of qualitative change began to gain momentum and slowly expand beyond traditional boundaries—and beyond the established socialist model. Two fundamental conclusions began to emerge: (1) central planning was unsustainable, as it was unable to carry the burden of

---

[2]Francois Houtard and Geneviève Lemercinier (1984, pp. 11–20) regard 50,000 as the likely figure. Gareth Porter (1972) in "The Myth of the Blood Bath" represents the opposite view, while Edwin Moise (1976) in "Land Reform and Land Reform Errors" comes to the conclusion that 15,000 is the more probable figure.

efficient resource allocation, and (2) the system of government ownership and bureaucratic management was unable to motivate human resources and mobilize the capacity for development inherent in the society. The central planning system proved wasteful and inefficient, as reflected in low growth rates, low capacity utilization, and low financial contributions to the budget. It showed what Kornai calls "investment hunger," which would be impossible to satisfy (Kornai, 1992, p. 463). Soviet and other sources of aid could uphold the system if provided in sufficiently large quantities, but such aid could not produce sustained development. New incentive structures had to be created.

A hostile environment and dwindling aid flows put economic efficiency in focus, as political and economic difficulties were aggravated by the failure of efforts such as the collectivization of agriculture. Under such circumstances, heretical phenomena such as the agricultural contract system, fence breaking, and private-sector activities gradually became accepted as necessary to resolving a critical food situation and other shortages. Modernization could not be built on an alienated peasantry. The "space" occupied by the party-and-state symbiosis had to be curtailed so that the energy of peasants, small businessmen, traders, and others could find release. The reform began to move beyond "personal plot socialism" (Sampson, 1987, p. 136).

These important changes in the perspective on "socialist development" were supported by developments taking place in other parts of the socialist world and in the international environment. China's reforms ran parallel. *Perestroika* emerged as a way of trying to bring the Soviet economy out of its vicious circle of stagnation.[3] The lesson drawn from the collapse of socialism in Eastern Europe was that these countries had undertaken too little reform too late. The conclusion that followed was that it was unwise to pursue far-reaching economic and political reforms simultaneously, but instead, one should go ahead with market reforms while ensuring political stability and continued party hegemony. At a somewhat later stage, aid from the (then) Soviet Union and Comecon (CMEA) ceased to be the fundamental vehicle on which development could rely—a change that in itself would inevitably have led to profound reforms.

Support from the IMF, the World Bank, and others—or the possibility of such support—put economic distortions, such as the sharply dual price-and-exchange-rate systems, in clear focus and made structural adjustment and stabilization key issues. In the case of Laos, the influences exerted by these

---

[3]Many parallels can be found between Vietnam's early reform measures and those introduced by Gorbachev as he tried to "combine the advantages of planning . . . with stimulating factors of the socialist market" (Gorbachev, 1988, p. 90).

international financial institutions, in an increasingly close dialogue over the years, seem to have been an important factor in the shaping of the reform.

The rapid development in neighboring countries like Thailand and South Korea became increasingly hard to ignore, standing in sharp contrast to the growing contradictions within the economies of Vietnam, Laos, and Cambodia. These neighboring countries obviously had something to offer that their own economies were in need of. Martin Stuart-Fox over-simplifies when noting that "the poverty of Vietnam is compared with the prosperity of Thailand, and the Lao leaders know which they prefer" (Stuart-Fox, 1991, p. 8). But the comparison did, indeed, have a deep and lasting impact on Lao thinking.

Socialist transformation was not abandoned as the ultimate goal for these countries, but a central assumption in this paper is that that goal has become an increasingly distant one, of clearly diminishing significance in daily economic and political life, even though the present era in the 1992 Vietnamese Constitution is being described as a "transitional period to socialism" (Vietnam, Socialist Republic of, 1992, p. 2).[4] The term actually appears only once in the lengthy political report recently presented to the Fifth Congress of the Lao party (Lao P.R.P., 1991). The market is proving to be the more efficient mechanism for allocating resources. Consequently, the heterodox and painful metamorphosis to the disorderly world of such a system has to be faced, and the meaning of socialism modified accordingly. The evolution of events transformed the revolutionary mindset and produced the reformer.

The emerging, applied meaning of socialism seems to be to "manage the market," provide physical and social infrastructure, and assure an increasingly better livelihood for the vast majority of the population. The Vietnamese attitude is, as we have seen, more ambivalent than the Lao one. All three countries have moved beyond Chen Yun's vision of the market as a bird in a cage, with planning acting as the cage, and beyond modified socialist visions such as Nove's "feasible socialism" (Ferdinand, 1989, p. 301; Nove, 1991).

---

[4]In the preamble to the Vietnamese *1992 Constitution* (Vietnam, Socialist Republic of, 1992), the present period is characterized as a "transitional period to socialism." When visiting the party school of the Communist Party of Vietnam in May 1992, the author of this chapter asked the first vice-director, with reference to this passage, in what way Vietnam today was building a socialist society, considering the development toward a market economy, the role attached to the private sector, the liberal foreign-investment laws, decollectivization, privatizations, and so on. The first vice-director responded that Vietnam wanted to build a society free from exploitation, and that the ownership of the means of production would be controlled by the people. Nobody could, for example, *own* land. This author pointed out that, according to the new constitution, people were "entitled by law to transfer the right to use the land." There would, hence, be a market in land. The first vice-director then went on to say that the ultimate objective was to assure that the people were well fed, happy, living a good life, enjoying education, and so on, in an equitable and democratic society.

The Vietnamese and Lao party congresses, however, have also confirmed that the countries shall remain one-party states. The market economy as well as the leading role of the party are written into the Lao constitution. The new Vietnamese constitution has an opening article (Article 4) that states that the Communist party, as the vanguard of the working class, should be "the force assuming leadership of the State and society" (Vietnam, Socialist Republic of, 1992, Article 4, p. 3). However, "all organizations of the party shall operate within the framework of the constitution and the law" (Vietnam, Socialist Republic of, 1992, Article 4, p. 3).

"Pluralism" was clearly rejected at the Seventh Congress of the Communist Party of Vietnam. In the July 1992 elections, the Fatherland front nominated a considerable number of non-party candidates, but truly independent candidates were not allowed to run (Hiebert, 1992, p. 21). In due time, this development may lead to the formation of some kind of loose factions, potentially challenging the principle of democratic centralism, according to which "the National Assembly, the People's Councils and other state bodies are organized and function" (Vietnam, Socialist Repubic of, 1992, Article 6).

It seems increasingly clear, as William Turley argues, that the actual objective of the leaders in Hanoi as well as in Vientiane is to establish and consolidate their version of the East Asian market-based one-party state, and that the regime in Phnom Penh would also prefer such a solution if that would be within the realm of the politically possible (Turley, 1991, p. 26).

While reform in Eastern Europe and the Soviet Union strongly emphasized political change, the emphasis in Asia is clearly on economic efficiency. At the Seventh Party Congress of the Communist Party of Vietnam, resigning Party-Secretary Nguyen Van Linh summarized the party's position as follows: "Incorrect political renovation leads to political instability. . . . An unstable political situation would create difficulties and obstacles for the entire renovation process" (quoting Linh in *The New York Times*, June, 25, 1991).

Vietnam and Laos—Cambodia being a special case after the signing of the Paris agreement—can be said to lack a model that they perceive as their own and are struggling to develop a new model around which consensus can be built—one that will allow them to regain a sense of "balance." However, two fundamental features of a new model have emerged. The market is replacing planning as the primary allocative mechanism, and the governments would like to build consensus around a modified one-party state system based on the (conflicting) ideas of participation and firm party control. (Turley has called this system "participatory authoritarianism.") This dream of combining one-party rule and legitimacy is, of course, as old as one-party rule, and as unlikely to be resolved in Vietnam and Laos as elsewhere. It is, however, most probably the constraint under which further political reform will evolve in Vietnam and Laos for quite some time to come.

Cambodia is treading a different path. Some kind of rudimentary—and unstable—multi-party system will come into being if the development allows for the implementation of the Paris agreement.[5] Immediately before the signing of the agreement, the ruling party in Phnom Penh decided to adopt a liberal political platform, according to which "the people have complete freedom to express their opinions, participate in meetings, engage in politics . . . [and] create . . . political parties" (Hiebert, 1991). The resolution illustrates that developments in Cambodia are no longer closely coordinated with Hanoi but determined by the political dynamics of the situation created by the Paris agreement on Cambodia.

In his book *Governing the Market. Theory and the Role of Government in East Asian Industrialization* (1990), Robert Wade analyzes the political system of one of East Asia's successful newly industrialized countries (NICs). He notes that the political system of the country clearly meets one condition of Chalmers Johnson's model for the political institutions in a developing country, namely, that of "a virtual monopoly of power in a single party or institution for a long period of time." Wade says that the state is both authoritarian and corporativist "with very limited scope for popular preferences in the selection of rulers" and "tight restrictions on interest groups." The country is, furthermore, "not merely a militarized regime; it is a militarized society," the military having "veto-power over the selection of the top-most political leaders." Civic society is weakly organized, and "indeed, even today the state shows resemblance to a Leninist party-state. It lacks the element of class struggle, and it explicitly sanctions private property and markets; but it shares with Leninist states a need to limit commitment to existing groups, a sense of urgency to develop, a comprehensive perspective on the development problem, and a tutelary notion of government." Since the 1970s we have seen some "softening of the authoritarian qualities of the regime." However, "what is striking," Wade thinks, "is how late this softening comes—long after the regime was well formalized and institutionalized, . . . long after the period of economic breakthrough, long after living standards

---

[5]It is futile to speculate about what might happen in the incomprehensible event of a return of Khmer Rouge to power. Phnom Penh would not be emptied again and money would not be banned, but such a return would most probably cause renewed persecution and suffering, as well as deteriorating relations between Cambodia and Vietnam. A Khmer Rouge return would have to be preceded by years of social deterioration causing widespread alienation. Pol Pot's control was confirmed in connection with the violent demonstrations (almost degenerating into slaying) that took place in late 1991, when Pol Pot's deputy Khieu Samphan reentered Phnom Penh to participate in the first meeting of the Supreme National Council (SNC) to be held inside the country.

began to rise for everyone." All through, "the government has continued to be preoccupied with the legitimacy question, with insuring its survival in power" (Wade, 1990, pp. 253-54).

The country in question is Taiwan. In spite of the fact that Taiwan and Vietnam have been worlds apart, there seem to be only a few words in Wade's description that do not fit Vietnam. His analysis captures not only essential features of the Vietnamese regime, but also the attitude toward political change that Vietnam is likely to show. Rapid economic development assuring legitimacy dominates the thinking of Vietnam's leaders. Political change may be introduced slowly, provided it does not cause any disruption. Laos is, in most respects, a parallel case, while the Paris agreement on Cambodia, as we have noted, determines the options of the Hun Sen government in Phnom Penh.

Ultimately, we have to address the following question: When does a "communist state" cease to be such a state in any meaningful sense of the word and become simply an authoritarian state? *The MIT dictionary of Modern Economics* gives the following definition of communism: "The term is . . . used to denote the planned economic system operated in the COME-CON countries, China and elsewhere, where the government has centralized economic decisions and taken control of productive activity" (Pearce, 1986, p. 71).

Clearly, none of the three Indochinese states is—or is about to become—communist in this sense of the word. Central planning has been abandoned, agriculture has been decollectivized, public enterprises are being divested (so far, primarily in Cambodia and Laos), private industry is allowed and is expanding, legislation is being adopted to guarantee the security of business operations and to promote free competition between public and private enterprises, foreign investments are encouraged, and the constitutions have been revised accordingly. The process is far from complete, and, at times, has been fraught with ambivalence. But, the direction is clear—and the alternatives, since the collapse of the Soviet system, unreal. Hence, in this important respect, the parties have de facto abandoned their original ideologies.

The other dimension of the concept of communism concerns the political system as such rather than production relationships; it is about the nature of the one-party system, a system deeply rooted in revolutionary tradition and Leninist theory and the tactics of the dictatorship of the proletariat. Neither Vietnam nor Laos has any intention of allowing multiple parties within the foreseeable future. "Democratic centralism" remains the principle according to which state organs should be organized. Preserving the one-party system, however, does not necessarily mean a de facto status quo. Both Vietnam and Laos are trying to separate party and state, enhance the role of the legislature and law, have more nonparty members elected to the legislatures, and create a more open debate before decisions are made. There are clear movements in that direction, an important example being the new Vietnamese constitution. It not only includes articles that guarantee different forms of ownership and encourage foreign investments, but also includes a number of provisions aimed at overhauling the state's administrative structure and strengthening the legal system. Achieving the latter is seen as a key element in the political reform program adopted by the Communist Party of Vietnam. The draft constitution was debated publicly over a number of months before being adopted by the National Assembly of Vietnam.

The fundamental principle of due process of law is not fully recognized in the revised Vietnamese constitution (in fact, in its true sense, it is inconceivable under one-party rule), but the position of the individual vis-à-vis the law is strengthened in a number of respects. The concept of human rights is mentioned in a new paragraph that says, "In the socialist Republic of Vietnam human rights are respected and protected in law" (Vietnam, Socialist Republic of, 1992, Article 50).[6] The ambition is, as the former minister of justice put it, to create "an equilibrium between state, discipline and democracy."[7]

A crucial question is to what extent change will be possible as long as the one-party system remains, considering the extent to which the party has penetrated society through the nomenklatura system with its loyalties, and influence over appointments, educational opportunities, and so on. Kornai's and Ferdinand's skepticism is justified given the ingrained nature of the system (Kornai, 1992; Ferdinand, 1989). A process of change, however, has undoubtedly begun, both with regard to the state-party relationship and with regard to the relationship between the state and enterprises. Civil service systems based on professionalism are emerging, and enterprises increasingly are treated as independent economic units, which have to face hardening budget constraints. The process will take time, and it will be only partial as long as the one-party system remains. Provided that the process continues, the differences between Vietnam's public administration and that of other authoritarian regimes may, however, have to be explained in terms of tradition and culture rather than simply in terms of Marxism-Leninism.

The role of the media is another crucial dimension. The nature of debate in the media remains controlled, but it has become considerably more open

---

[6]For a comment on the constitution, see "Cutting Red Tape—Review of Constitution to Streamline Government" (Hiebert, 1991a, p. 11).

[7]The statement was made in a meeting between the minister and the author of this chapter, held in Hanoi in the Ministry of Justice in January 1992.

than a decade ago (Hiebert, 1992a, pp. 21–22). Corruption within the goverment has, for example, become a common theme in Vietnamese papers. An increasingly large variety of books is also being published. Within the limits set by the party, the press is increasingly accepted as a kind of "socialist opposition."

In Vietnam, a fairly large number of people were arrested prior to the Seventh Party Congress. Most of them have since been released, as have all except a few of those who were put in reeducation camps after 1975. However, the Vietnamese regime is still (as reported by Asia Watch, Amnesty International, and Information and Censorship) arresting and imprisoning citizens for peacefully expressing views deemed to threaten "state interests," even though Amnesty International, in its most recent report, considers the situation to be improving.[8]

Assuming that the economic reform processes will continue and gradually lead to diversified economic systems, increasing tension will most probably develop between the economic and political systems. The profound changes that are taking place in the economic field cannot be limited to that sphere. To the extent that a developmental state takes shape, it will, as Sorensen puts it, tend to "undermine authoritarianism through its very success" (Sorensen, 1992, p. 49). Phenomena such as peasant households, private industries, service activities, growing foreign investments, decentralized contacts with foreign firms, Western aid, and the information flow that these structures generate, are all bound to have effects on the class character of the society and lead to the formation of diversified interest groups. Peasant associations, chambers of commerce, bar associations, and other coalitions of interest will demand to be allowed to have a voice, or express dissent and demand new exits.[9] The international community will certainly monitor to what extent the Vietnamese government allows other voices to be heard, using aid as an increasingly important lever. A crucial question is whether the international community will be satisfied with a gradual development toward "softening authoritarianism," allowing the Vietnamese and Lao regimes to

---

[8]For a recent critical account see Mirsky (1991, pp. 44–52). The author catches only a part of the complexity of the political situation, conveying a picture of a geriatric leadership that, disturbed by "the loss of the 'glorious past,'" is frightened by new ideas. For a more complex image, see "Art in the Time of Doi Moi" by Goll (1992, pp. 36–37).

[9]Ferdinand notes that "interests" were an illegitimate issue in socialist politics, a "dogmatic claim" that is being abandoned: "Although it has not been accepted that *any* interests can be expressed politically in a socialist regime, is now accepted that individual and group interests are a legitimate basis for political action" (Ferdinand, 1989, p. 306).

pursue their economic reform programs, or whether the international community will put demands on these countries that would be incompatible with the continued existence of the regimes themselves.

So far, Vietnam, Laos, and Cambodia undoubtedly have been willing to go further with economic reform than the "enlightened observer" was able to imagine, and further than Kornai considered possible under "communist rule." The communist one-party system is being transformed into a market-oriented one, ruled according to adapted principles of democratic centralism, or what the Lao People's Revolutionary Party, in the Political Report presented to the Fifth Congress, prefers to call "centralized democracy," (and what is called "socialist democracy" in the *Political Report of the Communist Party of Vietnam* to the Seventh Party Congress) (Vietnam Communist Party of, 1991). Concern about national development—and the legitimacy of the party—has prevailed over adherence to sacrosanct socialist ideals.

Further changes can be expected as the countries make progress in reforming their economies. To the extent that the parties in power can control events, those changes, however, are likely to be in the East Asian tradition of slow "moderating trends" (Wade, 1990), rather than bold leaps into uncertainty—especially if such steps may endanger political control. Communism will continue to be diluted, and, over time, will become increasingly difficult to distinguish from authoritarian systems surrounding it.

It appears to be no coincidence that the Vietnamese leaders have been very impressed by Singapore and have invited former Prime Minister Lee Kuan Yew to come and advise Vietnam.[10] Stan Stesser, reporter at large for *The New Yorker*, notes in a feature article about Singapore that "a political scientist who visits Singapore would regard the island state as fascinating, since its authoritarian government functions in many ways like that of a Communist state yet is dedicated whole-heartedly to the pursuit of capitalism" (Stesser, 1992, pp. 37–68). That may be close to the ultimate dream of those in power in Hanoi.[11]

From a radical socialist perspective, the transformation that Vietnam is undergoing is causing grave concern. After having noted that "in Vietnam the

[10]Lee Kuan Yew visited Vietnam in April 1992 and contributed a paper to a UNDP-financed seminar for senior officials.

[11]In his book *Vietnam at the Crossroads*, Michael C. Williams notes that "the Vietnamese Communist Party, if it is to survive, may end up being not that different from the Koumintang in Taiwan, the People's Action Party in Singapore of Golkar in Indonesia, models which many Vietnamese talk favorably of in private now. Some of the political reforms currently under discussion, such as divorcing the party from the government, would appear to encourage this trend. But if the party is going to move in this direction, it still has a lot to divest itself of from its past. But just as Vietnam's leadership already sees its economic future converging with that of ASEAN, so its political future may increasingly lie in that direction" (Williams, 1992, pp. 88–89).

'adjustment policy' is leading to the creation of private companies, the spread of private agricultural companies, the 'free market,' suppression of subsidies for consumption, the reduction of the public sector, and a very liberal set of laws for foreign investments," one of the authors of a recent book on the future of socialism concludes that "we cannot exclude the possibility that in those countries [Angola to Vietnam], rather than reform the state, the people will be forced to overthrow it [the government], less they pass through the bitter experience of neo-colonial restoration" (Gonzales, 1990, p. 230).

Vietnam's efforts to define a growth path within the Southeast Asian context are clearly alienating it from the intellectual tradition of which it has been such a central symbol. Principles such as "proletarian internationalism," which formed the basis of Ho Chi Minh's thinking, will most probably remain a part of the intellectual framework of the Communist Party of Vietnam, but as intellectual heritage rather than as a source of vanguard action. If one sees "Vietnamese communism as the product of a graft: the union between Vietnamese patriotism and Marxist-Leninist proletarian internationalist," then the former element is undoubtedly overshadowing the latter as rapid economic development becomes the "national project" (Huynh Kim Khanh, 1982, p. 20). The international situation prevailing after the dissolution of the Soviet Empire offers no "Marxist-Leninist" road toward that end. Nor does it, however, offer a market-economic road that is defined once and for all. The failed attempt to implement what has sometimes been called "the received ideas of socialism" should not be followed by an attempt to implement yet another "received" model (quoting Post and Wright, 1989, in Nixson, 1992, p. 4).

An important consequence of these changes for Indochina as a region is that each one of the three countries increasingly is going its own way in defining its development objectives and laying out a viable development strategy. In the process, the connotation of the concept of Indochina will continue to change.

The Diverging Paths of the Countries of Indochina

Vietnam's ouster of the Pol Pot regime in the beginning of 1979 and its installation of the present regime in Phnom Penh brought the region as close to the idea of a common destiny as it may ever come. Suddenly, three regimes with very similar ideologies were occupying the capitals of the three countries, with Vietnam as the dominating force and the guarantor of its security, and with the Soviet Union as its major source of international support. Military cooperation was regarded as crucial, and highest priority was given to "consolidating the combat alliances."[12] As early as 1950, the Vietnamese formulated the doctrine that Indochina comprised a "single strategic unit" (Turley, 1992b, p. 8 in draft chapter). The three governments foresaw cooperation in many fields, and in 1983, a Vietnam-Laos-Cambodia joint economic committee was established, with a plan to meet twice a year "to accelerate the economic cooperation and the coordination of national plans of development" (quoting *FBIS/APA*, February 25, 1983, in Chanda, 1986, p. 375).

Efforts under Vietnam's leadership, to integrate the three countries, however, did not advance very far, and today the centrifugal forces are considerably stronger than the integrating ones. Each country sees its comparative advantages as lying elsewhere. Even the present regimes see their future potentials in a different context as they adapt their development strategies to an outward-oriented development model. It is their hope that such a model will lead to the the economic and social development that was the dream of those who began the struggle for the independence of what France chose to call Indochina.

The word "sea change" has been used to describe the developments under way in the region, beyond the Third Indochina War and beyond the Cold War. In early 1989 a major change in the regional climate occurred when the then Thai Prime Minister Chattichai launched his slogan to "turn Indochina from a battlefield into a market place." Vietnam's interest in closer regional cooperation was expressed in unequivocal terms by Prime Minister Vo Van Kiet before his historic visit to Indonesia, Thailand, and Singapore in October of 1991 (*Bangkok Post*, October 21, 1991). Recently, the Prime Minister of traditionally hard-line Singapore declared that ASEAN "will help Indochinese countries return to the regional mainstream and rebuild their economies" (*The Nation*, January 16, 1992). The so-called Singapore Declaration adopted at the fourth ASEAN summit, held in late January 1992, illustrates that the idea of closer ties between ASEAN and the countries of Indochina is becoming a matter of mutual interest. *The Asian Wall Street Journal Weekly* reported that the leaders of the ASEAN countries "moved closer to eventual inclusion in ASEAN of Vietnam and Laos, urging closer ties with those countries and with Cambodia. Vietnam and Laos are expected to sign the ASEAN-created Treaty of Amity and Cooperation soon, a move seen widely as a prelude to eventual admission to the group" (Pura, 1992, p. 1). Vietnam and Laos signed the so-called Bali Declaration in connection with the

---

[12]For a vivid picture of the notion of Indochina prevailing at the time in the three countries, see Nayan Chanda, "Vietnam Uber Alles," June 20, 1980, pp. 28–29. Hanoi was clearly "the ideological capital of Indochina."

ministerial-level ASEAN meeting held in July 1992, and will attend future meetings as observers. Vietnam is, as Turley has noted, exchanging "the security interdependence of the Indochinese states for the greater rewards of cooperation in maintaining the peaceful environment it so badly needs for its development" (Turley, 1992b, p. 40).

The dynamics of the processes in the region are clearly such that they defy conventional wisdom. The future of Vietnam, Laos, and Cambodia cannot be told by looking back at the past century. Nor can one simply refer to the economic success stories surrounding them.

The paths of these three countries will diverge in the process, as they integrate with ASEAN and other structures, and as they continue their efforts to connect with the growing number of Asian countries that have come up behind Japan and the East Asian NICs as an increasingly impressive formation of flying geese.[13]

While the adaptation of market- and outward-oriented development models is an essential common feature, each country will face unique challenges, and difficulties. Twenty years from now, the three countries may have considerably different incomes per capita as they move on different growth paths.

Laos is the one among the three whose immediate future appears most predictable. Its future looks brighter than it has at any time since independence. The situation that the country finds itself in, as the process of structural adjustment and stabilization proceeds, is an entirely new one for the country. After decades of war, internal conflicts, antagonistic relations with important neighbors like China and Thailand, and experiments in socialist transformation, Laos is entering an era in which it may concentrate its resources on national development, and do so with considerable support from the international community. The point of departure for such an undertaking is its deep underdevelopment, characterized by weak institutions, subsistence farming, and widespread shifting cultivation. So far it has not been able to mobilize domestic financial resources for its development programs or begin to bridge its large trade deficit, as it has been excessively dependent on development assistance. Still, it stands a real chance of entering the next century as an emerging "developmental state," provided it is able to

---

[13]The image of a formation of geese has been used to describe how new countries have come up behind Japan, the lead goose, and developed their exports in niches which the leading geese have left behind, as they have moved on to the manufacture of technologically more advanced products. Different geese fly at different distances from the lead goose, depending on whether they are at the level of producing garments, assembling simple electronic equipment, or, in the most advanced cases, having significant research and development (R&D) programs of their own (Okita, 1989, p. 209).

match development assistance with domestic resources in a steady effort to reduce its poverty in a sustainable manner. A crucial test will be whether its political reform process keeps pace.

Assessing Vietnam's future prospects is a more complex task. Its endowments, including its developmental strength, are clearly richer than those of its Indochinese neighbors, and it could be entering an era of rapid growth led by agriculture and rapidly growing exports. During the last few years, it has overcome unprecedented external shocks with minimal external assistance, and recent developments, such as its export performance, are indications of growing strength. However, the economy is still plagued by inflation, caused by the financial demands of a public sector in need of profound reforms in the spirit of the bold reform package implemented in 1989. In 1989, China brought its inflation under control by reverting to administrative means rather than determined monetary and fiscal measures, thereby retarding the reform process. Vietnam, however, did not choose such a road. During 1992, it has instead pursued a less expansive credit policy than in the past and begun to reform its state-owned enterprise sector. By doing so, it has pushed its reform process into yet another stage, a stage during which it may begin to address its imbalances more directly, provided the IMF, the World Bank, and the Asian Development Bank are allowed to start adjustment lending. Vietnam would then be in a better position to reduce its budget deficit and let chronic loss-making state-owned enterprises go bankrupt. Hopefully 1992 will be the last year of U.S. embargo and the last year without financial support from international financial institutions. Such a movement away from isolation would accelerate and deepen ongoing state market reforms.

The combination of additional external resources and appropriate performance criteria will create a new climate for Vietnamese reform, a climate in which private investments and savings will increase. The credibility of those who favor further reforms will be enhanced, and party unity will demand less in terms of ambiguous consensus building. Vietnam will be on its way to joining the East Asian "geese formation."

Gradually, Vietnam will generate sufficient growth in the economy for the state to strengthen its crucial role in developing social and physical infrastructure, accelerating its inner reform. Considerable statecraft will be needed to exploit the growth opportunities in a way that will lead to a renewal of Vietnam's social commitments. In the process, the pressure for further political reform is likely to increase.

Cambodia's present situation is too uncertain for any single, definitive assessment of what its future may be. A number of scenarios can be explored. But the underlying determinants of Cambodia's future direction are political, not economic. Much hope was generated at the time of the Paris Conference on Cambodia in August of 1989, and again, when the Paris agreement was signed in the fall of 1991. Still, the country is far from a genuine solution. The appropriate conditions can only develop over time, as confidence is built. What happens will depend ultimately on the future role of the Khmer Rouge, which, in spite of the immense suffering it has caused the Cambodian people, is represented in the Supreme National Council, the "unique legitimate body and source of authority in Cambodia."

Close collaboration between Hun Sen and Norodom Sihanouk, chairman of the SNC, offers the best countervailing force.

During the last decade, we have seen how Cambodia, in spite of war, has undergone a partial recovery through the re-establishment of peasant agriculture, the growth of the private sector, through rudimentary education, and health care, and the gradual dismantling of central planning. Experience and necessity have produced a highly pragmatic approach to change and reform, and economic activities have, as a consequence, picked up. Still, the country will remain unable to address such crucial tasks as stabilization of the macroeconomy, reconstruction of infrastructure, or provision of adequate basic education or health services, and corruption will spread further, if the state is allowed to continue to disintegrate. Much depends on the international community, which also is responsible for the fact that the Khmer Rouge has reentered Phnom Penh. It is hoped that the international community will ensure that the writing of a new chapter has begun, a chapter that will make the Khmer Rouge a part of the era coming to a close rather than the one that has just begun.

References

Brown, MacAlister, and Josoph J. Zasloff. 1986. *Apprentice Revolutionaries: The Communist Movement in Laos, 1930–85.* Stanford: Hoover Institution Press.

Cady, John F. 1976. *Southeast Asia—Its Historical Development.* T M H Edition. New Delhi: Tata McGraw-Hill Publishing Company Ltd.

Chan, Steve. 1988. "Puff, the Magic Dragons: Reflections on the Political Economy of Japan, South Korea, and Taiwan." *Journal of Developing Societies* IV (July-October): pp. 208–25.

Chanda, Nayan. 1980. "Vietnam Uber Alles." *Far Eastern Economic Review* (20 June): pp. 28–29.

———. 1986. *Brother Enemy—the War After the War, A History of Indochina Since the Fall of Saigon.* New York: Macmillan Publishing Company.

————. 1992. "Cambodian Peace Accord May Be in Jeopardy as Economy Unravels Amid Government Crisis." *The Asian Wall Street Journal Weekly* 6 January, p. 2.

————. 1992b. "Cambodia: Ghost at the Feast." *Far Eastern Economic Review* July 2, 1992.

Ferdinand, Peter. 1989. *Communist Regimes in Comparative Perspective—The Evolution of the Soviet, Chinese and Yugoslav Models.* London and Savage, MD: Harvester Wheatsheaf and Barnes and Nobles.

Genberg, Hans. 1991. "On the Sequencing of Reforms in Eastern Europe." IMF Working Paper. Washington D.C.: International Monetary Fund.

Goll, Sally. "Art in the time of doi moi." *Far Eastern Economic Review* May 7, pp. 36-37.

Gonzales Casanova, Pablo. "The Third World and the Socialist Project Today." In William K. Tabb, ed., *The Future of Socialism—Perspectives from the Left.* New York: Monthly Review Press.

Gorbachev, Mikhail. 1988. *Perestroika—New Thinking for our Country and the World.* Updated version. London: Fontana/Collins.

Gunn, Geoffrey C. 1988. *Political Struggles In Laos (1930-1954).* Bangkok: D.K.

Hall, D.G.E. 1968. *A History of Southeast Asia.* Third edition. New York: St Martin's Press.

Hess, Gary H. 1990. *Vietnam and the United States—Origins and Legacy of War.* Boston: Twayne Publishers.

Hewitt, Ed A. 1988. *Reforming the Soviet Economy—Equity vs. Efficiency.* Washington D.C.: The Brookings Institution.

Hiebert, Murray. 1991a. "Cutting Red Tape." *Far Eastern Economic Review.* August 22, p. 11.

————. 1991b. "Exit Heng Samrin." *Far Eastern Economic Review* (October).

————. 1992a. "New Directions—Press Takes Bolder Stand on Corruption." *Far Eastern Economic Review* (20 February); pp. 21-22.

————. 1992b. "Red Capitalists—Private Enterprise Flourishes Despite Hurdles." *Far Eastern Economic Review* (20 February).

————. 1992c. "Election Strategy No Threat to Party Rule in July Polls." *Far Eastern Economic Review* July 9, p. 21.

Houtard, Francois, and Geneviève Lemercinier. 1984. *HAI VAN—Life in a Vietnamese Commune.* London: Zed Books Ltd.

Huynh Kim Khanh. 1982. *Vietnamese Communism 1925-1945.* Ithaca, N.Y., and London: Cornell University Press.

"Kiet Vows Closer Ties with ASEAN," *Bangkok Post,* 21 October 1991.

Kornai, Janos. 1983. *Contradictions and Dilemmas.* Budapest: Corvina.

————. 1990. *Vision and Reality, Market and State.* New York: Routledge.

————. 1991. *The Road to a Free Economy: Shifting from a Socialist System: The Example of Hungary.* New York: Norton.

————. 1992. *The Socialist System: The Political Economy of Communism.* Princeton, NJ: Princeton University Press.

Lao People's Democratic Republic (P.D.R.), Ministry of Economy, Planning and Finance, State Statistical Center. 1990a. "Basic Statistics about the Socio-Economic Development in the Lao P.D.R. for 15 years (1975–1990)." Vientiane: Lao P.D.R.

Lao P.D.R., Ministry of Economy, Planning, and Finance. 1990b. "Policy Framework for the Public Investment Program, (1991–1995)." Draft document prepared by a consultant team (PDP Australia Pty Ltd.) and financed by UNDP. November.

Lao P.D.R. 1991. "Socio-Economic Development Strategies." Vol. I. Document prepared for the UNDP Round Table meeting on Laos, Geneva, February, 1992.

Lao People's Revolutionary Party (P.R.P.). 1991. "Political Report of the Executive Committee of the Central Committee of the Lao People's Revolutionary Party presented at the Fifth Party Congress." Vientiane: Lao P.R.P.

Lindbeck, Assar. 1986. "Public Finance for Market-Oriented Developing Countries." Stockholm: Institute for International Economics. Mimeo.

Migdal, Joel S. 1988. *Strong Societies and Weak States.* Princeton: Princeton University Press.

Minh, Ho Chi. 1979. *Patriotism and Proletarian Internationalism.* Hanoi: Foreign Language Publishing House.

Mirsky, Jonathan. 1991. "Reconsidering Vietnam." *The New York Review of Books* (10 October): pp. 44–52.

Moise, Edwin. 1976. "Land Reform and Land Reform Errors." *Pacific Affairs* 46.

Ngo Long Vinh. 1988. "Some Aspects of Cooperativization in the Mekong Delta." In Marr and White, eds., *Postwar Vietnam: Dilemmas in Socialist Development.* Ithaca, N.Y.: Cornell University, Southeast Asia Program.

Nguyen Van Linh. 1989. *Answers by General Secretary of CPVCC Nguyen Van Linh.* Hanoi: Foreign Language Publishing House.

Nove, Alec. 1986. *Socialism, Economics and Development.* London: Allen and Unwin.

———. *The Economics of Feasible Socialism Revisited.* Second edition. London: Harper Collins Academics, 1991.

Okita, Saburo. 1989. *Japan in the World Economy of the 1980s.* Tokyo: University of Tokyo Press.

Phomvihane, Kaysone. 1980. *La Révolution Lao.* Moscow: Editions due Progrès.

Porter, Gareth. 1972. "The Myth of the Blood Bath." Cornell University Studies of the International Relations of East Asia, Interim Report No. 2. September, 1972. Ithaca, N.Y.: Cornell University.

Pura, Raphael. 1992. "ASEAN Leaders Set Course for Integrated Market." *The Asian Wall Street Journal Weekly* 3 February, p. 1.

Stesser, Stan. 1992. "A Reporter at Large (Singapore)—A Nation of Contradictions." *The New Yorker* 13 January, pp. 37–68.

Sheehan, Neil and Susan. 1991. "A Reporter at Large in Vietnam." *The New Yorker* 18 November, pp. 54–119.

Skocpol, Theda. 1985. "Bringing the State Back In: Strategies of Analysis in Current Research." In Evans et al., eds., *Bringing the State Back In.* London: Cambridge University Press.

Sorensen, George. 1991. *Democracy, Dictatorship and Development—Economic Development in Selected Regimes in Third World Countries.* New York: Macmillan Publishing Company.

————. 1992. *Democracy and the Developmental State.* Aarhus, Denmark: Institute of Political Science, University of Aarhus.

Stuart-Fox, Martin. 1991. "Laos at the Crossroads." *Indochina Issues 92* March.

Taylor, Lance. 1988. (1991 in paperback edition). "Varieties of Stabilization Experience—Towards Sensible Macroeconomics in the Third World." Wider Studies in Development Economics. Oxford: Clarendon Paperbacks.

Thayer, Nate. 1992. "The War Party—Khmer Rouge Intransigence Threatens Peace." *Far Eastern Economic Review* June 25, p. 12.

Tonnesson, Stein. 1991. *The Vietnamese Revolution of 1945—Roosevelt, Ho Chi Minh and de Gaulle in a World at War.* London: Sage Publications; Oslo: International Peace Research Institute (PRIO).

Turley, William, and Mark Selden. 1992a. *Reinventing Vietnamese Socialism: Doi Moi in Comparative Perspective.* Boulder, CO: Westview Press.

————. 1992b. "More Friends, Fewer Enemies—Vietnam's Policy Toward Indochina—ASEAN Reconciliation," in Simon Sheldon, ed., *Reinventing Vietnamese Socialism: Doi Moi in Comparative Perspective.* Armonk, NY: E.M. Sharpe (forthcoming).

UNICEF. 1989. "Kampuchea—Project Proposals for Supplementary Funds." Phnom Penh.

United Nations, Security Council. 1992. "Report of the Secretary General on Cambodia." S/23613. 19 February.

United Nations Development Program (UNDP). 1991. *Human Development Report.* New York: Oxford University Press.

————. 1992. *Human Development Report.* New York: Oxford University Press.

Vickery, Michael. 1991. *Cambodia After the Peace.* Penang: Samidzat.

Vietnam, Communist Party of. 1987. *Sixth National Congress of the Communist Party of Vietnam.* Hanoi: Foreign Languages Publishing House.

————. 1987b. *Sixth National Congress of the Communist Party of Vietnam: Documents.* Hanoi: Foreign Languages Publishing House.

————. 1990a. Draft "Platform for the Building of Socialism in the Transitional Period." Hanoi.

————. 1990b. Draft "Strategy for the Socioeconomic Stabilization and Development of our Country up to the Year 2000." Hanoi.

————. 1991. *Seventh National Congress: Documents.* Hanoi: Foreign Language Publishing House.

Vietnam, Socialist Republic of, National Assembly (VIIIth Legislature), Commission for the Revision of the Constitution. 1992a. Third draft of the 1980 Constitution. Hanoi.

————. 1992b. *Constitution of the Socialist Republic of Vietnam.* Hanoi.

Vietnam Courier. 1992. "The Second Plenum of the Central Committee of the Communist Party of Vietnam." (January).

Wade, Robert. 1990. *Governing the Market. Economic Theory and the Role of Government in East Asian Industrialization.* Princeton, NJ.: Princeton University Press.

White, Gordon. 1984. "Developmental States and Socialist Industrialization in the Third World." *The Journal of Development Studies* 21, no. 1.

Woodside, Alexander. 1989. "Peasants and the State in the Aftermath of the Vietnamese Revolution." *Journal of Peasant Studies* 16, no. 4: pp. 283-97.

World Bank. 1991. "The Challenges of Development." Country Economic Reports on Vietnam and Laos. *World Development Report* 1991. Washington D.C.: World Bank.

Appendix: Socioeconomic Data by Country

	Vietnam	Laos	Cambodia
Area, Population, GNP/capita			
Area (sq. km.)	332,000	237,000	181,040
Density/sq. km.	194	16	47
Population (million, 1990)	66.5	4.2	8.5[1]
Rate of growth	2.4	2.9	2.8
Life Expectancy, Infant Mortality, and Literacy			
Life expectancy at Birth	62.7 (1990)	49.7 (1990)	48 (1989)
Infant mortality			
(per 1,000, 1990)	46	104	120
Adult literacy[2] (%, 1990)	88	54	35.2
Mean years of schooling	4.7	2.9	2.0
GNP/capita (US $)	200 (est. 1990)	180 (1988)	130–200 (est. 1989)
Human Development Ranking in the UNDP Human Development Index (1992)[3]	101	129	135
Gross National Product (Ratios to GDP)			
GDP at market prices	100	100	100
Gross domestic investment	9.1	NA	NA
	(1990)	(est. 1990:19)	
Gross national savings	− 2.0	NA	NA
	(1988)	(est. 1990: + 3)	negative
Current account balance	− 2.1	− 12.9	NA
	(1990)	(1991)	
Export of goods (1991)	16–17	6.3	3
Import of goods (1991)	16–17	20.3	9
Annual Rate of Growth (%/GDP)			
1984–87	3.9	2.9	
1988	5.9	− 1.8	NA
1989	7.1	13.5	
1990	4.5	6.6	3
1991	3.0	4.0	4
Output—Value Added (%)			
Agriculture	40	60.8	45–52
Industry	30	13.8	12–17
Services (other)	30	25.4	31–43
			(diff. est.)
Government Finance (% of GNP)			
Current receipts	12.0	10.9	4.0
	(1990)	(1991)	(est. 1991)
Current expenditure	15.1	11.3	8.0
Current surplus	− 3.7	− 0.4	− 3.0

	Vietnam	Laos	Cambodia
Capital expenditure	3.9	9.1	NA
Total government expenditure	19.0	20.4	NA
Rate of Inflation			
1988	394	15	10
1989	35	76	50
1990	68	20	100
1991	70	11	150
Exchange Rate			
1986	125	95	
1988	2,047	480	
1989	3,946	576	210
1990	4,485	700	480
1991 (July)	9,000	700	800
1992 (March)[4]	11,450	700	800
External Debt (million $ US)[5]			
1990	7,950	636	1,411
out of which in convertible currency	3,500	340	279
Debt service ratio (%) (1990)	30 (scheduled) 9 (actual)	15	NA
Net Aid Flows (%/GDP)	1.5	21.6	NA

[1]Official estimates place the 1990 Cambodian population figure at 8.5 million. The figure is based on what is called a "census," which was undertaken in 1980. The possibility of a sizable margin of error is acknowledged by many because of the large-scale dislocation of people and the lack of technical personnel to undertake a proper population count at the time. A full-scale population census has not been undertaken since 1962.

[2]The figure for Vietnam is the official figure, generally assumed to be accurate. Until recently Laos's official figure has been as high as the Vietnamese one, but recent estimates by the UNDP and the World Bank has put it at 50 to 55, a figure which by now has been accepted by Laos as the best available estimate. The official Cambodian figure is 93%. No reliable figure is available, but one must assume that the actual figure is as low—or lower—than the estimated one for Laos. In a recent document published by one of the international financial institutions, the adult literacy rate is reported to be about 60 to 70%, the figure being yet another "guesstimate." In the 1992 *Human Development Report*, the figure is put as low as 35.2%.

[3]160 countries are included in the 1992 index. The index is based on three variables: life expectancy at birth, adult literacy rate/mean years of schooling, and real GDP per capita (PPP$).

[4]The parallel rate in Vietnam was, for some time, as high as 14,000, but was brought down during the first months of 1992 to a level close to the official rate. Major contributing factors were the government's sale of gold and a more restrictive monetary policy than in the past. Also the parallel rate in Cambodia has fallen from above 1,000 riel to a rate close to the official one. Increased inflows of foreign exchange, as a consequence of the rapid expansion of the foreign community in Phnom Penh, is supposed to be a main factor.

[5]The total debt figures are misleadingly high as the nonconvertible parts are converted into US $ at the rate of rubles 2.5 per $ or similar rates in that range. None of the countries will give priority to servicing the nonconvertible debt.

Sources: Official statistics: *World Development Report 1991* and other World Bank Data; *Human Development Report* 1991 and 1992; International Monetary Fund documents. Other data: Asian Development Bank documents; UNICEF reports on the situation of children and women; OECD, External Debt of Developing Countries (1991). The figures quoted for Cambodia come mainly from secondary sources, primarily Curtis (1990); Coady and DeSai (1990); Cheriyan and Fitzgerald (1989).

Index